RECIDIVISM

QUANTITATIVE STUDIES IN SOCIAL RELATIONS

Consulting Editor: Peter H. Rossi

UNIVERSITY OF MASSACHUSETTS
AMHERST, MASSACHUSETTS

Published

Michael D. Maltz, **RECIDIVISM**

Nancy Brandon Tuma and Michael T. Hannan, **SOCIAL DYNAMICS: Models and Methods**

Peter Schmidt and Ann D. Witte, **AN ECONOMIC ANALYSIS OF CRIME AND JUSTICE:** *Theory, Methods, and Applications*

Alexander Basilevsky and Derek Hum, **EXPERIMENTAL SOCIAL PROGRAMS AND ANALYTIC METHODS:** *An Evaluation of the U. S. Income Maintenance Projects*

Walter R. Gove and Michael Hughes, with contributions by Omer R. Galle, **OVERCROWDING IN THE HOUSEHOLD:** *An Analysis of Determinants and Effects*

Ronald S. Burt, **CORPORATE PROFITS AND COOPTATION:** *Networks of Market Constraints and Directorate Ties in the American Economy*

Peter H. Rossi, James D. Wright, and Andy B. Anderson (Eds.), **HANDBOOK OF SURVEY RESEARCH**

Joan Huber and Glenna Spitze, **SEX STRATIFICATION:** *Children, Housework, and Jobs*

Toby L. Parcel and Charles W. Mueller, **ASCRIPTION AND LABOR MARKETS:** *Race and Sex Differences in Earnings*

Paul G. Schervish, **THE STRUCTURAL DETERMINANTS OF UNEMPLOYMENT:** *Vulnerability and Power in Market Relations*

Irving Tallman, Ramona Marotz-Baden, and Pablo Pindas, **ADOLESCENT SOCIALIZATION IN CROSS-CULTURAL PERSPECTIVE:** *Planning for Social Change*

Robert F. Boruch and Joe S. Cecil (Eds.), **SOLUTIONS TO ETHICAL AND LEGAL PROBLEMS IN SOCIAL RESEARCH**

The list of titles in this series continues at the end of this volume

RECIDIVISM

MICHAEL D. MALTZ
Department of Criminal Justice
and Department of Quantitative Methods
University of Illinois at Chicago
Chicago, Illinois

1984

ACADEMIC PRESS, INC.
(Harcourt Brace Jovanovich, Publishers)
Orlando   San Diego   San Francisco   New York   London
Toronto   Montreal   Sydney   Tokyo   São Paulo

COPYRIGHT © 1984, BY ACADEMIC PRESS, INC.
ALL RIGHTS RESERVED.
NO PART OF THIS PUBLICATION MAY BE REPRODUCED OR
TRANSMITTED IN ANY FORM OR BY ANY MEANS, ELECTRONIC
OR MECHANICAL, INCLUDING PHOTOCOPY, RECORDING, OR ANY
INFORMATION STORAGE AND RETRIEVAL SYSTEM, WITHOUT
PERMISSION IN WRITING FROM THE PUBLISHER.

ACADEMIC PRESS, INC.
Orlando, Florida 32887

United Kingdom Edition published by
ACADEMIC PRESS, INC. (LONDON) LTD.
24/28 Oval Road, London NW1 7DX

Library of Congress Cataloging in Publication Data

Maltz, Michael D.
  Recidivism.

  (Quantitative studies in social relations)
  Includes bibliographical references and index.
    1. Recidivists--United States. 2. Corrections--
United States. I. Title. II. Series.
HV6049.M27 1984   364.3   83-15911
ISBN 0-12-468980-9 (alk. paper)

PRINTED IN THE UNITED STATES OF AMERICA

84 85 86 87   9 8 7 6 5 4 3 2 1

To my parents
For my sons

Contents

Preface xi
Acknowledgments xiii

1. Introduction

Purpose 2
Overview of the Book 3

2. Correctional Goals and Their Evaluation

Goals Related to the Offender 8
Goals Related to Society 13
Goals Related to the Correctional Institution 17
Summary 17

3. Recidivism as a Measure of Correctional Effectiveness

The Values in Evaluation 18
Practical Difficulties in Evaluation 20
Success as a Measure of Effectiveness 23
Appropriate Uses of Recidivism 25

4. What Works?

Nothing Works	27
Getting Tough Works	30
Policy Implications	40

5. Correctional Organization and Recidivism

The Parole Process	42
Limitations on Discretion in Parole Decision-Making	46
The Parole Process and Recidivism	47
Empirical Variations	50
Summary	53

6. Recidivism Definitions

Complete Information	54
Problems with Incomplete Criminal Justice Data	58
Data Problems in Controlling for Arrest Quality	60
Absconsion	61
Recidivism Defined in Practice	61
Proposed Recidivism Definitions	64

7. Recidivism Measures and Models

Characteristics of Models	68
Development of Models	69
The Model Underlying the One-Year Recidivism Rate	71
Models of Individual Failure Processes	75
Probability Distributions Used in Modeling Recidivism	77
Summary	86

8. Selection of a Recidivism Model

Characteristics of the Recidivism Process	88
Eyeballing	91

The Chi-Square Goodness-of-Fit Test	92
Split-Sample Model Validation	97
The Model's Use in Forecasting	99
A Quantitative Forecasting Test	105
Other Considerations in Model Selection	107
Summary	112

9. Using Model M_I to Analyze Recidivism Data

The Data-Collection Process	114
Data Analysis	116
Graphical Parameter Estimation	118
Confidence Intervals and Regions	121

10. Covariate and Nonparametric Methods

Covariate Methods and Offender Characteristics	127
Analyzing Treatment Effects Using Covariate Models	128
Using Covariate Models with Model M_I	129
Using Covariate Methods with Model M_L	134
Nonparametric Methods	135
Summary	136

11. Conclusion

Interpreting Recidivism Data	138
Analyzing Recidivism Data	139
Directions for Future Research	139
A Final Caution	141

Appendix A. Parameter Estimation for Model M_I: The Incomplete Exponential Distribution

Discrete-Time Version	143
Continuous-Time Version	153
The "Critical Time" Model of Releasee Behavior	157

Appendix B. Confidence Statements for Model M_I

Confidence Intervals and Regions	160
The Likelihood Function and the Joint Density Function	161
The Likelihood Function and Progressively Censored Data	164
Likelihood Ratio Test for the Normal Approximation	169
Summary	171

Appendix C. Tables for Estimating Sample Size and Length of Observation Period

Using the Tables	172
Trading Off between Population Size and Observation Time: An Example	173

Appendix D. Programs for Analyzing Recidivism Data and Examples of Their Use

Description of Variables Stored by Program MLEDATA.FORT	191
Example 1: Individual (KTYP = 1) Singly Censored (KCNS = 1) Data	192
Example 2: Grouped (KTYP = 2) Singly Censored (KCNS = 1) Data	196
Example 3: Individual (KTYP = 1) Progressively Censored (KCNS = 2) Data	199
Example 4: Grouped (KTYP = 2) Progressively Censored (KCNS = 2) Data	203

References   222

Index   237

Preface

The purpose of this book is to present a thorough analysis of the concept of recidivism. The first half of the book describes the role that different definitions of recidivism have played in evaluating correctional goals and programs and shows how improper policy conclusions have been based on studies that used inappropriate definitions of recidivism. It describes the many goals that the correctional system is called upon to achieve and specifies how recidivism is used in measuring their achievement. A taxonomy of recidivism definitions is proposed to make possible the comparison of recidivism statistics of two different studies.

The second half of the book addresses the problem of analyzing data on recidivism. Deficiencies in the standard method of analysis are noted, and different methods and models that overcome these deficiencies are described. Selection of the "best" method and model is addressed by noting the inappropriateness of the standard selection criterion, the chi-square goodness-of-fit test. New selection criteria are developed, including a graphical test based on the model's predictive ability. In addition, characteristics of the recidivism process are invoked to aid in the selection of an appropriate model. This model, based on the incomplete exponential distribution, is described and a number of examples of its use are presented. Appendixes containing tables, graphs, and computer programs (useful in estimating confidence regions) are provided, with examples of their use in analyzing correctional data.

The primary audience for the book will be members of the criminal justice research community, particularly individuals who use and teach research methods in criminal justice and corrections. Those involved in teaching and research in related policy areas should also find this volume useful. Having taught quantitative and statistical courses to graduate students for a number of years, I have always tried to tie the methods used to the subject at hand, and I assume that others do likewise. Therefore, I describe many of the methodological problems involved in developing an analytic technique, demonstrating how definitions can be clarified, showing how definitions suggest models of the process (and vice versa), detailing the concerns involved in selecting one model over competing models, and indicating how analytic techniques are developed based on the model.

Statisticians and operations researchers concerned with failure rate analysis in other contexts will also find this treatment useful, especially the discussion of model selection principles in Chapter 8 and of analytic procedures in Chapter 9. In addition, the appendixes on maximum likelihood and Bayesian estimation (Appendix A) and on confidence intervals and regions (Appendix B) will interest this audience.

This book can be read and understood by people with little technical or mathematical sophistication. This is especially true of the first six chapters, which focus on research design issues. However, even in those chapters a level of sophistication is required that is rarely found among those who have not had at least one course in research methods at the graduate level.

Chapters 7–10 require somewhat more mathematical ability to be understood. Those who have had a graduate course in statistical methods and some acquaintance with the exponential distribution should have little difficulty with this material. Most of the more difficult material is in the appendixes, which will be of interest to the mathematically sophisticated who may want an understanding of the mathematical and statistical underpinnings of the methods described in this book.

Acknowledgments

The research described herein was supported from 1977 to 1983 by the National Institute of Justice of the United States Department of Justice, under Grants 77-NI99-0073 (1977–1979), 79-NI-AX-0068 (1979–1981), and 81-IJ-CX-0064 (1981–1983). The points of view or opinions expressed in the book, however, are my own and do not necessarily represent those of the U.S. Department of Justice.

Stephen M. Pollock was the primary consultant on the quantitative aspects of the research. But to call him consultant does not do justice to the role he played in all aspects of the work. In essence, he is the coauthor of Chapters 7–9 and Appendixes A and B. Steve has the all-too-rare ability to understand the nature of a process, physical or behavioral or organizational, and to develop *useful* models of the process—exemplary of the best aspects of operations research.

Much of the material in the first half of this book is taken from a report on the first grant (Maltz, 1981b). Richard McCleary and I initiated this research, which was effectively supported by an advisory panel consisting of Melvin Axilbund, John P. Conrad, Lawrence A. Greenfeld, John Henning, and Gerald Strathman. Frank Merritt and Carl Harris consulted on various aspects of this research. The contributions of research assistants Louis Cainkar, Laura Frazier, and Steven Mihajlovic are also reflected in this book.

A number of people reviewed early drafts of the book and made valuable suggestions. They include Jan Chaiken, Marcia Chaiken, Jacqueline Cohen, Marcia Farr, Robert Figlio, David Fogel, Robert Holden, and Doug Thomson.

The search for data to test the methods was met with cooperation from our colleagues in various organizations throughout the country. They include George Cox (Georgia Department of Offender Rehabilitation), Peter Hoffman and Barbara Stone-Meierhoefer (U.S. Parole Commission), Howard Kitchener (U.S. Bureau of Prisons), Cheryl Ruby and Paul Litsky (National Council on Crime and Delinquency), and Ann Witte (University of North Carolina at Chapel Hill). I hope they have been provided with new ways of looking at correctional effectiveness. At least, this is one goal of this book; its measure of effectiveness will be in terms of the extent to which the recommended methods and procedures are adopted.

RECIDIVISM

1
Introduction

Recidivism, in a criminal justice context, can be defined as the reversion of an individual to criminal behavior after he or she has been convicted of a prior offense, sentenced, and (presumably) corrected. It results from the concatenation of failures: failure of the individual to live up to society's expectations—or failure of society to provide for the individual; a consequent failure of the individual to stay out of trouble; failure of the individual, as an offender, to escape arrest and conviction; failure of the individual as an inmate of a correctional institution to take advantage of correctional programs—or failure of the institution to provide programs that rehabilitate; and additional failures by the individual in continuing in a criminal career after release.

This book is an exploration of the concept of recidivism. It is not an analysis of how much there is, what causes it, or how it varies by offender type, correctional treatment, or jurisdiction, since (as the book shows) we truly do not know enough about recidivism to make either absolute or comparative statements about its extent. There are good reasons for our lack of knowledge. For the most part, recidivism has been defined on an ad hoc basis, without consideration of its true meaning; and it has been measured in ways remarkable for their inconsistency. Yet we find "recidivism rates"—based on different definitions applied in different contexts and measured in different ways—being compared to each other to determine which correctional program or which state is "better."

Determination of "how much" recidivism there is cannot be made without addressing some basic issues. The aim of this book is to address these issues, which are fundamental to the study of recidivism: How can recidivism be defined, and in what ways are these definitions applied in practice? In what contexts is it used? And finally, how do the characteristics of the process determine the way it should be measured? In other words, the focus of this book is on methodology, not on outcome. Only by using an appropriate methodology to measure a phenomenon can we obtain valid and reliable measures of outcome.

The word *methodology* frightens many people, among whom are a significant number of those trained in the social sciences. They equate methodology with statistics—F tests, t tests, Yule's q, Kendall's tau, ANOVA, ARIMA, and other assorted mystical procedures found in SPSS or SAS, to be invoked by incantations spoken in Job Control Language or, worse yet, FORTRAN. Yes, methodology does include statistics; and statistical (and computer) procedures are included in this book—whenever large numbers of data are used, statistics are used. But methodology is not only statistics, and an understanding of the nonstatistical aspects of methodology can make the statistical aspects more comprehensible. The book explains both the nonstatistical and statistical aspects of the methodology of measuring recidivism.

PURPOSE

My purpose in writing this book is to show how recidivism is being measured and to suggest how it should be measured. But my aim goes beyond that. Many people have an awareness of what recidivism is, or is supposed to be, but have never really given the concept much thought. I have found this to be equally true of those who do research on correctional effectiveness, those who compute recidivism statistics for administrative purposes, and those who merely read of such statistics. Researchers may suffer a slight twinge of uneasiness when calculating the 1-year recidivism rate,[1] but they are not sure why—or if they are, they make some prefatory and perfunctory disclaimers concerning the recidivism figures, but compute and present them as useful outcome measures regardless. They perform the computations in the same way that they or others have performed them before. In this way they feel that they are at least maintaining some semblance of consistency, perhaps as an article of faith that someone must have a good reason for using this method.

But there is no good reason for using this method. To explain why there is not, and to suggest an alternative method, this book examines the concept *recidivism* from several different viewpoints. It does not examine only the substantive part—how the way recidivism is defined affects the outcome measure; the contextual part—how the nature of the organizations involved in the study affects the outcome measure; or the statistical part—how different analytic techniques brought to bear on recidivism data produce different outcome measures. The fact is, these three aspects of recidivism are intertwined. The fact is, programs have been accepted or rejected based on muddy definitions of recidivism, in which the organizational contexts have had major impacts on outcomes, and in which data were analyzed using inappropriate techniques. The fact is, policies throughout the United States have been based on these studies—and have been wrong; and the fact is, too many technically competent people have paid too little attention to what has been measured,[2] in their rush to squeeze the last ounce of statistical significance out of "the data."

---

[1]The 1-year recidivism rate is the recidivism measure used most frequently in correctional studies. It represents the proportion of individuals released from a correctional program who are arrested, or prosecuted, or convicted, or returned to prison—the exact criterion varies from study to study—within a year of release from prison, or parole, or probation, or a halfway house; the date on which the offender's clock starts also differs from study to study.

[2]Nils Christie's article, "Is It Time to Stop Counting?" (Christie, 1976:75) refers to the penchant of many criminal justice researchers to quantify trivia (or analyze trivia that someone else has

When I was an undergraduate in engineering school there was a saying: An engineer measures it with a micrometer, marks it with a piece of chalk, and cuts it with an axe. This expression described the imbalance in precision one sometimes sees in engineering projects. A similar phenomenon holds true for social scientists, although the imbalance is in the opposite direction. It sometimes seems that a social scientist measures it with a series of ambiguous questions, marks it with a bunch of inconsistent coders, and cuts it to within three decimal places. Some balance in precision is needed, from the initial measurement process to the final preparation of results.

This book, then, aims at improving and balancing precision in recidivism methodology across the board, from how it is measured to how it is marked to how it is cut. The term methodology is not restricted to matters mathematical or statistical; definitional and contextual issues must also be included, and not only for the sake of completeness; the rationale for the statistical model of recidivism developed in this book is based on the substantive and organizational characteristics of the recidivism process. The definitional and contextual aspects of recidivism and the statistical aspects are interdependent; the two halves are intertwined.

OVERVIEW OF THE BOOK

The definitional and contextual aspects of recidivism are addressed in Chapters 2 through 6. Problems of modeling are discussed in Chapters 7 and 8, and statistical methods of measuring recidivism are treated in Chapters 9 and 10.

The Context of Recidivism

Recidivism is not the only measure used to evaluate correctional programs, because reduction in offender criminality is not the only goal of the criminal sanction. Chapters 2 and 3 put the measurement of recidivism in perspective. In Chapter 2 the different goals of the criminal sanction and of corrections are described, and appropriate measures of effectiveness are given. Some goals relate to the offender, others concern the behavior of society, while still others refer to the conditions of confinement. These goals cannot all be evaluated using recidivism as a measure of effectiveness. In fact, as Chapter 2 shows, recidivism is useful only for evaluating goals related to the offender. For only one of these goals can recidivism be used as the primary measure of effectiveness, while it is a secondary measure of effectiveness for two other offender-related goals.

The fact that recidivism can be used as a measure of correctional effectiveness

---

quantified) and ignore substance. He concludes, "It is not time to stop counting. But it is time to know more *before* counting, *while* counting and *after* counting."

does not mean that it should be so used. Chapter 3 discusses some of the reasons for not doing so. Using recidivism as a measure of correctional effectiveness implies that offenders—not society—need correcting, that we know how to correct offenders, and that correcting offenders will lead to reduced criminality. These assumptions are often implicit, yet some would dispute their validity. In addition, the fact that recidivism is a measure of failure rather than success is seen by some to cast a shadow over corrections; but measuring success is generally more difficult—and more intrusive into the ex-offender's life—than is measuring failure. Although recidivism may have been used improperly and too extensively in the past, there are a number of instances, described in Chapter 3, in which recidivism is both appropriate and useful as an outcome measure.

Using Recidivism as a Measure of Correctional Effectiveness

Two rather important examples of the improper use of recidivism to measure correctional effectiveness are described in Chapter 4. Both studies resulted in newspaper headlines and had major policy implications. Both were wrong, but for different reasons. The conclusion of the first study was that nothing works to correct offenders. The only reason for this pessimistic assessment was that no "silver bullet" was found that could be used to rehabilitate all offenders under all conditions. The second study, which claimed to have found the silver bullet for chronic juvenile offenders, did not consider the statistical nature of the data, which led to an overwhelmingly favorable assessment of energetic interventions in juveniles' subsequent careers. This study is an example of how statistical methodology can affect results, conclusions and, subsequently, policy.

Using the right methodology does not automatically ensure that recivids is used properly to evaluate programs. As Chapter 5 describes with respect to the parole process, the characteristics of the organization in which the study is conducted can have a major effect on recidivism outcomes, so that comparisons of studies in different jurisdictions are ill advised. Furthermore, different jurisdictions may use different definitions of recidivism, so much so that these comparisons are rendered meaningless.

Defining Recidivism

Recidivism definitions can be based on varying amounts of information, depending on the availability of data from the criminal justice system. In Chapter 6, this availability and its effect on recidivism measures are discussed, leading to the conclusion that recidivism definitions should be based on arrests or (parole or probation) violations. A taxonomy of recidivism definitions based on arrests and violations is proposed in this chapter. A researcher using this taxonomy will at

OVERVIEW OF THE BOOK 5

least be able to determine whether two studies have a chance of being comparable.

In summary, Chapters 2 through 6 explore how recidivism is used to study the subsequent behavior of released offenders. Recidivism's viability as a measure and examples of its definition and use (and misuse) are given. Methodological considerations relating to its definition and organizational context are described.

Considerations of Statistical Methodology

Chapters 7 through 10 explore the more quantitative methodological concerns. These include consideration of the models used to study recidivism, the means by which a model is selected, and how the selected model can be used to analyze recidivism data. Other methods of data analysis are also described.

Chapter 7 discusses modeling in the social sciences. The characteristics and development of models and their advantages and disadvantages are presented to set the stage for a critique of the 1-year recidivism rate,[3] the most frequently used model of recidivism. Next is a description of a family of recidivism models based on failure rate analysis, which makes more effective use of the data.

How to choose among these competing failure rate models is the subject of Chapter 8. Both informal (eyeballing) and formal methods of comparison (the chi-square goodness-of-fit test, split-sample model validation) are described and their deficiencies noted. Finally, a procedure is described for selecting a model based on the model's forecasting ability and on its versatility. This procedure strengthens the argument for using one particular model of the recidivism process, termed Model M_1, based on the incomplete exponential distribution.

Taking a model of the recidivism process and turning it into a set of procedures to analyze recidivism data is the subject of Chapter 9. Procedures are described to provide estimates of the model's parameters and associated confidence regions. For a special case of interest, graphical techniques can be used; the graphs are given and their use described in this chapter.

Chapter 9 also describes the relationship between the size of the confidence region and four statistics that summarize the data—number in the group under study, observation time, number of failures, and total failure time. Because the confidence region varies as a function of both sample size and observation time, this method provides an important side benefit. Since observation time and sample size affect level of confidence in the probability of recidivism, a researcher can choose the length of follow-up period based on the confidence level desired. This procedure makes the choice of length of follow-up time a rational one rather than one based on funding cycles, as it often is.

[3]See Note 1.

Chapter 10 contains a discussion and description of more advanced techniques that employ covariate and nonparametric methods. Covariate methods permit one to disentangle the various effects of offender or program characteristics on recidivism. Nonparametric methods are not based on any particular model of recidivism; covariate methods can also be used nonparametrically to analyze the effect of different characteristics on outcomes. The problems and potential contribution of these methods to the study of recidivism are described.

Four appendixes are provided. Appendix A derives the maximum likelihood and Bayesian procedures used to estimate the parameters of Model M_1. Appendix B describes the methods used to calculate confidence intervals and regions for these parameters and for associated forecasts. Appendix C provides tables describing the confidence regions for Model M_1, and gives an example of their use. Finally, Appendix D contains the listings of FORTRAN programs that can be used to provide maximum likelihood estimates and confidence regions for correctional data, and gives examples of their use.

2
Correctional Goals and Their Evaluation

Correction or rehabilitation of the offender is but one of the goals that society specifies for prisoner custodial and treatment programs. Sechrest *et al.* (1979:18) list seven goals of criminal sanctions:

1. to deter the offender from offending again by punishment or fear of punishment (without necessarily changing him or her in any other way);
2. to deter others from behaving as the offender has;
3. to incapacitate the offender and thus deprive him or her of the opportunity to offend again for a given period of time;
4. to forestall personal vengeance by those hurt by the offender;
5. to exact retribution from the offender and so set right the scales of moral justice;
6. to educate people morally or socially;
7. to rehabilitate or reform the offender.

These goals are value-laden goals: they focus on producing beneficial effects for society or on improving the future conduct of offenders.

Society also imposes limits on criminal sanctions and on the agencies that administer them, limits that can also be construed as correctional goals. Some of these goals relate to the essential fairness of the criminal sanction: they include proportionality and sentence equity. Still other correctional goals are more in the nature of administrative or managerial objectives. They include safety and humaneness in institutional care, and the protection of the incarcerated and of the institution staff and the public from incarcerated offenders.

Discussion of these correctional goals and how their achievement may be measured is the subject of this chapter. This discussion is not meant to be a full exploration of correctional and penal philosophy, which is the province of legal and moral philosophers, and well beyond the scope of this book. (A more thorough discussion of the goals of the criminal sanction is found in Gross and von Hirsch, 1981.) But this book is concerned with the evaluation of correctional outcomes, and correctional outcomes only have meaning with reference to correctional goals; hence, we should examine these goals to develop outcome measures for evaluative purposes.

Recidivism is not the only measure of correctional effectiveness, or even of rehabilitation, although many feel that it is. With such diverse correctional goals one cannot expect a single measure of effectiveness to cover the waterfront; measures of similar diversity are required. These measures are described in this chapter to put consideration of recidivism in the proper context, as a measure of effectiveness for some of the more important goals of corrections.

GOALS RELATED TO THE OFFENDER

Correctional goals can be divided into three general groups: those that relate to the offenders, those that relate to society at large, and those that relate to the correctional institution. Goals related to the offenders are concerned with reducing the number of crimes they commit, by "curing" them (rehabilitation), frightening them (special deterrence), or imprisoning them (incapacitation). A discussion of these offender-related goals follows.

Rehabilitation

The very word *rehabilitation* contains certain implications about offenders and correctional programs. It implies that:

1. Incarcerated individuals have problems, problems which are a direct cause of their criminal behavior;
2. correctional program personnel can diagnose these problems accurately, and have appropriate treatments available for the individuals;
3. these treatments will be properly applied; and
4. the problems will be "corrected" (or at least mitigated) as a result of these treatments.
5. In addition, the individuals' criminal behavior will begin to diminish as a result of mitigating the problems.

This sequence of implications forms a logical construct (see Figure 2-1), and is what is normally meant when rehabilitation or correction is considered to be the goal of the criminal sanction; it has been referred to as the "medical model" of corrections. This logical construct is quite appropriate for medical treatments, in which the causal links are physical and physiological and can be traced with appropriate instrumentation. But such a construct is a heavy burden to place on correctional treatments. Too little is known about behavioral change or the causes of criminal behavior to make this sequence of implications apply to corrections. Yet this model still may be appropriate for some offender types and some programs designed for them. An evaluation based on the goal of rehabilitation would gauge the extent to which this model of the correctional process actually applies.

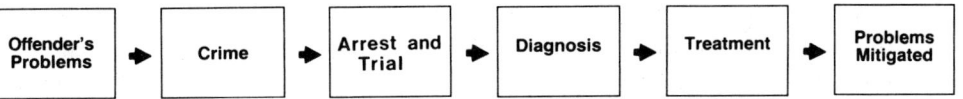

FIGURE 2-1 The logical construct of offender rehabilitation.

Although most offenders are sent to correctional institutions or participate in correctional programs, and the agencies administering these institutions and programs are called departments of corrections or offender rehabilitation, these titles are more wishful thinking than they are descriptive. One could hardly expect otherwise: programs and agencies should not be held responsible for what is basically an individual's choosing to continue to break the law, especially since such behavior occurs in environments beyond the control of correctional organizations.

An evaluation based on the goal of rehabilitation should be primarily a *process evaluation;*[1] that is, it should be primarily concerned with validating the logical construct previously described (and depicted in Figure 2-1): Did the offender have problems? Were they a direct cause of his criminal behavior? Were they diagnosed properly? and so on.

For example, an offender may be diagnosed as having psychological problems that led to his criminal behavior. Determining the nature of the offender's problems would require extensive psychological testing, both before and after treatment. In addition, an assessment of the diagnostic and treatment capabilities of the correctional agency would need to be undertaken, to determine whether the treatment program can actually be implemented in the agency. This assessment would concentrate on the process of rehabilitation, and not just on the bottom line of reduction in criminality.

Measurement problems in evaluating the goal of rehabilitation loom quite large, especially because of the nature of the agency administering the program (Martin *et al.,* 1981:15). Many would claim that an agency whose focus is primarily penal cannot serve any rehabilitative function. While such an extreme position may be overstated, it is a plausible working hypothesis that tests and treatments designed for willing participants on the outside are not entirely applicable to a captive audience of prisoners.

Of course, not all problems are psychological in nature; lack of education and job-related skills also affect the propensity of an individual to resort to crime. Process evaluations that focus on these more tangible aspects of rehabilitation would have fewer measurement problems.

---

[1]Every program has (or should have) a rationale, a raison d'etre, based on an empirical or theoretical body of knowledge, that explains why it is assumed that the treatment will cause or lead to certain outcomes. A process evaluation is an assessment of the extent to which the program was implemented properly and followed its rationale.

The last step in the logical construct (Figure 2-1) is the *impact evaluation*:[2] to what extent were treatment group members rehabilitated? This step implies measuring the extent of problem amelioration in the treatment group and comparing it to the improvement noted in a similar control (i.e., nontreatment) group. If there is a difference in improvement it may be attributed to the treatment, regardless of the nature of the process or the way the treatment worked.

The impact evaluation, in fact, is often done without the process evaluation and is considerably less satisfactory than one incorporating a process evaluation: it is important to know how a program worked (or why it did not) to determine its applicability under different circumstances and for different populations.

But impact evaluations of correctional programs often ignore program goals. Rehabilitation programs may be evaluated not on the basis of what the treatment is expected to accomplish, but rather on the basis of recidivism. Thus the question addressed is not, Did the treatment mitigate the problem addressed by the program?, but rather, Did the program (somehow) reduce the postrelease criminality of its participants? Recidivism, then, is employed as a measure of effectiveness for the goal of rehabilitation.

As von Hirsch (1976:11) points out,

> In the literature of rehabilitation, there is often considerable ambiguity whether the aim is to reduce recidivism (a form of crime prevention) or to help the offender with his own problems (a paternalistic goal). But treatment programs have generally been tested by measuring their effects on recidivism—suggesting that the goal of reducing recidivism is actually the primary one.

This is the stance taken by the National Academy of Sciences' Panel on Research on Rehabilitative Techniques (Sechrest *et al.*, 1979). The panel not only points out that recidivism is the "traditional measure" for evaluating rehabilitation programs, but also states that it is "the *sole criterion* against which rehabilitation ultimately must be measured" (Sechrest *et al.*, 1979:21, emphasis added: see also Martin *et al.*, 1981:8).

Considering the difficulties inherent in doing a process evaluation, this stance is understandable; a virtue is made of necessity. Counting the number of people rearrested is much easier than doing a process evaluation. But this stance is also troublesome. Looking only at the bottom line, recidivism, without consideration of how the program effected the outcome, is a shortsighted approach to program evaluation. I do not dispute the importance of considering recidivism in evaluating rehabilitation programs (after all, this book develops methods for doing so); however, I question the extreme position taken by Sechrest *et al.* (1979). Other

---

[2] An impact evaluation is an assessment of the extent to which the program goals are achieved, regardless of whether they were achieved by the program as described in the rationale, by the program in some unforeseen way, or by some other means. A control group is normally required to determine the program's effect. An impact evaluation cannot determine how the program caused the impact; a process evaluation is needed for that.

evaluative measures are often of much greater benefit in understanding a program's effectiveness than is recidivism alone.

Special Deterrence

Two different types of deterrence are distinguished by Zimring and Hawkins (1973): general deterrence and special deterrence. *General deterrence* is the reduction in criminal activity by the general public attributable to a planned intervention. The intervention may be one based on criminal justice system actions—for example, more police or increased penalties (Press, 1971; Campbell & Ross, 1968), or it may be based on individual or community actions—for example, Operation Whistlestop (Reed, 1978) or community organization (Cirel et al., 1977). *Special* (or individual) *deterrence* is the reduction in criminal activity by specific offenders, as a direct consequence of their fear of incarceration or some other sanction. It implies that these offenders have been convinced that the risk of additional penalties is not worth the potential rewards from continued criminal behavior.

Measurement of the extent of special deterrence is relatively straightforward. One need only trace the future criminal careers of the specific offenders, which is facilitated by the existence of criminal history records or "rap sheets."[3] One can study how a given sanction affects the recidivism rates of different types of offenders, or one can hold offender characteristics constant and vary the sanction.

Thus, recidivism is useful as a measure of the extent of special deterrence. However, since this same measure is also used for measuring rehabilitation, one cannot be certain which of these goals is being achieved: it may not be possible to disentangle the effects of the carrot (rehabilitation) from those of the stick (special deterrence) (Sechrest et al., 1979:21).

Incapacitation

Incapacitation means that an incarcerated offender cannot commit a crime, at least not against the general public, while incarcerated. To evaluate the extent to which crime is reduced as a result of incapacitation, one must estimate the number of crimes that would have been committed by the offender if incarcerated

---

[3] Anyone who has tried to use these records to study criminal behavior knows how glib a statement this is; criminal history records are notoriously incomplete and inaccurate. However, compared to studies of deterrence in other areas, the task is straightforward. For example, consider the problem of assessing the effectiveness of sanctions imposed on drunk drivers. There are no rap sheets showing the arrests and subsequent dispositions of people arrested for driving while intoxicated (DWI). To obtain such information might require a search of records in police departments and county court houses throughout a state, with much less expectation that the information is complete or accurate.

for a shorter period of time (or not at all). One can then show how different sentencing practices affect the total crime rate.

Estimating what would have happened had the offenders been free is a crucial component of an incapacitation evaluation. Early estimates of the incapacitation effect were based on simple models of the criminal behavior of offenders; see, for example, Marsh and Singer (1972), Avi-Itzhak and Shinnar (1973), Clarke (1974), Shinnar and Shinnar (1975), and Greenberg (1975). Their claims as to the extent of crime rate reduction due to incapacitation have been shown to be based on a variety of assumptions which may make the mathematics more tractable but do not typify offender behavior (Cohen, 1978).

More recently, empirical investigations into patterns of criminal activity have been conducted by Chaiken and Chaiken (1982). Their study, based on interviews with over 2000 incarcerated offenders in California, Michigan, and Texas, describes the variation in characteristics and criminal behavior among their respondents. They develop 10 different categories of offenders, based on the types of crimes committed by the offenders. Offense rates varied considerably; but the most active category, the "violent predators," committed crimes at the following high annual rates: robbery, 135; assault, 18; burglary, 516; forgery and fraud, 578; and drug dealing, 4088 (Chaiken & Chaiken, 1982a:56). There were indications that these offenders alternated between quiescent periods with relatively low crime rates and active periods marked by these very high crime rates.

These findings contradicted many of the assumptions of the early models of criminal behavior, thus invalidating their conclusions about incapacitative effects. The findings also suggested to some investigators that crime rates could be lowered significantly, without expanding prison capacity, by selectively incapacitating violent predators and other high-rate offenders for longer periods, while at the same time reducing the sentences of low-rate offenders. In fact, using the data from Chaiken and Chaiken (1982), Greenwood (1982) proposed doing just that. For example, he estimated (p. 85) that California could achieve a 15% reduction in robberies while reducing the prison population by 5%, if high-rate robbers are given longer sentences and low-rate offenders are given reduced sentences.

The crucial issue here is identification of high-rate offenders: is there some way to use routinely collected criminal justice data (as opposed to the self-report data used by Chaiken & Chaiken) to distinguish between high-rate offenders and others? Unfortunately, for the present the answer appears to be no. Greenwood (1982) attempted to identify high-rate offenders using a modification of Hoffman and Beck's (1974) Salient Factor Score. This method produces a very high number of false positives (Type 1 errors): upwards of half of the offenders predicted to be high- (or medium- or low-) rate offenders are misclassified (Greenwood, 1982:59). As the Chaikens (1982a:78) point out, "the specific collection of official data we had available did not permit discriminating the violent predators from the others." Cohen (1982) details other problems with selective incapacitation as a criminal justice policy.

This is not to say that identification of violent predators and other high-rate offenders will never be possible: only that it is not possible given the present state of affairs with respect to criminal justice data. It may be that other sources of data, for example, from schools or the juvenile justice system, will become available, permitting better identification to be made and better models to be constructed.

One of the unknown factors in such modeling efforts is the extent to which postrelease criminality is affected by incarceration. That is, will an individual upon release try to "make up for lost time" by increasing criminal activity, in effect nullifying the incapacitative effect? Or will the individual be more subdued after release, adding a deterrent effect to the incapacitative effect? An investigation of postrelease criminality (i.e., recidivism) would thus be useful in studying certain aspects of the incapacitative effect of incarceration.

Summary

We see that these three goals—rehabilitation, special deterrence, and incapacitation—which are concerned with the criminal behavior of a convicted offender, all use postrelease criminality, or recidivism, for their measurement. In the case of rehabilitation, recidivism should play a secondary role; for measuring special deterrence, recidivism is the only appropriate measure; and for estimating incapacitative effects, measures of recidivism permit the estimation of the number of crimes averted by the incarceration of offenders.

GOALS RELATED TO SOCIETY

Correctional goals are not directed solely at offenders. They focus on the general public as well. They include general deterrence—using the sanction imposed on offenders to deter others from committing crimes; forestalling vengeance—punishing lawbreakers so that the victims will not take the law into their own hands; moral and social education—using a trial and conviction as a morality play, and retribution and desert—fitting the punishment to the crime.

General Deterrence

General deterrence is based on the premise that the threat of a criminal penalty will convince potential offenders not to engage in criminal behavior. It is based on a sequence of assumptions concerning risk taking, how the threat of punishment is communicated, and the rationality of offender decision making, assumptions that are open to question (Cook, 1980). In recent years general deterrence has been studied extensively with respect to a number of criminal justice policies, two of the more prominent ones being capital punishment and gun control.

With regard to capital punishment, Ehrlich's (1973, 1975) conclusions about its deterrent effect on homicide have been hotly debated (Baldus & Cole, 1975; Bowers & Pierce, 1975; Forst, 1976; Passell, 1975). The relative infrequency of homicides and rarity of executions make the analysis quite sensitive to very small changes in the number of events. And changes in the assumptions implicit in the various analytic methods used make a considerable difference in the conclusions; see Klein *et al.* (1978). In addition, Barnett (1981a, 1981b) shows that the models used in these studies are for the most part inadequate in extracting the putative deterrent effect from the "noise" of the underlying stochastic process.

Another study of general deterrence focused on gun control. Deutsch and Alt (1977) reported that gun-related crimes in Boston were deterred by a new guncontrol law in Massachusetts. Although this conclusion was disputed (Hay & McCleary, 1979; Deutsch, 1979), subsequent research (Pierce & Bowers, 1979) using more data and more extensive analyses did show that certain crimes were deterred by the new law. (Wright *et al.* (1983:280–297) discuss the methodological and substantive issues surrounding the implementation of this law.)

Measuring the deterrent effect of a new policy requires the collection of data before and after the policy is implemented. One of the major threats to the validity of such studies is regression to the mean: this phenomenon can produce what looks like a deterrent effect when there really is none. For example, Campbell and Ross (1968) show how an apparent deterrent effect was generated by a new traffic enforcement policy. Following a year in which there was an unusually high number of traffic deaths, a new, stricter policy of traffic law enforcement was initiated. In the next year traffic deaths went down, but probably would have done so irrespective of the new policy: it would have been highly unlikely to have 2 consecutive years of unusually high traffic death rates. Therefore, care must be exercised to account for regression effects and other threats to validity when studying general deterrence.

Forestalling Vengeance

We entrust the criminal justice system with a monopoly on the legal use of coercive force. In return we expect that we will be protected from crime, and that the criminal justice system will punish offenders in the event that the protection proves ineffective and the offenders are known.

But offenders normally cannot be identified by their victims, so personal vengeance cannot for the most part be carried out. However, this does not mean that all vengeance is forestalled; it may be practiced vicariously. Many television programs use this theme; and the popularity of the recent movies *"Death Wish"* and "*Death Wish II,*" in which a man whose wife and daughter were assaulted goes after muggers and rapists, suggests that criminal sanctions do not completely eliminate all feelings of personal vengeance. In addition, vigilante groups have sprung up in many communities to augment what they see as ineffectual police activity (Marx & Archer, 1971, 1973). In Brazil, where the crime rate has grown dramatically in recent years, lynchings of criminal suspects have occurred (Hoge, 1979). Even in the United States we find reports of people "taking the law into their own hands" (Wattley, 1982), in some cases because of perceived inadequacies of the criminal justice system (Hirsley, 1983).

Measuring the effectiveness of criminal sanctions in forestalling vengeance is no easy task; in fact, it may not be possible. Public confidence in the criminal justice system is one possible measure, but it is a weak indicator of the extent to which private vengeance is eschewed. One possible contraindication might be sales of handguns; but one would need to determine the extent to which gun sales are attributable to fear or to vengeance.[4]

Moral and Social Education

The criminal law and its accompanying punishment serve notice to the public as to exactly what behaviors are proscribed. That is, the criminal law serves as a community's boundaries or radius of allowable activity "in the sense that its members tend to . . . regard any conduct which drifts outside that radius as somehow inappropriate or immoral" (Erikson, 1966:10). This announcement is an integral aspect of general deterrence: potential offenders cannot be deterred from committing crimes if they are unaware that the behavior is defined as criminal (or, alternatively, if they are aware that the law is rarely enforced). In that sense, the educational goal of the criminal sanction can be seen as an intermediate step between the sanction and deterrence. The announcement is intended to affect all citizens, not just offenders or potential offenders.

One of the more interesting facets of the deterrent effect of the Massachusetts gun law was the role played by the accompanying extensive publicity campaign. No more restrictive than laws in other locales, the law has significantly deterred gun-related offenses, a circumstance that Pierce and Bowers (1979) convincingly attribute to the publicity accompanying the law's enactment. It is also likely that the campaign's effect was not restricted to potential offenders: a major effect may have been in its encouragement of police, prosecutors, and judges to enforce the law fully.

Measurement of this goal would be based on surveys of the general population, to determine the extent to which people are aware of the criminal law, of its

---

[4]Wright *et al.* (1983) describe studies that have been conducted to determine the reasons for purchasing handguns.

accompanying penalties, and of the extent to which the laws are actually enforced.

Retribution and Desert

One of the purposes of criminal sanctions is to punish the offender because of the intentional harm he or she caused the victim. Retribution and desert focus on this concern. von Hirsch (1976:46) discusses the pejorative connotation of *retribution,* which seems to imply revenge, vindictiveness, and punishment out of proportion to the offense; while *desert* implies a measured punishment meted out rationally. Basing sanctions on desert or retribution implies that the punishment is to fit the crime, not the criminal: it should not be based on a prediction of future criminality (from an offender's past record); only the instant offense should be considered. But desert is a sword that cuts two ways—it would also mean that a first offender not be given special consideration.

It is difficult to develop a means of evaluating the extent to which these goals are achieved. As Morris (1974:75) notes, "Desert is, of course, not precisely quantifiable." One might gauge the public's perception of the degree of harm caused by each offense and to compare their perceptions with punishments for those offenses. The study by Sellin and Wolfgang (1964) on the public's perception of offense seriousness does this to some extent. However, as Reiss (1982) points out, crimes that are usually considered less serious, especially vandalism, may be the ones that "substantially contribute to the destruction of communities" (p. 584); we may need to give greater attention to juvenile crimes than we have in the past if punishment is to be based on a harm-based desert.

Proportionality and Sentence Equity

Retribution and desert are related to the concepts of proportionality (letting the punishment fit the crime and the past behavior of the offender) and sentence equity (giving like punishments to like offenders who commit like crimes).

Studies that have been concerned with these goals include those by the American Friends Service Committee (1971), Fogel (1979), and von Hirsch (1976). Their influence has been felt in the enactment of new laws and criminal codes in a number of states, in which sentencing guidelines are promulgated and the discretion of judges and parole authorities in changing sentences is curtailed.

Efforts have been undertaken to evaluate sentence equity. In particular, Barry and Greer (1981) have developed a measure of sentence disparity that can be used to study equity. Assessment of sentence proportionality would be based in part on an analysis of sentencing guidelines, to determine the extent to which the punishment does indeed fit the crime. However, the assessment should be based not only on the sentence as handed down, but on the sentence as served. This would require an examination of the whole criminal justice system, to determine the extent to which discretion in the system is used to distort the ideals of proportionality and sentence equity.

GOALS RELATED TO THE CORRECTIONAL INSTITUTION

Other goals focus on the administration of correctional institutions. They include the provision of adequate food, housing, and health care, the safety of residents and staff, and the prevention of escapes.

Measurement of these goals is facilitated by the existence of standards in these areas, promulgated by the Correctional Standards and Accreditation Project (American Correctional Association, 1981), and jails and prisons throughout the country are being upgraded to meet these standards. Others are being upgraded involuntarily, under court order following inmates' suits. Assessing the extent to which these goals are met is therefore straightforward.

SUMMARY

In this chapter we have reviewed the various goals of the correctional system and described how they may be measured. Some are fairly easy to measure (e.g., those related to institutional administration) because they are so clear-cut and because standards and standard measures exist for them. Other goals (forestalling vengeance, exacting retribution, sentence proportionality) are not so easy to measure; they are not well defined, nor are there standard ways to measure them.

In evaluating goals relating to the offender, we are on firmer ground because a useful measure does exist—that of recidivism. While recidivism is not truly a measure of rehabilitation, it does measure the extent to which rehabilitation reduces future criminality; furthermore, recidivism is a valid measure of special deterrence[5] and is useful in studying incapacitation. The next chapter examines arguments for and against using recidivism as a measure of correctional effectiveness.

---

[5]Not only *can* recidivism be used to measure special deterrence, it *should* be used. "To base extra punishment on a *belief* in deterrence is morally acceptable only as long as it is necessary. When facilities exist for the evaluation of sanction policies, failure to test policies while continuing to penalize offenders in the name of deterrent beliefs becomes morally obnoxious" (Zimring and Hawkins, 1973:43; emphasis in the original).

3
Recidivism as a Measure of Correctional Effectiveness

Recidivism, or postrelease criminality, is the outcome measure used most frequently in evaluating correctional programs. As mentioned in the last chapter, some consider recidivism to be the sole criterion for assessing correctional programs. But it has often been used indiscriminately without regard for its appropriateness or limitations. In this chapter I discuss some of its more salient limitations. First, I explore the values that are implicit whenever recidivism is used as an evaluation criterion. Next I discuss the practical problems encountered in using recidivism as a measure of correctional effectiveness. Alternative evaluation criteria are then discussed. Finally, I discuss what recidivism can tell us and when the use of recidivism is appropriate as an outcome measure.

THE VALUES IN EVALUATION

Whenever scientists do research, especially social research, they insert their personal values. Many would deny this, insisting that science is objective and therefore value neutral. Max Weber (1949) may have laid this illusion to rest in the social sciences, but as Heims (1980:360) notes, it continues to persist in the natural sciences:

> The ethos of science rests on two pillars, the politically useful myth of "value neutrality" and the article of faith most conducive to the growth of scientific bureaucracy, namely, that scientific innovations ("progress") and science-based technological innovations are *a priori* beneficial. While these two pillars clearly knock against each other, they continue to hold up the practice of science.

Clearly, research on corrections cannot be considered value free, even by its most objective practitioners. Among the values implicit in correctional studies are that the offender, not society, needs correcting; that we know how to, and should, change a person's behavior (for the better); that problem amelioration will lead directly and immediately to reduced recidivism; and that measuring failure is appropriate in correctional studies. These values are discussed below.

Offenders Need Correcting

Correctional evaluations often make the implicit assumption that it is the individual offender who needs correcting; yet some argue that the social and political system that created the criminogenic environment should be corrected. The increase in crime would thus be seen as a measure of the extent to which society is failing the individual, not the reverse. According to this argument, recidivism should be looked upon as an indicator of deficiencies in society in general (and in the criminal justice system in particular), not only of deficiencies in the individual offenders.

The assumption that the offender needs correcting may be incorrect for other reasons. No doubt there are some offenders whose criminal activity is promoted in some way by correctible defects: inability to read, lack of employable skills, personal or family problems. But some may choose to commit crimes because it is easier than working a straight 9-to-5 job, some because they enjoy risk-taking, some because of peer pressure. These reasons for committing crimes may be considered defects by some, but not by the offenders.

Critics of correctional evaluations have suggested looking beyond the goals of corrections to the goals of the criminal justice system in general, and evaluating programs on the basis of their contribution to these goals. One might consider a goal of the criminal justice system to be the reinforcement of societal values; another goal might be the reduction of harm to society due to crime. Not addressing these goals and focusing on recidivism is thus seen as shortsighted because its relevance to these overall goals may be marginal.

We Know How to Correct

A concentration on recidivism conveys the implication that we can do something to reduce the postrelease criminality of offenders, that we just have not found the right combination of treatment modalities yet. In other words, the offender is not responsible for his subsequent acts; it is we who have failed to provide for his rehabilitation. This view, of course, presumes that it is easy to change a person's behavior. But as Wilkins (1969:7) points out, "If it were possible to change from 'bad' to 'good' without much effort, changes from 'good' to 'bad' could probably be effected as simply and perhaps would involve a larger proportion of the population." As will be discussed in Chapter 4, our knowledge of "what works" in correcting offenders is quite limited; we do not yet know how or why offenders terminate their criminal careers.

Correcting Leads to Reduced Criminality

To label a program a success or failure on the basis of its participants' future criminality is to distort the true value of many programs. Good programs may be curtailed or eliminated because recidivism is the dominant measure of correctional effectiveness. If an illiterate offender has learned to read while in prison, but committed a crime after release because of a heroin habit or unemployment, this crime has nothing to do with the program's effectiveness. The program may have been quite successful, but success at one level does not automatically (or immediately) lead to success at another level. The underlying assumption that alleviating an individual's problems will cause him or her to turn away from criminal activity unfortunately is not always true.

But sometimes the assumption does hold: the criminal activity of some offenders may be reduced because of the program. However, it is not realistic to expect an instant and total conversion on the part of these offenders. Habits of a lifetime should not be expected to disappear immediately, no matter how successful the program. Since recidivism measures are normally based on behavior immediately after release, the program's beneficial effects may be underestimated.[1]

Failure as a Correctional Measure

When a program is evaluated using recidivism (i.e., failure), instead of criteria that highlight success, a particular set of values may be fostered among program evaluators. Their attention is given to program participants only when they fail; they are not asked to follow up and report on the successes of program participants. This can create a subtle bias in the program evaluation—program evaluators who are asked to document failures rather than successes may approach their task from a pessimistic point of view.

These criticisms of the use of recidivism as a measure of correctional effectiveness are based on the values inherent in its use. There are also criticisms of its use based on the more practical aspects of conducting correctional research.

PRACTICAL DIFFICULTIES IN EVALUATION

A number of practical difficulties arise in the evaluation of correctional programs. Some are present regardless of the outcome measure used; for example, one can rarely run a controlled experiment in corrections. Other difficulties relate

---

[1]Extreme care should be taken in pretest–posttest evaluations to ensure that the decline in criminality is real and not an artifact of the selection process. See Maltz *et al.* (1980) for a description of the artifact; it is also discussed in the next chapter.

to the choice of recidivism as an outcome measure: lack of a standard definition and poor data quality are common in recidivism studies. These and other problems are discussed below.

Research Design

The assumption that a particular correctional program causes the behavior of its participants to change is often doubtful. Even when all threats to validity have been accounted for, as in a well-designed correctional experiment, attribution may be faulty. For example, success may be due more to the personalities of the staff running the program than to the nature of the program: given that same staff, any program would show signs of success. One might say that this is true success anyway, since the staff are part of the program. But correctional experiments are normally run to test correctional treatments for widespread use. If they are successful only when implemented by a dedicated staff, the external validity of the experiment (i.e., its generalizability to other settings) is suspect.

But true experiments are the exception in correctional research. Sechrest *et al.* (1979:60) argue the case for true experiments, but it is an uphill battle. Rarely is it possible to form equivalent experimental and control groups, or to assign people randomly to one or the other, when doing correctional research. Prisoners are protected from being coerced into volunteering for experimental programs where they are subject to manipulation by researchers.[2] Therefore, quasi-experimental research designs[3] are the norm in correctional research; and quasi experiments contain many threats to validity.

For example, in a quasi experiment one may try to match the cohort volunteering for an experiment with a cohort of those who do not volunteer. Even if both cohorts have comparable distributions of age, race, prior offense records, education, etc., there is one important variable that cannot be accounted for: voluntarism. And prisoners volunteer to participate in experimental programs for a variety of reasons—motivation, boredom, a desire to impress the parole board, a real interest in the program, a desire to better themselves—some of which are quite relevant to correctional success. (Blumstein and Cohen [1979a] show how the effect of voluntarism can be addressed in a quasi-experimental evaluation of a prison-based college educational program.) Thus, a difference in recidivism rates between groups in a quasi-experimental program evaluation may be attributed to the program, but is actually due to the hidden difference between the groups.

---

[2] It is often moot as to who is manipulating whom. Courses in research methodology rarely spend time on describing how con artists try to put one over on researchers.

[3] Quasi-experimental designs use "nonequivalent groups that differ from each other in many ways other than the presence of a treatment whose effects are being tested. The task confronting persons who try to interpret the results from quasi experiments is basically one of separating the effects of a treatment from those due to the initial noncomparability between the average units in each treatment group; only the effects of the treatment are of research interest" (Cook & Campbell, 1979:6).

Recidivism Definitions

There is no consistent definition of recidivism. One program may use a follow-up time of 1 year, another of 6 months.[4] Follow-up time may be computed starting with release from prison or with release from parole. The recidivating event may be a technical violation of the conditions of parole, or it may be a return to prison. There are so many possible variations in the method of computing recidivism that one doubts if more than a handful of the hundreds of correctional evaluations are truly comparable. Nor is there any way of deciding which of the many variations is most applicable for a given situation (Sechrest *et al.*, 1979:73).

Data Quality

The ideal situation with respect to recidivism data would be one in which everything was known about every crime committed and who committed it. In that way we would have complete data on every recidivating event. However, we do not even have information about every crime, let alone information about who committed it.

Recidivism data are based on reported crimes, not all crimes. Studies of crime-reporting behavior (LEAA, 1977:9) have shown that only about half of the crimes reported to Census Bureau interviewers are reported to the police. When studying crime, then, one can supplement data on crimes reported to the police with survey data to get a more complete picture of the crime problem. However, the same does not hold true for recidivism data. We could, perhaps, conduct a survey of all individuals we are following up, asking them whether and when they committed crimes; but the validity of such data would indeed be questionable. In studying recidivism, we therefore must use data based on arrests and parole violations, not data based on crimes, whether self-reported by offenders or victims.

Using only officially reported events creates another problem. Such data are very sensitive to policy shifts within the data-collecting agencies. For example, parole officers may be told to be lenient with their parolees (if the prisons are overcrowded) or to tighten up on parole (if the parole agency has been receiving unfavorable publicity). The recidivism rates in the two situations would doubtless be quite different. Changes in police arrest policies may have a similar effect. The extent to which policy shifts of this kind affect recidivism statistics is not known.

[4]The National Advisory Commission on Criminal Justice Standards and Goals (1973:529) recommends a follow-up time of 3 years. "*While this is an arbitrary figure,* it is chosen because the few recidivism studies that have followed offenders for more than three years have shown that most recidivism occurs within three years of release from supervision" (emphasis added). The effect of choice of follow-up period is discussed in Chapters 7 and 9.

Because of the measure's variability (described in greater detail in Chapters 5 and 6) one cannot state with any degree of assurance whether a given recidivism rate is high or low; there is no "normal" recidivism rate as there is a normal body temperature.[5] Therefore, recidivism can only be used as a comparative measure.

Another problem with recidivism data is that all recidivism events are given the same weight. Everything is either black or white, success or failure; there are no shadings of gray, no middle ground. "A great deal of information is lost when something as complex as possible criminal activity that may or may not culminate in detection, arrest, and conviction is finally expressed as a simple dichotomy" (Sechrest *et al.*, 1979:71).

One approach to this problem is to weight the event according to its perceived seriousness (Sellin & Wolfgang, 1964; Moberg & Ericson, 1972); but this approach also has deficiencies. An individual may have his parole revoked ostensibly for a technical violation, but actually because he committed another crime. Or he may be arrested for a crime he did not commit and is subsequently released, but is considered a recidivist because an arrest is one of the events used to define recidivism. Furthermore, although the Sellin–Wolfgang Crime Seriousness Index is a step forward in crime measurement, it is far from perfect as a measure of crime (Maltz, 1975), let alone recidivism. Should not any crime no matter what its seriousness be considered an act of recidivism? After considering all these factors, one wonders how useful it would be to employ a measure more complicated than a simple dichotomy.

SUCCESS AS A MEASURE OF EFFECTIVENESS

Recidivism may be thought of as a measure of success as well as failure. That is, those who do not fail could be considered successes. But this is a very limited and pessimistic view of success—not (having been discovered) getting into trouble. A measure of success should be based on positive accomplishments, not on the absence of negative findings.

Measuring Success

It is failure that is recorded by agencies, not success. Evaluators are inclined to use the data collected by these agencies for their evaluation because it is much easier (and less expensive) than collecting new evaluative data. Despite the well-known problems in using official data for research purposes (Kitsuse & Cicourel,

[5]Analogizing recidivism to body temperature is apt for another reason. Both are gross measures of a phenomenon, but neither can be used to diagnose the subject of the investigation—additional variables must be measured for diagnostic purposes.

1963; Maltz, 1972), they are used because they already exist. Their very existence inhibits the collection of more relevant data, since the cost of collecting reliable and valid data is quite high. Aside from economic considerations, very often evaluators are not given access to better sources of data for reasons of privacy and confidentiality.

Measuring success is more intrusive than measuring failure. To determine how successful an individual is, one would need to investigate that person's employment situation, family situation, and other aspects of his or her personal life. One cannot expect ex-offenders to volunteer to give this information to evaluators, just because the evaluators feel the need to measure success. And even if all ex-offenders could be counted on to provide the information, it would be necessary to determine the extent of exaggeration and dissembling in their statements.

The cost of data collection and verification would be quite high if success data had to be collected especially for the evaluation. However, this type of information is routinely collected by parole and probation officers. For special evaluations these officers could use standardized collection instruments and procedures for gathering information on employment, educational attainment, family stability, and other relevant variables. Additional procedures, similar to those used by survey research organizations, could be implemented to check on data reliability and validity. Measuring success of parolees or probationers, then, may be feasible—if cooperation is forthcoming from the parole or probation agency.

Data Requirements for Measuring Success

Success must be defined with respect to a goal. The goal should be defined with some degree of precision; the sources of data used to measure the extent of goal attainment should be specified; and the method of analyzing the data should be specified, since it will also affect the evaluation.

For example, employment is a common goal of correctional programs. One can use a number of different definitions to determine the extent of its attainment:

- number placed in any job,
- number placed in a job employing the skills acquired in the program,
- number placed in a job who remain for a specified follow-up time, or
- number placed, controlling for employability and/or for the local employment rate, etc.

The specific measures used should reflect the perceived goals of the correctional program.

Similarly, a number of different sources of data can be used to measure employment:

- evaluators may rely on a program participant's word concerning his employment,

- they may have a telephone conversation with the participant's employer, or
- they may visit the workplace to assess job placement firsthand.

These data sources vary considerably in terms of reliability, validity, and cost of collection.

The analysis of employment data can be accomplished in a number of different ways:

- employment can be looked upon as a binary variable (employed/not employed) or a continuous variable (hours worked per week),
- a person's entire employment history can be analyzed, or
- a single point in time (say, 6 months) can be selected to determine the fraction of program participants employed at that time.

Each method of analysis will produce different evaluation findings.

Each operationalization of the goal of employment has its own strengths and weaknesses. One should try to determine the extent to which the measured quantity actually represents the goal—for example, do program personnel tell the participants, "Just stick with this job for 6 months, so we can get a good evaluation?" This consideration is crucial in gauging how well the goal was achieved (impact evaluation) and how effective the program was in contributing to its achievement (process evaluation).

Performance measures other than employment are also useful in gauging program success, and also have similar problems. Grizzle (1979) discusses a number of different performance measures and their applicability to evaluating correctional programs.

APPROPRIATE USES OF RECIDIVISM

We see, then, that there are many valid criticisms of recidivism as a measure of effectiveness. It reflects certain values about offenders and society that may be unwarranted; it implies that we know how to correct; it is a measure of failure, not success. Even if we accept recidivism as a measure, we find that it is difficult to measure with precision; even if it could be measured precisely, there are no set standards with which to compare measurements; and even if standards existed, interpretation of the findings are likely to be flawed.

But problems of this nature are common to the measurement of virtually all social phenomena. The measurement of poverty, educational attainment, intelligence, employment, self-esteem, socioeconomic status, social structure, or peer-group relationships is no less difficult than the measurement of recidivism. Doubtless none of these measures will ever be defined as precisely as physical measures such as temperature or pressure. But to defer correctional evaluation until we have more precise measures "would seem to elevate the pursuit of neatness and false precision over truth" (Chaiken, 1982).

This is not to say that all uses of recidivism as a measure of correctional effectiveness are appropriate, especially when evaluating rehabilitation programs. But recidivism is still quite useful as a program measure, as a correlate measure if not always as the primary measure.[6] In conjunction with other measures of effectiveness it can be used to evaluate selection criteria for halfway houses or for community-based correctional programs. It can be used to estimate the extent of special deterrence. It is very useful in studying the effects of different policies on the criminal justice system.

One of the more important uses of recidivism analyses is in estimating the characteristics of offender populations. Knowing how many people recidivate, the frequency with which they do so, when they terminate their criminal careers, and other characteristics of their offending behavior is useful in many policy-related areas. Empirical and theoretical studies of offender behavior (Wolfgang, Figlio & Sellin, 1972; Blumstein & Cohen, 1979b; Blumstein & Moitra, 1980; Blumstein & Graddy, 1982; Chaiken & Chaiken, 1982) employ recidivism statistics to determine various characteristics of offenders (length of criminal careers, arrest switch matrixes, prevalence and incidence of criminal activity); and virtually all studies of criminal justice system workload require modeling or measuring recidivism (Belkin, Blumstein & Glass, 1973; Blumstein, 1975; Blumstein & Larson, 1971).

Recidivism can be used to analyze certain questions relating to the cessation of criminal activity: Is there a certain age when most offenders terminate their criminal activity? How does it vary by offender characteristics, by type of criminal career path, by other factors? Thus, recidivism can be used to study criminal career characteristics. Furthermore, some rehabilitation programs actually do result in offenders being rehabilitated, either because of the nature of the program or the type of offender at which it is directed (e.g., certain types of delinquency programs).

There are also instances in which the use of recidivism can lead to inappropriate conclusions. The next chapter discusses two studies of correctional programs that used recidivism as the primary measure of correctional effectiveness. These studies came to conclusions that, albeit incorrect, have greatly influenced correctional policy in recent years.

---

[6]Concerning this point I take issue with Sechrest *et al.* (1979:21), who state that criminal behavior, not "offender growth, insight, or happiness is the sole criterion" for measuring the worth of rehabilitative programs. Offender employability, offender literacy, and even offender growth, insight, or happiness *are* relevant criteria if the rehabilitative programs were directed toward those ends.

4

What Works?

Recidivism, with one operational definition or another, has been the dominant outcome measure used in studies evaluating correctional programs. Two of these studies have recently received a great deal of attention. Both lead to conclusions that question the efficacy of correctional programs in reducing postrelease criminality. One conclusion, based on comparisons of control groups with groups in experimental programs, is that "nothing works," that is, no program seems to be the key to reducing recidivism. The second conclusion, based on comparisons of the preintervention and postrelease behavior of chronic juvenile delinquents, is that "getting tough works"; that is, a substantial reduction in delinquent behavior is almost guaranteed with any intervention, and the tougher the intervention the greater the reduction.

Both of these conclusions are quite strong and unequivocal. Both are open to question. This chapter discusses the background leading to these conclusions and the questions that have arisen about their validity.

NOTHING WORKS

Over the past few decades literally hundreds of correctional programs have been evaluated. In an effort to use the information generated by these studies to plan correctional programs, the New York State Governor's Special Committee on Criminal Offenders funded a review and reanalysis of these studies. This reanalysis was completed in 1971 and published in 1975 (Lipton, Martinson & Wilks, 1975), but publication in 1974 of its major conclusions, summarized by Martinson, had a strong impact in correctional circles. Martinson's "bald summary" stated that, *"With few and isolated exceptions, the rehabilitative efforts that have been reported so far have had no appreciable effect on recidivism"* (Martinson, 1974; emphasis in the original). This conclusion was based on an evaluation of studies published between 1945 and 1967 that were in the open literature or available from "agencies conducting evaluation research on treatment in the United States, Canada, and Western Europe" (Lipton *et al.*, 1975). Over 1000 studies were identified, but only 231 of them met the rigor that would permit reanalysis. There were 286 separable findings from these studies, classified in Table 4-1 according to the nature of the treatment (11 types) and the nature of the outcome measure used (7 types). As can be seen, almost half of the

TABLE 4-1
Treatment Methods by Outcome Measures

Treatment methods	Recidivism	Institutional adjustment	Vocational adjustment	Educational achievement	Drug and alcohol readdiction	Personality and attitude change	Community adjustment	Total
Probation	18	0	1	1	0	3	0	23
Imprisonment	19	2	0	0	0	10	0	31
Parole	18	0	0	0	3	4	0	25
Casework and individual counseling	7	1	2	0	3	3	2	18
Skill development	15	3	5	9	1	3	4	40
Individual psychotherapy	12	4	3	1	1	5	1	27
Group methods	19	6	2	1	2	21	3	54
Milieu therapy	20	5	0	0	1	8	4	38
Partial physical custody	4	0	0	0	1	0	1	6
Medical methods	5	2	1	0	4	9	1	22
Leisure-time activities	1	1	0	0	0	0	0	2
	138	24	14	12	16	66	16	286

Source: Lipton, Martinson, and Wilks, 1975, p. 8.

findings used recidivism as the outcome measure, and this measure was given the most attention in the book.[1]

The report's conclusion sparked considerable controversy (e.g., Klockars, 1975; Martinson, 1975; Martinson et al., 1976). Palmer (1978) provided one of the more comprehensive responses to this and other criticisms of correctional intervention. He pointed out that almost half of the studies cited in Lipton et al. (1975) had positive or partly positive findings. That no single treatment was shown to work across the board—under all conditions, for all types of offenders—should not be taken as a negative finding if it was effective for some types. Palmer contended that it is the search for rapid and glamorous solutions that has caused rehabilitation to fall into disrepute, that what is needed is patience and precision in formulating a correctional research program.

Martinson's criticism extended beyond this interpretation of past research. He took correctional researchers to task for making overly optimistic claims about treatments, claims that were not borne out in subsequent evaluations. And the little or no effect on crime rates from all the past research was construed by Martinson to demonstrate the failure of correctional intervention. Both of these criticisms were seen by Palmer to be beside the point: the exaggeration of claims does not negate a treatment's actual benefits;[2] and the participation of a small group of specific types of offenders in a correctional treatment program should not be expected to reduce criminality among all types of offenders in society.[3]

The findings of Lipton et al. (1975) were given strong support in two more works. Greenberg (1977) surveyed studies published from the late 1960s through 1975, and reached the same conclusion as Lipton et al. (1975) regarding the effectiveness of correctional programs in reducing recidivism. And Fienberg and Grambsch (1979) were commissioned by the National Academy of Sciences (NAS) Panel on Research on Rehabilitative Techniques (Sechrest et al., 1979) to reanalyze a random sample of the studies cited by Lipton et al. (1975). They also found no cause to doubt the general thrust of the Lipton et al. (1975) findings, which they characterized as a "reasonably accurate portrayal."

These more recent reviews went further than Lipton et al. (1975) and looked more critically at the programs being evaluated. In commenting on the nature of correctional studies, Sechrest et al. (1979) noted that most of the programs that have been evaluated were designed to be carried out in institutions; they suspected that rehabilitation research has often been "dictated more by practicalities

---

[1] However, distinctions were not made as to how recidivism was defined among these studies. Chapter 6 describes the various operational definitions used in these and other studies of correctional programs.

[2] A new program is often oversold by its advocates, who see little prospect of implementing it unless it is billed as a major breakthrough.

[3] Apparently Martinson later changed his mind about the effectiveness of correctional programs (Martinson, 1979).

than by logic" (p. 95). Greenberg (1977:141) found that descriptions of many of the treatments studied were vague or nonexistent; their theoretical underpinnings were often not made explicit; and when they were made explicit, they tended "to border on the preposterous." Sechrest et al. (1979:40) also questioned whether the treatment was sufficient in intensity or duration, and whether the integrity of the treatment was maintained. The studies of correctional treatments also had many flaws in their research designs; according to Sechrest et al. (1979:60): "The thousands of extant studies on rehabilitation scarcely add up to a single trustworthy conclusion."

What emerges from this review of correctional research is almost as pessimistic as the conclusion that nothing works. It is that much of the research on rehabilitation completed thus far has been too weak to permit any valid conclusions to be made. And even when potentially promising treatments are found, little effort is made to follow up on them or to attempt to replicate them under other conditions or in different jurisdictions. In other words, we lack a coherent body of knowledge about correctional program effectiveness.

In a subsequent report on correctional research, the NAS Panel on Research on Rehabilitative Techniques concluded that, far from abandoning rehabilitation as a goal of corrections, efforts to find what does work under what circumstances should be made more systematic (Martin et al., 1981). However, such efforts depend on stable funding patterns for correctional research, something that has been noticeably absent in recent years.

GETTING TOUGH WORKS

A recent evaluation of a correctional program (Murray, Thomson & Israel, 1978; Murray & Cox, 1979b) received a lot of coverage by the media and generated a great deal of controversy in correctional circles (Murray, 1978a, 1978b, 1979; Maltz, 1980; Maltz & Pollock, 1980; Maltz et al., 1980; Gordon et al., 1978; New York Times, 1978; McCleary et al., 1979; Kiernan, 1979). The finding, based on an evaluation of the Unified Delinquency Intervention Services (UDIS) Program of the Illinois Department of Corrections, is that the delinquency rate of chronic juvenile offenders decreases substantially (i.e., there is a "suppression effect") following a court-mandated intervention. This was the case whether the intervention was community-based or institution-based. Both of the intensive programs ("energetic correctional interventions") they examined achieved a 60–70% reduction in delinquent activity. Figure 4-1, taken from Murray and Cox (1979b), is a dramatic representation of this suppression effect.

The UDIS evaluation employed a quasi-experimental research design, which can create artifacts that appear to be true findings; however, it was not the quasi-

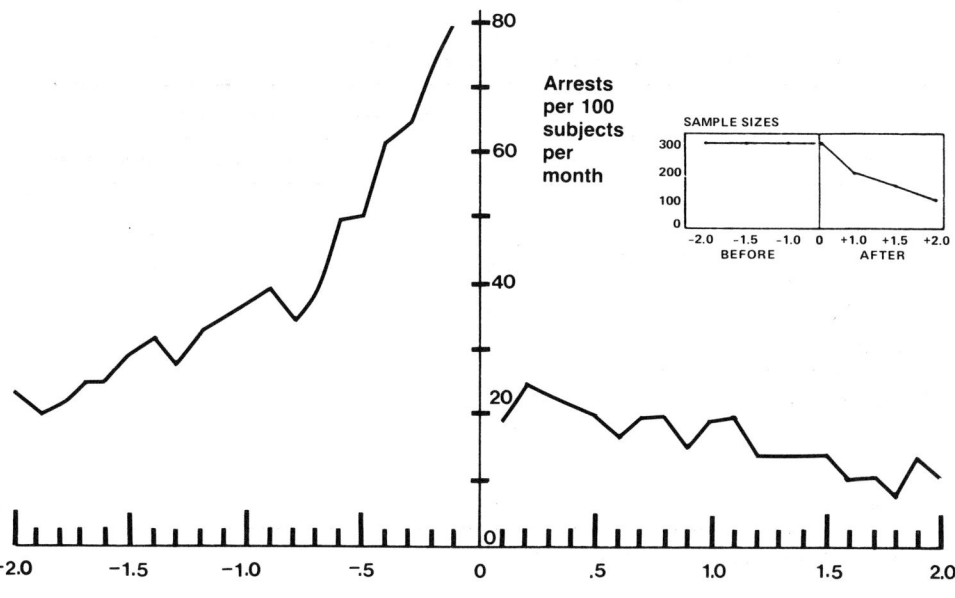

FIGURE 4-1 Arrests in the 2 years before and after institutionalization, for chronic juvenile offenders. (Source: Murray and Cox, p. 39 in *Beyond Probation*. Copyright © 1979 by Sage Publications, Inc., reprinted by permission.)

experimental design that caused an artifact. In fact, the findings paralleled those of two earlier experimental studies: Empey and Lubeck (1971) and Empey and Erickson (1972) found similar reductions in delinquent activity in an experimental setting—for both experimental and control groups, whether the intervention was probation or incarceration. Tables 4-2 and 4-3 give the before–after data for these studies. These supporting findings, and their apparent application to all kinds of interventions, have given strength to the inference that "getting tough works," that an energetic intervention will produce a profound reduction in delinquent activity.

This conclusion emerging from the UDIS evaluation has been linked by many to Martinson's (1974) conclusion. The net impression that remains from these two studies is that all offenders should be sent to prison, and that no one treatment works much better than any other. On the basis of this impression there has been a revision in the thinking of many involved in correctional policy making and research. A get-tough policy, which has often been cited by many as the solution to crime, is now felt to be strongly supported by current research. This is not the case.

Before discussing the UDIS finding, it should be noted that this evaluation did

TABLE 4-2

Before and After Comparisons—Silverlake Experiment

	Average annual police contact rate	
Group type	Year before intervention	Year after intervention
Completers		
Experimental	2.70	.42
Control	2.90	.40
Runaways		
Experimental	2.77	1.02
Control	2.38	1.15
In-program failures		
Experimental	2.58	.92
Control	3.38	1.08
Total		
Experimental	2.71	.73
Control	2.60	.74

Source: Empey and Lubeck, 1971, pp. 258–261.

not use the standard operational definition of recidivism, that is, rearrest (or reconviction) within 1 year (or some other time period). Rather, arrest rates before intervention (treatment) were compared with arrest rates after intervention.[4] This measure was used because the evaluators felt that it was unrealistic to expect a treatment to effect an immediate and total cessation of delinquent activity; reduced activity should also be considered a successful outcome.

In virtually every before–after comparison evaluators made, they found a reduction in arrest rate, ranging from a low of 47% for wilderness programs to a high of 82% for intensive care residential programs (Murray & Cox, 1979b:118). They therefore concluded that the interventions, regardless of type, all suppressed delinquent behavior; anything done to these chronic delinquents appeared to work, and work well.

Unfortunately, most of the suppresion effect of Figure 4-1 is probably only an artifact of the juvenile justice process. The artifact is quite similar to the regression-to-the-mean artifacts discussed by Campbell and Ross (1968) and Campbell and Erlebacher (1970). In those papers, however, the artifact was attributed to the quasi-experimental research designs that were used, whereas the selection artifact that gives rise to an illusory suppression effect can occur using either experimental (Empey and Lubeck, 1971; Empey & Erickson, 1972) or quasi-experimental (Murray & Cox, 1979b) designs.

The selection artifact can be caused by a number of circumstances, of which

---

[4]Actually, the data are based on police contacts, not arrests. However, since police contacts of juveniles are equivalent to arrests of adults, the term *arrest* will be used throughout.

TABLE 4-3

Before and After Comparisons—Provo Experiment

	Average annual arrest rate							
	Years before intervention				Years after intervention			
Group type	4	3	2	1	1	2	3	4
Probation								
Experimental	.18	.29	.64	3.52	.55	.42	.11	.08
Control	.34	.38	.65	2.87	.70	.23	.08	.41
Incarceration								
Experimental	.30	.65	1.48	3.57	1.19	.84	.29	.19
Control	.27	.60	1.71	4.43	1.71	1.63	1.20	.74

Source: Empey and Erickson, 1972, pp. 209–211.

two have been mathematically analyzed. The following sections describe these two circumstances.

One Explanation: Offenders Alternate between Active and Quiescent States

One model of offender behavior is that the offender is in either of two states: State 1 (active), in which his arrest rate is μ_1; and State 2 (quiescent), in which his arrest rate is μ_2 (less than μ_1). There are indications from self-report data (Chaiken and Chaiken, 1982a) that this model of behavior accords with reality for high-rate offenders.[5]

Transitions between these two states can be modeled by a continuous-time Markov process, with α and β the transition rates from State 1 to 2, and 2 to 1, respectively. It can be shown (Maltz and Pollock, 1980) that a group of offenders with these characteristics would exhibit an arrest rate rising exponentially from a steady-state value. Figure 4-2 shows this model superimposed on the data of Figure 4-1, using values of $\mu_1 = 1.69$, $\mu_2 = .08$, $\alpha = .119$, and $\beta = .06$.

What this model shows is that a group of offenders with an average arrest rate of about .88 arrests per month (10.6 per year), but alternating between 1.69 arrests per month (20 per year) and .08 arrests per month (1 per year), can appear to have arrest rates growing uncontrollably when viewed retrospectively. But this exponential buildup is merely due to the fact that most of them were in their active state when intervention occurred. The apparent suppression effect is obtained by comparing this artifactual buildup in arrest rate to the average rate that would characterize arrest behavior after release.

[5]This behavior can be noted in Tables 2.13–2.15 of their study.

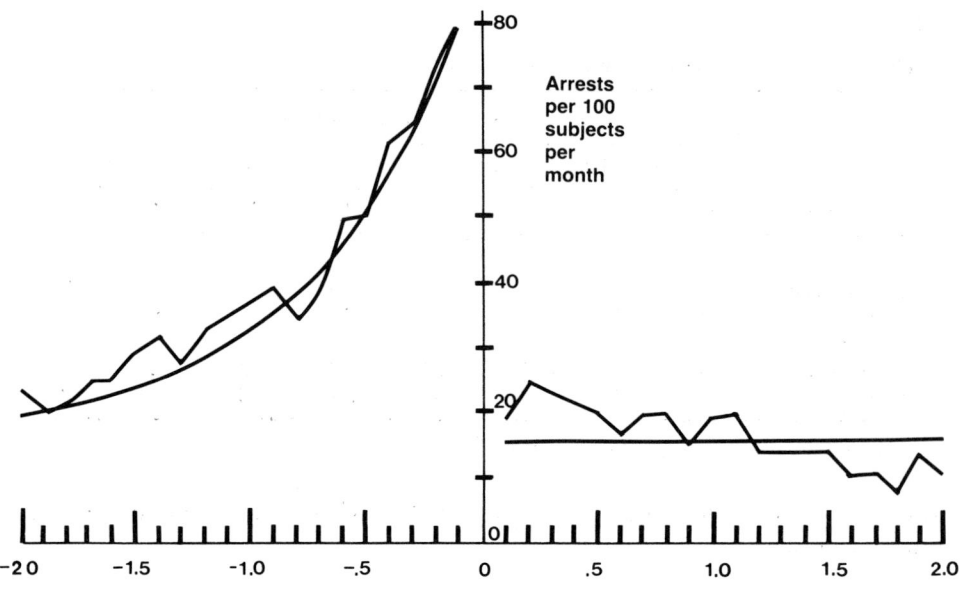

FIGURE 4-2 Graph of a Markov model of offender behavior, superimposed on the data of Figure 4-1. (Source: Murray and Cox, p. 39 in *Beyond Probation*. Copyright © 1979 by Sage Publications, Inc., reprinted by permission.)

Another Explanation: Selection Due to an Unusually High Arrest Rate

The previous section showed how an artifact is generated by nonconstant (but on average stationary) offender behavior. This section describes how one can be generated *even if offenders have constant offense rates,* if judges select offenders for formal intervention because they have had high arrest rates in the recent past. This high arrest rate can be generated by normal statistical variation, so that it regresses to the mean after release (Maltz and Pollock, 1980; Tierney, 1983; Pollock & Farrell, 1984). The artifact occurs because arrests are a biased subsample of crimes.

The fact that arrests are a biased subsample of crimes was noted by Blumstein and Larson (1971), who described the way the bias is generated. Criminological studies since that time have paid lip service to the distinction between arrests and crimes, but often treat arrest statistics as representative of crime statistics.[6]

Regression effects are counterintuitive and difficult to apply. The reasons they are have been studied by psychologists and decision theorists. As Kahneman and

---

[6]This error has been made so often that its consequences are usually ignored. But the consequences can be substantial; in fact, much criminological research might be more appropriately termed "arrestological" research because it is based on crime known to the police, that is, arrests.

Tversky (1982:66) note, "Regression effects typically violate the intuition that the predicted outcome should be maximally representative of the input information." They provide an example of this phenomenon:

> In a discussion of flight training, experienced instructors noted that praise for an exceptionally smooth landing is typically followed by a poorer landing on the next try, while harsh criticism after a rough landing is usually followed by an improvement on the next try. The instructors concluded that verbal rewards are detrimental to learning, while verbal punishments are beneficial, contrary to accepted psychological doctrine. This conclusion is unwarranted because of the presence of regression to the mean. As in other cases of repeated examination, an improvement will usually follow a poor performance, and a deterioration will usually follow an outstanding performance, even if the instructor does not respond to the trainee's achievement on the first attempt. Because the instructors had praised their trainees after good landings and admonished them after poor ones, they reached the erroneous and potentially harmful conclusion that punishment is more effective than reward. (Kahneman and Tversky, 1974:1127, copyright 1974 by the AAAS)

and conclude that, "the failure to understand the effect of regression leads one to overestimate the effectiveness of punishment and to underestimate the effectiveness of reward."

An Analogy

The general properties of the regression-to-the-mean phenomenon are illustrated in the following analogy. Instead of considering the delinquency of a relatively small group of chronic juvenile offenders, consider an illegal behavior in which most of us occasionally indulge—exceeding the speed limit.

Suppose that I have been exceeding the speed limit with regularity for the past 20 years, and that my driving record is punctuated with arrests for speeding about once every 2 years. This year, however, I am arrested three times for speeding, even though my driving behavior has not changed—I am just unlucky. As a consequence of this record, I am not fined but rather am required to attend a driving school (an experimental treatment), along with a hundred others with similar driving records.

Upon completion of this treatment my classmates and I continue to drive as before. Perhaps one or two of us will incur three more arrests within the next year (assuming that our licenses are not revoked—but of course they would not be, or else the evaluators would not be able to keep track of our posttreatment driving habits!), but again this has more to do with luck than with changed driving behavior: all of us continue to exceed the speed limit with regularity.

What will a before–after comparison of arrests show? Quite obviously, a decline: my classmates and I were selected for treatment specifically because of our high arrest rate immediately prior to intervention. Afterwards, even if our driving behavior does not change at all, the arrest rates of my classmates and me will (on average) revert back to once every 2 years, although one or two unlucky souls among us may again be rearrested three times in the next year. Aggregate before–after arrest records for the class, therefore, will show a dramatic rise in arrest rates just prior to intervention and a decline in arrest rates afterwards—without any changes in driving behavior! This is a selection effect, caused by selecting extreme cases that then regress to the mean.

However similar speeding and delinquency may appear to be, they are not the same thing. How well does this analogy concerning speeding apply to delinquency?

Necessary Conditions for the Artifact

It may not be apparent from the description of the artifact given in the last section, but four conditions conspire to produce the artifact: (1) individuals are selected for treatment based on an unusually high arrest rate in the immediate past; (2) this unusually high arrest rate is based on a relatively small number of arrests; (3) the probability of arrest for any given infraction is very low;[7] and (4) arrests are independent of offense behavior. The first condition ensures that the arrest rates immediately prior to intervention are higher than average, so that only those with high prior arrest rates are given treatment. The second, third, and fourth conditions make it very likely that this high arrest rate (and therefore selection for treatment) was due to a spate of bad luck rather than to a higher-than-normal infraction rate. It is reasonable to assume that these four conditions hold for delinquent behavior as well as for driving behavior.

Selection Based on an Unusually High Arrest Rate   A high arrest rate is the selection mechanism for the chronic delinquents studied by Murray and Cox (1979b). In fact, the definition of *chronic deliquent* is based on a high arrest rate[8] (in much the same way that a *chronic speeder* would be defined by a high arrest—not infraction—rate). I do not mean to imply that these offenders are not actually chronic ones. Except for the few truly incompetent or unlucky individuals who are arrested every time they violate the law, those known as chronic offenders are in fact much more active offenders than their arrest records imply. Not only that, but there are many other chronic offenders who are not labeled as such because they have less extreme (delinquency or driving) records as measured by arrests.

So if only chronic offenders are studied, we ensure that selection is based on an unusually high arrest rate. It has also been shown (Terry, 1967) that judges select individuals for intervention based on their arrest rates. That is, other things

---

[7]For example, a person who speeds 100 times a year—twice a week—and averages one ticket a year has an arrest probability of .01.

[8]The New York City Police Department has a Felony Augmentation Program that uses an offender's high arrest rate as a means of selecting whom to target. Its guidelines for priorities for investigation and prosecution specify that targeted individuals "have a prior arrest history of at least two robberies or one robbery and one violent felony offense that had occurred in Manhattan within the last 36 months" (Chambers, 1981:119).

being equal, the higher the arrest rate in the recent past, the greater the probability of intervention. Thus, the first condition (high arrest rate → selection) holds for juvenile offenders as well as for the speeding analogy.

As an interesting sidelight of this condition, consider the following hypothetical situation which, according to juvenile officials, is not far from the truth: a youth is caught committing a delinquent act. After conferring with a police youth officer (it is his first offense), the victim decides not to make a formal complaint. The youth is arrested again for delinquency. This time the victim complains, but the youth officer still handles it informally. Another arrest, and the officer brings the youth into the police station, calls the youth's parents, and warns them all that the next time the offense will be dealt with more severely. After the fourth arrest the youth is referred to the juvenile probation officer, who also warns the youth and his parents. The next time he is arrested for a delinquent act the youth is actually brought before the court, but he is put in a diversion program rather than on trial. It is the sixth arrest that finally results in intervention, that is, in a formal disposition. In other words, at least six delinquent acts (remember, these are only the ones for which he was arrested) have taken place, according to this scenario, before formal intervention occurs. If the youth had terminated his delinquent career at an earlier point (i.e., with five or fewer arrests) he would not have been subject to formal intervention.[9]

A Small Number of Arrests An arrest rate of 24 per year can be based on 24 arrests over a year's time, on 12 arrests in 6 months, on 4 arrests in 2 months, or even on 2 arrests in a 1-month period. If it is based on 24 arrests in a year, the probability is very small that the real arrest rate is considerably higher or lower. But if the arrest rate is based on, say, 4 arrests in a 2-month period, it is quite likely that the actual rate is considerably different from 24 arrests per year; a 50% swing in either direction would not be unexpected.

This condition undoubtedly exists for the chronic juvenile offenders as it does for the speeding example. No judge who feels that 24 arrests per year is unusually high would permit a juvenile (or a driver) to be arrested at this rate for a full year. The offender would certainly be sentenced well before he had a chance to establish his arrest rate based on such a high number of arrests.

A Low Arrest Probability The probability of being arrested for a delinquent act is quite low; it is not as low as it is for speeding, perhaps, but various estimates (Boland and Wilson, 1978; Blumstein and Cohen, 1979b) put it at under one-tenth. Murray and Cox generally agree with this estimate.

To see why a low arrest probability is a necessary condition for generation of

---

[9]This scenario gives rise to an interesting conjecture: the more layers in the juvenile justice process, the more arrests it takes to get selected for a correctional intervention. Therefore, the more layers in the juvenile justice process, the greater the build-up in arrest rate prior to intervention and the greater the apparent suppression effect after release from treatment. As far as I know, this conjecture has not been studied.

the artifact, consider two situations, one in which the arrest probability is .9, the other in which it is .1. In the first situation the arrest rate is an excellent proxy measure of the crime rate: as the crime rate increases or decreases, so does the arrest rate, although at a slightly attenuated level.

However, if the probability of arrest is .1, changes in the arrest rate do not necessarily reflect changes in the crime rate. This would occur only if there is a highly improbable connection between arrests and crimes, as described in the next section.

The Arrest Process Is Independent of the Crime Process If arrests occur for only a small fraction of offenses, what would it take for the arrest rate to be a good proxy for the crime rate? There would have to be some *deterministic dependency* between arrests and offenses, for example, if an individual were arrested for the seventh, seventeenth, twenty-seventh, etc., offense, as in Figure 4-3. Then one could say, "To determine the offense rate at any given point in time, find the arrest rate and multiply it by 10."

But the chances of such an occurrence are ridiculously small. Every tenth offense can no more be expected to result in arrest than can every sixth roll of the dice be expected to result in a seven, merely because the chances of rolling a seven are one in six.

It is more likely that arrests will occur on average for 1 out of 10 offenses, but in an unpredictable (stochastic) manner and that arrests will be independent of offenses, as in Figure 4-4. Note that there are periods in which arrests cluster as well as periods of no arrests, that is, the pattern of arrests is random but averages out to one-tenth of the number of offenses.

Murray and Cox dispute this argument. They feel that arrests will mirror offenses accurately, that there is regularity in the pattern of arrests and offenses:

> The probability that a delinquent will be caught, given that he has just committed an offense, is considerably less than one. This drives a wedge between observed reality and actual reality . . . [but] does not in itself pose a threat to [our assertion that the observations are accurate]. If, for example, we always observe exactly one-half of the offenses that are committed by the subjects in the sample, then what we observe as increases and decreases per unit time *will be exactly correct* [emphasis added]. (Murray and Cox, p. 49 in *Beyond Probation*. Copyright © 1979 by Sage Publications, Inc., reprinted by permission.)

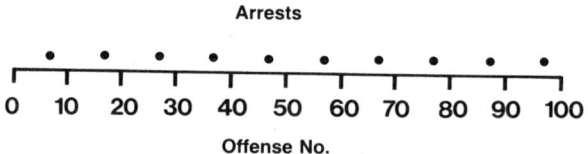

FIGURE 4-3 A deterministic relationship between arrests and offenses (one arrest for every tenth offense).

GETTING TOUGH WORKS 39

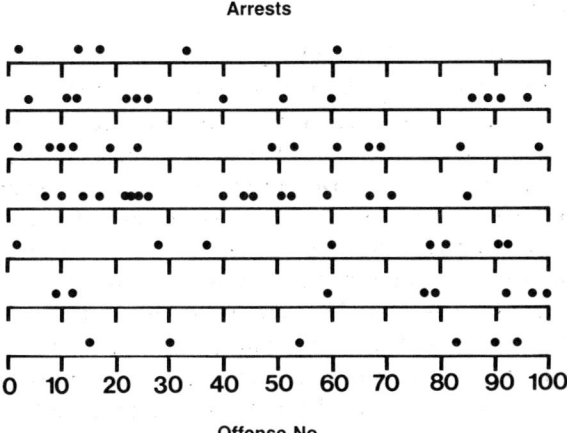

FIGURE 4-4 Arrests independent of offenses, with a probability of arrest of .1.

In other words, their argument is based on the assumption that Figure 4-3 is a truer representation of reality than Figure 4-4. Were the probability of arrest .9, I would agree with them; then the 10% of hidden offenses would not drastically alter the underlying pattern. Were the probability of arrest even .5, as they imply in the above quote, they could make a strong case for their argument. But their argument has little validity when the upper estimate for the probability of arrest is .1.

Figure 4-4 shows what happens when the probability of arrest is .1, but is not related deterministically to the offense number, as in Figure 4-3. Note that there are periods in which there are many arrests and periods of no arrests—in other words, a stochastic pattern of arrests. Figure 4-3 reflects the situation when arrests and crime are not independent, Figure 4-4 the situation when they are independent. Although it cannot be proved which assumption is correct (offenders would have to tell us about their offenses for which they were not arrested), it seems to me to be highly unlikely that Figure 4-3 represents reality.

A more formal mathematical argument can be made in support of this assertion. Haight (1967:25) refers to a finding by Renyi concerning processes of this nature. If we consider the occurrence of offenses by an individual to be a point process generated by some distribution (either deterministic or stochastic), then the observed points (those violations that result in arrest) are a "thinned" point process, thinned because not all of the events are observed. Renyi found that if the thinning process is independent of the original process (i.e., if the arrest process is independent of the offense-generating process) and if most of the points are thinned out, then the result (the thinned process, that which we observe) is a Poisson process.

Size of the Artifact

Thus the four conditions necessary for generating a selection artifact are present in the delinquency process: selection for the cohort requires a high arrest rate just prior to intervention; it is based on relatively few arrests; the probability of arrest for any given offense is low; and the arrest process is independent of the crime process. The question is not *whether* the artifact exists so much as it is *the extent* to which it exists. I do not mean to imply that no reduction in delinquent activity will ever ensue following intervention, only that it cannot be calculated merely by a before–after comparison. Part of the reduction may be due to treatment and the rest to artifact. The part attributable to the artifact would be directly related to the probability of arrest; the greater the proportion of offenses gotten away with by the offenders, the greater the contribution of the artifact. Unfortunately, the exact relationship between the arrest probability and the magnitude of the artifact is not known.[10]

POLICY IMPLICATIONS

The two responses, "nothing works" and "getting tough works" are very attractive to legislators and correctional policymakers. They have been given the impression that research has at last found the "silver bullet" for corrections: lock 'em up. Unlike so many other research results, this is a definitive answer that is easily understood and readily applied. Furthermore, it appeals to those who feel that too much attention and care are given the offender and not enough are given the victim.

But the first answer oversimplifies a complex set of issues, and the second answer is wrong. A seemingly equivocal answer ("Under these conditions one can expect this result 30% of the time") or the researcher's all-too-frequent response, "We need to do more research," may not be considered helpful, but with our present state of knowledge these are the only answers that can be given with any degree of confidence.[11] A well-planned program of research is needed to provide more definitive answers.

The conclusions of the NAS Panel on Research on Rehabilitative Techniques

---

[10]Charles Murray and I continue to disagree on the nature of the suppression effect. He maintains that a variety of characteristics in the UDIS data argue against an important role for a statistical artifact. I maintain that, because the data consist solely of arrest activity, the suppression effect is mostly artifactual.

[11]Upon hearing a number of experts testify before his committee, all to the tune of "On the one hand . . .; but on the other hand . . . ," a senator was heard to say with exasperation, "I wish we had some one-handed scientists!" Unfortunately, the problems we face are not necessarily one-handed problems.

(Martin et al., 1981) recommends such a program as a necessary precondition to further research in corrections. They conclude (pp. 22–24):

> The search for rehabilitative techniques and programs has borne little fruit; this is discouraging but should not be cause for the abandonment of efforts to find more effective rehabilitation strategies. . . . It is now time to undertake more systematic, long-term, and focused research that will have a substantial probability of improving techniques and programs that can then be evaluated in ways that will produce more definitive conclusions. [Such a] research strategy involves a number of component elements:
> 1. Rehabilitative research must be guided by theory.
> 2. Intervention programs and research should be developed jointly as a coordinated activity designed to test detailed theoretical propositions explicitly.
> 3. Intervention programs must be designed for and tested with a theoretically suggested, clearly specified target population.
> 4. In assessing any intervention program, the strength of the intervention should be systematically varied and evaluated.
> 5. The integrity with which an intervention program's intended activities or components are implemented must be carefully examined.
> 6. The timing of the interventions in terms of the age and stage in the criminal career of the program client population requires further study.
> 7. A new strategy of search is needed to determine what interventions might work.
> 8. Rehabilitation research must test interventions developed at multiple loci of intervention; the family, the school, the workplace, the community, as well as the individual.

The NAS Panel found a number of treatment and intervention directions that do have promise of working, for certain target populations and under certain conditions. They include interventions at the family level and through schools, employment, community, and the individual (Martin et al., 1981:135–173). These potential interventions are grounded in theory-based research; they require additional research as well as improved evaluation techniques, as part of a systematic research program, to bring them to fruition.

An important factor in planning and coordinating a correctional research program is ensuring that the results of different studies within the program are comparable, so that programs can be "evaluated in ways that will produce more definitive conclusions." Similar settings and standardized operational definitions and analytic techniques are required. The next chapter discusses the way outcomes are affected by the criminal justice setting; succeeding chapters focus on definitions and analytic techniques.

5
Correctional Organization and Recidivism

In the previous chapter an example was given of how the organizational context (i.e., the juvenile justice system) of a study may have affected the measurement of its outcome. In this chapter I describe other organizational aspects of the criminal justice system and their effect on outcome measurement: the criminal courts, in their roles of sentencing and supervision of probation; correctional agencies, from halfway houses to work-release programs to prisons, and the correctional programs they offer; and parole boards and agencies, in their roles of determining the conditions of release and monitoring parolees' behavior to ensure that they comply with the conditions of release. Differences in these organizations limit direct state-to-state comparisons of correctional outcome.

These organizations will not all be studied in depth. This chapter describes the characteristics and variants of just one process—parole—and shows how the legal and organizational characteristics of courts and correctional and parole agencies can influence measures of recidivism. It is instructive to focus on parole because parolees constitute a significant proportion of prison releasees. Furthermore, we have greater knowledge of their characteristics and of their postrelease behavior than for other releasees, since parole agencies are required to keep such records on all of their clients. Understanding how state parole agencies differ and how interaction among all parts of the criminal justice system affects the parole decision is necessary in interpreting how parole outcomes vary from state to state.

THE PAROLE PROCESS

Sutherland and Cressey (1970:584) provide this definition of parole:

Parole is the act of releasing or the status of being released from a penal or reformatory institution in which one has served a part of his maximum sentence, on condition of maintaining good behavior and remaining in the custody and under the guidance of the institution or some other agency approved by the state until a final discharge is granted.

There are many variants to this basic definition. One can view parole or conditional release as a process with a number of stages and actors responsible for the process in each of its stages. The stages in a typical parole process are

- sentencing as a means of defining parole eligibility,
- conditional release from a sentence, and
- supervision (followed by discharge from or revocation of parole).

The actors in each of these stages are

- courts,
- parole and pardon boards, and
- parole field agencies and supervising agents.

The parole process is thus fully defined by a description of its stages, a description of the role of the actors in each of the stages, and a description of the relationships among actors in each of the stages. The following description of a parole process is typical of that found in many states.[1]

Sentencing

The parole process is initiated in a sentencing court—the first stage. By setting minimum and maximum sentences, the court defines the time of parole eligibility. For example, a sentenced offender might become eligible for parole

- after serving the minimum time of the sentence (less time off for good behavior)[2] or 20 years, whichever is less (in some states this includes life sentences); or
- after serving one-third of the maximum term (less time off for good behavior) or 20 years, whichever is less.

The sentencing court thus sets a time after which the sentenced offender is eligible for parole. In some cases the sentencing court may so restrict this time that, in effect, it takes the parole decision-making function away from the parole board.

Conditional Release

The second stage of the parole process consists of a conditional release or parole decision by the state parole board. The board's decision-making task has four aspects:

---

[1]This description of parole is based on the Illinois parole process as it existed prior to 1978, when determinate sentencing legislation was enacted. Many states still have similar organizational structures for parole.

[2]"Good time" is the time subtracted from a prisoner's sentence for good behavior while in prison. One characteristic of the justice model of corrections (Fogel, 1979) is the vesting of good time so that all of it cannot be taken away, once accumulated, for subsequent infractions of institution rules.

- deciding whether to release,
- deciding the time of release,
- deciding the conditions of release, and
- deciding the time of discharge from supervision.

The decision in each case must meet specific legal criteria, including an explanation or justification that is clear enough to permit its appeal to a court. Each decision must also be based on or must acknowledge data collected from other actors. The sentencing court and the state department of corrections furnish documents and reports related to each decision. For the most part, however, the interaction of these two actors with the board at this stage is pro forma.

Parole Supervision

The third stage of the parole process consists of a period of parole supervision, terminated either by discharge from supervision or by revocation of parole. A parole officer is assigned to each case, and the board interacts with the parole officer in two ways. First, the officer is charged with enforcing the general conditions as well as any case-specific conditions of the release. For example, the parole board may release a person conditional upon his participation in a special treatment program; the parole officer must enforce this special condition. Second, the parole officer must participate in the decision to discharge the parolee from supervision or to revoke his parole. With respect to a discharge from supervision, the parole board continually evaluates parolee behavior for a period of time to determine whether discharge is warranted. At the end of this period, given satisfactory performance and on the recommendation of the parole officer, the board issues a discharge order which operates as a commutation of sentence.

Of course, parole officers must report to the parole board all behaviors which appear to violate the conditions of release. The key word is *appear*. In those cases in which a new crime is involved, there will be little question as to whether the behavior violates the conditions of release. But in other cases the behavior may be interpreted ambiguously, so the validity of the charge must be tested. Differences in the interpretation by different parole officers will result in different de facto revocation criteria.

Parole officers may have full police powers in the arrest and retaking of parolees. While the parole officer must request a warrant, a parolee can be detained pending issuance of the warrant.

Once the warrant has been issued, it must be heard by an officer designated by the parole board, to determine whether there is cause for a revocation hearing. The hearing officer is usually an employee of the department of corrections or parole board, so the charge, issuance of warrant, and preliminary hearing on the warrant are all handled internally.

If the charge is upheld, a revocation hearing must be held by the parole board. On the basis of this hearing the board may decide either to revoke parole or to continue parole with or without modification of the original conditions. The board may decide, for example, that the original conditions were too restrictive and may continue parole with fewer restrictions. Or the board may decide that the original conditions were not restrictive or explicit enough and may continue parole with more restrictions. If the board decides to revoke parole, however, the parolee may be required to serve the remainder of his sentence in prison (although a second conditional release is not precluded).

When a new crime is involved, the parole officer in charge would be notified by the police, given an in-state arrest.[3] Once this occurs, negotiations may take place between the police, prosecutors, and parole officers. The charge may be dropped, it may be reduced to a technical violation with subsequent repercussions, or prosecution may ensue with a post conviction sentencing option of revocation of or return to parole. There are thus several alternatives available to the system in the handling of alleged repeat offenders who are parolees; processing options present greater latitude, due to the involvement and decision-making power of another organization—the parole system. By contrast, when a person is arrested who is not on parole but who has been mandatorily released, the only alternatives are whether to proceed or not. Given that the alleged offender has served time in prison, it is likely that he or she would be formally processed. Thus, the same behavioral action does not always lead to the same disposition.

There is usually a clear distinction in the parolee's record between parole revocation for a technical violation of the conditions of release (e.g., failing to continue in a drug treatment program) and revocation in lieu of prosecution for a new offense. (The Uniform Parole Reporting System makes such a distinction in the data it collects from the states.)

As can be seen from this description, each of the three stages—determining parole eligibility, determining of release conditions, and supervising parolees—is associated with a decision by one of the three actors—the court, the parole board, and the parole agency. The relative freedom enjoyed by each of the actors in each stage is limited by actions of the actors at a prior stage. For example, the parole board may limit the decision-making function of the parole agency by setting conditions that are too restrictive or not restrictive enough. And the court, in its determination of parole eligibility, may limit the decision-making function of the parole board. In addition, the court's decision-making function is circumscribed by prosecutorial actions—which charges are brought against the alleged offender; and by legislative actions—what sentences the law permits.

---

[3]If the parolee is arrested out of state, there is no guarantee that the parole officer would be notified.

LIMITATIONS ON DISCRETION IN PAROLE DECISION-MAKING

Although this description of the parole process is quite general, there is still considerable variation among the states in how parole is defined. The variation is due primarily to the limits on decision-making discretion placed on the actors by state legislatures. Following is a summary of the differences.

Sentencing

Sentencing is set by the court, but the degree of latitude the court is permitted in sentencing varies considerably from state to state. Considered here are three general types of sentencing:

1. *Indeterminate sentencing:* There is wide discretion in the imposition of a sentence. The matter may be left entirely to the parole authorities, in which case the offender may enter prison without any idea of how long his or her sentence will be. Or it may be determined by a judge, who may impose prison terms of any length or range of lengths within board guidelines. Or there may be a combination of these two conditions, and the parole board may "even out" major discrepancies in sentences for similar situations.

2. *Modified indeterminate sentencing:* The sentencing court may impose a sentence that is charge-dependent, but may select a range from within this category. For example, if a certain charge is liable to a Class B penalty, for which the maximum sentence may be set between 5 and 10 years, the judge may select the maximum sentence anywhere between these two figures. If it is set at 6 years, and state law sets the minimum sentence at one-third the maximum, the offender leaves the courtroom knowing that he or she must serve at least 2 years and may serve at most 6 years—less any good time accrued while in prison.

3. *Determinate sentencing:* The sentencing court imposes a sentence based primarily on the charge.[4] The judge's discretion is limited to adding to the sentence if there are aggravating circumstances or reducing the sentence if there are mitigating circumstances. A limit is placed on the change in sentence length due to aggravation or mitigation; for example, if a certain charge is liable to a Class B penalty, which is a nominal 5 years but may be set anywhere between 4 and 6 years, the offender leaves the courtroom knowing a single number for the sentence (again, less good time). An additional feature of determinate sentencing is that the legislature may prescribe the circumstances which are allowed to be considered in aggravation or mitigation, and the judge may be required to document the circumstances considered in determination of sentence length.

[4]The offender's prior record may also affect sentence length. For example, a life sentence may be mandatory if an offender has a record of three prior felony convictions. But these conditions are also nondiscretionary, that is, determinate.

Conditional Release

The types of sentencing alternatives available to a state determine the nature of discretion in decision making on conditional release, as summarized here:

1. *Indeterminate sentencing:* Parole eligibility may be set by the court or the parole board. In this situation, prisoners often attempt to curry favor with the authorities: they may join the Jaycees or an AA program or start going to chapel in an attempt to improve their chances of being paroled.

2. *Determinate or modified indeterminate sentencing:* The date of release is known by the offender when he or she is sentenced: the minimum sentence length, less any good time accrued. In some cases additional conditions may be imposed on the offender. Mandatory release may occur under determinate sentencing, in which case there are no postrelease conditions to which the ex-offender must adhere. Mandatory release may also occur under indeterminate sentencing if parole is denied and the prisoner serves the full sentence.

Parole Supervision

Parole supervision does not vary to any great extent among the states. The primary difference is with regard to which agency directs the supervision: the parole board directly or an independent agency working cooperatively with the parole board.

As to parole outcome, however, it appears that the structure of supervision within the parole process makes little difference. The state-to-state differences that had existed in the past have been greatly reduced or eliminated by Supreme Court decisions in *Morrissey* v. *Brewer* (408 U.S. 471, 1972) and *Gagnon* v. *Scarpelli* (411 U.S. 778, 1973). These decisions accorded parolees due process rights in revocation procedures, such as their right to notification of the facts of the case, to be heard on their own behalf, to cross-examine witnesses, and to receive a written statement of the final decision and the reasons for it (Merritt, 1980). While the decisions in *Morrissey* and *Gagnon* leave some discretion to the states, the residual discretion is small. For all practical purposes, the only formal difference in the parole process among the states is the extent of authority vested in the courts and parole boards.

THE PAROLE PROCESS AND RECIDIVISM

The locus of authority for sentencing and release, as described in the last section, does not affect recidivism statistics directly. Yet its impact is substantial when the entire criminal process is considered.

Sentencing and Sentencing Alternatives

In recent years the trend has been for legislatures to limit the discretion of courts and parole boards. There has been a general shift toward determinate sentencing, vested good time, and parole eligibility determined by time served rather than program participation. This trend has been toward the legislative package known as "the justice model" (Fogel, 1979).

But discretion is not necessarily reduced by this legislative action. There seems to be some immutable "law of conservation of discretion" that shifts discretion to another level (Alschuler, 1978). For example, without determinate sentencing a prosecutor is able to drive a harder (plea) bargain if the assigned judge is known to favor long sentences. With sentences fixed by law, plea bargaining may simply be based only on the charges rather than on the sentencing philosophy of the judge as well. So the prosecutor effectively determines the sentence given the offender.[5]

Another discretionary aspect of the sentencing process is in the type of correctional program open to the offender. The extent to which probation, work release, halfway houses, community treatment centers, and other alternatives less severe than prison are used varies considerably among the states. But as Morris (1974:11) has noted, the use of alternatives to prison results in "reducing the intensity and severity of control but increasing the numbers under control." A state that makes extensive use of these alternatives would be expected to have a higher recidivism rate for its parolees than would a state that uses these alternatives sparingly. In the latter type of state, the offenders considered to be "better risks" are given these alternatives, thus increasing the average risk level of those going to prison. Similar "skimming" of the lower-risk offenders would be manifested when comparing the recidivism rates of parolees to those denied parole.[6]

In comparing programs across states, therefore, care should be taken to ensure that the populations under study are similar. One means of doing so is to consider the proportion of people in each state sentenced to the various alternatives. If the proportions are quite different, then comparisons are not likely to be very instructive; unfortunately, even if the proportions are similar the populations can be dissimilar if the selection criteria are different.

---

[5]Plea bargaining is not easy to eliminate, especially in jurisdictions with crowded dockets. But even in jurisdictions with less crowded dockets it seems to survive all attempts to eradicate it. In Alaska, for example, plea bargaining was outlawed by the state legislature. But according to a recent report (Rubenstein & White, 1979) the practice still continues.

[6]For example, Martinson and Wilks (1977) noted the higher recidivism rate of prisoners denied parole than of parolees. However, they misinterpreted this difference as demonstrating the effectiveness of parole rather than as being a consequence of the parole boards' selection of the best risks for parole.

Release on Parole

Parole boards have been criticized for arbitrariness in determining who is released (e.g., von Hirsch, 1976; Fogel, 1979). But another aspect of the release decision has not been given as much attention—the timing of release. Eck (1979) and Berk et al. (1982) have shown, in two different states, how the number of people paroled in any given time period is strongly correlated with the number of people sentenced to prison during that period.[7] This policy serves to stabilize prison populations, which may be a partial explanation of why prison populations seemed to have a "natural" level in eighteenth-century France (Quetelet, 1842) and in twentieth-century Canada, Norway, and the United States (Blumstein and Cohen, 1973; Blumstein et al., 1977).

The impact of this policy would be seen in comparing cohorts of parolees from year to year. A surge in the number of persons sent to prison (perhaps reflecting new legislation, an increase in the number of judges, or a new prosecutorial policy toward plea bargaining) would cause an increase in the number of prisoners paroled. The only way for the parole board to accomplish this would be for it to lower its standards for release, resulting in a poorer-risk cohort for that year (at least, poorer in the board's estimation).

Parole Supervision

Although parole officers do not set policy, they do carry out the policies set by their supervisors, for example, a strict revocation policy (say, in the aftermath of a highly publicized crime committed by a parolee) or a very lenient revocation policy (in response, say, to prison overcrowding). But parole supervision is not a constant entity; parole officers do not necessarily carry out their duties in the same way. In recounting the experience of California's Special Intensive Parole Unit (SIPU) program, Conrad (1981) noted

> In Oakland, for example, the SIPU agent was an irrepressible enthusiast who kept his office open until late hours at night to dispense advice to, and to conduct bull sessions with any parolee who cared to happen in, as most of his caseload seemed to enjoy doing. His violation rate was extremely low, and I never saw any reason to believe that there was a special ambience in Oakland which favored parole success. Across the bay in San Francisco the SIPU agent was an enthusiast of another stripe. He liked to rise in the small hours of the morning so that he could descend on unemployed parolees and remind them that early birds get the available worms and slug-a-beds do not. How he managed to conduct these sunrise raids on his charges without dismemberment on his person I have never understood, but his parole violation rate was high, even after he was convinced of the unwisdom of the strenuous counseling technique he had adopted.

Variation in outcomes, then, is not only a function of legislative or policy

---

[7] Eck used monthly data and Berk et al. used annual data. But the conclusions are similar.

differences; the personal attributes of the actors also influence recidivism rates.

Another factor influencing program outcomes lies somewhere between agency policy and personal proclivity. This might be termed an agency's "style." Wilson (1968) identified three dominant styles of policing, which he termed the legalistic, watchman, and service styles. Similar styles are doubtless characteristic of correctional agencies. However, studies of correctional agencies tend to be of single entities (e.g., Jacobs, 1978; McCleary, 1978) rather than comparative or cross-sectional studies. And police departments are geographically compact, while correctional organizations are dispersed throughout a state. Therefore, a single style may not be so dominant in a correctional organization as in a police department; there may be major differences between rural and urban (or upstate and downstate) parole supervision styles, for example.

EMPIRICAL VARIATIONS

Not all factors that have an impact on recidivism can be found by reviewing agency policy statements or by reading the literature. Some can be found only by visiting the agencies themselves. As part of this research effort eleven state correctional agencies were visited[8] to determine how their characteristics and policies might affect the outcome measures used to study correctional programs. Our brief visits did not enable us to analyze an agency's "style" in any depth, but we were able to obtain insights into other factors that affect recidivism statistics. We obtained information on the outcome measures used, the populations followed up, the events that define recidivism, and the length of follow-up times, as well as organizational factors that work to produce variations in recidivism rates.

Outcome Measures Used

All routine evaluations in these 11 states use recidivism as the outcome variable of interest. No measures of success are used. Reasons given for not measuring success were, "It is too difficult to collect such data," "It violates privacy rights," "It is not part of our mission," and "The cost of data collection is too high for measures that have little bearing on policy." Thus, the evaluations are failure-based. Even given more research money, many officials contended it would not be used to develop success measures. Some officials reported that recidivism data are collected only to satisfy other agencies that demand such data—such as the Law Enforcement Assistance Administration, the state legisla-

---

[8]The states visited were California, Florida, Georgia, Maine, Massachusetts, Michigan, Minnesota, Texas, Washington, and Wisconsin.

ture, or the National Council on Crime and Delinquency—or to forecast prison populations.

Populations Followed Up

Some variation was found in the types of populations followed up. Four states tracked only parolees, while three followed up all persons released, including parolees, mandatory conditional releasees, and mandatory releasees. Another state studied all but those mandatorily released while still another followed up a cohort of parolees and a cohort of those mandatorily released.

Naturally, such differences will have an effect on observed failure rates. Since parolees are considered better risks upon release, one would anticipate that states that follow up only parolees would have a lower recidivism rate, ceteris paribus, than states that follow up those released under any status.

Parolees, however, are subject to more behavioral constraints than those mandatorily released. A violation of the technical conditions of parole can result in parole revocation and consequent readmission to prison. Parolees may also be under closer and more systematic observation. The greater observation of parolees, then, may work in the opposite direction; that is, parolees might also be expected to have a higher recidivism rate.[9]

Recidivating Events

The states generally agreed as to which events are defined as incidents of failure. Six states considered return to prison as the only indicator of failure. Thus, absconders, technical violators, and those convicted of new crimes would only be documented as failures if these actions led to subsequent recommitment to prison. Furthermore, only one state counted returns to prison if they occurred in another state.

Some states' definitions approached the pragmatic conception of a failure more rigorously. One state included a new major conviction with subsequent continuation on parole as a failing event, while another included a jail sentence of 30 days or more as an indicator of failure.

Finally, one state utilized a fairly comprehensive definition of recidivism, including parolee at-large for 6 months or longer; death in the commission of a crime or from drug overdose; any new conviction which resulted in one of six types of sanctions; felony arrest and charge, guilt admitted, no further trial; and return to prison for felony conviction in any state.

---

[9]Care should be taken to distinguish between the two effects described here. The first effect is that the recidivism rate is expected to be lower because a population of parolees is expected to have a lower-than-average offense rate than a population that includes those denied parole. The second effect is that closer observation of parolees may increase the probability of arrest for any given offense.

Absconsion

The interpretation of absconsion in recidivism measurement varies across states. Officials' estimates of the proportion of parolees who abscond ranged from 2 to 10 percent. One state considers all officially recorded absconders as failures, while another considers them failures if they have been in that status for at least 6 months, or if there is an outstanding felony warrant for their arrest. The remaining states consider them nonrecidivists (i.e., successes, by default), if they are not returned to prison in-state during the duration of their follow-up.[10]

Event Time

The date of occurrence of a recidivating event is the time at which the recidivist interacts with the system that records the interaction. For example, in the case of return to prison, the date of the recidivating event is the date the individual is on the books as having returned to prison. Events are not traced back to the time of the actual act (e.g., arrest) that caused subsequent system actions. Recidivism is calculated using information relating to reimprisonment, and only the information that is of ultimate concern to the correctional agency may be formally documented. In special evaluations, however, FBI or state rap sheet data may be used to define failure, and date of arrest would be used as event time.

Follow-up Period

The range of maximum follow-up periods for the states visited was from 1 to 4 years, the most common being 1 year. Of course, not all of the parolees are followed up for the 4 years in those states that track parolees for that length of time; only those whose paroles are that long or longer are followed up for 4 years. Thus, recidivism statistics for the fourth year would be biased because they would reflect the behavior of only that subset of parolees for whom a 4-year parole is considered necessary.

Organizational Factors in Reporting Failure Events

Parole officers use considerable discretion when deciding whether to report technical violations and institute revocation procedures (Lerman, 1968; McCleary, 1978). One parole official interviewed admitted, "There is great pressure on

---

[10]This points out one of the problems in measuring recidivism. Most studies of recidivism rely on criminal records, or "rap sheets," for their data. But rap sheets record events—arrests, prosecutions, dispositions, etc.—and an absconsion is not an event so much as it is the absence of an event (e.g., the parolee did not check in with his agent). Since this nonevent may not be included on the rap sheet, the parolee is not considered a recidivist or is still considered a success.

parole officers not to return parolees due to the overcrowded situation of our prisons." Thus, the capacity of the state to incarcerate, the number of "free beds," could have an eventual effect on failure rates, especially those based on return to prison.

Other factors also affect the underreporting of parole violations. According to officials, the amount of paperwork required to process violations could have an effect on the stringency of reporting, especially when considered in relation to officer–client ratios. Departmental policy on revocations, as mandated by internal and external organizational constraints and contingencies, will also affect the eventual rate of return. Court decisions related to parole have made it more difficult for parole officers to revoke parole. Whereas considerable discretion was given to parole officers to revoke, some officials say that such discretion now operates in the reverse, and that they have considerable discretion not to revoke.

Agency Perspective

The view of correctional agencies is that the postrelease behavior of individuals who once were in their custody is not their responsibility. This is especially true in times of tight budgetary constraints, when maintaining livable conditions in institutions or keeping parole caseloads at a reasonable level takes priority over studying recidivism.

Also, agency officials are closer to the source of data used to evaluate programs, and are therefore much more cautious in making inferences based on such data. One official explained that evaluations that relied on data from parole officer reports were discontinued because "we came to consider them too biased to use, because information collected on parolees was generally in narrative form and primarily reflective of the parole officer's personal attitude toward his client."

SUMMARY

Variations in parole organization, policies, and practice, as well as variations in the types of releasees followed up, will be reflected in variations in the observed rates of recidivism.

This chapter has described how certain characteristics of correctional organizations affect recidivism. Differences in the characteristics may create differences in the populations under study, in the way the program is conducted, or in the type of data collected. Another significant factor limiting comparisons is the lack of consistency in defining recidivism. This problem, and a suggested solution, are taken up in the next chapter.

6
Recidivism Definitions

When recidivism is discussed in a correctional context, its meaning seems fairly clear. The word is derived from the Latin *recidere,* to fall back. A recidivist is one who, after release from custody for having committed a crime, is not rehabilitated. Instead, he or she falls back, or relapses, into former behavior patterns and commits more crimes.

This conceptual definition of recidivism may seem quite straightforward; however, an operational definition, one that permits measurement, is not so simple. The information on which measurement of recidivism is based is rarely complete, and even when it is complete, there is no consistency in the way the data are analyzed: there is "considerable variation in the way recidivism is measured" (National Advisory Commission, 1973: 512).

This chapter discusses variations in the way recidivism is defined. The problems encountered in formulating a clear definition are described by first assuming that all conceivable information one would need concerning an individual's criminal behavior is available. Next it is shown how more realistic assumptions about information affect the definitions. A description is then given of how recidivism is defined in practice. The chapter concludes with recommendations concerning the operational definition of recidivism.

COMPLETE INFORMATION

First consider the measurement of recidivism when complete information is available. By "complete information" I mean that every crime committed by the individuals under study, whether an arrest ensues or not, is known to the evaluators. Even under this unlikely condition there is a problem since the word *crime* covers a lot of ground.

For example, a child molester may be arrested, convicted, and sentenced to a correctional program specifically designed to treat such offenders. Upon release he may actually have been corrected so that he no longer molests children. If he then turns to armed robbery or to forgery, should we consider him a recidivist? In one sense he is a recidivist, since he committed another crime after release. However, the crime is of an entirely different nature; the origianl harmful behavior has ceased and a different set of harmful behaviors is manifested. Should we consider a person a recidivist if he shifts frome one crime type to a totally different type?

Of course, it is possible to label a person a recidivist only if he commits the same crime type for which he was originally convicted. However, this definition implies that all offenders are specialists, which is contradicted by the available (and mounting) evidence (Petersilia, 1980; Chaiken & Chaiken, 1982; Goldstein, 1982; Miller & Dinitz, 1982). Furthermore, if there is a separate category of recidivism for each offense, there will be correspondingly less information about each category. One might consider using four categories of crime: property crime,[1] personal crime, public-order crime, and white-collar crime. But there are no clear dividing lines among these categories, since many crimes (e.g., robbery or arson) can cross the boundaries.

To a great extent the nature of the correctional program dictates the definition of recidivism. In the preceding example the individual would not be considered a recidivist if the program being evaluated were aimed at modifying the behavior of child molesters, but would be considered a recidivist if the program were, for example, a study of the effectiveness of different parole caseloads. Thus, both crime type and program type must be considered in defining recidivism.

Complete Criminal Justice System Information

Now let us consider the best of all possible *realistic* worlds: the evaluators do not have information about all *crimes* committed by individuals in the cohort, but do have complete information about all of their transactions with the criminal justice system—arrests, indictments, prosecutions, convictions, and sentences. This goal is achievable—the U.S. Department of Justice has provided funds for states to develop Offender-Based Transaction Systems (OBTS), which are designed to collect such data. A number of states currently have substantial OBTS data-collection and analysis capability.

The fundamental question now is, To what extent can an individual's criminal record be used as an indicator of his or her behavior? We know that it has major weaknesses (see Chapters 3 and 4 for a discussion of some of these). Since the criminal record is the only indicator (other than, possibly, self-reports), the goal should be to understand these weaknesses and use the criminal record in a way that minimizes their effect on the behavioral measure used.

---

[1] Robbery is usually categorized as a personal or violent crime, not a property crime. The reason is that the victim has been placed in danger by the offender. But in studying recidivism we are concerned with the *offender's* behavior, not the *victim's*. Since robbery is an *instrumental* crime—committed to obtain money—more than it is an *expressive* crime—committed to fulfill psychic needs—it would appear that one who engages in robbery would have more in common with one who engages in property crime than with one who engages in murder, rape or assault. In fact, Sokal (1974: 1121) found that robbery was more strongly associated with auto theft than with any other index crime.

One problem may be determining who is truly a recidivist and who is a first offender. Many states have laws prohibiting disclosure of juvenile records (Greenwood *et al.*, 1980; Frazier, 1981), so that youthful indiscretions and delinquent activities do not haunt people for the rest of their lives. This policy means that, upon reaching the age at which he or she can be tried as an adult, a person is considered to be a first offender, regardless of past record. However, juvenile records can often be used for research purposes if appropriate safeguards are taken.

It is important to determine *when* the behavior occurred. Normally, the date of arrest (or of violation, for parolees and probationers) is the only indicator of time. If arrest date coincides with offense date (which is the exception rather than the rule), then arrest date is a good indicator. For the purposes of the analytic techniques described in later chapters, however, it is sufficient if offense and arrest occur within a few days of each other. It is not unreasonable to assume that this is ordinarily the case. In fact, Greenwood *et al.* (1977) found that about 90% of all cases (whether an arrest occurred or not) were closed by police within a week of occurrence of the crime; for cases in which an arrest occurred, this number would doubtless be higher.

A more important question in defining recidivism is whether one should use a "raw" arrest (one not necessarily followed by a conviction) as an indicator. In dealing with named individuals there can be only one appropriate answer: an arrest must be followed by a conviction before it can be used as an indicator of behavior; a person should not be assumed guilty merely because he or she has been arrested. However, recidivism studies deal with statistical descriptors of *cohorts* rather than named individuals, so the ethical problem of using raw arrests is minimized.

From a social science perspective, the primary consideration is how to use the availabe data to develop the most appropriate indicator, the one that is closest to what we think of as recidivism. In practical terms, this boils down to a choice between using raw arrest data or using data from arrests only if they are followed by conviction.[2]

The argument against using raw arrests is based on the standard for arrest being much less rigorous than that for conviction. Probable cause is sufficient to arrest an individual; proof beyond reasonable doubt is needed for conviction. Furthermore, the arrest of a person released from prison (i.e., known to have been an offender) is much more likely to occur than the arrest of a person with no prior record. For example, suppose that a person convicted of child molesting has actually been rehabilitated. This does not make him immune from arrest; on

---

[2]One might also consider using prosecutorial action as a quality-control check on arrests. That is, if the prosecutor presses charges there is a stronger presumption that the arrest is valid. However, obtaining data from this part of the criminal justice system is often more difficult than obtaining data from police, courts, and correctional agencies. This problem will be discussed later in the chapter.

the contrary, that person may be subject (and subjected) to arrest frequently, whenever a child is molested anywhere nearby. An arrest of this type should not be an indicator of recidivism.

Arrests are used for purposes other than detaining suspects or those known to have committed crimes. It may be that the police have a policy of harassing ex-offenders to encourage them to leave the jurisdiction (as did the Lenaxa, Kansas police—see Westin & Baker, 1972: 87). Or they may use computerized offender files when looking for suspects, and thus make more arrests of ex-offenders. Furthermore, a great deal of pressure is placed on the police to clear crimes by arrest, so they may be inclined to make arrests without sufficient cause. I am reminded of that memorable line uttered by Claude Raines, the impeccable chief of police in the movie *Casasblanca*: "Round up the usual suspects."

Thus, using raw arrest data to indicate recidivism will produce Type 1 errors, that is, it will *include* those who should be *excluded*—to the extent that the police arrest individuals who have not committed offenses. But Type 2 errors, *excluding* those who should be *included,* also occur. In a great many cases people known to be guilty of a crime are not convicted or even arrested, and for reasons totally unconnected with the quality of the evidence or the strength of the case:

- An offender may be put in a diversion program in lieu of prosecution.
- He or she may be granted immunity from prosecution in return for testimony.
- The case may be continued so many times that witnesses finally die, move away, or just get discouraged from showing up for trial.
- He or she may offer to make restitution to the victim if the victim agrees to drop charges or withhold testimony.
- The case may be insignificant compared to other cases awaiting prosecution and is consequently dropped.
- Since the time of the arrest the offender has committed a more serious offense for which he or she will be prosecuted, in lieu of prosecution for the earlier arrest.
- The charge on which the individual is convicted may bear little resemblance to the offense committed, due to plea bargaining.[3]

Thus, the basic problem, even when complete information about offenders and their "transactions" with the criminal justice system is available, is the difference between *de facto* and *de jure* recidivism. Legal definitions of offenses, arrests, and charges are the basis of the only data obtainable from the criminal justice system and must be used by evaluators in assessing behavioral charac-

---

[3]Determinate or "flat time" sentencing (Fogel, 1979), which limits the sentencing discretion of judges, is becoming more and more widespread. One consequence of this trend may be an increase in plea bargaining by prosecutors, effectively moving sentencing discretion to this stage of the criminal justice process.

teristics. Were the legal definitions reflective of what actually occurred, the problem would be minimized. But the data are distorted because sentences are based on these definitions of criminal conduct—a burglary may be charged as burglary, criminal trespass, malicious mischief, vandalism, or larceny, which is not very helpful when one is trying to reconstruct what happened.

One can see, then, the problems associated with an operational definition of recidivism using criminal history records, even when the records are complete. On the one hand we have errors of commission, if we call an arrestee a recidivist when he or she has actually not committed an offense. On the other hand we have errors of omission, if arrestees who are factually guilty are labeled nonrecidivists because they have not been convicted for the variety of reasons discussed. Based on the empirical data relating to these errors, Blumstein and Cohen (1979b: 565) concluded that "the errors of commission associated with truly false arrests are believed to be far less serious than the errors of omission that would occur if the more stringent standard of conviction were required." This position is also taken in this book: arrest is a better indicator of offender conduct than conviction. However, it may be advisable to use some sort of check on the quality of the arrest. This issue is treated later in this chapter, in the discussion of how recidivism should be operationalized.

PROBLEMS WITH INCOMPLETE CRIMINAL JUSTICE DATA

In the last section it was assumed that complete information about an individual's transactions with the criminal justice system was available; however, some of this information may be lacking. Many different agencies report on these transactions, but in most states there is no single repository for the data. This is in part attributable to the many jurisdictions and governmental levels involved in the criminal justice process in a state.

Enforcement Data

A state's enforcement agencies are found at all levels of government: municipal (local police), county (sheriff's offices), and state (highway patrols, bureaus of investigation). Centralized reporting of crime and arrest data was initiated over 50 years ago and has been improved and expanded over the years (Maltz, 1977). It now includes virtually all enforcement agencies.

All enforcement agencies report felony arrests to the National Crime Information Center (NCIC), a service provided for state and local agencies by the Federal Bureau of Investigation (FBI). In the past these reports went directly to the FBI; but recently many states have established Statistical Analysis Centers (SACs), funded by the Justice Department, to compile these data and forward them to the FBI. These states are able to provide researchers with virtually complete felony arrest data.

Prosecutorial and Court Data

With few exceptions, criminal courts and prosecutors' offices are county agencies.[4] There is no single repository of data from them akin to the NCIC program for felony arrests. Statistical Analysis Centers are charged with collecting all criminal justice data, but their collection of prosecutorial and trial data has not proceeded as rapidly as has their collection of data from enforcement agencies. However, many of the larger prosecutors' offices have been funded by the Justice Department to install the Prosecutor's Management Information System (PROMIS [National Institute of Justice, 1977]) or similar computer-based information storage and retrieval systems. Data from these offices should be more complete than can be anticipated from other jurisdictions.

Correctional Data

Correctional data are generated at both the county (jail) and state (prison, halfway house) level. But few states presently include jail data in their statewide correctional statistics. Here, too, developments are promising. The Justice Department has funded states to create Offender-Based State Correctional Information Systems (OBSCIS), to compile state correctional data at all levels. At the present time, however, few states can routinely track individuals who have been given jail sentences, with any assurance of completeness.

State-Specific Data

Even if all of the information from within the state were available for analysis, it would still be incomplete for offenders who are rearrested, prosecuted, and/or convicted in another state. If only data from the state conducting the study are used—which is always so when "return to prison" is the recidivism indicator—recidivism rates may be dependent on geography. For example, state-specific recidivism rates for states like Rhode Island and Nevada may be lower than expected due only to the proximity of their major population centers to bordering states. Since states have different regulations limiting the dissemination of such data for interstate (and intrastate) use (Office of Technology Assessment, 1978),

---

[4]This refers to "courts of original jurisdiction," that is, it excludes appellate courts. In some states the attorney general's office has limited criminal jurisdiction as well. Also, in some states the courts are funded by the state, but even in these states records are normally kept at the county level.

one cannot count on the availability of "foreign" data for an evaluation. However, arrest data would in any case be more accessible to another state than prosecutorial, court, or correctional data.

Summary

So we see another reason for using arrest as the indicator of choice in studying recidivism: prosecutorial, court, and correctional data are not yet as complete or as reliable as arrest data supplied by enforcement agencies. Add to this the argument that arrest charges are generally more descriptive of offender behavior than the charges at prosecution or the charges on which a person is convicted, and a strong case is made for using arrest as the indicator of recidivism.

DATA PROBLEMS IN CONTROLLING FOR ARREST QUALITY

Recidivism need not be determined by arrest alone. One can attempt to reduce Type 1 errors (resulting from improper arrests) by looking at subsequent criminal justice transactions based on the arrest. If recidivism is defined as "arrest only if followed by affirmative prosecutorial action," records must be examined to see if an indictment, information, or other prosecutorial action has taken place. To examine these records the analyst must go through all files in a prosecutor's office. Except for the few offices that have been automated, this usually means that every case folder in the office must be examined to determine the name of the defendant, the nature of the original charge at arrest, whether the charges have been dropped or pursued further, and the present disposition of the case. This information is usually handwritten on the outside of the folder by staff attorneys whose penmanship rivals that of the medical profession for illegibility and encryption. In other words, the task is not so straightforward as it seems, especially since many of the folders are likely to be in briefcases, in piles on (and under) desks, in attorneys' homes or cars, or in other locations convenient for the attorneys but not for the researcher. Although this particular check on the quality of the arrest would be useful, one cannot be sure of getting complete and accurate data.

Recidivism may also be defined as "arrest only if followed by conviction." Determining if a conviction ensued is less difficult a task than determining the nature of the prosecutor's response. The FBI's NCIC compiles data on arrests and subsequent dispositions. However, the NCIC program is largely voluntary, so complete disposition information cannot be guaranteed. Although the quality of dispositional data is improving, there can easily be a delay of many months before the data are transmitted to NCIC or to a state repository of criminal justice information. For the present the researcher should not expect to have complete dispositional data available.

ABSCONSION

Another disposition related to the parole process must be considered in the definition of recidivism. If a person absconds, that is, stops reporting to the parole officer and cannot be located, should he or she be considered a recidivist? In some states, perversely enough, an absconder is treated by default as a *success*. If no action is taken against the absconder because he or she cannot be found, that person is carried on the books as not having failed—because there was no record of parole violation, or arrest or other adverse action being taken. Even if this oversight is corrected, the question of how to treat absconsions is still not answered. No doubt many parolees abscond because of fear of arrest, but absconsion should not automatically be treated as a failure; it should depend on the purposes of the study and on the way recidivism is defined. For example, if a felony arrest is the recidivism criterion, absconsion alone would not be considered a recidivism event (unless the absconsion was to avoid a felony arrest).

RECIDIVISM DEFINED IN PRACTICE

Most states use data only from their own state when conducting an evaluation. They do so not because of any theories about offender mobility, but because of the uncertainty and difficulty of obtaining data from other states and because of a certain parochialism and fear of using data collected by others; there may be a feeling that different standards and criteria are used in their data collection, and that other states' data are not as reliable as theirs.

For special evaluations, FBI data may be used in follow-ups, so that all arrests are included; but this is the exception, not the rule. And even when FBI data are used, it is often very difficult to determine if a conviction resulted from an arrest: Kitchener *et al.* (1977) found this to be so in their study of releasees from federal prisons, even though they had the FBI's NCIC data available to them; and Hoffman and Stone-Meierhoefer (1980) found that disposition data were often missing. Telephone follow-ups to the arresting jurisdictions were required to fill in the gaps.

But arrests, whether or not followed by convictions, are not the only indicators of recidivism that are used in evaluations. For example, Waldo and Chiricos (1977) used 18 different measures of recidivism in a study of a work release program. For the present study, to determine the way recidivism has been defined in practice, some 90 studies that used recidivism as an outcome measure were reviewed. The studies were in the open literature and/or were cited by Lipton *et al.* (1975). The definitions were into separated general categories. Here are these categories and some of their qualifying conditions:

- Arrest: number of arrests; recorded police contact; court appearance; time elapsed before the first arrest; did conviction result?
- Reconviction: jail or prison sentence; felony or less; sentence.
- Incarceration: type of facility ; seriousness of offense.
- Parole violation: nature of the violation; seriousness of the infraction; was it police-initiated?
- Parole suspension: new offense; number of suspensions.
- Parole revocation: new offense; seriousness of the offense; average number of good days on parole.
- Offense: seriousness; number; new offense.
- Absconding: was an absconder warrant issued?
- Probation: proportion redetained; length of time detained; number of violations; violation warrant.

Each of these definitions has been used frequently in correctional research.[5] In some studies more than one definition (e.g., "either parole revocation or ar-

---

[5]Examples of their use include

1. Arrest. Arrest for a new offense (Inciardi, 1971; Fishman, 1977; Cox, 1977); court appearance within 1 year after release (Coates *et al.*, 1978); criminal arrest (Hoffman & Stone-Meierhoefer, 1979); recorded police contact (Wolfgang *et al.*, 1972; Murray & Cox, 1979); number of arrests (Waldo & Chiricos, 1977).

2. Reconviction. Reconviction of a felony (Hopkins, 1976); reconviction or recall for unsatisfactory conduct (Hood, 1966); any new conviction resulting in a sentence of 60 days or more (Gottfredson & Ballard, 1966; Bennett & Ziegler, 1975; Beck & Hoffman, 1976); any new conviction for a felony or felony-like offense (Kitchener *et al.*, 1977); conviction of a further offense (Wilkins, 1958).

3. Incarceration. Jail sentence of more than 3 days and return to prison for either a new offense or a technical violation (Burkhart & Sathmary, 1964); return to prison (Jacobson & McGee, 1965; Waldo & Chiricos, 1977); return to prison as a parole violator or due to outstanding absconder warrant (Gottfredson & Ballard, 1966); number of commitments to an institution with or without adjudication (Boston University, 1966); return to prison for an administrative violation (Beck & Hoffman, 1976); recommitted to prison with conviction(s) for major offense, same jurisdiction or any other jurisdction (Mosely & Gerould, 1975); return to prison for at least 30 days within 1 year of release (LeClair, 1977); return to prison as a parole violator (Kitchener *et al.*, 1977).

4. Parole Violation. Alcholic criminality: arrests and fines for drunkenness, disorderly conduct (Hansen & Teilman, 1954); issuance of a parole violation warrant whether subject was reinstitutionalized or not (Garrity, 1956); violating rules of parole (Kusuda & Babst, 1964); issuance of a parole violation warrant by District Court or Board of Parole for technical violations or new felony offenses (Lohman, 1967); parole violation (Kantrowitz, 1977); parole violation warrant (Hoffman & Stone-Meierhoefer, 1979).

5. Parole Suspension. Parole suspension with or without a new offense (Narloch *et al.*, 1959); suspension (California, 1956); number of parole suspensions (Werner & Palmer, 1976).

TABLE 6-1

Recidivism Definitions Used in Recent Studies

Definitions	Frequency
Offense data	
Recorded police contact	2
New offense	16
Severity of offense	12
Arrest	20
Parole–probation infractions	
Parole suspension	8
Parole revocation	8
Technical violation	26
Absconding	10
Probation violation	3
Court appearance	3
Reconviction	22
Sentencing	8
Return to prison	39

Source: Compiled from those studies marked with an asterisk in the References.

rest") of recidivism was used. And even when two studies used the same *general* definition of recidivism (e.g., incarceration), they may have used different *specific* definitions (e.g., "return to prison" vs. "return to prison with conviction for a major offense"). Despite this lack of comparability, the definitions used in about 90 studies were tabulated; they are listed in the References and denoted by an asterisk. The tabulation listed in Table 6-1 should be taken as indicative of the popularity of different measures.

There can be major differences in the conclusions one comes to regarding correctional effectiveness, depending on which recidivism measure is used. Hoffman & Stone-Meierhoefer (1980) have shown how varying the way recidi-

---

6. Parole Revocation. Revocation of parole (Johnson, 1962); parole revocation or bad discharge (Guttman, 1963).

7. Offense. New Offense or violation of the rules of supervision within 2 years (Babst & Mannering, 1965); mean number of offenses during a 12-month follow-up period, seriousness of the offense (McEachern & Taylor, 1967; Waldo & Chiricos, 1977).

8. Absconding. Absconding (Kusuda & Babst, 1964; Inciardi, 1971; Mosely & Gerould, 1975); absconder warrant (Gottfredson & Ballard, 1966; Beck & Hoffman, 1976).

9. Probation. Observed reconviction rate compared with expected conviction rate (Great Britain, 1964); drunk arrest rate for municipal court (Ditman & Crawford, 1965); unfavorable dismissal from probation (Feistman, 1966); number of months before successful completion of probation (Kawaguchi & Siff, 1967).

vism is operationalized can produce different interpretations of which program or cohort is better. Obviously, what is needed is a way to systematize the operational definitions of recidivism.

PROPOSED RECIDIVISM DEFINITIONS

I do not propose to prescribe one single operational definition of recidivism. Rather, I propose to describe some of the more useful definitions in some logical way. The goal is similar to the goal of economists in developing a set of definitions of "money." Economists talk not of money in general, but of M1, currency plus demand deposits, or of M2, M1 plus time deposits other than large certificates of deposit. These have (sometimes) been found to be useful indicators in charting the economy's course. A similar language is suggested below for recidivism.

Recidivism is normally measured in terms of the time interval between two events: time of release and time of recidivism. (Of course, those who do not recidivate do not experience the second event.) For example, many studies of correctional programs report the "1-year recidivism rate," which is the fraction of program participants who experience a recidivating event within 1 year of release.

The release event can be one of a number of events: release from incarceration, release from parole supervision, release from a work–study program or halfway house. The choice of event can depend on the nature of the program being evaluated. For instance, to evaluate a prison vocational program one would consider release from prison to be the release event whether or not the participants were on parole.[6] To evaluate a parole program the release event would be release from parole supervision.

Occasionally it may be necessary to look beyond recorded dates to determine when the release event occurred. For example, when a prison releasee enters a halfway house he may find himself essentially incarcerated for the first few weeks, until he gets his bearings in his new surroundings. (He may be permitted out to work and for other activities, but never without supervision.) In this case the actual date of release may not be the date he leaves the prison, but the date he is released on his own to the outside world.

The recidivism event depends upon the nature of the release event. If the release event was release to parole or probation supervision, the recidivism event may be a technical violation (of the conditions of parole or probation or of the rules of the halfway house); it may be revocation of parole or probation in lieu of

---

[6]Naturally, one would control inter alia for parole participation.

a trial for a new offense (whether or not followed by an additional disposition); or it may be return to prison.

Not all of the release–recidivism pairs will be defined below. My concern has been to operationalize recidivism in ways that are reasonable from theoretical and data-acquisition standpoints. The definitions are based on the events that terminate the time interval, because the date of release (when the recidivism clock starts) is both less ambiguous and more dependent on the program under evaluation (see p. 55). They are listed in order of the most restrictive to least restrictive definition.

R_{ac}—Arrest and Conviction. The time interval runs from date of release to date of arrest, but it is counted as a recidivism event only if the arrest results in conviction. An absconder is treated as having failed on the date of absconsion if an absconder warrant is issued for an arrest.

R_{ap}—Arrest and Prosecution. The time interval runs from date of release to date of arrest, but it is counted as a recidivism event only if some prosecutorial action is taken against the arrestee: charges filed, grand jury presentation, indictment, etc. This definition also includes R_{ac}.

R_a—Arrest. The time interval runs from date of release to date of arrest, regardless of whether prosecution or conviction ensues. This definition also includes R_{ap}.

R_{vc}—Violation and Return to Custody. The time interval runs from date of release to date of violation of the terms of release (i.e., parole or probation), but it is counted as a recidivism event only if the violator is returned to custody.[7] This definition also includes R_{ap}.

R_v—Violation. The time interval runs from date of release to date of violation of the terms of release, whether or not the individual was returned to custody. Absconders are treated as having recidivated from the date of absconsion. This definition also includes R_{vc}.

These definitions can be modified in two ways. First, if data from only one state are used to calculate arrest recidivism, then it can be denoted as r_a to distinguish it from R_a, in which arrest data from every state are used. Second, if only felony arrest data are used, it can be denoted by R_A to distinguish it from R_a which denotes that data from misdemeanor arrests are also used.

Another measure of recidivism that has been used is "return to prison." The time interval usually runs from date of release to date of return to prison, not to the date of the arrest that led to the prison sentence. This measure may be useful

---

[7]Hoffman and Stone-Merierhoefer (1979) use this criterion, but add "killed during the commission of a crime." Naturally, this should be considered a recidivism event, but it may not always be recorded. In any event, it occurs so infrequently that its exclusion (should the data not be available) would not greatly affect the results.

TABLE 6-2

Characteristics of Proposed Recidivism Definitions

Recidivating event	Recidivism definitions							
	r_V	r_{vc}	r_a	r_A	r_{ap}	r_{Ap}	r_{ac}	r_{Ac}
Violation of parole or probation conditions	X	—	—	—	—	—	—	—
Violation and return to custody	X	X	—	—	—	—	—	—
Any arrest	X	—	X	—	—	—	—	—
Felony arrest	X	—	X	X	—	—	—	—
Charges filed	X	X	X	X	X	—	—	—
Felony charges filed	X	X	X	X	X	X	—	—
Conviction	X	X	X	X	X	X	X	—
Felony conviction	X	X	X	X	X	X	X	X

NB: Lowercase "r" refers to single-state data.

to prison officials, for planning budgets and expected occupancy rates. However, it is *not* useful as an indicator of offender behavior because it includes criminal justice processing time. The time interval is thus the sum of the following time intervals: release to arrest, arrest to hearing, hearing to trial, trial to sentencing, and sentencing to recommitment. Only the first time interval relates to offender behavior; the others reflect the behavior of the criminal justice system.

Table 6-2 summarizes these definitions. The recidivism definition of choice appears to be R_a, arrest recidivism, for the present. (For studying parole or probation cohorts, R_v would appear to be the most appropriate, since technical violations may mask new offenses.) R_{ap} might be preferred were there data to support it, but this is not presently the case[8]; therefore, the choice is between using raw arrests or arrests followed by convictions. And despite the fact that raw arrest figures include some for which no offense occurred, their number is probably considerably smaller than the number of felony arrests of guilty persons for whom no conviction resulted. Moreover, arrest data are more accessible than disposition data. The choice is dictated, therefore, as much by data availability and completeness as by theoretical considerations.

Other Sources of Noncomparability

I do not mean to imply that use of the same recidivism measure by different programs or jurisdictions will automatically result in comparable findings. This is far from the case. Differences in laws, policies, and procedures among juris-

---

[8]Some jurisdictions in a state may have complete and accurate prosecutorial data (e.g., they may have a PROMIS system); however, if other prosecutors' offices have inadequate data collection systems, data involving offenders working in more than one county will be of questionable quality.

dictions will still prevent direct comparisons. For example, suppose one state makes little use of probation while another uses it heavily. Then a cohort of prison releasees from the first state will probably have a higher percentage of good risks than will a cohort from the latter state, and therefore a lower recidivism rate. Or suppose one state has a computerized data-collection system used by parole officers, while in another jurisdiction parole officers turn in longhand reports on their parolee caseload. Then information about technical violations is likely to be considerably more variable in quality (and often richer) in the latter case than in the former. Not all of these differences can be accounted for. However, foreknowledge of their presence and their potential effect on recidivism measurement is necessary in developing evaluation designs and in interpreting results.

7
Recidivism Measures and Models

Although definitions of recidivism may have varied considerably in the past, the method of measuring it has been consistent. Most of the studies cited in the last chapter analyzed recidivism data in the same way: members of the experimental and control groups were tracked for a given period of time;[1] the percentage of recidivists in each group was calculated; and the two percentages were then compared using an appropriate statistical test.

Implicit in this method of analyzing recidivism data is a model of the underlying behavior of the groups under study, although the model may not be immediately apparent. The relationship between the methods used to measure recidivism and the models they imply is the subject of this chapter. The first two sections discuss general characteristics of models and their development. Next, the model underlying the 1-year recidivism rate is described, followed by descriptions of other recidivism models that have been proposed as alternatives.

CHARACTERISTICS OF MODELS

A model is a simplified representation of reality, one that contains the salient features of the system or process under study. There are physical models (e.g., of an airplane, for testing in a wind tunnel), semantic or verbal models (e.g., a description of a neurosis), and symbolic or mathematical models (e.g., of the times of failure of a cohort of parolees). It is the last type that will be discussed in this chapter.

In all cases, however, a good model should be "a representation of reality in manipulable form" (Howard, 1970). Its manipulability is its *raison d'etre,* permitting one to see how the system or process under study is affected by different inputs, or how changes in its form can affect system behavior. A model's manipulability permits "experimentation" (e.g., changing the length or camber of an airplane's wings) without having to change the actual system. Models may

---

[1]The period of time is usually 1 year, resulting in the "1-year recidivism rate." Similarly, cancer studies use the "5-year survival rate" as their benchmark.

also provide insight into processes upon which experimentation is impossible (e.g., motions of the solar system) or undesirable (e.g., the behavior of individuals under extreme stress). They can aid in developing theories to explain the behavior of a process, and in gaining insight into its characteristics. They permit one to extrapolate beyond available data, and thus to reduce the length of time needed to study a phenomenon. And they permit these experiments to be conducted at a much lower cost than if one had to use the actual system.

DEVELOPMENT OF MODELS

Models describe how the variables of interest are related to each other. The relationships may turn out to be rather complicated, requiring a great deal of analytic work to determine their structure. In fact, it is often the case that a research knows (or suspects) only that certain variables are useful in describing a process, but not how they interact, that is, whether the outcome is an additive or multiplicative (or some other) function of the variables. In such cases exploratory analyses are undertaken, using various functional forms, to see how best to characterize the system. Daniel and Wood (1971) give some concrete examples and suggestions of how such exploratory analyses may be conducted.

Unfortunately, not every researcher attempts a thoughtful application of exploratory analyses in developing models. Some "models" reported on in the social science literature are no more than the results of applying a canned statistical package to the data, without consideration of whether the package is best for the purpose or whether the data are in the most appropriate form.

For example, Barnett (1982, 1983) shows how a linear regression of salary against years of service can produce a finding of sex discrimination in salaries where none exists. He argues that a linear model is inappropriate in this case, since it implies that dollar-value increases in salary are the same regardless of salary level. However, salary increases are usually based on a percentage of present salary, so an exponential or geometric relationship between salary and years of service is more appropriate.

In another example, Maltz (1981a) compares two models of cigarette smuggling. The first is regression model in which little consideration is given to the nature of the relationship among variables. He shows that this model is greatly inferior to a regression model that structures the relationship among variables according to geographical and market characteristics of the smuggling process. Such a model, based on an understanding of the underlying process, simplifies a model's structure and makes it more useful as a predictive tool.

In many other cases researchers do attempt to model the process accurately, but pay insufficient attention to the stochastic properties of the data. For example, Barnett (1981a, 1981b) reviewed studies examining the putative deterrent effect of the death penalty on homicide. He found that none of the models employed could distinguish the deterrent effect from the natural (stochastic) variation in homicide rates. Chapter 4 of this book describes how ignoring the stochastic nature of arrests can lead one to interpret regression to the mean as a "suppression effect."

A good model, therefore, is one that incorporates the known characteristics of the process under study and of the data it generates. In developing such a model, a balance must be struck between completeness and conciseness. Not all variables are equally useful; in fact, selection of the appropriate variables and how they are related constitute the art of modeling (Morris, 1967; Pollock, 1976). The analyst is guided not only by a strong knowledge of the process but by personal values and experience as well, in choosing those characteristics that are seen as important to study. Model development is also guided by the principle that a simple model is better than a complicated model, if both provide about the same explanatory power.[2]

But finding such concise models is no simple task. Our knowledge of social phenomena is much more limited and less precise than our knowledge of physical phenomena. Knowledge of fluid dynamics permits an analyst to develop a complex model of the effect of wing length and camber on airplane drag. Our knowledge of social dynamics has not reached the same level of accuracy. Therefore, in conducting social research we still must subject the empirical data to a variety of analyses to see if we can uncover any patterns of social interaction.

Furthermore, patterns of social interaction are liable to change. Whereas fluid dynamics relationships do not vary, social dynamics relationships can change greatly over time and distance.

Finding patterns of social interaction is much easier when studying people collectively than when studying individuals.[3] A good example of this is the behavior of people in waiting lines or queues (Gross & Harris, 1974), whether they are waiting for service in a supermarket or for a response from a police patrol car (Larson & Odoni, 1981). And models of consumer behavior have been found useful in studying purchasing habits (Bagozzi, 1980). These models cannot predict the behavior of any one individual. That is, we are unable to tell if a person will switch to a shorter line at the checkout counter or whether a person will buy a new brand of soap; but the models can be used to estimate the percentage of people who will behave in a particular way, and the estimates are

---

[2]The Law of Parsimony, generally known as Occam's razor, states, "Entities are not to be multiplied beyond necessity." Antoine de Saint-Exupery (1939) expressed the same concept more elegantly: "If anything at all, perfection is finally attained not when there is no longer anything to add, but when there is no longer anything to take away, when a body has been stripped down to its nakedness."

[3]The same is true in the physical sciences. It is easier to model the flow of wind over a wing than to chart the progress of a single molecule of air over the wing.

superior to those obtained when the known characteristics of queuing or consumer behavior are ignored.

Three important structural features will be used in characterizing the recidivism process:

1. Our focus is primarily on the behavior of groups rather than individuals. Individual characteristics and their effect on recidivism are described in Chapter 10.[4]
2. The outcome measure of recidivism is binary: success or failure. Although success and failure are of course multivalued, we assume that these two alternatives serve to describe the outcome adequately.[5]
3. For those who fail, the time to failure is an outcome variable of interest. For those who do not fail, the length of exposure time without failing is important. Note that if the 1-year recidivism rate is used, we do not record the actual time to failure, but only whether this time is greater or less than 1 year.

THE MODEL UNDERLYING THE ONE-YEAR RECIDIVISM RATE

Before describing the model underlying the 1-year recidivism rate, three terms must be clarified: *1 year, recidivism,* and *rate.* As previously mentioned, the time period used most often in recidivism studies is *1 year.* This choice may be due more to funding cycles than to more research-oriented reasons; if the program evaluation is funded for only a year, then a year's data is the most that can be collected. However, other time periods have also been used. A more appropriate term might be *fixed-period.*

Recidivism and failure are used interchangeably in this book. The term failure is used because so many of the statistical techniques referred to in this and succeeding chapters have been developed for failure processes, of which recidivism is but one type.

The term *rate,* when used in the context of the 1-year recidivism rate, is actually the *fraction* or *percentage* of individuals who recidivate (or fail) within 1 year of their release. However, a rate is normally considered to be time based. For example, rate of speed is measured in miles per hour. When describing the 1-year recidivism rate, we will conform to criminological usage and use *rate* to

---

[4]See also Schmidt and Witte (1980) and Barton and Turnbull (1981), who direct their attention to covariate models, which attempt to describe an individual's recidivism behavior.

[5]Chapter 3 describes the difficulties in using a more refined measure of program outcome than the binary success–failure. With data of poor or of highly variable quality it is pointless to make a finer distinction.

mean fraction or percentage; however, *failure rate* will denote a time-based rate, for example, the number of failures per month. This will be explained more fully in the next section.

The 1-year recidivism rate, then, can more aptly be labeled the *fixed-period failure fraction,* with a fixed period of 1 year. This measure of recidivism requires the analyst to fix a point in time (1 year after release) and determine the fraction of program particpants who have failed within that length of time. This is obviously not the total number of failures, since others will undoubtedly fail after this time: rarely is the time interval long enough to observe most of the eventual failures.[6] A statistical test is then used to make a confidence statement about this fraction, and often to determine whether there is a significant difference between two fractions describing different programs or populations.

Although 1 year is the observation period used most often to calculate recidivism, sometimes it is 6 months, or sometimes periods of 2 years or longer. The reason for ignoring time beyond 1 year is quite practical: agencies funding correctional research want results and do not want to wait as long as, say, the 3 years suggested by the National Advisory Commission (NAC) on Criminal Justice Standards and Goals (NAC, 1973: 93) to get the results of a study. So studies are often trimmed to meet the time (and funding) goals set by the agencies.

Time is fixed in this method of analysis specifically so that a difference-of-proportions statistical test can be used. This test is based on the classic urn model of probability theory: two urns contain both white and red marbles (representing successes and failures, respectively). A sample of N marbles is drawn from one urn, and the sample contains n red marbles (failures), yielding a fraction n/N. A samle of M marbles is drawn from the other urn, and it contains m red marbles, a fraction m/M. The difference-of-proportions test is used to test the hypothesis that the two urns contain the same proportion of red marbles. The urn model is a *static* model. Time does not come into the picture at all. The red marbles have been and will always be red.

However, in the recidivism situation the "marbles" all start out white, and each may or may not turn red as time goes on. The results obtained using this static measure would be useful if a certain amount of continuity could be assumed in the failure process; that is, if it could be assumed that a program that is better (i.e., has a significantly lower percentage of failures) at the end of 1 year would continue to be better thereafter. Without this assumption the results are of little utility: if the program did not remain better in the long run, then what good is an interim measure?

But this assumption of continuity does not always hold. For example, a study

---

[6]An exception to this is the study by Kitchener *et al.* (1977). They report on an 18-year follow-up of a cohort of individuals released from federal prison. The number of failures kept increasing throughout, but at a negligible rate after 10 years.

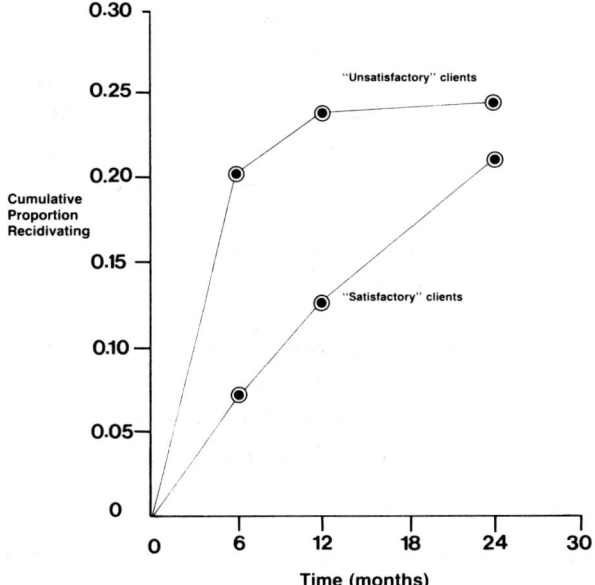

FIGURE 7-1 The recidivism experience of two groups of clients released from Minnesota halfway houses. (Source: Minnesota, 1976: 196.)

of residential correctional programs (Minnesota, 1976: 196) found that "unsatisfactory" clients released from halfway houses had a 1-year recidivism rate of 23.8%, compared to 12.8% for "satisfactory" clients,[7] a difference that was statistically significant. By the end of the second year, however, recidivism for the unsatisfactory clients had risen slightly, to 24.5%, while recidivism for the satisfactory clients had climbed over 8%, to 21.1%—and the difference was no longer statistically significant. If those trends continued for another year, the unsatisfactory clients would have the lower of the two recidivism percentages (Figure 7-1). In this case, then, fixing a single point in time at which to make recidivism calculations is clearly misleading.

Thus, one of the implicit characteristics of the model underlying the 1-year recidivism rate is that cumulative recidivism rates of different groups are "nested" and do not cross. As can be seen from Figure 7-1, this assumption is tenuous at best.

Furthermore, much useful evaluative information is discarded using this method. For example, consider a correctional treatment program that started releasing

[7]"Unsatisfactory" clients were those who did not complete their residence satisfactorily, for reasons that included revocation or conviction for additional offenses while in residence, as well as other, noncriminal reasons. All others were considered "satisfactory."

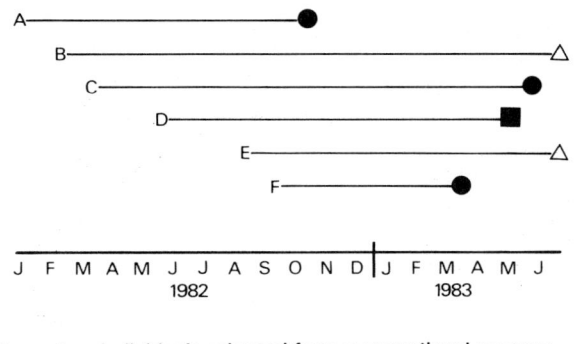

FIGURE 7-2 Recidivism histories of program releasees.

offenders on January 1, 1982, and that completed its data collection by July 1, 1983. Figure 7-2 shows the time traces of some of the program participants. Person A was released in January 1982, became a recidivist in October 1982, and is considered a failure. Person B was released in February 1982, did not fail at all during the evaluation period, and is considered a success. Person C was released in March 1982, but failed in May 1983; since the failure occurred after a year had elapsed, this person too is considered a success. Person D was released in May 1982 and was only tracked for 11 months; this person might have moved away or died. Since the observation period is less than 1 year, person D cannot be included in the evaluation. Nor can person E, who was also tracked for less than 1 year (August 1982–June 1983).

Furthermore, person F, who was tracked from September 1982 and became a recidivist in March 1983, cannot be included in the evaluation. The reason is that none of the people released after July 1982 can be tracked for a full year. Therefore, there can be no successes from person E on, only failures (those who fail before July 1983). Including these failures would bias the results, making the recidivism rate appear higher than it actually is.

In fact, there is a hidden bias in the results even if we only include people released before July 1, 1982. To illustrate this bias more concretely, suppose that two individuals are released simultaneously. Both intend to leave the jurisdiction at the end of 10 months. The first is arrested in the eighth month and becomes a recidivist; the second is not arrested and leaves the jurisdiction after 10 months. The first person is tallied as a recidivist; the second is not counted at all because he or she was not observed for a full year. Thus, instead of showing that 50% of these individuals are recidivists, the 1-year recidivism rate would be 100%.[8]

Furthermore, information is being discarded. Failure times greater than 1 year are ignored. Those with observation periods of less than 1 year are not to be included; nor are those who are released within 1 year of data cutoff. One way around this is to run the program for only 6 months, so that all program participants are released from January to June 1982. Data collection could then commence in January 1983 and run through June 1983. However, it seems absurd to stop running a program merely because of the idiosyncracies of a faulty measurement technique.

MODELS OF INDIVIDUAL FAILURE PROCESSES

Thus, we have seen that the 1-year recidivism rate is a static measure of recidivism. It results in a misleading and biased estimate of recidivism, and it does not make full use of existing data. However, other recidivism measures developed in the past decade overcome these problems. They are based on models of recidivism using failure-rate analysis, for which estimates are made of individual recidivism characteristics. The characteristics of failure rates and individual recidivism processes are described below.

Defining Failure Rate

Failure-rate (or reliability) models (Barlow & Proschan, 1975; Mann et al., 1974; Kalbfleisch & Prentice, 1980), which were originally used to analyze the reliability of electronic equipment and machinery (Nelson, 1982) and the efficacy of biomedical treatments (Gross & Clark, 1975), have been put to use in studying recidivism. As discussed earlier, the failure rate of these models is not the same as the "recidivism rate" used by criminologists. The recidivism rate is actually a percentage, the fraction of offenders who have become recidivists within a fixed observation period. For example, the unsatisfactory clients of Figure 7-1 had 6-month, 1-year, and 2-year recidivism percentages of 22.0, 23.8, and 24.5.

However, the average failure rate[9] for this group for the first 6 months is $22.0/6 = 3.67\%$ per month (see Table 7-1). For the next 6 months the calculation of the average failure rate is more complicated. Since only 78% of the population has survived (without failing) to 6 months, the additional 1.8% of

---

[8]This effect will always bias the 1-year recidivism rate upward, because it only counts the failures among those whose exposure times are (or would have been) less than 1 year.

[9]As previously stated, the term *failure rate* will be used instead of *recidivism rate* to denote the time rate of recidivism. This conforms with statistical usage.

TABLE 7-1

Failure Rate Calculations for Figure 7-1

Time (months)	Time interval (months)	Failure fraction (%)	% of population at start	Mean failure rate (%/month)
		Unsatisfactory clients		
6	6	22.0	100.0	$22/1.0 \times 6 = 3.67$
12	6	23.8	78.0	$1.8/0.780 \times 6 = 0.38$
24	12	24.5	76.2	$0.7/0.762 \times 12 = 0.08$
		Satisfactory clients		
6	6	7.2	100.0	$7.2/1.0 \times 6 = 1.2$
12	6	12.8	92.8	$5.6/0.928 \times 6 = 1.0$
24	12	21.0	87.2	$8.2/0.872 \times 12 = 0.78$

failures actually represents the failure of $1.8/0.78 = 2.32\%$ of the surviving population. The average failure rate for the second 6 months, then, is $2.32/6 = 0.38\%$ per month. Using similar calculations, the average failure rate for the second year is found to be 0.08% per month. The corresponding average failure rates for the satisfactory clients are 1.2, 1.0, and 0.78% per month. Note that the failure rates for both groups are decreasing, for the unsatisfactory clients faster than for the satisfactory clients; and that after the first 6 months the failure rate for the unsatisfactory clients is lower than for the satisfactory clients.

The source for Figure 7-1 (Minnesota, 1976: 196) only presents data for three points in time. However, the date of each person's failure is known. Therefore, it is conceivable to have monthly data points for the cumulative percentage of failures, and to calculate the average failure rate not for a 6-month period but for each month, or even for a smaller period of time.[10]

Failure rates can be decreasing (e.g., Table 7-1), increasing, or constant (i.e., DFR, IFR or CFR processes). A constant failure rate (CFR) does not mean that a constant *number* fail in each time interval; rather, it means that a constant *percentage of those surviving* fail in each time interval. For example, if there were 100 people in the program at the start of the sixteenth month and if 10 people fail in the time interval between the sixteenth and seventeenth month, then the failure rate in month 17 is $10/100 = 0.1$/month. If 9 people subsequently fail during month 17, since the number of people remaining at the start of month 17 is $100 - 10 = 90$, the failure rate in month 18 is $9/90 = 0.1$/month again. That is, a different *number* fail, but the same *proportion* fails if the failure rate is constant.

[10] In fact, it is possible to define an instantaneous failure rate at time t. This is the percentage of failures in the interval $[t, t + dt]$, divided by dt, as dt becomes small.

Probability of Recidivism for an Individual

It is not known beforehand which individuals will fail, or when they will fail. But the past behavior of similar groups is known, and certain regular patterns may have been discerned in population failure statistics over time. This regularity may be described in statistical or probabilistic terms; for example, one may estimate that between 52 and 68% of the population will fail within 18 months of release, with 90% confidence in this estimate.

Based on this regularity, what can we then say about each individual in the group? We do not know *a priori* which individuals will or will not fail; if we did, we would not need to study the group's recidivism. In fact, the best we can do is use group statistics to make inferences about individual behavior. An example will serve to explain the rationale behind this inference.

Suppose that, based on the data, we estimate that 60% of the population will eventually fail. This is a *population* characteristic. Since we do not know who the 60% will be, we use a model in which the probability of recidivism for every individual in the population is 0.6. This suggests that each individual has the same probability of failing, which may not seem useful: we know that different releasee characteristics are associated with recidivism,[11] for example, age at first arrest, educational attainment, or involvement with drugs. However, were we to restrict our attention to people with the same characteristics (e.g., all heroin users with fifth-grade educations who were first arrested at age 15), recidivism would still not be a deterministic event, but rather an essentially probabilistic one.[12] Moreover, since we cannot distinguish between individuals *a priori*, the only logical alternative is to apply the same probability of recidivism to each individual. This probability can be shown, by appropriate statistical methods, to be the fraction of the population that is expected to fail. We are merely expressing the limited extent of our knowledge of each individual, and basing it on the statistics of the group.

We therefore can look at the group's cumulative proportion failing over time (e.g., Figure 7-1) and interpret it as the probability that any individual will fail by that time.

PROBABILITY DISTRIBUTIONS USED IN MODELING RECIDIVISM

We have seen that the phenomenon of recidivism is not deterministic, at least from the standpoint of the researcher. We cannot tell who will fail, only that on

---

[11]Chapter 10 addresses the case in which individual characteristics can be used to specify individualized models.

[12]Covariate models of recidivism typically explain about 10 to 20% of the variation in recidivism, so 80 to 90% of the variation would remain.

the average so many will fail by a certain time. The most convenient way to describe this relationship is by a probability distribution. For each individual in the group, this would be a function describing the probability of an individual failing by a given time:

$$P(t) = \text{Probability (failure by time } t)$$

This is also called the cumulative distribution function (cdf). It should not be confused with the probability density function (pdf), which is its derivative and equivalent to the frequency distribution of failures over time.

Figure 7-1 is an example of a cdf, from which certain properties should be apparent. First, it is zero when time is at zero; no one can have failed before release.[13] Second, it cannot decrease over time; no one who has failed can "unfail." Third, it cannot exceed 100%; there can be at most 1 failure per person.

A cdf may be generated by empirical data (Figure 7-1). It may also be generated by a model of the recidivism process, one in which the general shape is specific to the model and the data are used to estimate the model's parameters. This section describes 6 models that have been used to characterize recidivism.

Model M_E: Exponential Distribution (CFR Model)

Stollmack and Harris broke new ground in the study of correctional programs, in their paper "Failure Rate Analysis Applied to Recidivism Data" (1974). They were the first to recognize recidivism as a failure process and to apply failure-rate techniques to study the effectiveness of correctional programs. They used a constant failure-rate model, which gives rise to an exponential distribution (Figure 7-3), in which the probability that an individual will fail before time t, $P_E(t)$, is given as[14]

$$P_E(t) = 1 - \exp(-\phi t) \tag{7.1}$$

where ϕ is the (constant) failure rate.

The constant failure-rate (CFR) model is not only the chronological precursor to the other models to be discussed, it is also implicit in many of them since the exponential distribution is a special case of other distributions. This model is very simple: it has only one parameter—ϕ. Methods of estimating ϕ from data are very well known.[15]

---

[13]Wainer develops a model in which there are recidivists at the start. However, this model "does not reflect the actual process of recidivism" (Wainer, 1981: 820).

[14]The subscript E denotes that this is the probability distribution for the exponential distribution.

[15]For example, the maximum likelihood estimator for ϕ is simply the total number of failures divided by the sum of all the failure times and all the observation times (for those who have not failed). See Appendix A for the procedures used in parameter estimation.

PROBABILITY DISTRIBUTIONS USED IN MODELING RECIDIVISM

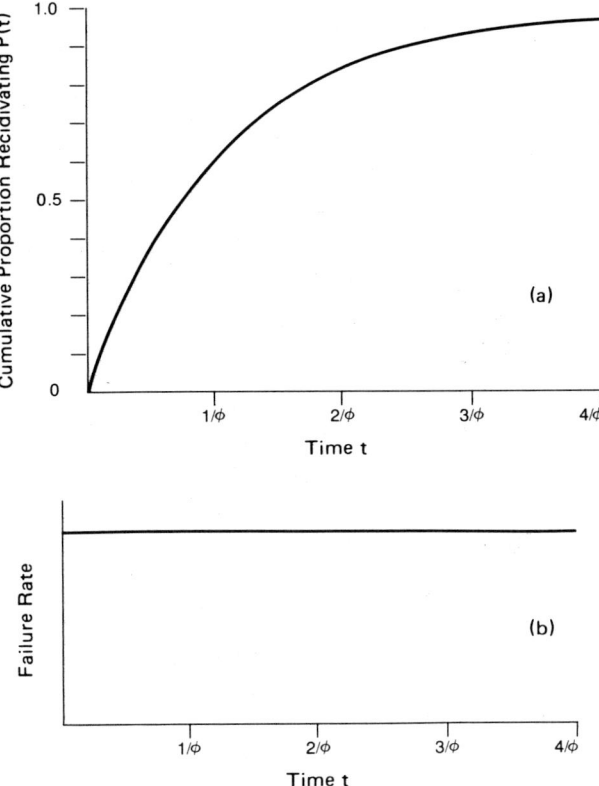

FIGURE 7-3 The exponential distribution $P_E(t) = 1 - e^{-\phi t}$: (a) cumulative distribution function, (b) failure rate.

In their numerical example, Stollmack and Harris used such a model to evaluate a halfway house project in Washington, D.C. They first used the difference-of-proportions test with time fixed at 1 year. This test failed to show any significant difference between the experimental and comparison groups. Using model M_E, however, they found a significant difference between the failure rates ϕ of the two groups.

Model M_I: Incomplete Exponential Distribution (DFR Model)

Model M_I is a generalization of Model M_E. It has the same shape (Figure 7-4); however, it allows for the eventuality that not all members of the group under study will fail. That is, the probability of an individual failing before time t, $P_I(t)$ is given by

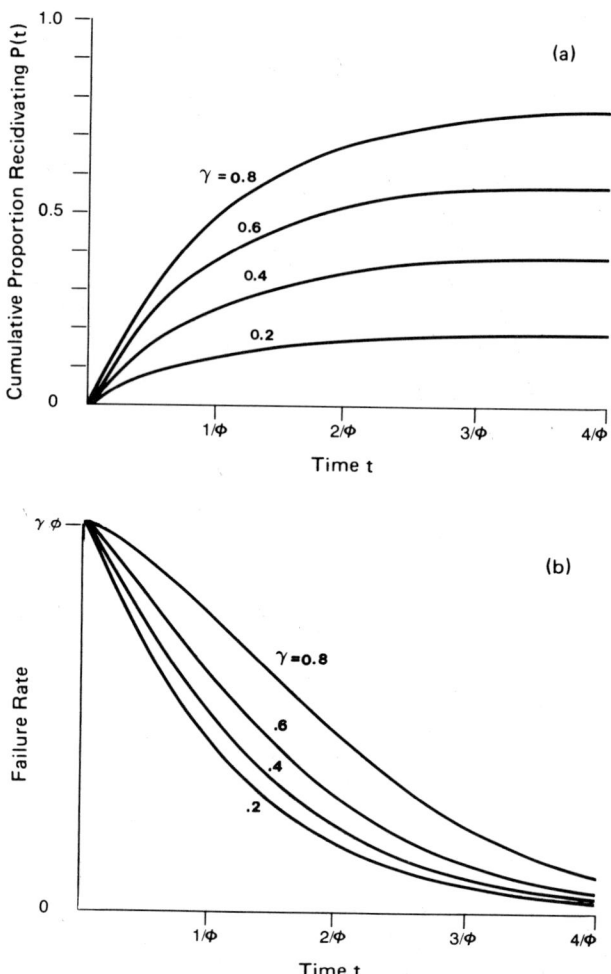

FIGURE 7-4 The incomplete exponential distribution $P_I(t) = \gamma(1 - e^{-\phi t})$: (a) cumulative distribution function, (b) failure rate.

$$P_I(t) = \gamma[1 - \exp(-\phi t)] \qquad (7.2)$$

where γ is the probability of an individual eventually failing and ϕ is that person's failure rate should he or she do so.

This distribution is said to be "degenerate at infinity" (Nelson, 1982: 53), because a proportion $(1 - \gamma)$ survive forever. A variant of this distribution was first used by Boag (1949), to estimate the proportion of patients cured by cancer; later studies (Berkson & Gage, 1952; Cutler & Axtell, 1963; Haybittle, 1965) extended this method in other biomedical applications. In addition, this class of distributions has been used to study the success of an advertising campaign (Anscombe, 1961); automobile scrappage rates (Golomb & Bunch, 1978); the length of time needed to solve a problem (Regal & Larntz, 1978); occupational injury patterns (Chung, 1983); and recidivism (Partanen, 1969; Carr-Hill & Carr-Hill, 1972; Maltz & McCleary, 1977; Greenberg, 1978).

Note that this model has two paremeters, γ and ϕ, while Model M_E only has one. The failure rate for the group decreases over time, i.e., is DFR (Figure 7-4B).

Equation 7.2 can be termed the continuous-time version of Model M_I, because it gives the probability of failure at any instant of time. Another useful representation of M_I is the discrete-time version:

$$P_I(i) = \gamma(1 - q^i) \qquad (7.3)$$

In this case time is considered to be measured in discrete intervals (e.g., months) and P_I is interpreted as the probability of failing before or within time interval i. This version of Model M_I is useful for analyzing grouped data, in which the number of people with failure (exposure) times in each of the intervals is known.

Model M_H: Hyperexponential Distribution (DFR Model)

Another DFR model was proposed by Bloom (1979; Bloom & Singer, 1979), which is also degenerate at infinity, that is, in which not all individuals fail. In this model the failure rate $h_H(t)$ starts out at some value b and decays exponentially at rate c, so that (see Figure 7-5b)

$$h_H(t) = b \exp(-ct) \qquad (7.4)$$

This leads to a probability of failure by time t of

$$P_H(t) = 1 - \exp\{-b/c(1 - \exp[-ct])\} \qquad (7.5)$$

This model was developed because of a belief that an individual's failure rate would naturally tend to decrease the longer he or she was out of prison. An exponentially decreasing failure rate was chosen for this DFR model. The parameter c is a scale parameter, and b/c can be considered a shape parameter. Figure 7-5a shows how $P_H(t)$ varies as the ratio b/c varies.

Model M_W: Weibull Distribution (IFR, CFR, or DFR Model)

Harris and Moitra (1978a) use a Weibull distribution to analyze recidivism data. It is another two-parameter variant of the exponential distribution:

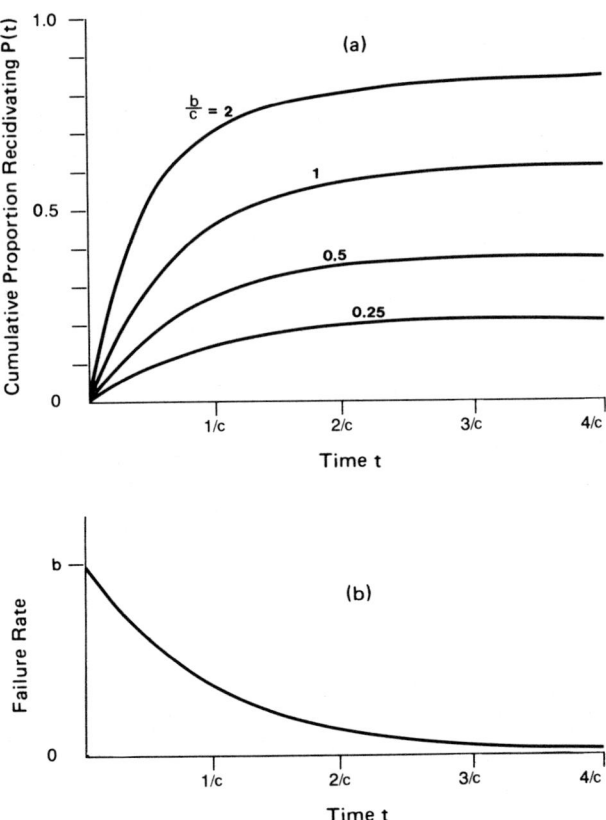

FIGURE 7-5 The hyperexponential distribution $P_H(t) = 1 - e^{-(b/c)(1-e^{-ct})}$: (a) cumulative distribution function, (b) failure rate.

$$P_W(t) = 1 - \exp[-(at)^b] \qquad (7.6)$$

in which a is the scale parameter and b is the shape parameter. The Weibull distribution can have an increasing, decreasing, or constant failure rate. It is IFR if $b < 1$, DFR if $b > 1$, and constant if $b = 1$. Figure 7-6 shows how the failure rate and the probability of failure before time t varies with b.

Because of its versatility, the Weibull distribution is used in many life-testing applications. It is also useful in studies of extreme value distributions.

Model M_L: Lognormal Distribution (IFR, CFR and DFR Model)

Witte and Schmidt (1977) employed a model of recidivism based on the lognormal distribution, another two-parameter distribution. The probability of failing before time t for the lognormal distribution is given by

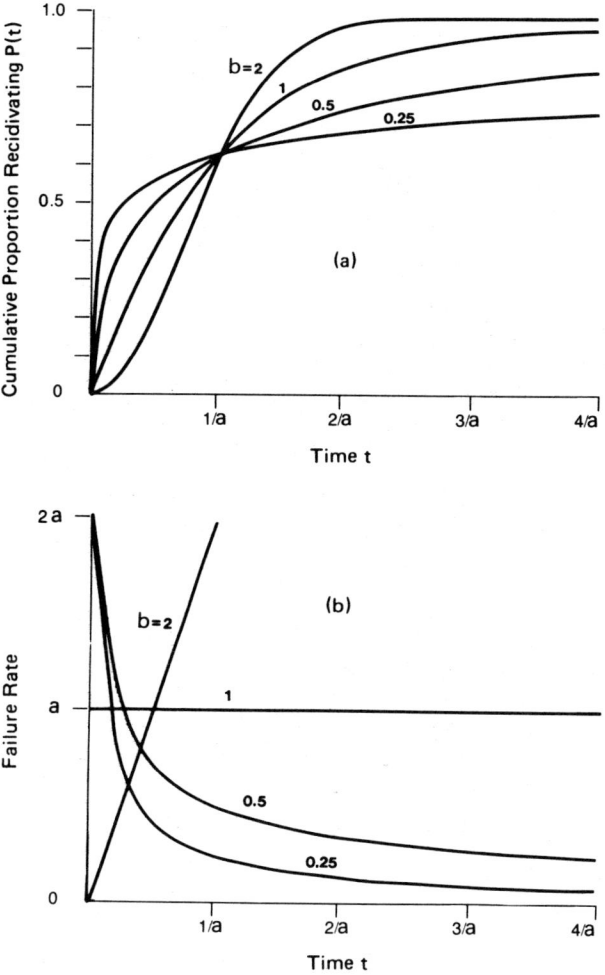

FIGURE 7-6 The Weibull distribution $P_w(t) = 1 - e^{-(at)^b}$: (a) cumulative distribution function; (b) failure rate.

$$P_L(t) = [\sigma\sqrt{2\pi}]^{-1} \int_0^t \exp[-(\ln t - \mu)^2/(2\sigma^2)]dt/t \qquad (7.7)$$

where μ is the location parameter and σ is the shape parameter of the lognormal distribution. Figure 7-7 shows how the shapes of the distribution and the failure rate are affected by the shape parameter. The lognormal distribution is IFR initially and then becomes DFR; however, with a suitable choice of σ it can describe a distribution with a primarily increasing, decreasing, or (relatively) constant failure rate.

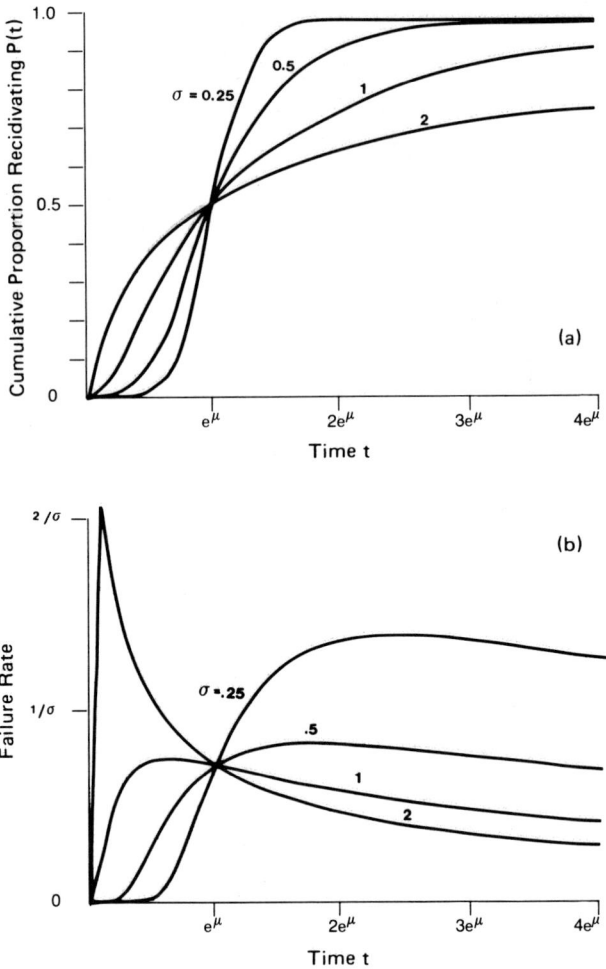

FIGURE 7-7 The lognormal distribution $P_L(t) = \dfrac{1}{\sigma\sqrt{2\pi}}\displaystyle\int_0^t e^{-\frac{1}{2}[(\ln t - \mu)/\sigma]^2} dt/t$: (a) cumulative distribution function, (b) failure rate.

Model M_M: Mixed Exponential Distribution (DFR Model)

The mixed exponential distribution, Model M_M, is a natural extension of Model M_1. For this model the recidivism process is considered to be one in which a person either fails with failure rate ϕ_1, or at a much lower failure rate ϕ_2. If γ is the probability that an individual has the ϕ_1 failure rate, then the probability of failure by time t is

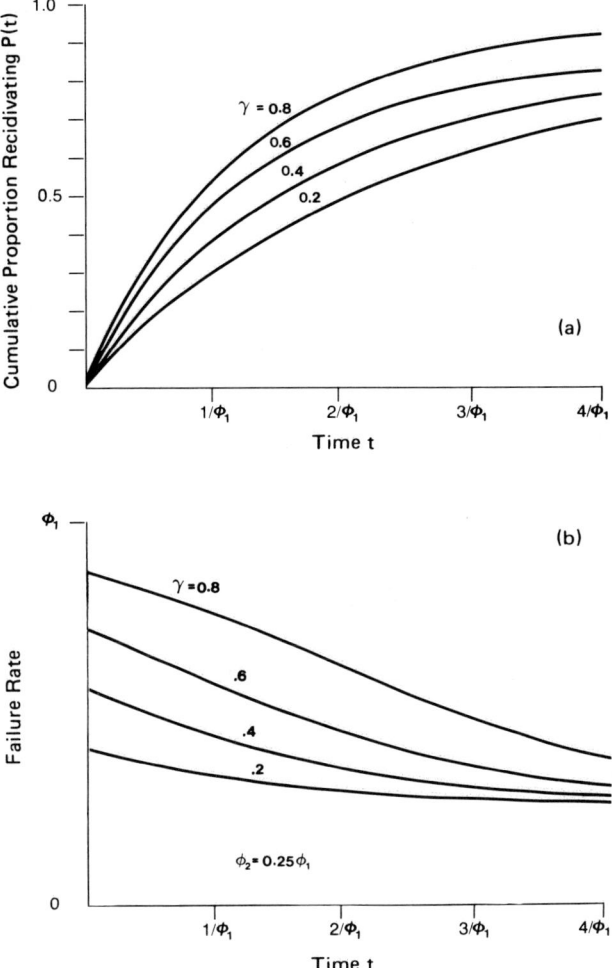

FIGURE 7-8 The mixed exponential distribution $[P_M(t) = 1 - \gamma e^{-\phi_1 t} - (1 - \gamma)e^{-\phi_2 t}]$, showing the effect of γ with $\phi_2/\phi_1 = 0.25$: (a) cumulative distribution function, (b) failure rate.

$$P_M(t) = \gamma[1 - \exp(-\phi_1 t)] + (1 - \gamma)[1 - \exp(-\phi_2 t)] \qquad (7.8)$$

If we choose the convention $\phi_2 < \phi_1$, then the lower failure rate ϕ_2 might be hypothesized to be the rate at which a general population (with the same characteristics) would be expected to fail: an ambient failure rate.

Note that setting $\phi_2 = 0$ results in M_I, and setting $\gamma = 1$ results in M_E. Figures

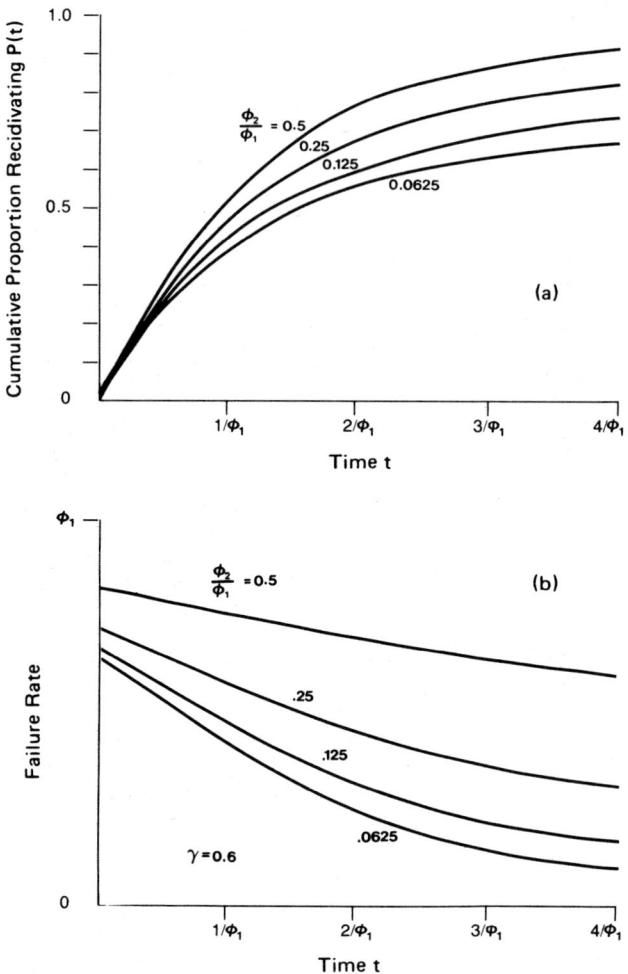

FIGURE 7-9 The mixed exponential distribution $[P_M(t) = 1 - \gamma e^{-\phi_1 t} - (1-\gamma)e^{-\phi_2 t}]$, showing the effect of ϕ_2/ϕ_1 with $\gamma = 0.6$: (a) cumulative distribution function, (b) failure rate.

7-8 and 7-9 depict this distribution and its failure rate. It is described at greater length in Harris *et al.* (1981).

SUMMARY

This chapter has analyzed the 1-year recidivism rate and explained why the 1-year recidivism rate is a faulty measure of recidivism. Six distributions used to

TABLE 7-2

Properties of Distributions Used to Model Recidivism

	Distribution	Failure rate	Asymptotic value
M_E:	Exponential	Constant	1
M_I:	Incomplete exponential	Decreasing	≤ 1
M_H:	Hyperexponential	Decreasing	< 1
M_W:	Weibull	Increasing or constant or decreasing	1
M_L:	Lognormal	Increasing, then decreasing	1
M_M:	Mixed exponential	Decreasing	1

model the recidivism process and measure recidivism have been described. The properties most useful in distinguishing them are the type of failure rate they exhibit and the distribution's asymptotic value, the value to which it rises. Table 7.2 lists these properties of the 6 distributions.

These distributions reflect different assumptions about the underlying model of recidivism. This gives rise to the question, Which model should we select? and to the more fundamental question, *On what basis* would model selection be made? These questions are addressed in the next chapter.

8
Selection of a Recidivism Model

The problem of selecting one model among the many proposed for a process is not trivial. Although the problem has been recognized and dealt with in some fields (Gass, 1983; Gass & Thompson, 1980; Greenberger *et al.*, 1976), no general rules or procedures for model selection have been propounded. A host of different criteria can be used to define the best model, and different criteria apply in different circumstances; for this reason model selection (called *model criticism* by Box & Tiao, 1973: 8) is still more of an art than a codified set of procedures.

Selecting the best model can be based on the characteristics of the process under study, or models may be compared by "eyeballing," that is, by visually inspecting the goodness of fit of each model to the data. Both of these methods are nonquantitative and based on the judgment and knowledge of the observer; they are described in the first two sections of this chapter. Quantitative model selection procedures can also be employed; among the most frequently used are the chi-square goodness-of-fit test and the split-sample model validation procedure. Their characteristics, and their deficiencies as procedures for selecting a recidivism model, are noted in the next two sections. A quantitative test useful in selecting models of the recidivism process under study is then described. Finally, other considerations for selecting a model are discussed in the concluding section.

CHARACTERISTICS OF THE RECIDIVISM PROCESS

As explained in Chapter 7, this book focuses on the study of groups, on binary (success/failure) outcomes, and on the use of time to failure (for recidivists) and length of exposure time without failing (for nonrecidivists) as relevant measures. These restrictions are not greatly limiting, since most empirical studies of recidivism generate data with these characteristics. A few of these studies will be described, to provide some knowledge of how recidivism varies over time.

The study with the longest period of observation—18 years—was conducted by Kitchener *et al.* (1977). This was a long-term follow-up of the cohort studied originally by Glaser (1964). The original study traced the subsequent criminality of about 1000 individuals released from federal prisons in 1956, through 1962; Kitchener *et al.* (1977) extended it through 1974. Figure 8-1 shows the cumula-

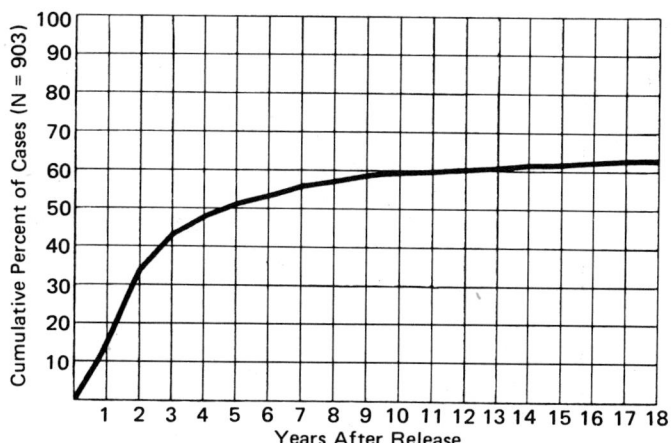

FIGURE 8-1 Cumulative proportion recidivating within 18 years of release from prison. (U.S. Bureau of Prisons data from Kitchener et al., 1977:10.)

tive distribution of failures for this cohort. As can be seen, about one-third of the cohort did not fail during the 18-year follow-up period, nor does it appear likely that they ever will.

This type of cohort behavior, that is, one in which not everyone is expected to fail, is far from atypical. The same general behavior is found in the Minnesota study described earlier (Figure 7-1), and in recent studies of people released from British prisons (Figure 8-2), as well as in other studies discussed later in this chapter (Figures 8-3 to 8-9). In none of these studies does it appear likely that everyone will eventually fail.

Almost all failure-rate models studied in reliability theory (e.g., Barlow & Proschan, 1975; Kalbfleisch & Prentice, 1980; Mann et al., 1974) assume that all individuals will eventually fail. Reliability theory concerns itself largely with the failure of electronic or mechanical components, for which this assumption is largely valid.[1] However, to assume that everyone released from a correctional program (whose purpose is to *prevent* failure) will eventually fail is, at worst, unconscionable, and at best, unduly pessimistic. That everyone fails may turn out to be the case, but should not be implicit in the model.

Both empirical evidence and logic, therefore, suggest that four of the seven candidate models—M_E (exponential distribution), M_W (Weibull distribution), M_L (lognormal distribution), and M_M (mixed exponential distribution)—need not be considered, since the probability of failing for all four approaches 1.0 as

---

[1] However, reliability theory may have to be reconsidered with regard to electronic components. Microchips have been made that are so reliable that failure will not occur before the equipment is itself technologically obsolete. An incomplete distribution may be the best way to model the reliability of such a device.

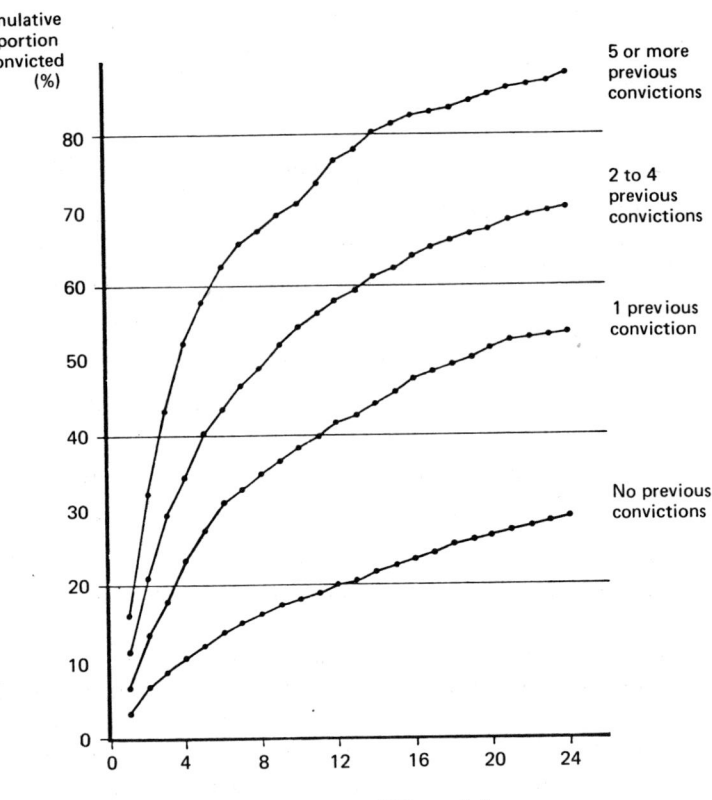

FIGURE 8-2 Cumulative proportion reconvicted within 6 years of release from prison, by number of previous convictions. (Figure is from Pillpotts & Lancucki, 1979:23, British Crown copyright, and reproduced with the permission of the Controller of Her Britannic Majesty's Stationery Office.)

the observation time increases. However, other characteristics of the process should be considered as well in selecting a model.

One such characteristic is the nature of the recidivism event. The event is clearly not the commission of a crime or the violation of the conditions of parole or probation. Indeed, we do not have information on all crimes or violations that were committed. However, we should have information on all crimes or violations that come to the attention of the authorities. It is this *recorded* information that is defined as a failure event in recidivism studies (see Chapter 6). Using the same arguments that were used in explaining the regression artifact in Chapter 4,[2] then, the following assertion can be made: given that an individual will

[2]That is, we do not have statistics on the point process that generates *crimes*, only on the thinned point process of *arrests:* Because most of the points are thinned out and because the thinning process is independent of the original process, the thinned points tend to occur as a Poisson process; hence, the interoccurrence times (and, in particular, the time to first arrest) are distributed exponentially.

eventually fail, the time to failure can be modeled by an exponential distribution. It should be noted that there is no way of knowing beforehand whether a particular individual will or will not eventually fail; if there were a way, the study would be unnecessary.

This argument suggests that Model M_I (incomplete exponential distribution) is the most appropriate for modeling recidivism. However, another model of the recidivism process generates the same shape distribution as shown in these figures. This model, Model M_H (hyperexponential distribution), is based on a different argument. According to Bloom and Singer (1979: 615), "this model is based on the premise that the longer releasees avoid criminal behavior the less likely they are to commit future crimes." For this reason Model M_H has a failure rate that decreases over time;[3] Bloom and Singer posit that the failure rate should decrease exponentially (Figure 7-5b). However, they give no justification for choosing an exponentially decreasing failure rate instead of some other functional form.

Another difficulty with Bloom and Singer's explanation is the assumption that the lack of a *recorded* failure event (i.e., an arrest) means that the individual has not committed a crime. Furthermore, as will be seen later, this model results in a distribution that is often almost identical to that of Model M_I, but is neither as versatile nor as easily interpreted as Model M_I. For these reasons Model M_I would be the model of choice based on the characteristics of the process under study.

EYEBALLING

Eyeballing, to see which model fits best, does have its advantages. Slight differences can be considered that more formal (quantitative) techniques would miss. Complex or subtle selection criteria that may defy quantification can be included. Furthermore, eyeballing may furnish some insight into what one should use for criteria in developing formal techniques.[4]

As an example of how eyeballing can be used, consider Figure 8-3, which depicts four models of recidivism (M_I, M_M, M_H, and M_W) and the data from which they were generated, using maximum likelihood estimation procedures to select parameters. (Appendix A describes these procedures for Model M_I.)

Eyeballing the four models is instructive. Model M_W provides the best fit in the early months, but diverges strongly in later months. Model M_M appears to

---

[3]Proschan (1963) has another explanation of why a decreasing failure rate is to be expected. If different subgroups have different (constant) failure rates, then the resulting pooled data will *always* exhibit a decreasing failure rate—those with high failure rates fail early, so as time increases the remaining group has a lower and lower mean failure rate.

[4]For example, if one is using the model to project future numbers of failures, the fit in later months may be more important than in the early months.

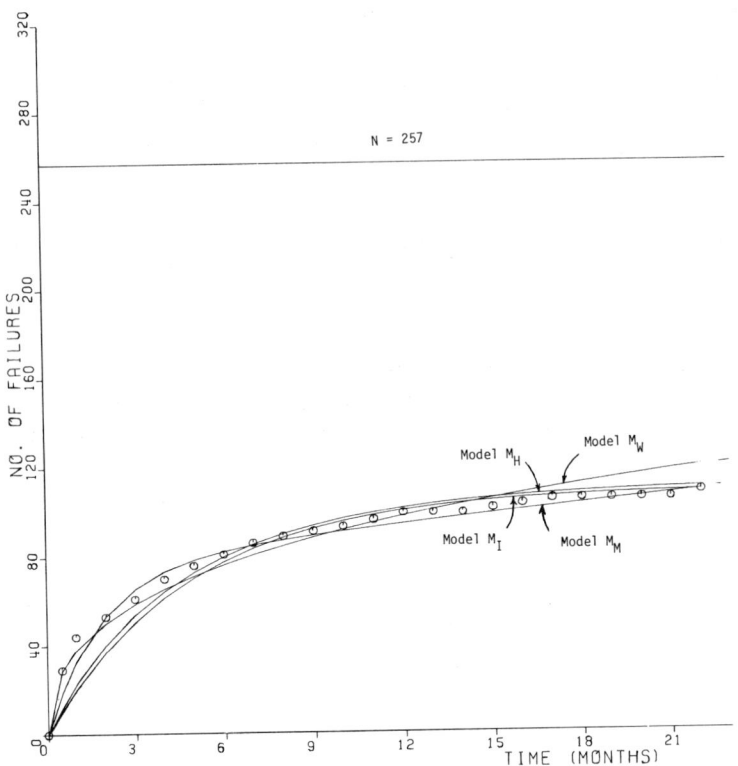

FIGURE 8-3 Fitting models to Illinois data: incomplete exponential model (M_I), mixed exponential model (M_M), Weibull model (M_W), hyperexponential model (M_H).

provide the best overall fit, while Models M_H and M_I provide excellent fits in later months and are essentially indistinguishable from each other.

But by itself, eyeballing is not really a suitable technique for making a rational, defensible choice among models. The findings are not necessarily replicable over time, nor are they likely to be the same for different people. Furthermore, eyeballing cannot be used to estimate *how much* better one model is then another. For this purpose one needs a quantitative measure for model selection.

THE CHI-SQUARE GOODNESS-OF-FIT TEST

The test used most often to compare different models is the chi-square goodness-of-fit test (Mann *et al.*, 1974: 350). It is applied to each distribution to determine how well it fits the empirical data. This test has been used frequently

TABLE 8-1

Four Models of Recidivism Compared to Data for 257 Illinois Parolees

Time interval (months)	Actual number failing during that interval	Forecast number of failures			
		Model $M_I{}^a$	Model $M_M{}^b$	Model $M_W{}^c$	Model $M_H{}^d$
0–0.5	29	10.756	18.737	28.592	12.122
0.5–1	15	9.696	14.485	9.407	10.589
1–2	9	16.620	20.005	12.146	17.457
2–3	8	13.506	12.305	8.586	13.607
3–4	9	10.975	7.817	6.821	10.730
4–5	6	8.918	5.198	5.728	8.543
5–6	5	7.247	3.668	4.971	6.858
6–7	5	5.889	2.772	4.410	5.543
7–8	3 ⎫ 5	8.675	4.177	7.598	8.185
8–9	2 ⎭				
9–10	2 ⎫ 5	5.728	3.374	6.428	5.500
10–11	3 ⎭				
11–12	3 ⎫	6.280	5.995	10.548	6.310
12–13	0				
13–14	0 ⎬ 5				
14–15	2 ⎭				
15–16	2 ⎫	3.720	9.717	13.986	4.183
16–17	2				
17–18	0				
18–19	0 ⎬ 7				
19–20	0				
20–21	0				
21–22	3 ⎭				
Over 22	149	148.988	148.751	137.779	147.373
Value of chi-square statistic		46.53	17.65	13.50	36.81
Degrees of freedom		10	9	10	10
Significance level (%)		$\approx 10^{-6}$	3.95	19.7	.00006

[a] Model M_I: Incomplete exponential distribution: $F(t) = \gamma[1 - \exp(-\phi t)]$; $\gamma = 0.4247$; $\phi = 0.2075$.

[b] Model M_M: Mixed exponential distribution: $F(t) = \gamma[1 - \exp(-\phi_1 t)] + (1 - \gamma)[1 - \exp(-\phi_2 t)]$; $\gamma = 0.5411$; $\phi_1 = 0.2942$; $\phi_2 = 0.0090$.

[c] Model M_W: Weibull distribution: $F(t)$ REQ $1 - \exp[-(at)^b]$; $a = 0.01553$; $b = 0.44$.

[d] Model M_H: Hyperexponential distribution: $F(t) = 1 - \exp\{-(b/c)[1 - \exp(-ct)]\}$; $b = 0.101$; $c = 0.178$.

in recidivism model selection, especially in comparing different models using Illinois parole data (Taylor, 1971).[5] Table 8-1 gives the chi-square statistics for the four models depicted in Figure 8-3.

Compare this assessment with the qualitative (eyeball) assessment described previously. According to the chi-square statistic, it is M_W that fits the data best! This is followed by Model M_M, and the two remaining models fit least well according to this test. The results are almost the direct converse of what common sense, at least according to the eyeballing technique, suggests.

The reason for this result is simply that the use of the chi-square goodness-of-fit test is not always warranted. This is especially true in the situation depicted in Figure 8-3. The explanation requires an understanding of the chi-square test. Its primary intended use is in studying categorical data. The chi-square statistic is defined as:

$$\chi^2 = \Sigma \frac{(f_i - np_i)^2}{np_i} = \Sigma \frac{(\text{observed}_i - \text{expected}_i)^2}{\text{expected}_i},$$

where p_i is the probability that an outcome falls in category i, f_i is the observed frequency of outcomes falling in category i, and n is the total number of observations ($\Sigma f_i = n$). No value of f_i should be less than 5 for best results.

For example, suppose we wish to test a die to see if it is fair ($p_i = 1/6$, $i = 1, 2, \ldots, 6$) by throwing it 120 times (Lindgren, 1976: 424). We obtain these results: 18 ones, 23 twos, 16 threes, 21 fours, 18 fives, and 24 sixes. It is easy to verify that

$$\chi^2 = \frac{(18 - 20)^2}{20} + \cdots + \frac{(24 - 20)^2}{20} = 2.5$$

in this case. This number is a measure of how far the observed outcomes deviate from our model of the process, the model being the probabilities p_1 through p_6 that define a fair die. For $df = 5$, the value of $\chi^2 = 2.5$ produces $p = .2235$, so the fair die model cannot be rejected.[6]

Now how might we use the chi-square test to select *among* models? For

---

[5]Data sets are often given an importance far beyond the extent to which they ought to be relied on. This is certainly the case with the data set depicted in Figure 8-3 and tabulated in Table 8-1. The original data were from a study in which the method of data collection was not described in any detail and whose validity is therefore suspect, especially since, as described on pp. 73–75, unnoticed censoring can bias a cohort considerably. However, this data set is one of the most widely used for testing models of recidivism; it has been used by Maltz & McCleary (1977), Miley (1978), Harris & Moitra (1978), Bloom (1979), Harris et al. (1981), Stein & Lloyd (1981), and Wainer (1981). So it cannot be ignored. Other data sets are more useful and reliable for model selection and testing; some are presented later in this chapter.

[6]In a chi-square test, the value of p is the probability that the hypothesis (that the model fits the data) can be rejected: If p is smaller than about .9, the hypothesis is not ordinarily rejected.

instance, suppose we had a second model of the die: the probability of an odd number is $p_{odd} = 18/120$ and of an even number $p_{even} = 22/120$. For this case we would obtain $\chi^2 = 0.49$ ($df = 4$, $p = .0255$), that is, a substantially better fit.[7] Does this mean that Model 2 is better than Model 1? Obviously not: the fair die model provides a sufficiently accurate fit for it not to be rejected. The chi-square test is thus seen to be a poor one for model selection.

Furthermore, there is no difficulty in applying the chi-square test in this case, because the data are unambiguously categorical: one of the six faces of the die must come up. This cannot be said of the data in the continuous models of Figure 8-3 and Table 8-1. To apply the chi-square test here, we first must aggregate the data into intervals within which there are at least five observations (the brackets in Table 8-1). Then "the continuous model to be tested must be approximated by a discrete one obtained by round-off, replacing the given sample space by a finite system of class intervals. Whether by reason of the necessary approximation or its failure to use or recognize order in the sample space, *the chi-square test appears to be generally less satisfactory for continuous models*" (Lindgren, 1976: 486; emphasis added).

It should also be noted that the chi-square test cannot be used when the data are progressively censored,[8] which is often the case in recidivism and other failure-rate models (see Barton and Turnbull, 1981: 85). The sample size can change dramatically due to censoring, and the chi-square test does not apply when this occurs; an implicit assumption of this test is that the entire distribution is available.

It is also difficult to apply this test to large samples. Green and Kolesar (1983) describe a queuing model which gives a very good (albeit not perfect) fit to the empirical data. However, since they have almost 3500 data points and since the data do not precisely mirror the model, the chi-square statistic suggests that the model should be rejected.

Another problem with using the chi-square test to select a model is best illustrated with another example (Harris *et al.*, 1981). Models M_I and M_M (incomplete and mixed exponential distributions, respectively—see Figure 8-4) were fit to data from a study of a North Carolina work release program (Witte & Schmidt, 1977). Table 8-2 gives the data, the parameters of the two models (obtained using maximum likelihood estimation), and the chi-square statistic for

---

[7] A critic might suggest that this is cheating; after all, the values 18/120 and 22/120 for p_{odd} and P_{even} were chosen after looking at the data. But this is exactly what is done whenever the chi-square goodness-of-fit test is used: first the data produce the model parameters, and then the test is used to see how well the data fit the model.

[8] Data can be *singly* censored or *progressively* censored. When they are *singly* censored, all of the observation times are truncated or censored, after the same length of time (e.g., 12 months); and therefore all failure times are smaller than this length of time. When data are *progressively* censored, individual observation times are not all truncated after the same length of time; that is, people may be lost to observation after different lengths of observation time.

TABLE 8-2

Two Models of Recidivism Compared to Data for 649 North Carolina Prison Releasees

Time interval (months)	Actual number failing during that interval	Forecast number of failures	
		Model $M_I{}^a$	Model $M_M{}^b$
0–1	32	43.737	44.630
1–2	45	39.665	40.320
2–3	30	35.972	36.429
3–4	27	32.623	32.916
4–5	45	29.586	29.744
5–6	28	26.830	26.880
6–7	24	24.333	24.294
7–8	27	22.067	21.959
8–9	23	20.13	19.851
9–10	20	18.149	17.948
10–11	22	16.459	16.229
11–12	8	14.927	14.678
12–13	14 ⎫ 26	25.814	25.289
13–14	12 ⎭		
14–15	13 ⎫ 24	21.231	20.709
15–16	11 ⎭		
16–17	3 ⎫ 12	17.461	16.975
17–18	9 ⎭		
18–19	7 ⎫ 12	14.361	13.930
19–20	5 ⎭		
20–21	2 ⎫ 5	11.812	11.448
21–22	3 ⎭		
22–23	8 ⎫ 15	9.714	9.425
23–24	7 ⎭		
24–25	4 ⎫ 9	7.990	7.775
25–26	5 ⎭		
26–27	3 ⎫ 7	6.71	6.430
27–28	4 ⎭		
28–29	1 ⎫ 5	5.405	5.333
29–30	4 ⎭		
30–31	1 ⎫ 2	4.445	4.439
31–32	1 ⎭		
32–33	3 ⎫ 3	3.656	3.710
33–34	0 ⎭		
34–35	1 ⎫ 3	3.007	3.115
35–36	2 ⎭		
36–37	0 ⎫		
37–38	3 ⎬ 3	4.507	4.864
38–39	0 ⎪		
39–40	0 ⎭		
40–41	3 ⎫		
41–42	1 ⎬ 5	3.049	3.559
42–43	1 ⎪		
43–44	0 ⎭		

TABLE 8-2 (*Continued*)

Time interval (months)	Actual number failing during that interval		Forecast number of failures	
			Model $M_I{}^a$	Model $M_M{}^b$
44–45	1 ⎫			
45–46	0 ⎬ 3		1.620	2.081
46–47	2 ⎭			
Over 47	176		175.997	176.040
Value of chi-square statistic			34.842	31.441
Degrees of freedom			26	25
Significance level (%)			11.5	17.5

^{a} Model M_I: Incomplete exponential distribution: $F(t) = \gamma[1 - \exp(-\phi t)]$; $\gamma = 0.7329$; $\phi = 0.09773$.

^{b} Model M_M: Mixed exponential distribution: $F(t) = \gamma[1 - \exp(-\phi_1 t)] + (1 - \gamma)[1 - \exp(-\phi_2 t)]$; $\gamma = 0.7127$; $\phi_1 = 0.1022$; $\phi_2 = 0.00142$.

them. Were we to judge the models using only this statistic we would select Model M_M ($\chi^2 = 31.441$, $df = 25$, $p = .175$) as better than Model M_I ($\chi^2 = 34.842$, $df = 26$, $p = .115$). As expected, the model with an additional parameter provides a better fit to the data. But this does not mean that the *model* is better or that the additional parameter is needed: in fact, visual comparison of the two models with the data does not provide any guidance as to which is better. The question is then whether it is worth increasing the model's complexity by 50% (by adding a third parameter) to obtain a slightly lower chi-square statistic. Probably it is not, unless the more complex model has other virtues to recommend it.

The chi-square goodness-of-fit test, then, does not appear to be well suited for selecting the best model. The next section describes another technique that is often used in model selection.

SPLIT-SAMPLE MODEL VALIDATION

Another technique used frequently to validate a model is to split the population under study. Each member of the subject population is randomly assigned to one of two groups. The first group (the estimation sample) is used to develop the model, that is, to determine which independent variables are significantly associated with the outcome variable(s), and the relative weight assigned to each independent variable. The model thus developed is then applied to the other group (the validation sample) to see how well the model predicts the outcome for

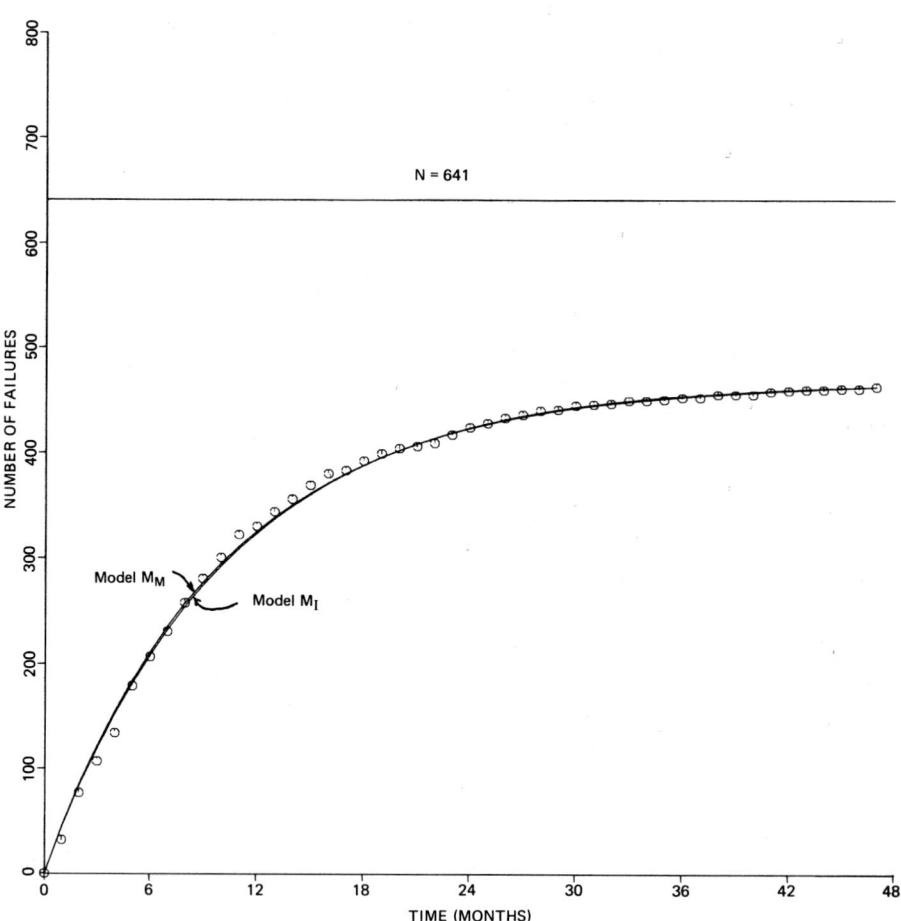

FIGURE 8-4 Fitting models to North Carolina data: incomplete exponential model (M_I), mixed exponential model (M_M).

it. This method is often used in the development of regression models (e.g., Schmidt & Witte, 1980).

However, this method *does not* validate a model. At best, what it validates is the equivalence of the two groups, the estimation sample and the validation sample. It tests whether the two groups have the same statistical characteristics; if they do, they will invariably produce similar results. The validity of the *model* is untested, because it has only been tested against a sample almost identical to the one that produced it, not against competing models.

For instance, let us assume that we wish to model a process in which, unknown to us, the outcome variable is not a simple linear function of the independent variables, but instead has a more complicated relationship. However, we assume incorrectly that the relationship is linear; we use linear regression to determine the relationship among the variables, using only the estimation sample. This will result in a model of the process which, when applied to the validation sample, will provide about the same fit as it did to the estimation sample. This model is the best *linear* model, but it is not the best model because it is premised on an incorrect assumption.

Thus, one cannot always use standard methods—the chi-square goodness-of-fit test and model validation using a split sample—to select a best model. However, there are alternatives. The next section describes an approach based on the purpose of the modeling effort.

THE MODEL'S USE IN FORECASTING

This section describes an approach to model selection based on the ability of the model to forecast beyond the given data. This ability is one of the criteria that appears to be implicit in model selection by eyeballing. Why this may be an implicit criterion can be understood by referring to Figure 8-5, which extrapolates the cumulative number of failures out to 36 months for the four models described in Figure 8-3 and Table 8-1. That is, one implicit criterion may be based in part on an estimate of future behavior—beyond the given data.

Indeed, one of the purposes of modeling the recidivism process is to make forecasts beyond the given data, for two reasons: first, we may wish to base policy on our estimates of future conduct; and second, evaluation studies rarely include observation times long enough for the probability of eventual recidivism to be estimated (with one exception—see Kitchener *et al.*, 1977), and we may wish to estimate this probability.

Model M_I was qualitatively tested for its forecasting ability in cooperation with the Research Unit of the U.S. Parole Commission. This agency provided data from a 6-year follow-up study of 1806 parolees released in 1970 (Hoffman & Stone-Meierhoefer, 1979), but did not give the data all at once. Instead, the following "arm's-length" procedure was used:

Data were provided on failures that occurred during the first 6 months after release for four cohorts: "very good risks," "good risks," "fair risks," and "poor risks." Risk level was based on the individual's Salient Factor Score (Hoffman & Beck, 1974), a score determined by the individual's prior criminality, education, employment, and personal characteristics. From the first 6 months of data the two parameters of Model M_I were estimated, as were the expected total number of failures for every 6 months over the remaining $5\frac{1}{2}$ years. These estimates were then sent to the Research Unit of the U.S. Parole Commission.

This arm's-length procedure was repeated twice. That is, failure data for

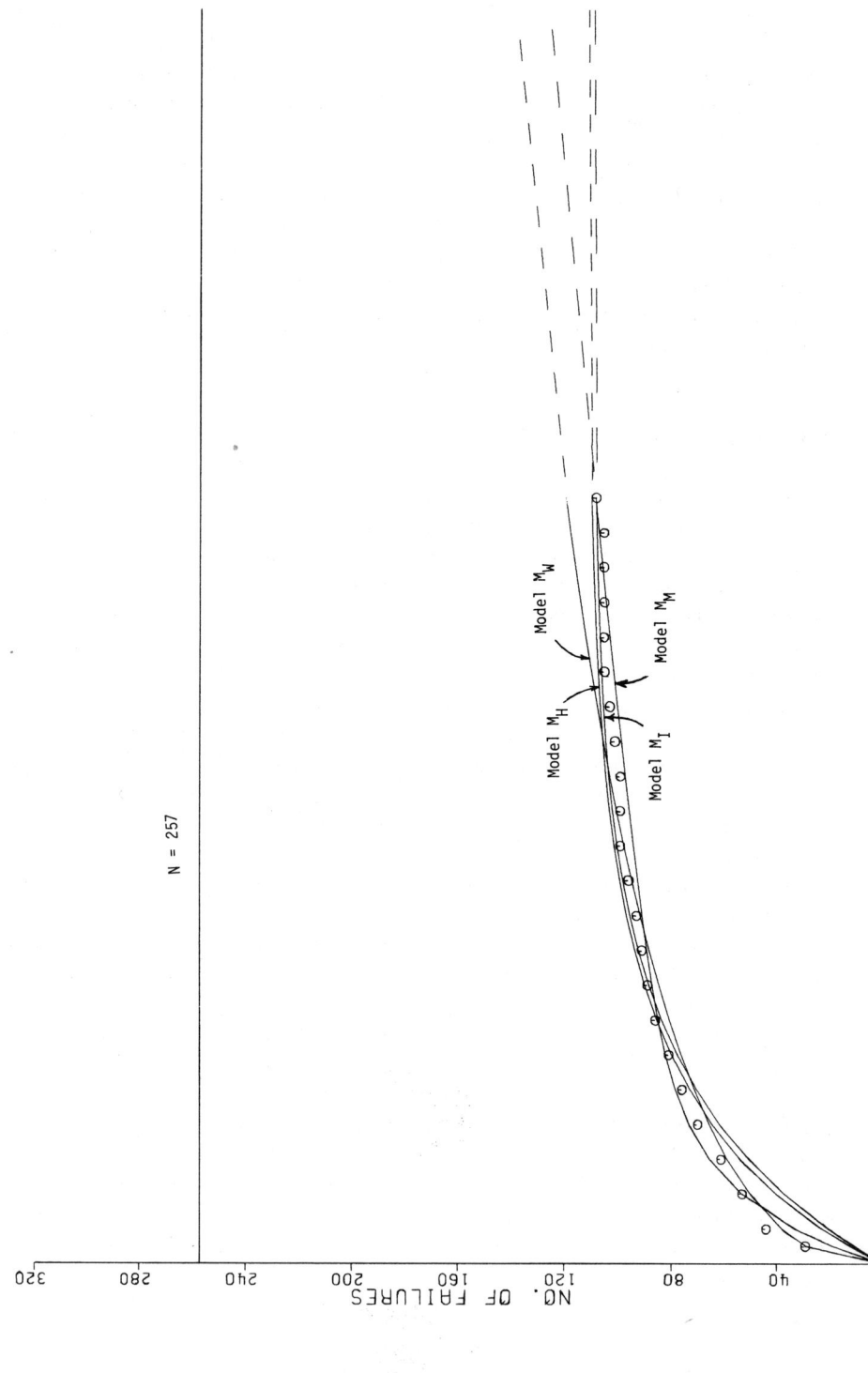

THE MODEL'S USE IN FORECASTING

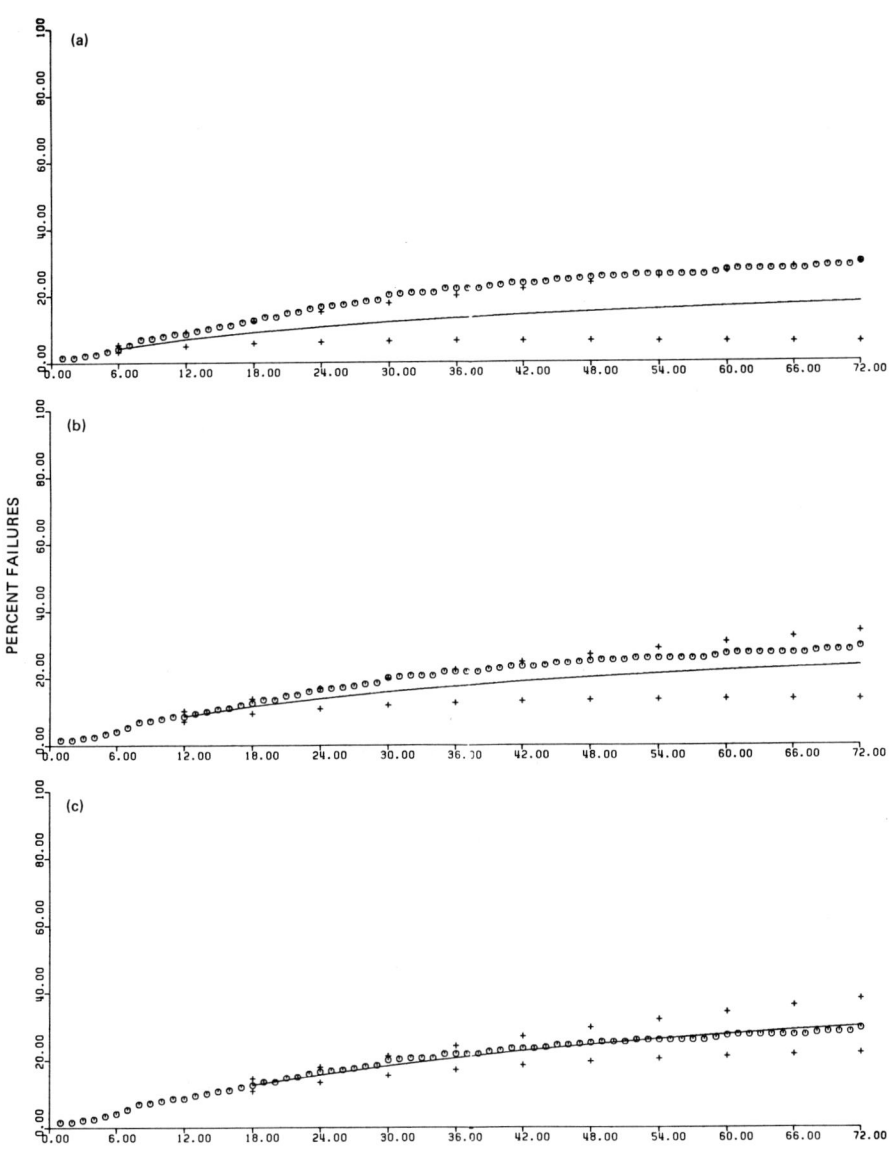

FIGURE 8-6 Failure estimation for a very-good-risk cohort for (a) 6-month estimate, (b) 12-month estimate, and (c) 18-month estimate, using U.S. Parole Commission data ($N = 319$). Forecast estimate depicted by ———, ± 1 s.d. of the estimate shown by $+$.

8 SELECTION OF A RECIDIVISM MODEL

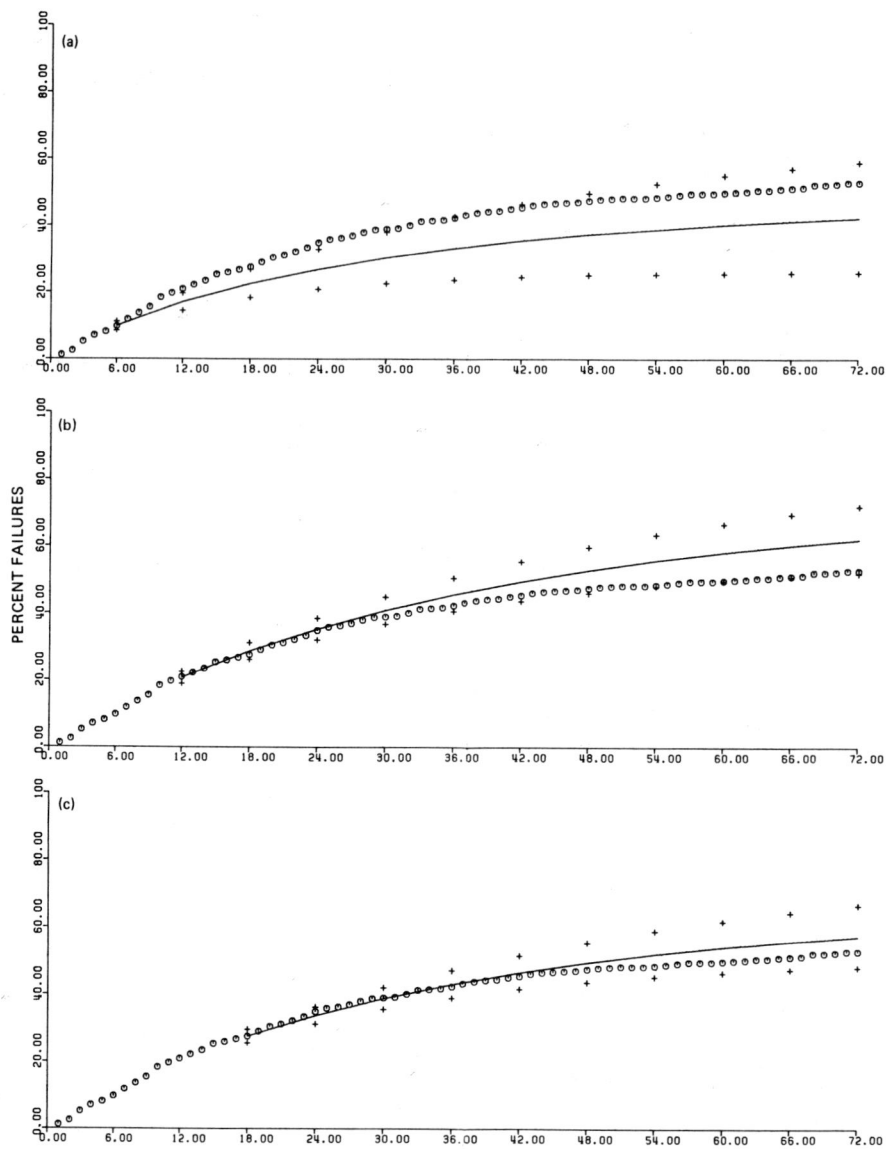

FIGURE 8-7 Failure estimation for a good-risk cohort for (a) 6-month estimate, (b) 12-month estimate, and (c) 18-month estimate using U.S. Parole Commission data ($N = 483$). Forecast estimate depicted by———, ±1 s.d. of the estimate shown by +.

THE MODEL'S USE IN FORECASTING

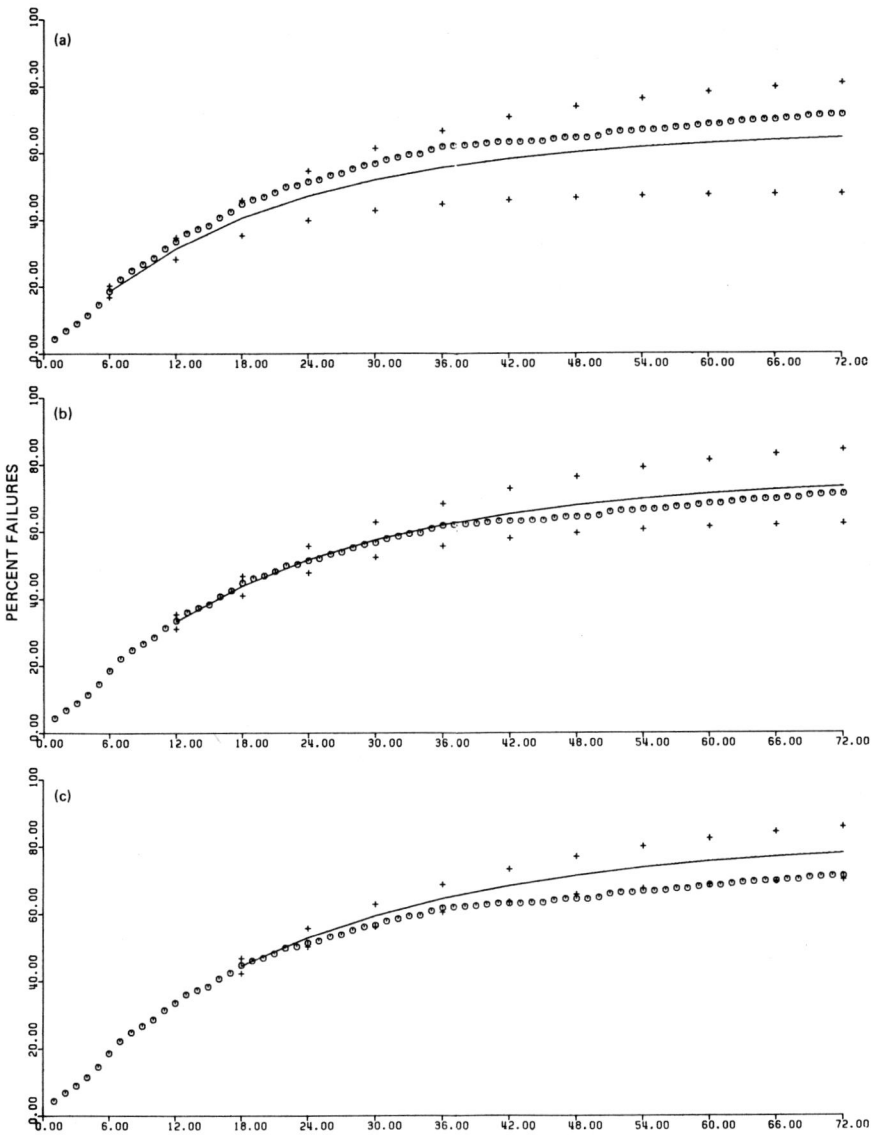

FIGURE 8-8 Failure estimation for a fair-risk cohort for (a) 6-month estimate, (b) 12-month estimate, and (c) 18-month estimate, using U.S. Parole Commission data ($N = 472$). Forecast estimate depicted by——, ±1 s.d. of the estimate shown by +.

8 SELECTION OF A RECIDIVISM MODEL

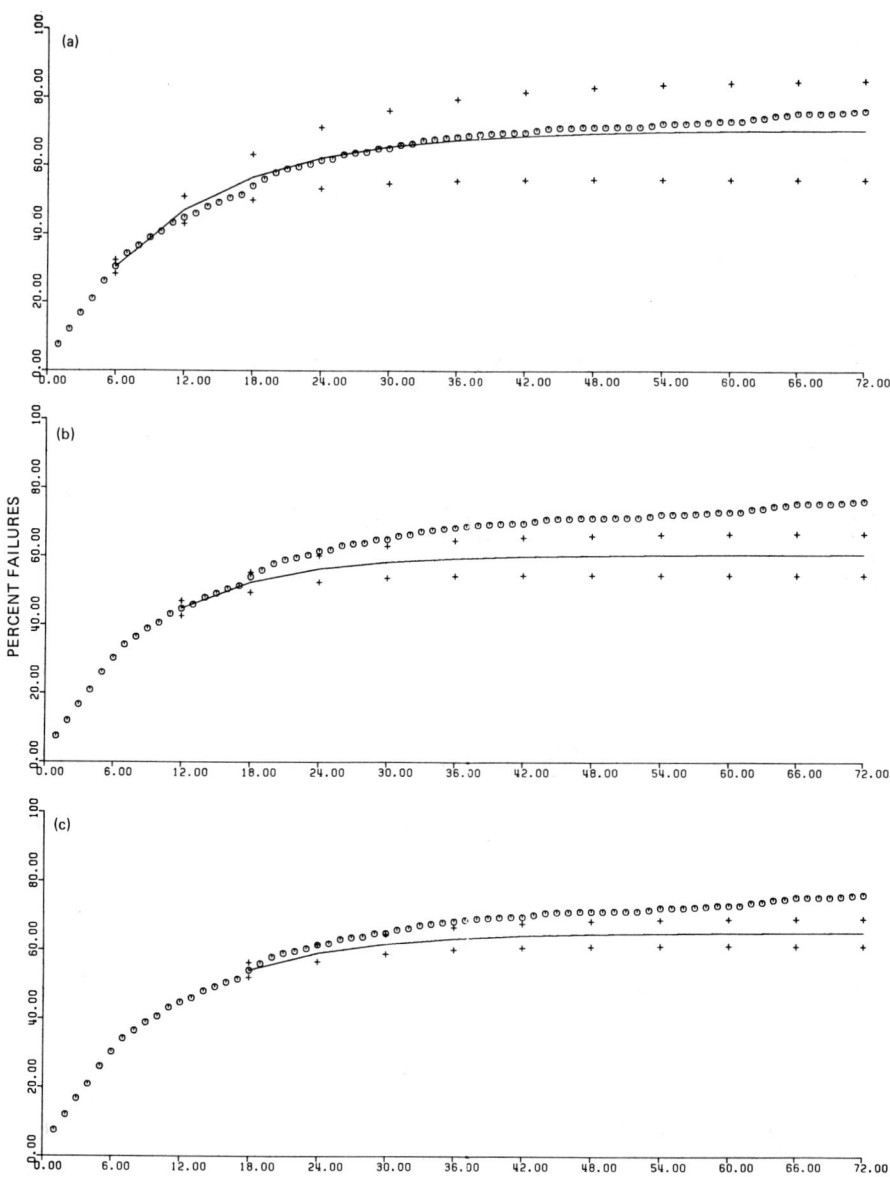

FIGURE 8-9 Falure estimation for a poor-risk cohort for (a) 6-month estimate, (b) 12-month estimate, and (c) 18-month estimate, using U.S. Parole Commission data ($N = 532$). Forecast estimate depicted by———, ±1 s.d. of the estimate shown by +.

months 7–12 were made available to us, based on which we made updated estimates; and this was repeated again for months 13–18. Following this, we were given the data for the entire 6 years so we could compare our predictions with the actual number of failures.[9]

Figures 8-6 to 8-9 show the resulting forecasts. Each of these figures presents the estimates out to 6 years, with the top curve based on 6 months of data, the middle curve, 12 months, and the bottom curve, 18 months. The actual data are represented by circles; the estimate is represented by a solid line; and the one standard deviation bounds on the estimate are represented by + symbols. As can be seen, the actual data generally fall within the $1-\sigma$ envelope of the forecast for the very-good, good, and fair-risk cohorts. The estimation procedure does not do as well for the poor-risk cohort. To some extent, the relatively poor fit for the poor-risk cohort points out the limits of applicability of Model M_I. Recall that this model assumes that only a fraction of the population will eventually fail, and that the rest will be rehabilitated, that is, will revert to an ambient failure rate of zero. However, it may well be that the poor-risk cohort is comprised of such poor risks that the ambient failure rate cannot be assumed to be zero, as is the case with other cohorts; so Model M_M (mixed exponential distribution) may be more appropriate for this cohort.

This test shows that forecasting is quite possible using Model M_I; it also suggests how a more quantitative test of forecasting ability might be developed, one that can be used to select among competing models.

A QUANTITATIVE FORECASTING TEST

One way to compare the forecasting ability of two models is to truncate the data early and forecast to a known point. For example, we have 22 months of data for the Illinois cohort, so we can use 22 months as a target point. Then, if we wish to test a model's forecasting ability using 6 months of data, we estimate the model's parameters using only the first 6 months of data. Based on these parameter estimates we can forecast the number of failures expected by month 22. This can be done using varying cutoff points, from 21 months down to the point where we no longer have sufficient data to make a valid estimate.

---

[9]The data were not entirely accurate because of the way they were calculated. The number of months of failure was calculated by the U.S. Parole Commission Research Unit by subtracting the month of release from the failure month. This procedure does not always produce the correct number of months. Consider a person released on January 31 who fails 1 day later: he would be recorded as having been out 1 month before failing. Conversely, a person released on January 1 who fails 30 days later would be recorded as being out 0 months before failing. These inaccuracies in the data militated against using maximum likelihood techniques; instead, we used Bayesian techniques. See Appendix A for the method used.

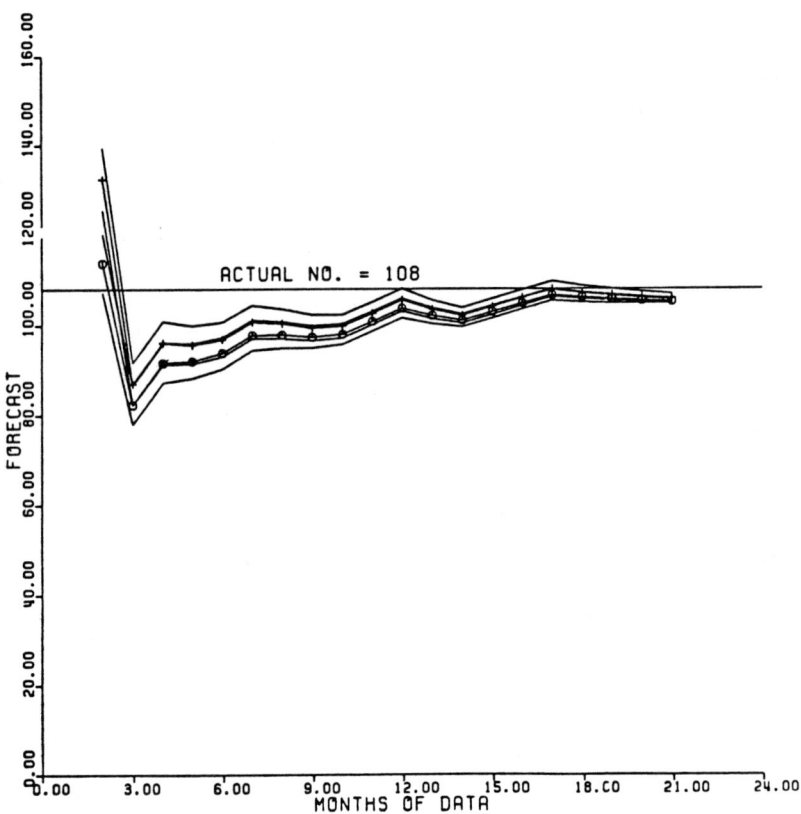

FIGURE 8-10 Comparing two models' forecasting of the number of failures at 22 months, using Illinois data: Model M_I (0), Model M_H (+).

This method is used to compare the forecasts of Models M_I and M_H for the Illinois cohort (Maltz & McLeary, 1977, and Figure 8-3). These two models are compared because they provide similar fits to the known data; however, their functional forms are sufficiently different that they may not provide similar forecasts beyond the known data. Figure 8-10 shows such forecasts for these two models. Confidence intervals (their width is one standard deviation) are included in the figure; they are derived in Appendix B. Note that Model M_H provides a slightly better forecast than Model M_I, although the forecasts are within one standard deviation of each other from 2 through 21 months.

Similar comparisons between these two models are shown in Figures 8-11 through 8-15, using data from the North Carolina and U.S. Parole Commission cohorts, respectively. As can be seen, Model M_I is clearly better in Figure 8-11, but in other cases neither model is always better.

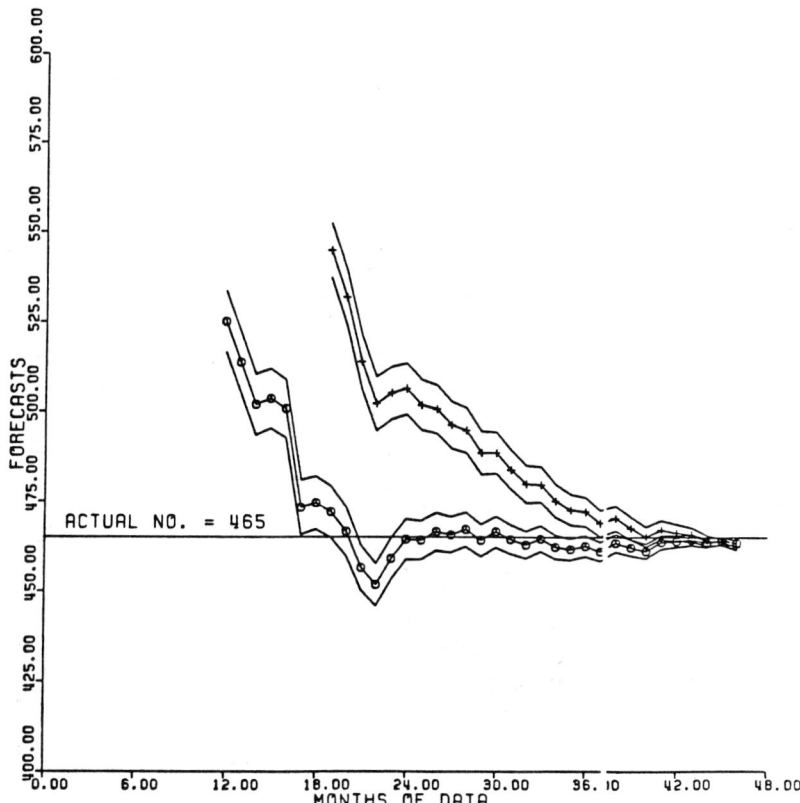

FIGURE 8-11 Comparing two models' forecasting of the number of failures at 47 months, using North Carolina data: Model M_I (0), Model M_H (+).

OTHER CONSIDERATIONS IN MODEL SELECTION

From the foregoing discussion it is clear that model selection in general and for recidivism in particular is not a matter of applying a simple test. Other factors should also be considered, such as the model's versatility and interpretability. These factors are described below.

Model Versatility

A model based on the exponential distribution has a number of useful properties. For example, it is the continuous-time analog of the geometric distribution, which is appropriate to use when time is given in discrete intervals (e.g., number of months between release and failure) and the data are grouped in these inter-

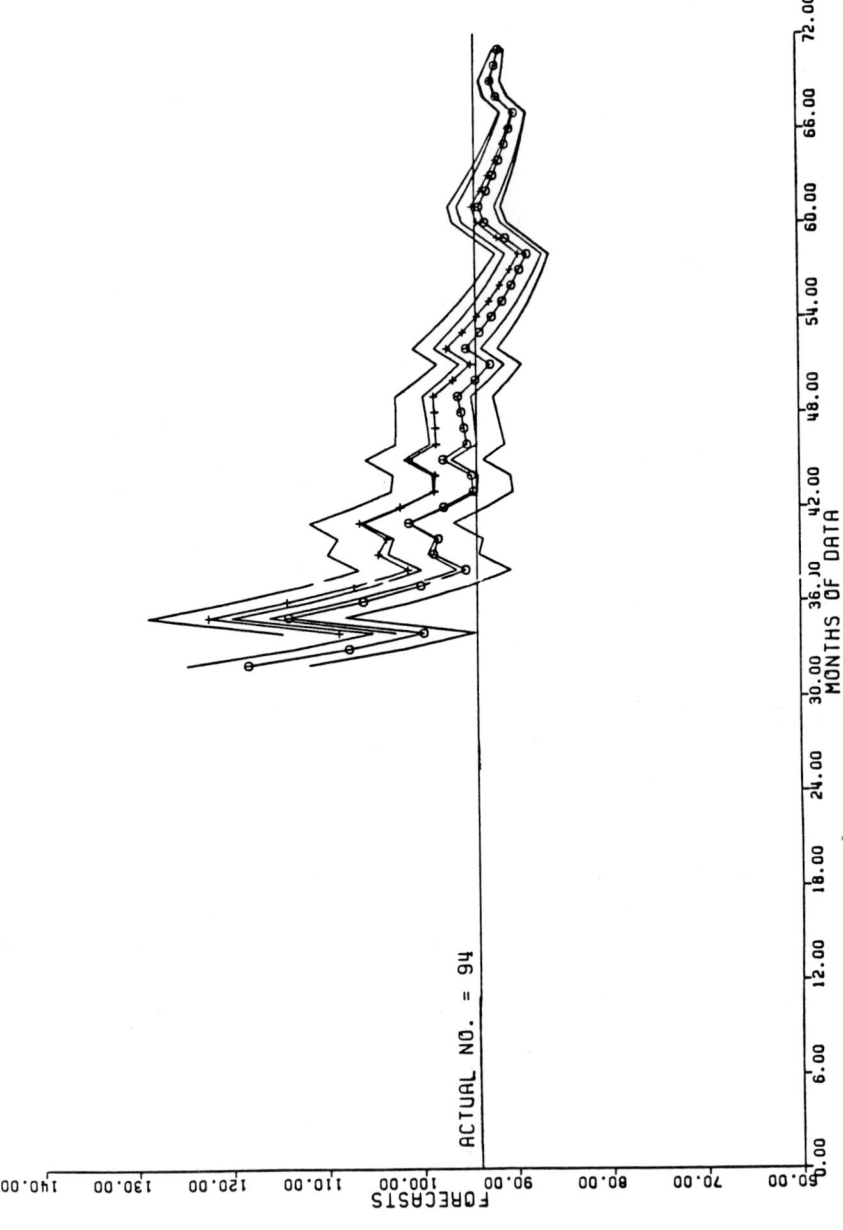

FIGURE 8-12 Comparing two models' forecasting of the number of failures at 72 Months, using U.S. Parole Commission Data ("very good risk" cohort): Model M_I (0), Model M_H (+).

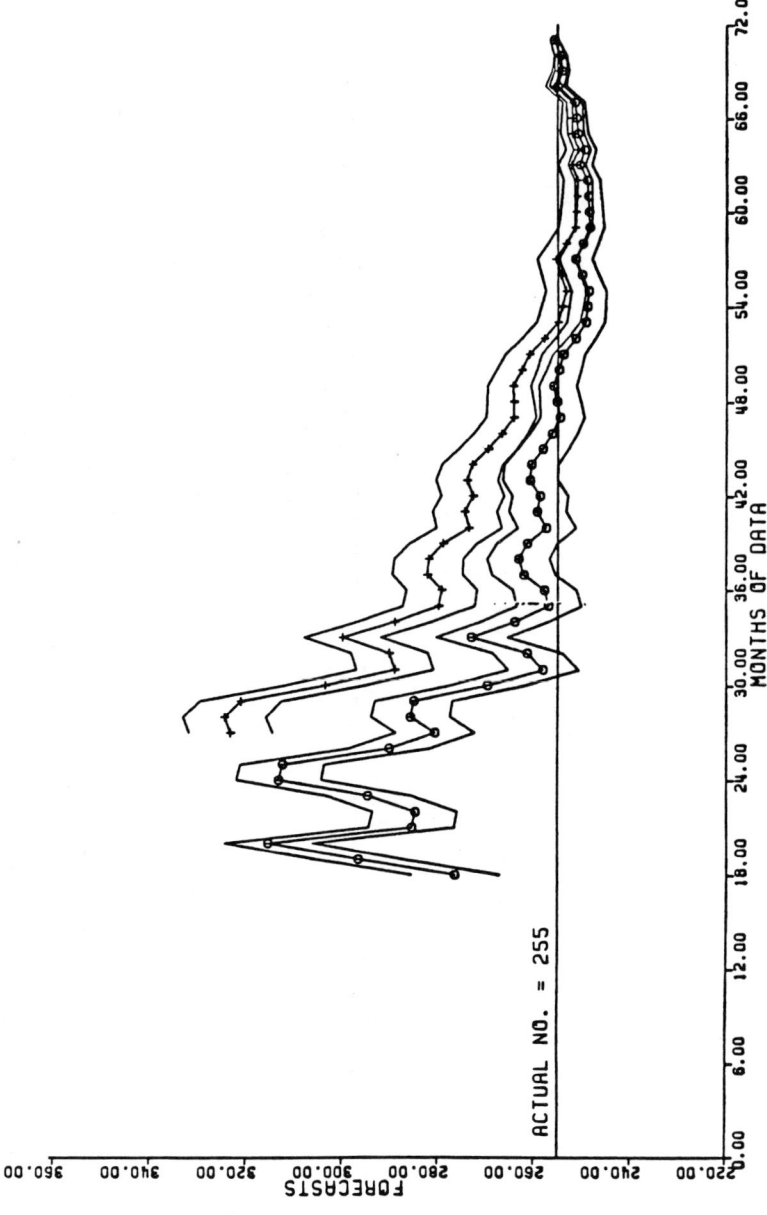

FIGURE 8-13 Comparing two models' forecasting of the number of failures at 72 months, using U.S. Parole Commission Data ("good risk" cohort): Model M_I (0), Model M_H (+).

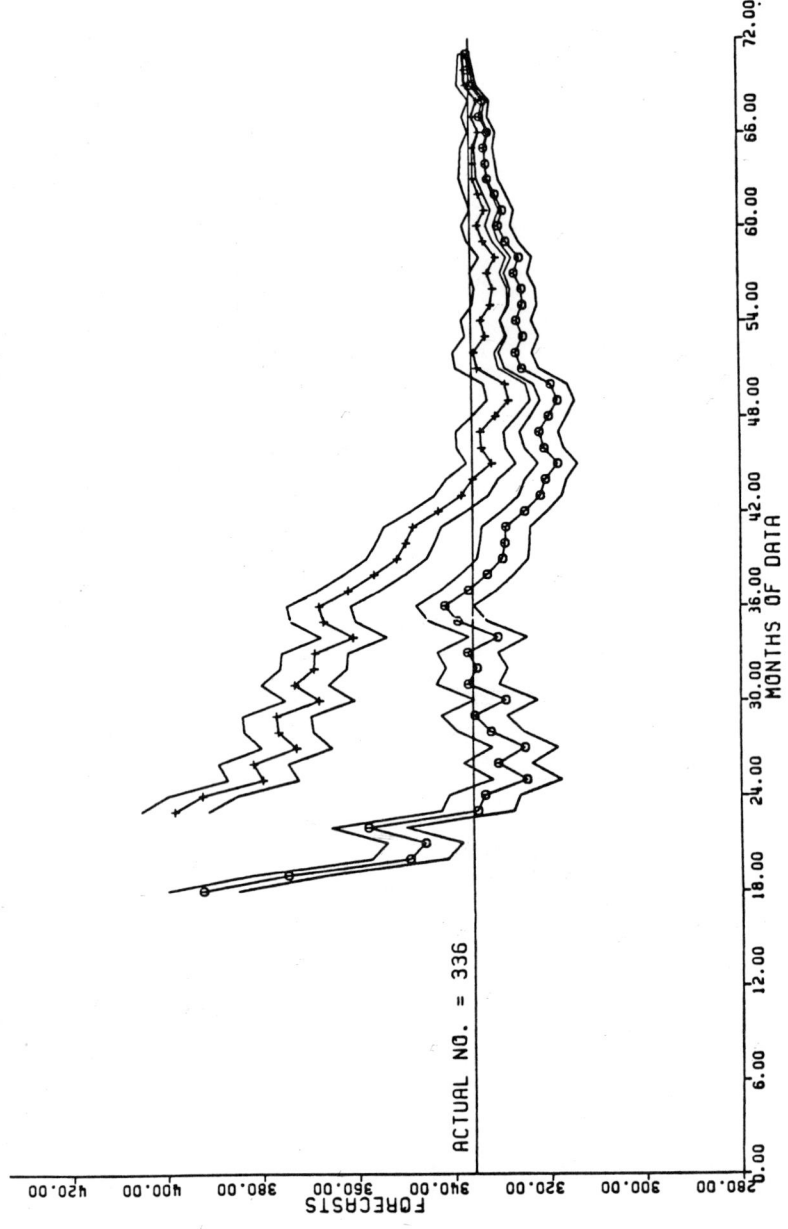

FIGURE 8-14 Comparing two models' forecasting of the number of failures at 72 months, using U.S. Parole Commission Data ("fair risk" cohort): Model M_I (0), Model M_H (+).

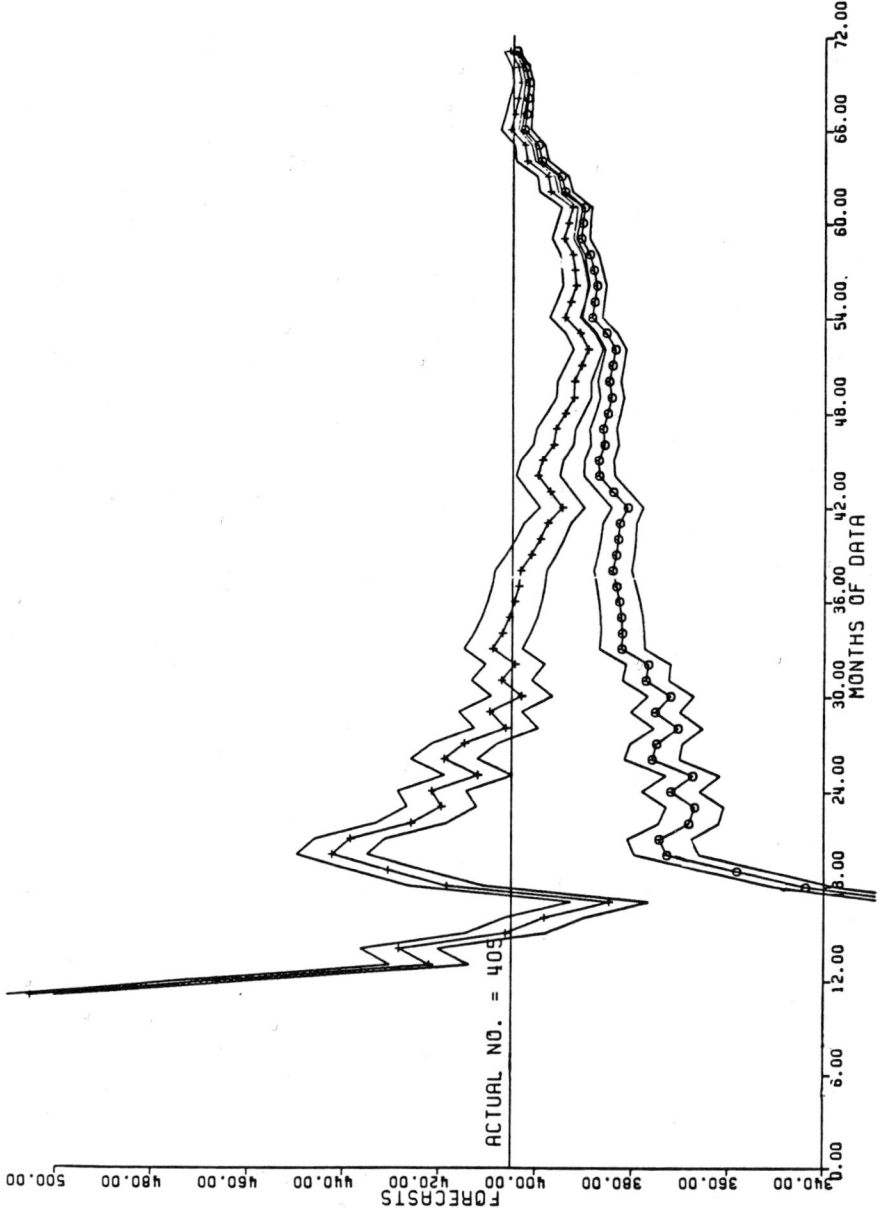

FIGURE 8-15 Comparing two models' forecasting of the number of failures at 72 months, using U.S. Parole Commission Data ("poor risk" cohort): (Model M_I (0), Model M_H (+).

vals. Handling grouped data is more convenient than handling a different time of failure for each individual. Furthermore, derivations of estimates are simple when using grouped data; see Appendix A for derivations of the maximum likelihood and Bayesian estimators for the discrete-time version of Model M_I.

The fact that Model M_I is related to Models M_E and M_M by suitable choices of parameters (see Equations 7.1, 7.2, and 7.8) is another of its virtues. It also suggests an approach to model specification: if Model M_I provides consistently low forecasts (as it does for the poor-risk cohort of Figures 8-9 and 8-15), then it may be advisable to use Model M_M. If it appears that the estimate for γ is fairly close to 1.0, then it may be that Model M_E is the proper choice.

Model Interpretability

Another advantage of Model M_I is that its parameters γ and ϕ have substantive meaning: γ is the propability that an individual will eventually recidivate, and ϕ is the conditional failure rate, conditional on the individual eventually recidivating. That is, γ is a measure of one's *propensity* to fail and ϕ is a measure of *how fast* one does so, should one eventually fail.[10] The corresponding parameters of Models M_E and M_M have the same substantive meanings. In contrast to these parameters, those of Models M_L, M_H and M_W have no substantive meaning with respect to the recidivism process.

There is another advantage to the interpretability of Model M_I's parameter γ: it suggests a new, more useful definition of recidivism. Whereas previous definitions were based on the 1-year recidivism rate, the use of Model M_I permits recidivism to be defined as "the probability of eventually recidivating" (or "the fraction of the group eventually expected to recidivate") *and* "the rate at which the eventual recidivists fail."

These additional advantages of Model M_I strengthen the argument for its use. However, the well-known properties of the exponential, lognormal, and Weibull distributions and the availability of computer software for estimating their parameters and associated confidence intervals make computing their properties much easier. Software is not (yet) readily available for computing the corresponding parameters for Model M_I; however, annotated FORTRAN programs for making these computations are provided in Appendix D.

SUMMARY

This chapter has described how a particular model of the recidivism process was selected. The standard chi-square goodness-of-fit test was considered and

---

[10] For the discrete-time version of Model M_I (Equation 7.3), γ has the same meaning and q is an individual's conditional probability of not failing in a given month, conditional on eventual failure. That is, q is a measure of *how slowly* an eventual recidivist fails.

SUMMARY

found to be misleading; in its place a graphical test based on model forecasting ability was used. The results of this test, and indications from other, nonquantitative criteria, led us to conclude that Model M_I (incomplete exponential distribution) is the preferred model of the recidivism process.[11] In Chapter 9 the properties of Model M_I are given in greater detail, and various techniques are described to make it useful.

---

[11]Variants of this model, M_E (exponential distribution) and M_M (mixed exponential distribution), may be appropriate when—as with the cohort of Figure 8-9—the population under study consists of such poor risks that essentially everyone is eventually expected to fail.

9
Using Model M_I to Analyze Recidivism Data

Once an appropriate model of the recidivism process has been selected, the model can be used to provide a set of techniques for reducing the data to useful information. In studying recidivism using Model M_I, this information includes γ, the probability of an individual eventually recidivating (or alternatively, the fraction of the cohort expected to recidivate eventually), and ϕ, the failure rate (or q, the probability of surviving to the next time period) for those who do eventually recidivate. The model can also provide statements about confidence limits that can be placed on these parameters.

The techniques for obtaining this information must start with the data-collection process, which is described in the first section of this chapter. Once the data have been collected, the model's parameters can then be estimated. A set of FORTRAN programs for this purpose is described in the next section; the listings are provided in Appendix D.

A computer analysis is not always necessary. If the data are singly censored (i.e., if all nonfailures have the same exposure time, as in the Illinois, North Carolina, and U.S. Parole Commission cohorts previously described), some simple graphical techniques can be used to estimate the model's parameters and their confidence limits. The third section describes the techniques and demonstrates their use.

Knowing point estimates of the model's parameters (γ and ϕ or q) is rarely enough by itself; it is also necessary to know how precise the estimates are. In the last section the development of confidence regions for these estimates is described, and the relationship between the confidence regions and the study's sample size and observation time is tabulated. This relationship can be used to provide guidelines for designing a recidivism study.

THE DATA-COLLECTION PROCESS

Most studies that use recidivism as an outcome measure are of two types, correctional program evaluations or studies of offenders' careers. The former are more common and usually control for offender characteristics; however, relatively few of them can actually make definitive statements about programs because of weak experimental designs (see pp. 20–22).

Studies of offenders' careers are designed to determine certain characteristics: when their careers tend to terminate, offense rates for nonterminators, and how offense rates vary by offender characteristics. It is interesting that these studies rarely control for type of correctional program in which the offender was involved; there seems to be an implicit assumption that such programs have little effect on offenders' later careers.[1]

The data requirements for measuring recidivism using Model M_1 are simple. They are the same as for other survival models, such as those included in the Statistical Package for the Social Sciences (SPSS), other computer analysis systems, or the other models described in Chapter 7. All that is needed is the length of time from release to recidivism, for those who recidivate during their observation times; or the length of time from release to cessation of data collection, for those who have not recidivated during their observation times. These three events—release, recidivism, cessation of data collection—require additional explanation.

Date of Release

When an individual is released from prison with no supervision after release, that date is clearly the date of release. But if he or she is released on parole or to the custody of a work-release program or halfway house, all of which include supervision while nominally free, the date of release is ambiguous: it can be considered either the date of release from prison or release from supervision. Which of these dates should be used depends on the goal of the recidivism study and on the extent of supervision; for example, if the study's goal is to determine the effectiveness of a work-release program, then release from the program would be the logical choice for release date.

Date of Recidivating Event

There are many possible definitions of recidivism, as described in Chapter 6. The one that has been selected should be used consistently (and identified) so that inappropriate comparisons are not made; Hoffman and Stone-Meierhoefer (1980) and Griswold (1978) show how different definitions applied to the same data set will produce radically different results and conclusions about program effectiveness.

The time of occurrence of the recidivating event should be based insofar as

---

[1] It is also true that the data sources used in such studies do not keep records of programs, so the researchers cannot be faulted entirely.

possible on the behavior of the offender, not on the behavior of the criminal justice system. That is, it would be preferable to use date of the offense as the date of recidivism, instead of the date of arrest, arraignment, indictment, prosecution, conviction, or return to prison. In most cases, however, the only dates (conveniently *and consistently*) available to researchers are the dates of transactions between the offender and the criminal justice system. Date of occurrence of the crime is not normally included, so date of arrest (or in some cases, date of issuance of a warrant for arrest) is usually the best choice for date of recidivating event.

Date of Cessation of Data Collection

In most studies data collection stops on a specific calendar date (e.g., December 31, 1982), so that the books can be closed and analyses begun. This date would normally be the date of cessation of data collection for those who have not yet recidivated. If, however, an individual has died or has moved from the jurisdiction, data collection cannot proceed beyond that date, so it becomes the relevant cessation date.

It often happens that the evaluator discovers some failures that occurred after the closing date but before the analysis has been completed. The question is then whether this information should be incorporated into the analysis. It should not be, because failure data would be extended past the deadline while success data would not be so extended, which would bias the findings toward a higher probability of recidivism. Pages 73–75 explain these types of bias in greater detail.

The primary reason for collecting these time data is to calculate time intervals: length of time to recidivism, for recidivists; or length of exposure time without failing, for nonrecidivists. However, they may also be used to test for time-based effects; for example, do individuals released in the early stages of a program fare better or worse than those released later?, or, have recidivism patterns changed due to changes in parole (or other) policies that occurred in the middle of data collection? Knowing the actual date of release, in addition to the necessary time interval information, will permit subsequent analyses of this nature.

DATA ANALYSIS

Once the data are collected they must be analyzed to develop estimates of the model's parameters. Appendix A describes the maximum likelihood estimation procedures used for parameter estimation.

Two computer programs have been written to enter and analyze the data, respectively. Appendix D contains the listings of these FORTRAN programs, described in the following section, and provides four examples of their use.

Data Entry Program

Program MLEDATA (an acronym for Maximum Likelihood Estimation DATA) is an interactive program designed to permit data entry from a computer terminal. It accepts failure time data in either of two forms, individual or grouped. That is, failure time data can either be entered separately for each individual, or they can be grouped into intervals so that the number of people failing in each time interval can be entered. The same two alternatives exist for entering exposure data; however, if the data are singly censored, only a single datum, the maximum exposure time, is entered for all nonfailures.

Individual time data are obviously more accurate than grouped data. But this accuracy may be misleading, because what we would like to know is the date of commission of the crime, not the date of the arrest. Data grouped into (equal) intervals may thus be sufficiently accurate.

Using grouped data is preferable when the number in the population under study is large (say, over 100). In such a circumstance it is more convenient to group observations (i.e., failure and observation times) by time intervals.

Parameter Estimation Program

Program MLECALC (an acronym for Maximum Likelihood Estimate CALculation) uses either continuous or discrete-time interval data and calculates the maximum likelihood estimates of the parameters of Model M_I. If *individual time data* have been used, the program calculates γ, the probability of eventually recidivating, and ϕ, the failure rate of those who do eventually recidivate. The units of ϕ are the reciprocal of the time interval units; that is, if time intervals are measured in days, then ϕ is in units of 1/days.

If *grouped data* have been used, the program calculates γ, as before, and q, the conditional probability that an eventual failure does not fail in any given time interval. Both γ and q are probabilities and have no dimensions (and must be between 0 and 1); however, if months are used as the time interval, then q is defined as the conditional probability that an eventual failure does not fail in any given month.

Program MLECALC uses a two-dimensional Newton-Raphson procedure to find the maximum of the likelihood function. It does so by calculating the first and second partial derivatives of the log likelihood functions with respect to the model's parameters, and using this information to drive the first partial derivatives to zero (Gross & Clark, 1975: 205). The number of calculations required is approximately proportional to the number of data entered, so for studies of large populations it may be doubly advantageous to use grouped data.

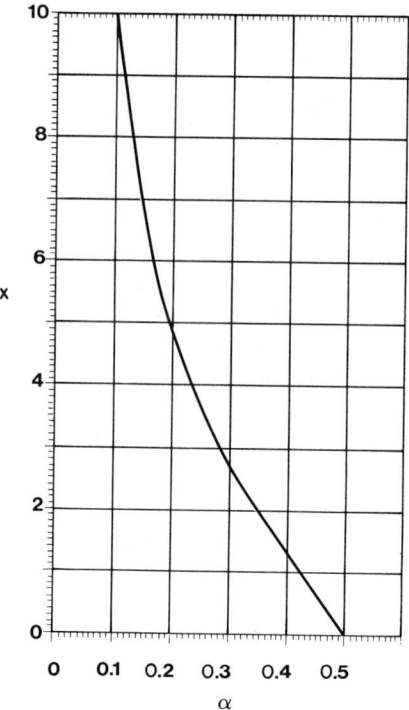

FIGURE 9-1 Graph of Equation 9.1, $1/x - 1/(e^x - 1) = \alpha$. A full-page graph of this equation is found in Appendix A on page 156.

GRAPHICAL PARAMETER ESTIMATION

When the data are singly censored, the model's parameters can be estimated graphically, since the equations used in maximum likelihood estimation simplify to a single equation. The particular equation depends upon whether the data are individual or grouped.

Individual Time Interval Data

When individual time interval data are used, the appropriate equations are (see Appendix A, Equations A.20′ and A.21′)

$$1/x - 1/(e^x - 1) = \bar{t}/\tau = \alpha \qquad (9.1)$$

$$\hat{\phi} = x/\tau \qquad (9.2)$$

$$\hat{\gamma} = K/N\,(1 - e^{-x}) \qquad (9.3)$$

where K is the total number of recidivists, $\bar{t}$ is the mean failure time (the sum of all failure times divided by K), τ is the exposure time for all nonfailures (as

GRAPHICAL PARAMETER ESTIMATION

TABLE 9-1

Sample Calculations for Graphical Solutions

Continuous-time version of $M_1{}^a$		Discrete-time version of $M_1{}^b$		
Failure time (days)	Exposure time (days)	Month	Number failing	Number lost to follow-up
14	365	1	3	0
19	365	2	2	0
24	365	3	2	0
37	365	4	1	0
44	365	5	0	0
75	365	6	0	0
83	365	7	1	0
100	365	8	0	0
207	365	9	0	0
	365	10	0	0
	365	11	0	0
		12	0	11
603 person-days			24 person-months	

$^a \bar{T} = 603/9 = 67.0$ days; $\alpha = 67.0/365 = .1836$.
$^b \bar{T} = 24/9 = 2.67$ months; $\alpha = 2.67/12 = .222$.

explained earlier, the data must be singly censored for this graphical technique to be used), α is the ratio of $\bar{T}$ to τ, and N is the total number in the group under study. Figure 9-1 is a graph of Equation 9.1.[2] It is used in the following manner: first, α is calculated from the failure and exposure data. Then the value of x is found from Figure 9-1, and $\hat{\phi}$ is calculated[3] from Equation 9.2. Finally, $\hat{\gamma}$ is calculated using Equation 9.3.

An example demonstrates the use of this graphical technique. Suppose that 20 people are being followed up for 1 year and 9 of them recidivate, on days 14, 19, 24, 37, 44, 75, 83, 100, and 207, respectively, after their release. The remaining eleven do not recidivate during the 365 days of observation. For this example we have $\bar{T} = 603/9 = 67$ days and $\tau = 365$ days, resulting in $\alpha = .1836$—see Table 9-1(a).

One can locate $\alpha = .1836$ on the graph[4] and estimate $x = 5.27$ (the actual value of x is 5.3033). The value of $\hat{\phi}$ is obtained from Equation 9.2 to be $5.27/365 = 0.0144$/day.

The parameter $\hat{\gamma}$ can be obtained quite readily from Equation 9.3: $\hat{\gamma} = .4523$ (the actual value of $\hat{\gamma}$ is .45225).

[2] The curve is only plotted to $x = 10$; beyond this value $x = 1/\alpha$ is a very good approximation.
[3] The circumflex (ˆ) over a variable denotes that it is the maximum likelihood estimate of the parameter it symbolizes.
[4] Note that α cannot exceed .5. If it does, Model M_1 cannot be used; either the model does not apply or the observation time has not been long enough. See Appendix A for a fuller explanation.

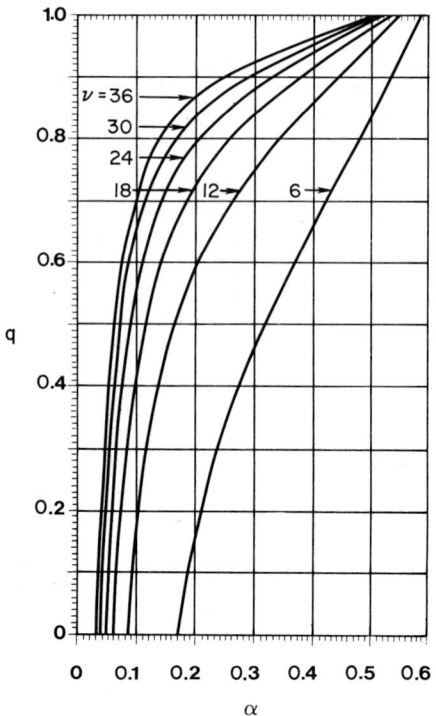

FIGURE 9-2 Graph of Equation 9.4, $1/[v(1 - q)] - 1/(q^{-v} - 1) = \alpha$.

Grouped Time Data

When grouped time data are used the appropriate equations are (see Appendix A, Equations A.20 and A.21)

$$1/(v(1 - \hat{q})) - 1/(\hat{q}^{-v} - 1) = \bar{t}/v = \alpha \qquad (9.4)$$

$$\hat{\gamma} = K/N(1 - \hat{q}^v) \qquad (9.5)$$

where v is the maximum exposure time interval and, as before, α is the ratio of mean failure time (for recidivists) to mean exposure time (for nonrecidivists). However, in this case $\bar{t}$ is calculated using $\bar{t} = \Sigma\, ik_i/K$, where k_i is the number of people who fail in time interval i. Dividing $\bar{t}$ by v results in α. As before, this equation is valid only if the data are singly censored, that is, only if all nonfailures are tracked to the same maximum exposure time interval v. For this equation α must be between $1/v$ and $.5\,(1 + 1/v)$.[5] Figure 9-2 is a plot of q versus α, from Equation 9.4.

The data from the last example can also be used to demonstrate this graphical

---

[5]For large values of v one can use the approximation $v(1 - \hat{q}) = 1/\alpha$.

technique. The data are first grouped into months.[6] Failures after 14, 19, 24; 37, 44; 75, 83; 100; and 207 days translate into three failures in month 1, two in month 2, two in month 3, one in month 4, and one in month 7; see Table 9-1(b). The maximum exposure time interval v is 12 months. The ratio of mean failure time to maximum exposure time is thus $\alpha = (24/9)/12 = .222$, somewhat higher than its value in the case with individual time data. From Figure 9-2 the value of $\hat{q}$ is estimated to be .63 (its actual value is .6317). Using Equation 9.5 with the estimated value of $\hat{q}$ results in an estimate for $\hat{\gamma}$ of .452 (its actual value is .4518).

The continuous-data and grouped-data estimates are quite close. If we set one month equal to $365/12 = 30.4$ days, using the continuous model we find that the probability of an eventual recidivist not failing in any given month is $e^{-0.0144 \times 30.4} = .6428$; this is compared to $\hat{q} = .63$. Using the continuous version, the value of $\hat{\gamma}$ is .4523; for the grouped version it is .4518. Thus the results using the two versions are quite consistent.

CONFIDENCE INTERVALS AND REGIONS

A parameter estimate is a random variable; therefore, it is important to provide some measure of the error of estimation. A confidence interval is such a measure. A 95% confidence interval means that 95% of the intervals constructed using the same method to analyze a process (but using different data sets generated by the process) will contain the true value of the parameter (Mann et al., 1974: 86).

The concept of confidence intervals can be expanded to that of confidence regions for two parameters. A 95% confidence region is one constructed from the data in such a way that, if the true parameters were known and different data sets based on these parameters were generated and a region constructed for each sample, 95% of these regions would contain the parameters.

To construct a confidence region for the parameters of Model M_I, we must first obtain the joint probability density function of the two parameters. It can be shown empirically (see Appendix B) that the joint density function can be represented by the likelihood function.

When the data are singly censored, four statistics completely determine the likelihood function, and therefore the joint density function. These statistics are α, the ratio of mean failure time to maximum exposure time; K, the number of failures; N, the total number of individuals in the group under study; and v, the maximum exposure interval.[7] Then the relationship between the four statistics

---

[6]Although months vary in length from 28 to 31 days, this variation would not normally have a major effect on the results.

[7]When individual data are used (continuous-time version of Model M_I), we use τ, the maximum exposure time, in place of v, the maximum exposure interval, for the last statistic.

and the confidence regions can be explored. This relationship can then be extended to cases in which the data are not singly censored. These steps are described in this section.

Confidence Intervals for Singly Censored Data

The joint density function contours depicted in Figures 9-3 and 9-4 (taken from Appendix B) give some indication of the relationship between the size of

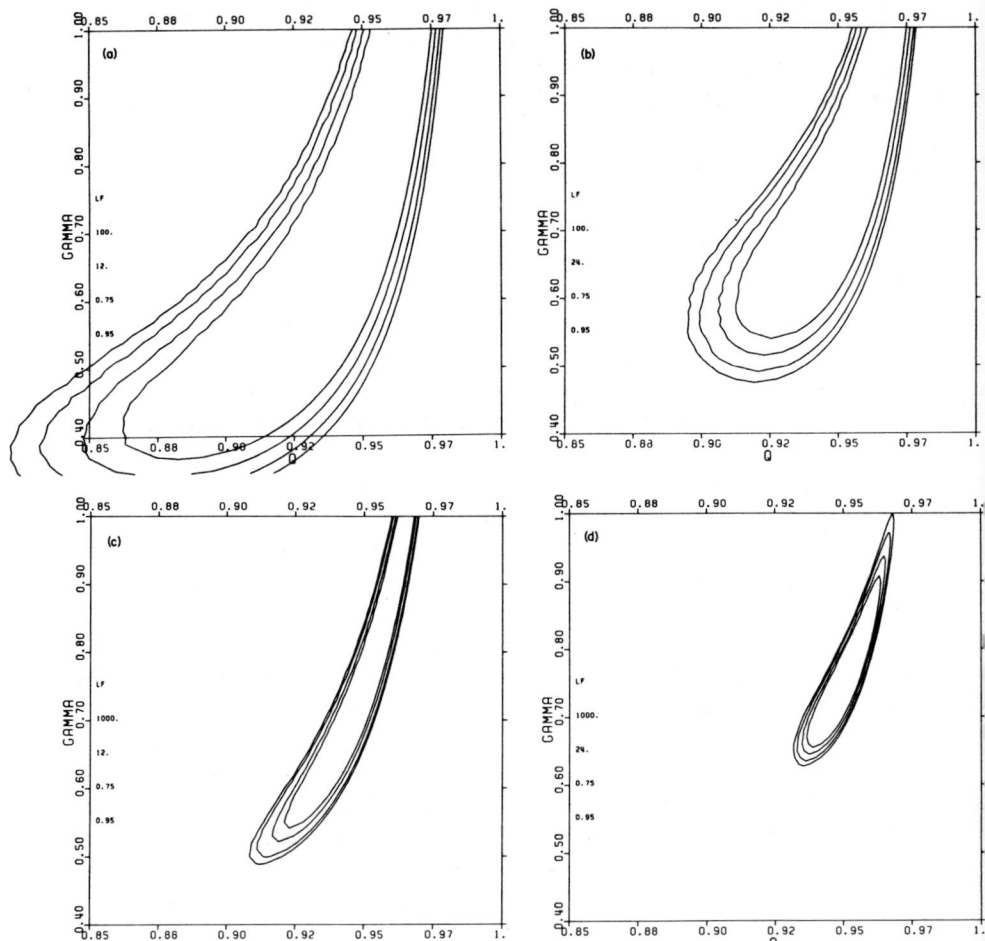

FIGURE 9-3 Joint probability density function for singly censored data, $\hat{\gamma} = 0.75$, $\hat{q} = 0.95$ (90, 95, 98, and 99% contours shown): (a) $N = 100$ subjects, $\nu = 12$ months; (b) $N = 100$ subjects, $\nu = 24$ months; (c) $N = 1000$ subjects, $\nu = 12$ months; (d) $N = 1000$ subjects, $\nu = 24$ months.

CONFIDENCE INTERVALS AND REGIONS

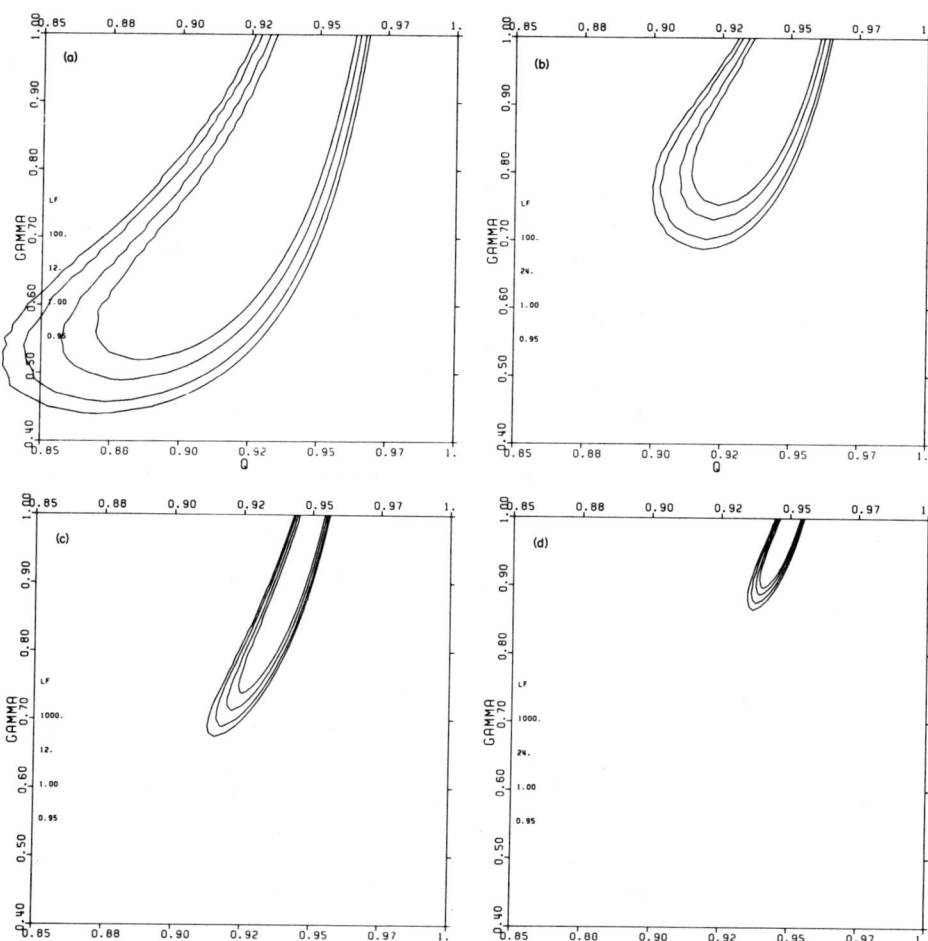

FIGURE 9-4 Joint probability density function for singly censored data, $\hat{\gamma} = 1.0$, $\hat{q} = 0.95$ (90, 95, 98, and 99% contours shown): (a) $N = 100$ subjects, $\nu = 12$ months; (b) $N = 100$ subjects, $\nu = 24$ months; (c) $N = 1000$ subjects, $\nu = 12$ months; (d) $N = 1000$ subjects, $\nu = 24$ months.

the confidence regions and the sample size and observation time for two different values of $\hat{\gamma}$ and $\hat{q}$. Doubling the maximum observation time has about the same effect on the confidence interval for $\hat{\gamma}$ as does a tenfold jump in sample size. However, the confidence interval for $\hat{q}$ is barely affected when the maximum observation time is doubled, while it is more than halved when a sample size 10 times larger is used. Appendix C contains tables showing the relationship between the size of the confidence regions and the values of $\hat{\gamma}$, $\hat{q}$, N, and ν. These tables are of assistance in designing studies that use recidivism as a measure of effectiveness, because they show the size of the confidence regions achievable with different sample sizes and observation times.

Confidence Intervals for Progressively Censored Data

The tables shown in Appendix C were generated for singly censored data sets. However, most data sets are not singly censored, even when the study is designed to have a single maximum observation time for all individuals. For example, imagine a correctional experiment in which all participants were released simultaneously, with plans to track them for 12 months. Some may die in the interim and others may leave the jurisdiction, thus precluding their being tracked for the full 12 months. When this occurs, the first inclination is to eliminate those with short observation times from the study. But this will bias the outcome, as explained on pages 73–75.

A second alternative is to keep these data, but then the tables cannot be used. However, in many cases it is possible to find a singly censored equivalent to a progressively censored data set. Appendix B describes the process for doing this, and includes the mathematical relationships used to develop the statistics of the equivalent singly censored problem.

When Is a Normal Approximation Appropriate?

As Appendix A has shown, the likelihood function sometimes approximates a bivariate normal distribution quite closely. When it does, standard confidence procedures and significance tests can be applied (e.g., see Lloyd & Joe, 1979).

The standard deviation of γ can be estimated using the second partial derivatives to calculate estimates of the variances and covariance of γ and ϕ (Gross & Clark, 1975: 50). They are obtained for singly censored data sets from the following relationships:

1. Continuous-time version:

$$\text{Var}(\gamma) = \left[\frac{K}{\phi^2} - \left(\frac{K}{\phi} - T\right)\Big/\tau + \left(\frac{K}{\phi} - T\right)^2 \Big/ (N - K) \right] \Big/ \Delta \tag{9.6}$$

$$\text{Var}(\phi) = \frac{NK}{(N - K)\gamma^2 \Delta} \tag{9.7}$$

$$\text{Cov}(\gamma, \phi) = N\left(\frac{K}{\phi} - T\right) \Big/ (N - K)\gamma \Delta \tag{9.8}$$

where

$$\Delta = \frac{N}{(N - K)\gamma^2} \left[T\left(\frac{2K}{\phi} - T\right) - \frac{K}{\tau}\left(\frac{K}{\phi} - T\right) \right]$$

CONFIDENCE INTERVALS AND REGIONS

2. Discrete-time version:

$$\text{Var}(\gamma) = \left[\frac{\theta^2}{N-K} - \frac{(\nu-1)\theta}{q} + \frac{T-K}{q^2} + \frac{K}{(1-q)^2}\right]\Big/\Delta \quad (9.9)$$

$$\text{Var}(q) = \frac{NK}{(N-K)\gamma^2\Delta} \quad (9.10)$$

$$\text{Cov}(\gamma, q) = \frac{-N\theta}{(N-K)\gamma\Delta} \quad (9.11)$$

where

$$\theta = \frac{K}{1-q} - \frac{T-K}{q}$$

and

$$\Delta = \frac{N(T-K)}{(N-K)\gamma^2 q}\left[\frac{(\nu+1)K - T}{q} + \frac{K\left(2 - \frac{(\nu-1)K}{T-K}\right)}{1-q}\right]$$

Estimates of standard deviations are obtained by taking the appropriate square roots. However, before making these calculations it is worthwhile to see if the estimates have any utility. We will consider a normal approximation to be appropriate if the maximum height of the likelihood function along the line $\gamma = 1.0$ is less than $\frac{1}{20}$ the height of the likelihood function at its maximum. (This would make the situation depicted in Figure 8-5 of Appendix B close to a borderline case. The likelihood ratio for those data is 15.)

Figure 9-5 shows the conditions on α, K/N, and N under which this holds, for the continuous-time version of M_1. Note that there is a restricted range of α in

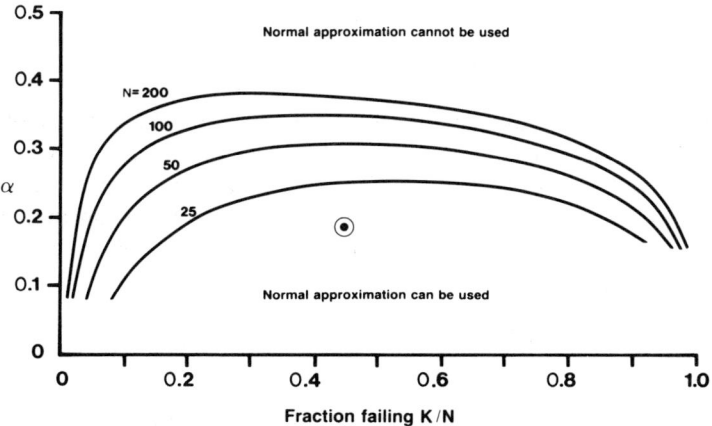

FIGURE 9-5 Region in which the joint density function can be approximated by a bivariate normal distribution (continuous-time version of Model M_1).

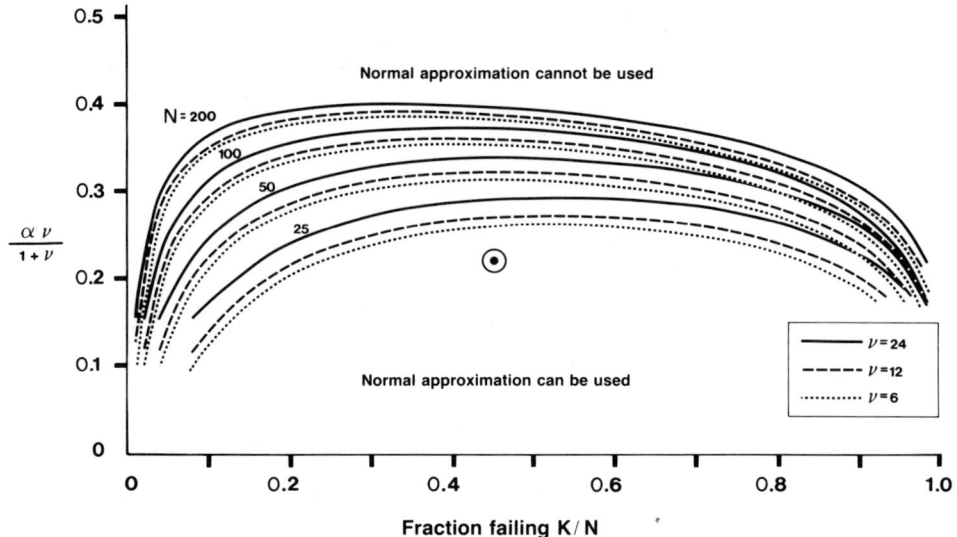

FIGURE 9-6 Region in which the joint density function can be approximated by a bivariate normal distribution (discrete-time version of Model M_1).

which the normal approximation can be used at both the high and low ends of K/N. For high values of K/N the maximum of the likelihood function is too close to the line at which the likelihood function is truncated ($\gamma = 1$) to permit the normal approximation; for low values there is apparently insufficient failure information, that is, not enough data for a trend to be discernible.

Applying the example shown in Table 9-1(a), we see that $\alpha = .1836$ is below the curve at $K/N = 9/20 = .45$. Therefore, the variance–covariance matrix calculated from Equations 9.6 through 9.8 can be used to characterize the joint probability density function of γ and ϕ. For this problem we obtain $\sigma_\gamma = .1119$, $\sigma_\phi = .0048$, and the correlation coefficient $\rho = .0357$.

Figure 9-6 shows the same relationship for the discrete-time version of Model M_1. Note that the allowable region increases as ν increases. The value $\alpha = .222$ is again[8] below the curve at $K/N = .45$, so, as before, the variance–covariance matrix can be used to describe the joint probability density function. For the example of Table 9-1(b) and using Equations 9.9 to 9.11, we obtain $\sigma_\gamma = .1118$, $\sigma_q = .1044$ and $\rho = .0328$.

---

[8]To see this, one must extrapolate from $\bar{N} = 25$, $\nu = 12$, to $N = 20$, $\nu = 12$.

10
Covariate and Nonparametric Methods

The methods developed in the last chapter can be used to analyze the recidivism behavior of a group of people released from a correctional setting. They are also useful in understanding how behavior may be affected by individual characteristics when a covariate approach is introduced into the models.

This chapter explores the possibility of using covariate methods to analyze recidivism data. These methods attempt to disentangle the effects of various offender or program characteristics on recidivism. The first section describes their use in looking at offender characteristics, and the next section their use in assessing treatment effects. Their use with Model M_I (incomplete exponential distribution) and with Model M_L (lognormal distribution) is explored in the following two sections.

Other methods of data analysis do not rely on a specific model of the process under study; they are called nonparametric methods. Their use in analyzing recidivism data is described in the concluding section.

COVARIATE METHODS AND OFFENDER CHARACTERISTICS

Covariate models posit a relationship between individual outcomes and individual characteristics. That is, the outcomes are assumed to vary in some regular way with the characteristics of the individuals under study.[1] For example, those with less education or a poorer employment record may be expected to have higher probabilities of recidivism, or shorter mean times to recidivism.

The choice of a covariate model should of course be dictated by the same factors discussed in Chapter 7. Unfortunately, however, the choice is frequently predicated on the availability of computer software to analyze the large amount of information produced for such a study.

That software takes precedence over process characteristics is not surprising,

---

[1]The fact that two variables covary or are correlated in some way does not necessarily imply that there is a causal relationship between them.

considering the potential complexity of covariate models. Furthermore, the method used most often—linear regression—has been found to work fairly well even if the data violate the method's implicit assumptions (linearity, heteroskedasticity, etc.), as long as the violations are not too extreme. Such methods are potentially useful in sorting out the independent variables that appear to be most strongly associated with the outcome variable.

It must also be kept in mind that the variables used in covariate models are not the most important variables, only the most important *measured* variables. They do not include such important factors as the individuals' emotional stability in crisis situations, their degree of impulsiveness, whether they are risk averse or risk preferring, the quality of their interactions with their parents as a child, and age they first left home,[2] any one of which may be more important than (although correlated with) the standard variables collected in correctional studies: drug or alcohol use, age at first arrest, number of rule violations while incarcerated, and type of offense for which convicted. Thus, although using covariate models is an improvement over not using them, they do not substitute for random assignment.

Another caveat with covariate models concerns the intepretation of their results. A covariate analysis may show, for instance, that a higher probability of recidivism is associated with individuals who are younger at first arrest. But it cannot predict what particular *individuals* will do; it can only predict, to some extent, what *cohorts* with different mixes of individuals might do. Applying such findings to individuals can be improper, as exemplified by Greenwood's (1982) reanalysis of the Chaikens' (1982a) data. He showed that those scoring higher on a crime predictor scale did, on average, have higher crime rates; however, the percentage of cases incorrectly predicted was so high as to render the scale useless as a prediction device.

A third caveat in using covariate methods is common to other methods as well. What is termed statistically significant relationship between an independent variable and the outcome variable may merely reflect a large sample size and a minor relationship rather than a substantively significant finding. It is also important to know if the difference involves an important variable or a trivial one, and a policy-related variable or one that policies cannot affect.

ANALYZING TREATMENT EFFECTS USING COVARIATE MODELS

Covariate models are also used when a true experimental design is not possible. Schmidt and Witte (1980) report on such a study of a correctional program.

[2]Glaser (1964), McCord and McCord (1959), Pritchard (1979), and Robins and Wish (1977) describe variables having an effect on recidivism that are normally not measured in recidivism studies.

If the research design does not permit random assignment of individuals to treatment and nontreatment groups, it is highly likely that the characteristics of the two groups will differ in some measurable ways, so that their aggregate outcomes cannot be compared readily. In this eventuality, Schmidt and Witte maintain that the use of covariate models "will allow control for the factors identified [as likely to affect the outcome]" (1980: 586).

This statement is somewhat misleading. If all of the relevant factors are identified, then the statement is correct; but this is rarely the case. Two selection procedures predominate in correctional programs: self-selection (volunteering for a new treatment) and judicial selection. In the first case, the treatment program may be filled only with volunteers, while the nontreatment group consists largely of individuals with similar characteristics who did not volunteer for the treatment. These two groups may be matched on all *measurable* characteristics, but they are not matched on an important variable—voluntarism. In fact, the choice of whether to participate in a new treatment program may be the most important difference between the two groups. For example, it may be a significant indicator of an individual's decision to terminate his or her criminal career, so the treatment group would be more likely to have a lower recidivism rate regardless of the nature or efficacy of the treatment.

In the second case, the decision of which individuals go into which programs is made by judges. Judges base their decisions on unmeasured as well as measured characteristics, and the unmeasured characteristics can weigh heavily in the decision. Only if it could be shown that judges' decisions are not based on factors important to success could a covariate model be said to control for all relevant factors.

In other words, when assignment of individuals to treatment is nonrandom, there is no validity to the assumption that the groups are equivalent, or that their nonequivalence can be accounted for by using covariate models.

USING COVARIATE MODELS WITH MODEL M_I

Two approaches to covariate analysis using Model M_I are described in this section. The first, based on multivariate techniques, turns out to be of little utility. A description of the approach and possible reasons for its failure follows. An alternative approach, partitioning the data according to specific covariate values, is then described.

Multivariate Parametric Models

We assume that each individual i has a unique probability γ_i of ultimately recidivating and (if a recidivist) that this person has a unique probability q_i of surviving another month without recidivating. We further assume that a small number of individual characteristics is primarily responsible for individual variations in γ_i and q_i, so that

$$\gamma_i = f(x_{i1}, x_{i2}, \ldots, x_{im}) + \epsilon_i \tag{10.1}$$

and

$$q_i = q(x_{i1}, x_{i2}, \ldots, x_{im}) + \delta_i \tag{10.2}$$

where x_{ij} is the jth characteristic of individual i, and where ϵ_i and δ_i are error terms.

A common approach is to assume that the relationship between independent and dependent variables is linear, so that

$$\gamma_i = a_0 + a_1 x_{i1} + a_2 x_{i2} + \cdots + a_m x_{im} + \epsilon_i$$

and

$$q_i = b_0 + b_1 x_{i1} + b_2 x_{i2} + \cdots + b_m x_{im} + \delta_i$$

These relationships ignore the fact that γ_i and q_i are restricted to be between 0 and 1. However, the following relationships can be used for f and g in Equations 10-1 and 10-2:

$$1 - \gamma_i = (1 - a_0) a_1 x_{i1} a_2 x_{i2}, \ldots, a_m x_{im} \epsilon_i \tag{10.3}$$

and

$$q_i = b_0 b_1 x_{i1} b_2 x_{i2}, \ldots, b_m x_{im} \delta_i \tag{10.4}$$

Note that large values of x_i produce "worse" behavior; that is, γ_i decreases and q_i increases as any x_{ij} increases. Since γ_i and q_i must be between 0 and 1, a_j and b_j must be restricted to be between 0 and 1. Equations 10.3 and 10.4 are linear when logarithms are taken of both sides. The coefficients a_j and b_j can then be estimated by maximizing the (log) likelihood function generated using these two equations, with the appropriate constraints.

The maximization problem was attempted for four data sets, from North Carolina, Georgia, Iowa, and the U.S. Bureau of Prisons. Two nonlinear unconstrained procedures were used: PRAXIS, a NASA-originated conjugate direction method without derivative information; and a Fletcher-Reeves conjugate gradient method. The results were unsatisfactory, for a number of computational reasons.

First, if the number of individual variables is even as low as 4 (i.e., $m = 4$), the solution space contains 10 ($= 2m + 2$) variables—and normally, many more than 4 variables are used. Perhaps because of this, the log likelihood function is extremely flat in the vicinity of the maximum, leading to convergence problems. This means that statistical statements about the quality of estimates for the a_j and b_j are almost meaningless.

USING COVARIATE MODELS WITH MODEL M_I

Second, for many data sets of interest n is of the order of 1000. This requires an appreciable amount of computation every time the log likelihood function is evaluated—by whatever optimization algorithm is used.

Third, the specific form used in the analysis (Equations 10.3 and 10.4) may not be appropriate for the process under study. It may well be that other forms for the functions f and g in Equations 10.1 and 10.2 would produce better results.

Therefore, although covariate analysis employing many variables may appear to be an attractive technique, for this problem, at least, it has many drawbacks. Nor does it necessarily lead to insights into postrelease behavior.

Covariate Analysis by Partitioning the Data

An alternative technique can be used to provide some insight into the relationship between recidivism parameters and independent variables. Data can be partitioned into a number of categories for an independent variable, then each category analyzed as a separate group using the methods described in Chapter 9.

A number of different data sets were analyzed using this approach. They include studies conducted in Iowa (Iowa, 1979), Georgia (Cox, 1977), North Carolina (Schmidt & Witte, 1980), and federal prison systems (Kitchener et al., 1977). Unfortunately, they did not all collect the same data, so not all of the covariates can be compared.

However, one covariate that can be investigated for all four data sets is age at release. Figures 10-1 to 10-4 show the effect of age at release on estimates and

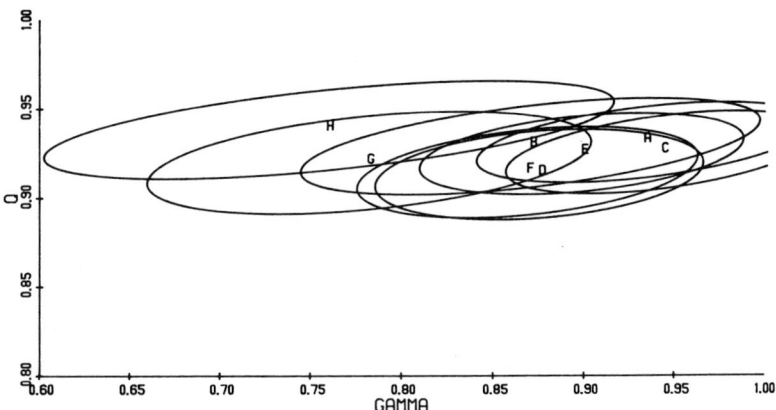

FIGURE 10-1 Effect of age at release on 90% confidence regions on estimates of γ and q using North Carolina data: 20 or less (A); 21–22 (B); 22–24.5 (C); 24.5–28 (D); 28–34 (E); 34–40 (F); 40–47 (G); 48 and over (H).

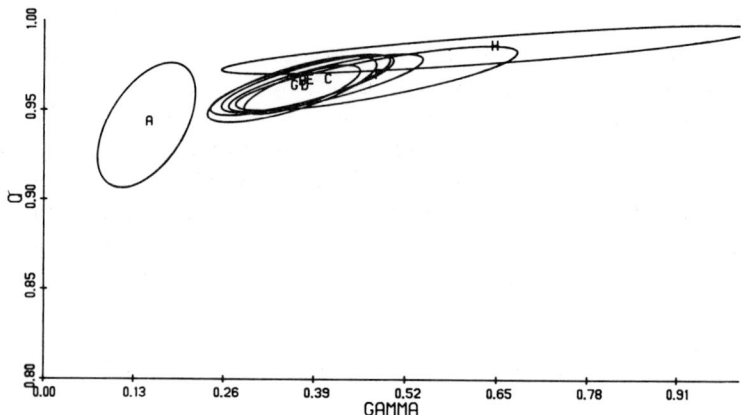

FIGURE 10-2 Effect of age at release on 90% confidence regions on estimates of γ and q using Iowa data. 19 or less (A); 20–21 (B); 22–23 (C); 24–26 (D); 27–29 (E); 30–35 (F); 36–46 (G); 47 and over (H).

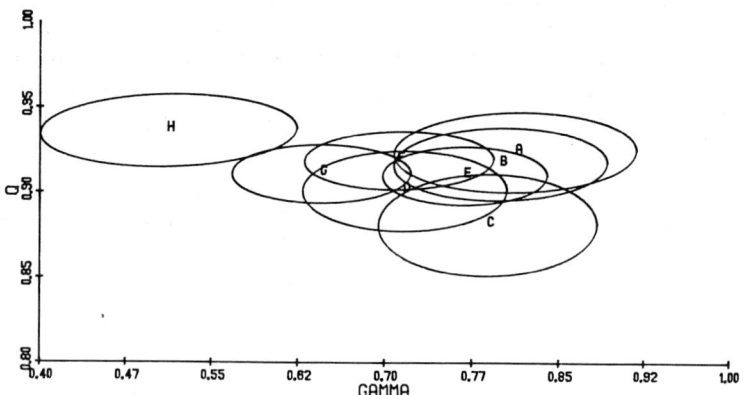

FIGURE 10-3 Effect of age at release on 90% confidence regions on estimates of γ and q using U.S. Bureau of Prisons data. 19 or less (A); 20–21 (B); 22–23 (C); 24–26 (D); 27–30 (E); 31–35 (F); 36–46 (G); 47 and over (H).

confidence regions for γ and q. The ellipses represent 90% contours about the mean of the likelihood function.[3]

As can be seen, there appears to be some regularity to the relationship between age at release and the recidivism parameters. In three of the four cases, γ, the

---

[3]There is little difference between the mean and maximum values of the likelihood function for three of the four cohorts. For the Georgia data, however, it was found that for many cases of interest the maximum value of the likelihood function was at γ = 1, so the mean value was used. Bayesian techniques were therefore used. See Appendix A for a description of these techniques.

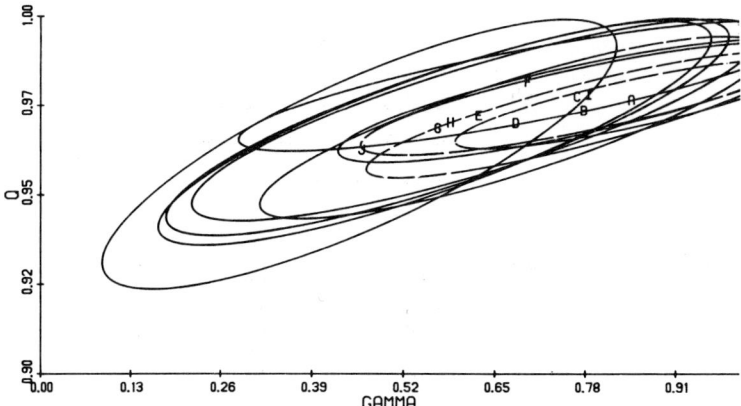

FIGURE 10-4 Effect of age at release on 90% confidence regions on estimates of γ and q using Georgia data. 17.8–22.3 (A); 22.3–23.6 (B); 23.6–24.6 (C); 24.6–25.6 (D); 25.6–26.9 (E); 26.9–28.7 (F); 28.7–31.3 (G); 31.3–35.1 (H); 35.1–41.2 (I); 41.2 and over (J).

probability of eventually recidivating, decreases as the age at release increases; but there seems to be no effect of age at release on q, the conditional probability of an eventual recidivist not failing in any given month.

The variations exhibited in the estimates of γ and q (or ϕ) can provide insight into the general characteristics of different cohorts. The higher the value of γ, the more likely an individual in the cohort will recidivate. The lower the value of q (or the higher the value of ϕ), the faster he or she will do so. This suggests a taxonomy of cohorts as depicted in Figure 10-5. Those in quadrants I and IV are easy to typify. The best risks are in quadrant I, those who are less likely to recidivate (and who recidivate at a low rate).[4] Those in quadrant IV are the worst risks; they have the highest probability of recidivating, and do so at high rates. Chronic juvenile offenders would fall in this quadrant, as would other unskilled offenders. In fact, the relationship between the parameters and employment record (Figure 10-6), as might be expected, show the cohorts fitting primarily into these two quadrants.

Quadrants II and III are more difficult to typify. Perhaps those with a high probability of recidivism and a low rate of rearrest (quadrant II) might be considered "professionals," while those in quadrant III might typify the "occasional bunglers." These insights are not profound, but they do serve to show how the two-parameter model might be used in interpreting differences among different programs or offender populations.

---

[4]Caution should be used in interpreting a low frequency of arrest (high q or low ϕ). It may mean that individuals in this cohort commit fewer crimes, but it may also mean that they are more skilled in avoiding arrest.

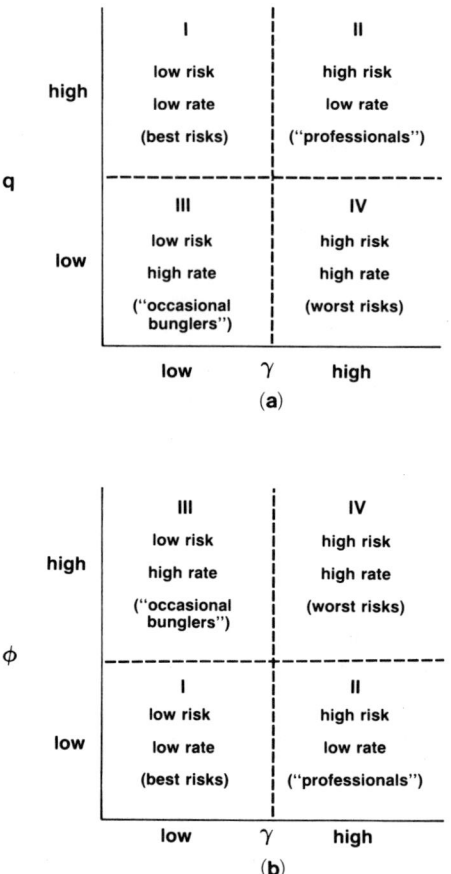

FIGURE 10-5 Categorizing cohorts using model parameters: (a) γ versus q, (b) γ versus ϕ.

USING COVARIATE METHODS WITH MODEL M_L

Schmidt and Witte (1980) analyzed data from the North Carolina Department of Corrections using Model M_L (lognormal distribution; see Section E5 of Chapter 7) to characterize length of time to recidivism. This model was used because "it fit the data considerably better" than an exponential or a normal model. These three models were the only ones investigated, apparently because regression methods are well developed for them, allowing one to determine the effect of covariates on the outcome. The method Schmidt and Witte used was developed by Amemiya and Boskin (1974) for censored (or truncated) observations.

Schmidt and Witte explored how recidivism was affected by a number of

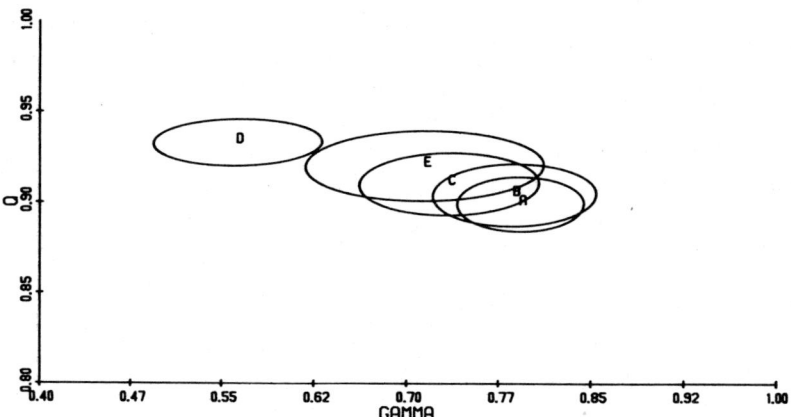

FIGURE 10-6 Effect of employment in the 2 years prior to imprisonment on estimates of γ and q: U.S. Bureau of Prisons data.

factors relating to the individual (alcohol usage, age at release, etc.) as well as by correctional programs, in particular, work release programs. The relationship they calculated was then used to evaluate a specific work release program. They found statistically significant differences between actual and predicted number of recidivists during the early months of the work release program, but "no significant differences between actual and predicted numbers of returnees beyond six months." Their evaluation is ambiguous, since the actual number of returnees is some 12% higher than predicted, yet the program is characterized as providing "superior performance." Aside from this ambiguity, attribution of the performance to the program cannot be made, because there is no way of knowing whether the group under study "differs significantly from the system norm in a way not controlled for by our models" (p. 595). In other words, without ensuring some degree of equivalence between groups being compared, evaluation of a program is tenuous at best, regardless of the sophistication of the methods used.

We see, then, that covariate methods are presently limited in their ability to mine data for additional insights, regardless of the model of recidivism used.

NONPARAMETRIC METHODS

All of the methods described thus far are based on specific models of recidivism. That is, they assume that individuals fail (in the aggregate) according to certain patterns as specified by the model, and that the statistical problem is merely one of determining the model's parameters (and confidence bounds).

Other statistical methods also exist to analyze failure data, methods that are not based on specific models. These nonparametric methods have been used to study recidivism. Turnbull (1977) analyzed the data analyzed parametrically by Stollmack and Harris (1974); he found it encouraging that the two methods produced essentially the same significance level (.028 versus .024) in distinguishing between two groups of releasees.

Barton and Turnbull (1981) use another method, due to Kaplan and Meier (1958), to analyze data on parolees released from two Connecticut institutions. This method permits the estimation of probabilities of recidivating by a certain time. They show both graphically and analytically that the two institutions' releasees have a statistically significant difference in the probability of recidivating by 12 months.

The primary advantage to using nonparametric methods is that no assumptions need be made about the process generating the data. However, this advantage is turned into a disadvantage if it means ignoring known information about the process; as Turnbull (1977: 707) notes, "First, a parametric model may allow one to gain more insight into the structure of the underlying phenomena. Second, it is easier to incorporate a parametric model into some larger model of the general correctional system [e.g., JUSSIM, a justice system simulation model; see Blumstein, 1975]. Last, [if one uses nonparametric methods when a parametric method is valid] there is loss of [statistical] power for small sample sizes."

Two nonparametric tests of significance are used by Turnbull for studying recidivism data. Both are based on the rank order of (failure and observation) times, not on the times themselves. Therefore, some of the information available for analysis is not used, which limits its efficiency.

Some nonparametric techniques can be used with regression models to include the effect of covariates on outcomes. For example, if two different groups have markedly different age distributions or education levels, there are nonparametric analytic methods that permit adjustment for such inhomogeneities. Barton and Turnbull (1979, 1981; see also Barton, 1978) reanalyze the Conneticut data using such nonparametric methods. The analyses showed that the originally significant difference between the releasees of the two institutions (found by looking at aggregate data) largely disappeared after adjustment for the covariates.

SUMMARY

Covariate and nonparametric methods have been used in analyzing recidivism data. At present, however, they are still in the experimental stage and need considerable refinement and testing before they can be routinely used to analyze correctional programs. In fact, nonparametric methods may not be the best approach. As Barton and Turnbull (1981: 98) point out, "As further studies of recidivism data are performed, it may become possible to choose an appropriate *parametric* model for increasing the small sample power of testing procedures'' (emphasis added).

One other point of interest should be noted. The North Carolina and Connecticot studies both were unable to attribute differences (or lack thereof) to specific variables because of the lack of control over the research design. Only if two groups are equivalent—or alternatively, only if individuals have been assigned randomly to the two groups—can attribution be made with validity.

11
Conclusion

This book has described the development of a method of studying recidivism. It has detailed how recidivism data are affected by different definitions of recidivism. It has shown how to analyze recidivism data to estimate the probability of an individual eventually recidivating and the failure rate for those who are expected to recidivate.

INTERPRETING RECIDIVISM DATA

The most practical definition of recidivism has been found to be one based on arrest. Following Thorsten Sellin's dictum about crime indexes—*"the value of a crime for index purposes decreases as the distance from the crime itself in terms of procedure increases"* (Sellin, 1931: 346; emphasis in the original)—an arrest-based recidivism definition was shown to be more useful and accurate than one based on prosecution, conviction, or return to prison. This is not to say that prosecution or conviction cannot be used as a quality-control check on arrest (i.e., by counting an arrest as a recidivism event only if followed by prosecution or conviction); rather, it means that the date of the event should be the arrest, since it is procedurally (and temporally) closer to the crime.

But resolving the definitional problem will not be itself resolve the issue of comparability of recidivism statistics across jurisdictions. Each state is *sui generis*: a state that places 10% of its convicted offenders on probation cannot be compared directly with one that places 30% on probation. A state with overcrowded prisons, in which the parole board and parole officers are urged to keep parolees out on the street if at all possible, cannot be compared directly with a state that is closing prisons. A state with determinate sentencing cannot be compared directly with a state with indeterminate sentencing. And variations in recidivism statistics may be even greater between urban and rural jurisdictions within a state than they are between states. In other words, one should be extremely careful before making inferences based on recidivism rates, notwithstanding the use of the same definition of recidivism and the same analytic techniques.

This should not be taken as a recommendation for a total proscription against the use of recidivism as a measure of correctional effectiveness. Carefully designed experiments (and quasi experiments) will still be useful in making limited inferences about programs, and will be useful in shedding light on the nature of offender behavior and the response it engenders from the criminal justice system. But blanket statements about programs or states, so avidly sought by those intent on making headlines, can rarely be gleaned from the data and will usually be misleading.

ANALYZING RECIDIVISM DATA

An arrest-based definition was shown to be more useful not only because it is closer to the crime; another reason concerns the statistical properties of crimes and arrests. The probability of arrest is largely independent of the probability of commission of a crime; that is, crime reflects the behavior of the individual and arrest reflects the behavior of the criminal justice system. This independence was shown to mean that, for those individuals in a group under study that do recidivate, the times to rearrest are distributed exponentially. Based on this characteristic of the process, and on considerable empirical verification that rearrests follow an exponential pattern, a model of offender behavior, Model M_I, based on an incomplete exponential distribution, was proposed and analyzed.

Model M_I's two parameters were estimated in standard ways, using maximum likelihood or Bayesian estimation procedures. Developing the confidence regions for the parameter estimates was shown to be more difficult, due to constraints on the values of the parameter estimates. It was shown how computer-based graphical procedures can be used to depict the confidence regions (Appendix D) for any particular data set, or the size of confidence regions can be estimated using the tables given in Appendix C. And if the sample size and observation time are sufficiently large, as determined by Figures 9-5 and 9-6, then the joint probability density function of the parameters was shown to be approximately bivariate normal, so that the asymptotic estimates of the parameter variances and covariances can be used to develop confidence regions.

DIRECTIONS FOR FUTURE RESEARCH

There are a number of promising areas for additional research. One area opened up by new analytic techniques is secondary analysis of existing data. Many of the data sets from past studies still exist, either in the agencies or universities where they were conducted, or in data repositories such as the Criminal Justice Archive and Information Network (CJAIN) or the Inter-University Consortium for Political and Social Research (ICPSR), both at the University of Michigan. Reanalyzing these data sets using consistent definitions of recidivism and new analytic techniques may provide fresh insights into offender behavior or program effectiveness.

Other promising areas for research lie in the further development of the analytic techniques. They include obtaining a greater understanding of the nature of the likelihood function, the development of confidence regions and statistical tests, and the development of covariate methods.

From all the empirical evidence thus far collected, it appears that the likelihood function has at most one local maximum. A proof to this effect (or if it is not the case, a specification of conditions under which it is true) would be of value. That it is true for singly censored data can be seen by inspection of Equation A.8; however, when the data are progressively censored it may not hold. There may be pathological data sets (e.g., in which the censoring is U-shaped, with a large number with short censoring times and a large number with long censoring times and few with medium censoring times) in which more than one local maximum exists. This property of the likelihood function should be studied.

Anscombe's (1961) transformation of the variables in the likelihood function for the case of singly censored data (see Equation A.7) may be useful in the estimation of confidence regions. The transformation simplifies the likelihood function by decoupling it into the product of two distributions. Although it produces other complications, the properties of the likelihood function under the transformation of variables should be investigated further.

The sample size and observation period required for a given confidence interval can be estimated using the tables in Appendix C. However, it may be possible to find empirically a simple relationship to estimate the confidence interval. Although we can depict the way the size of the confidence regions vary according to the four variables of interest (γ, q, N, and v; see Figures 9-3 and 9-4) and tabulate various contour points, a simple relationship would be much more useful in setting sample sizes and follow-up times for correctional evaluation studies.

Most significance tests are based on the normal and other tabulated distributions. However, because of the truncation of the joint density function at $\gamma = 1$, these tests cannot be used (except when the conditions noted in Chapter 9 and Figure 9-5 and 9-6 hold). Eyeballing, to see if two distributions appear to be distinct, might be useful, since the joint density functions can be depicted graphically. Other more formal tests may be more useful; among them are likelihood ratio tests and those based on Akaike's information criterion (Akaike, 1974). These other approaches should be explored.

The lack of success at using a covariate model in conjunction with Model M_1 should not foreclose this line of research. Other covariate approaches may be more appropriate for this particular model, and may provide the discrimination that was lacking in the approach described in Chapter 10. This is another research area that needs to be explored.

A FINAL CAUTION

It must be emphasized again that these methodological advances improve the utility of recidivism as a measure of effectiveness only to the extent that the measure is applicable. Improved statistical techniques are worthless if they are applied to inappropriate data or if the results are improperly interpreted. Sir Josiah Stamp's (1929: 258) caution about official statistics is quite appropriate:

> The individual source of the statistics may easily be the weakest link. Harold Cox tells a story of his life as a young man in India. He quoted some statistics to a Judge, an Englishman, and a very good fellow. His friend said, "Cox, when you are a bit older, you will not quote Indian statistics with that assurance. The Government are very keen on amassing statistics—they collect them, add them, raise them to the nth power, take the cube root and prepare wonderful diagrams. But what you must never forget is that every one of these figures comes in the first place from the *chowty dar* [village watchman], who just puts down what he damn pleases."

In this book we have prepared many "wonderful diagrams;" whether they have any significance (other than aesthetic) is in the hands of those who provide the data.

APPENDIX A

Parameter Estimation for Model M_I: The Incomplete Exponential Distribution

Equations 7.2 and 7.3 represent Model M_I, the incomplete exponential distribution, in continuous- and discrete-time versions, respectively. Equation 7.2 is the continuous-time version of M_I, the probability of an individual failing before time t:

$$P_I(t) = \gamma(1 - e^{-\phi t}) \qquad (A.1)$$

Equation 7.3 is the discrete-time version, the probability of an individual failing before the end of time interval[1] i:

$$P_I(i) = \gamma(1 - q^i) \qquad (A.2)$$

This appendix describes estimation of the parameters of Model M_I for both the continuous-time and discrete-time versions. Two estimation procedures are described: maximum likelihood and Bayesian. Maximum likelihood estimation produces modal estimates of the parameters; Bayesian estimation produces mean estimates, weighted according to prior knowledge of the parameters. Since the procedures are essentially the same for both versions, they will be fully explained for only the discrete-time version, in the first section of this appendix; the equivalent equations for the continuous-time version will be provided in the second section, with a prime (') appended to the equation number to key it to the appropriate equation in the first section. In addition, another model of offender behavior that gives rise to the same cumulative probability of recidivating (Equation A.1) as does Model M_I is described in the third section.

---
[1]All time intervals are assumed to be equal in length.

DISCRETE-TIME VERSION

In the following section the likelihood function for Model M_1 is derived and its characteristics described. The next section describes maximum likelihood estimation procedures for the general case and the following section describes them for the special case of singly censored data. Bayesian estimation procedures for the special case are derived in the last section.

The Likelihood Function for Model M_I

Equation A.2 describes the probability that an individual will fail before the end of time interval i, that is, before or in time interval i. The probability of failing in interval i is merely the probability of failing before or in interval i, less the probability of failing before or in interval $(i - 1)$:

$$p_F(i) = \gamma(1 - q^i) - \gamma(1 - q^{i-1}) = \gamma q^i(1 - q) \qquad (A.3)$$

where the subscript F denotes failure.

Note that $p_F(i)$ is the product of three terms: (1) γ, the probability that the individual is a recidivist; (2) q^{i-1}, the probability that the individual has not failed in the first $i - 1$ intervals; and (3) $1 - q$, the probability that he or she fails in the ith interval.

The probability that an individual has not failed by month i is given by

$$P_S(i) = (1 - \gamma) + \gamma q^i \qquad (A.4)$$

where the subscript S denotes success. The first term in Equation A.4 represents the probability that an individual is a nonrecidivist; the second term is the probability that he or she is an eventual recidivist who has gone through i months without yet failing.

Equations A.3 and A.4 are the building blocks of the likelihood function. We now assume that all individuals in the population under study act independently, so that the joint probability of individual successes and failures is just the product of the probabilities associated with each individual's success or failure.

Suppose we have data for v months, with k_i individuals failing in interval i and m_i individuals succeeding[2] through interval i, $i = 1, 2, \ldots, v$. The probability of obtaining these particular data k_i and m_i for a population with parameters γ and q is

$$P[\{k_i\}, \{m_i\}; \gamma, q] = \prod_{i=1}^{v} p_F(i)^{k_i} P_S(i)^{m_i}$$

[2]That is, observations for m_i individuals terminate (are "censored" or "truncated") in interval i without their having (yet) failed.

or, by using Equations A.3 and A.4 and combining terms,

$$P[\{k_i\}, \{m_i\}; \gamma, q] = \gamma^K q^{T-K}(1-q)^K \prod_{i=1}^{v}(1 - \gamma + \gamma q^i)^{m_i} \quad (A.5)$$

where $K = \Sigma k_i$ is the number of failures and $T = \Sigma i k_i$ is the total number of intervals experienced by the recidivists. This is the likelihood function of Model M_I. It may be written as $L_D(\gamma, q)$, where the subscript D denotes that this is the discrete-time version of the likelihood function.

L_D is defined only in the square region $\phi \leq \gamma \leq 1, 0 < q < 1$. It can readily be seen from Equation A.5 that L_D is zero along three sides of the unit square. Note also that this equation simplifies when the data are singly censored (i.e., truncated so that all nonfailures have their exposure times terminated in a single time interval, and so that no failure time exceeds this time interval). Then all of the m_i in Equation A.5 but the last are zero, and that last m_i, m_v, equals $N - K$, the number who have not (yet) recidivated. The likelihood function simplifies to

$$L_D(\gamma, q) = \gamma^K q^{T-K}(1-q)^K (1 - \gamma + \gamma q^v)^{N-K} \quad (A.6)$$

Note that for this model all of the data are summarized by two statistics that are characteristics of the study and by two statistics that result from the study: (1) N, the total number in the population under study, and v, the observation time for those who have not (yet) recidivated, are the study's characteristics; and (2) K, the number of failures in the population as of time interval v, and T, the total number of time intervals the failures were exposed before failing, are the study's "output." If these four "sufficient statistics" (Lindgren, 1976: 226) are given, the likelihood function (A.6) is completely specified.

Some of the properties of the likelihood function can be illustrated by considering a population of $(N =) 10$ individuals, of whom $(K =) 6$ fail—3 in the third time interval, 2 in the fourth interval, and 1 in the fifth interval. In this case T, the total number of exposure time intervals for the failures, is $(3 \times 3) + (2 \times 4) + (1 \times 5) = 22$ intervals.

The length of observation time chosen for the study—v—has a strong effect on the likelihood function. Figure A-1 shows its effect. In Figure A-1(a) the censoring time v is 24 months; in Figure A-1(b) it is 18 months; and in Figure A-1(c) it is 12 months. Figure A-1(a) can be approximated quite closely by a bivariate normal probability density function, which is useful for making confidence statements about parameter estimates (see Appendix B) or for testing hypotheses. The approximation is not as good for Figure A-1(b) and is unquestionably bad for Figure A-1(c); Figure A-2 depicts the difference between the actual likelihood function and the best-fitting bivariate normal probability density function for these three cases.

In all three cases, however, a local maximum exists; but this is not always

DISCRETE-TIME VERSION

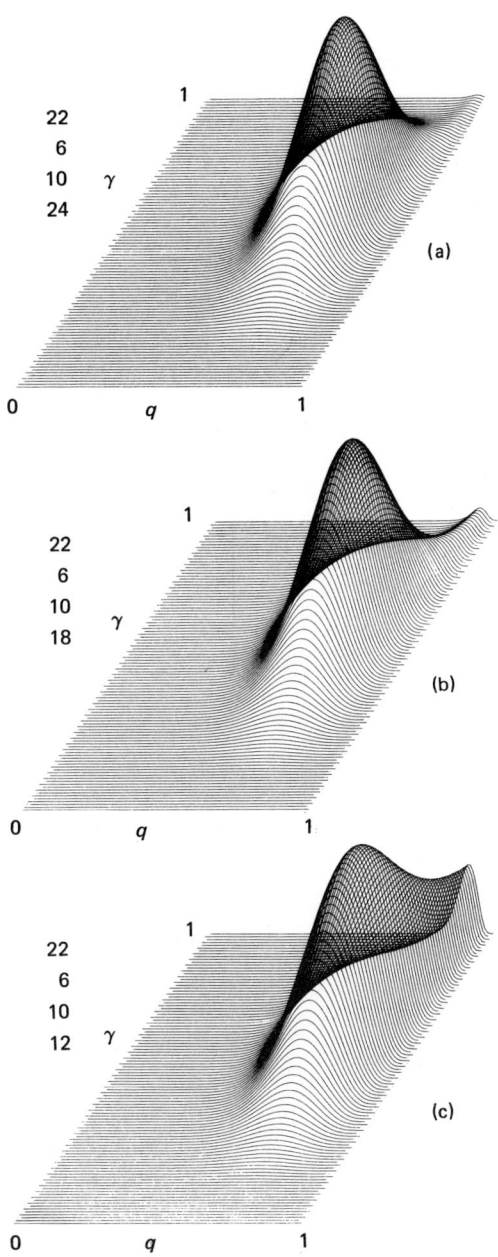

FIGURE A-1 Likelihood functions for $T = 22, K = 6, N = 10$: (a) $\nu = 24$, (b) $\nu = 18$, (c) $\nu = 12$.

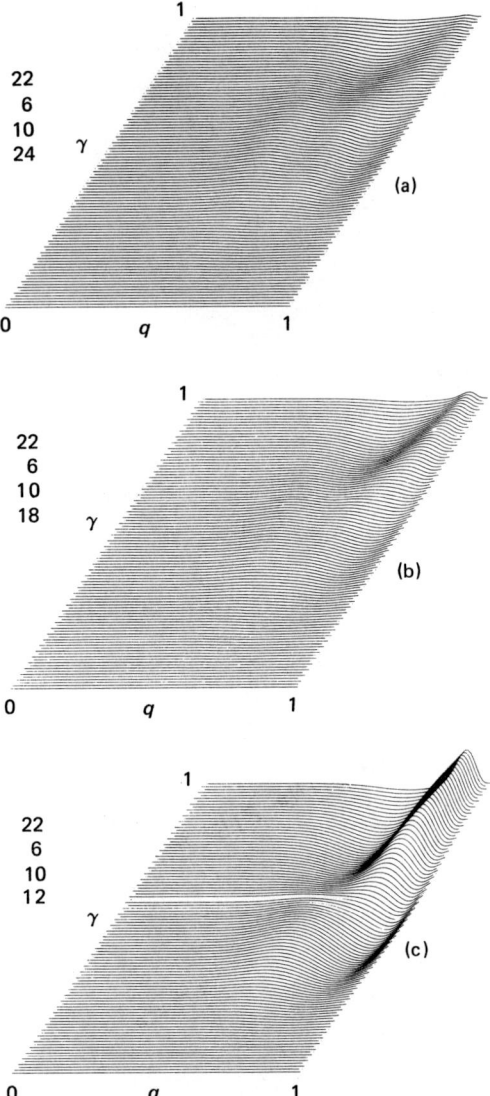

FIGURE A-2 Error associated with approximating the likelihood functions of Figre A-1 by a Normal Distribution, for $T = 22$, $K = 6$, $N = 10$: (a) $\nu = 24$; (b) $\nu = 18$; (c) $\nu = 12$.

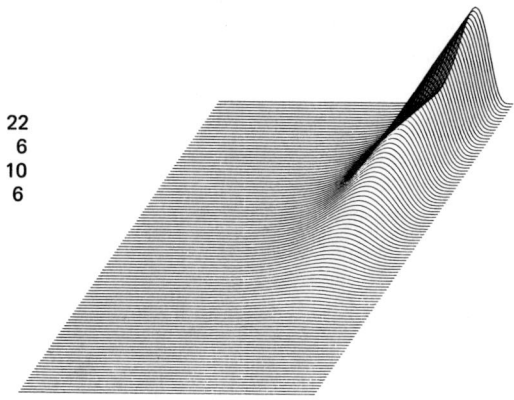

FIGURE A-3 Likelihood Function for $T = 22$, $K = 6$, $N = 10$, with $v = 6$.

true. Figure A-3 depicts the situation when the observation time v is reduced to six time intervals; in this case the maximum is on the border of the allowable region. Problems associated with this behavior of the likelihood function are discussed in the following section and in Appendix B.

A transformation of variables for the singly censored case "decouples" the likelihood function into the product of two functions (Anscombe, 1961). By defining

$$y = \gamma(1 - q^v) \tag{A.7}$$

Equation A.6 becomes

$$L'_D(y, q) = y^K(1 - y)^{N-K} \frac{q^{T-K}(1 - q)^K}{(1 - q^v)^K} \tag{A.8}$$

This is the product of a beta function [of the form $B(K + 1, N - K + 1)$; see Johnson & Kotz, 1970b: 37] and a function which is almost beta.[3] The beta function $B(a,b)$ is unimodal when a and b are greater than 1. Therefore, this transformation shows that there is at most one local maximum of the likelihood function.

Maximum Likelihood Estimation

The maximum of the likelihood function may be on the border of the allowable region, or it may be at an interior point. If it is on the border it must occur on the

---

[3] The right-hand side of Equation A.7 behaves like a beta function if the denominator is nearly constant within a few standard deviations of $q = 1 - K/T$. This is the case if K, T, and v are sufficiently large and if K/T is not very close to either 0 or 1.

line $\gamma = 1$, since L_D is zero on the other three borders (see Equation A.5). Substituting this into Equation A.5 results in

$$L_D(1, q) = q^{T-K}(1-q)^K \prod_{i=1}^{\nu} (q^i)^{m_i} = q^{S-K}(1-q)^K \qquad (A.9)$$

where $S = T + \Sigma \, im_i$. This is a beta function of the form $B(K+1, S-K+1)$. It is easy to verify that this function reaches its maximum value at $q = (S-K)/S$. From the definitions of S and T, we see that S is merely the sum total of all observation intervals, for both failures and successes.

If the maximum is at an interior point, the partial derivatives of the log likelihood function[4] with respect to γ and q are set to zero. Then the resulting equations are solved for γ and q. These values, denoted as $\hat{\gamma}$ and $\hat{q}$, are the maximum likelihood estimates of γ and q.[5]

The log likelihood function is, from Equation A.5,

$$l = \ln L_0 = K \ln \gamma + (T-K) \ln q + K \ln(1-q)$$

$$+ \sum_{i=1}^{\nu} m_i \ln(1 - \gamma + \gamma q^i)$$

The first partial derivatives are

$$l_\gamma = \frac{K}{\gamma} - \sum_{i=1}^{\nu} m_i \left(\frac{1-q^i}{1-\gamma+\gamma q^i} \right) \qquad (A.10)$$

$$l_q = \frac{T-K}{q} - \frac{K}{1-q} + \sum_{i=1}^{\nu} \frac{m_i \gamma i q^{i-1}}{1-\gamma+\gamma q^i} \qquad (A.11)$$

The maximum likelihood estimates $\hat{\gamma}$ and $\hat{q}$ set these two equations to zero. In general they can only be found by a series of approximations,[6] such as the Newton–Raphson procedure. In this procedure a Taylor series expansion is taken about the point γ, q. If we ignore higher-order terms, this results in

$$l_\gamma(\gamma + d\gamma, q + dq) = l_\gamma(\gamma, q) + l_{\gamma\gamma}(\gamma, q) \, d\gamma + l_{\gamma q}(\gamma, q) \, dq \qquad (A.12)$$

[4]The logarithm of the likelihood function has its maximum at the same point as does the likelihood function itself. The log likelihood function is used in maximum likelihood estimation procedures because it is often more tractable mathematically than the likelihood function.

[5]In analyzing the likelihood functions of a large number of diverse data sets, none as yet has been found to have more than one maximum. It should be noted that the likelihood function is nonnegative, so if only one point satisfies the equations it must be a maximum.

[6]The two equations can be solved analytically for a special case of interest; it is described on page 150.

$$l_q(\gamma + d\gamma, q + dq) = l_q(\gamma, q) + l_{\gamma q}(\gamma, q)d\gamma + l_{qq}(\gamma, q)dq \quad (A.13)$$

where the second partial derivatives are

$$l_{\gamma\gamma} = -\frac{K}{\gamma^2} - \sum m_i \left(\frac{1-q^i}{1-\gamma+\gamma q^i}\right)^2 \quad (A.14)$$

$$l_{\gamma q} = \sum \frac{m_i i q^{i-1}}{(1-\gamma+\gamma q^i)^2} \quad (A.15)$$

$$l_{qq} = -\frac{T-K}{q^2} - \frac{K}{(1-q)^2}$$

$$+ \sum m_i \left[\frac{\gamma i(i-1)q^{i-2}}{1-\gamma+\gamma q^i} - \left(\frac{\gamma i q^{i-1}}{1-\gamma+\gamma q^i}\right)^2\right] \quad (A.16)$$

We wish to choose $d\gamma$ and dq such that the left-hand sides of Equations A.12 and A.13 are zero. We therefore obtain

$$l_{\gamma\gamma}d\gamma + l_{\gamma q}dq = -l_\gamma$$
$$l_{\gamma q}d\gamma + l_{qq}dq = -l_q$$

where all partial derivatives are evaluated at γ, q. These equations can be solved for $d\gamma$ and dq to obtain

$$d\gamma = -(l_{qq}l_\gamma - l_{\gamma q}l_q)/\Delta$$
$$dq = -(-l_{\gamma q}l_\gamma + l_{\gamma\gamma}l_q)/\Delta$$

where

$$\Delta = l_{\gamma\gamma}l_{qq} - l_{\gamma q}^2$$

The new estimates become the old estimates incremented by $d\gamma$ and dq; that is, $\gamma + d\gamma \Rightarrow \gamma$ and $q + dq \Rightarrow q$. Since the Taylor series expansion ignored the effect of higher-order terms, the new values of γ and q do not necessarily set Equations A.12 and A.13 to zero. However, if the function is fairly regular, or if the starting point is sufficiently close to the maximum, iterating this process will cause it to converge rapidly to $\hat{\gamma}$, $\hat{q}$. It is repeated until the new estimates are sufficiently close to the previous ones (e.g., until $(d\gamma/\gamma)^2 + (dq/q)^2 < \epsilon$). A computer program to estimate $\hat{\gamma}$ and $\hat{q}$ is listed in Appendix D.

Note that the second partial derivatives of the log likelihood function are used in this estimation procedure. When evaluated at the maximum of the likelihood function, they are the components of the negative of the information matrix (Gross & Clark, 1975: 50). The inverse of this matrix is used to estimate the variance–covariance matrix. Therefore, after finding $\hat{\gamma}$ and $\hat{q}$ using this procedure the variance–covariance matrix is also estimated.[7]

Maximum Likelihood Estimation for Singly Censored Data

A special case of interest occurs when the data are singly censored at v. Equation A.6 is the likelihood function for this case, and the first partial derivatives of the log likelihood function are

$$l_\gamma = \frac{K}{\gamma} - (N - K)\left(\frac{1 - q^v}{1 - \gamma + \gamma q^v}\right) \quad \text{(A.17)}$$

$$l_q = \frac{T - K}{q} - \frac{K}{1 - q} + (N - K)\frac{\gamma v q^{v-1}}{1 - \gamma + \gamma q^v} \quad \text{(A.18)}$$

To find $\hat{\gamma}$ and $\hat{q}$ these two equations are set to zero. Algebraic manipulation of Equations A.17 and A.18 results in

$$\frac{1}{v(1 - \hat{q})} - \frac{1}{(\hat{q}^{-v} - 1)} = \frac{T}{Kv} = \frac{\bar{t}}{v} \overset{\Delta}{=} \alpha \quad \text{(A.19)}$$

$$\hat{\gamma} = \frac{K}{N(1 - \hat{q}^v)} \quad \text{(A.20)}$$

Equation A.19 can be solved for q; all that is needed for this calculation is the mean number of failure intervals $\bar{t}\,(= T/K)$ and the exposure time v. Their ratio α and the value of v completely determine the value of $\hat{q}$.

The relationship between α and $\hat{q}$ (Equation A.19) is plotted in Figure A-4 for different values of v. For values of α below .1 we can use the approximation $v(1 - q) = 1/\alpha$. It can also be shown that this equation is valid only for

$$1/v < \alpha < (1 + 1/v)/2. \quad \text{(A.21)}$$

Once $\hat{q}$ is known, $\hat{\gamma}$ can be obtained from Equation A.20. Comparing this equation with Equation A.2, we see that the maximum likelihood estimate solution is required to pass through the first and last data points.

Bayesian Estimation

Prior information about possible values of the model's parameters can be used in estimating the parameters of Model M_1, using a Bayesian approach. For the

---

[7]The fact that γ cannot exceed 1 means that the likelihood function may be truncated; therefore, the information matrix may be a poor estimator of the variance–covariance matrix, from which confidence regions are estimated. See Appendix B for an alternative means of obtaining confidence regions for maximum likelihood estimates.

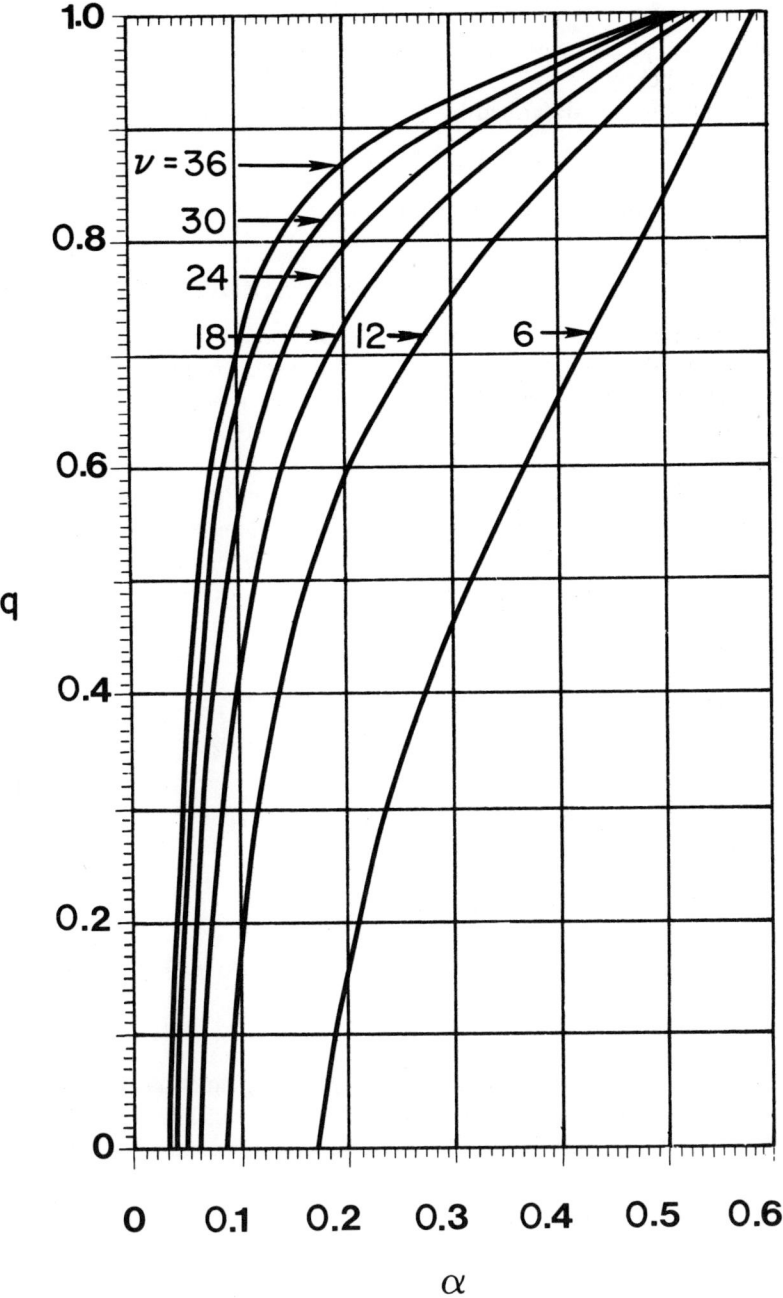

FIGURE A-4 Graph of $1/(\nu(1-q)) - 1/(q^{-\nu} - 1) = \alpha$.

special case of singly censored data the computations are easy to perform; they are described below.

Bayes's theorem is described by the following equation:

$$P(B|A) = P(A|B)P(A)/P(B) \tag{A.22}$$

If we consider B to be the model's parameters γ and q, and A to be the data, this becomes

$$f(\gamma, q|\text{data}) = P(\text{data}|\gamma, q)f^0(\gamma, q)/P(\text{data}) \tag{A.23}$$

That is, assume that we have prior information about the values of γ and q, as exemplified by the term $f^0(\gamma, q)$, the a priori joint probability density function of γ and q. The first term on the right is the probability of obtaining the data we did obtain, for given values of γ and q; this is merely the likelihood function, Equation A.6. The denominator on the right side, $P(\text{data})$, can be obtained by integrating the product of the likelihood function and the a priori joint density function over the entire range of γ and q. In performing these computations we obtain the a posteriori joint density function of γ and q, having taken into account the influence of our prior knowledge of γ and q and of the data.

The likelihood function for singly censored data (Equation A.6) can be rewritten as

$$L_D = \gamma^K q^{T-K}(1-q)^K(1-\gamma)^{N-K}\left[1 + \frac{\gamma}{1-\gamma}q^v\right]^{N-K} \tag{A.24}$$

The term in the brackets can be rewritten as a summation:

$$\left[1 + \frac{\gamma}{1-\gamma}q^v\right]^{N-K} = \sum_{i=0}^{N-K}\binom{N-K}{i}\left(\frac{\gamma}{1-\gamma}q^v\right)^i$$

so the likelihood function can be represented by

$$L_D(\gamma, q|N, v, K, T) = \sum_{i=0}^{N-K}\binom{N-K}{i}\gamma^{K+i}(1-\gamma)^{N-K-i}q^{T-K+iv}(1-q)^K \tag{A.25}$$

Assume that we have a prior joint probability density function (pdf) of γ and q, $f^0(\gamma, q)$. After observing the data (summarized by the sufficient statistics N, v, K and T), we wish to determine the posterior pdf $f(\gamma, q|N, v, K, T)$. From Bayes's theorem this is

$$f(\gamma, q|N, v, K, T) = CL_D(\gamma, q|N, v, K, T)f_0(\gamma, q) \tag{A.26}$$

where

$$\frac{1}{C} = \int_0^1\int_0^1 L_D(\gamma, q|N, v, K, T)f^0(\gamma, q)\,d\gamma\,dq \tag{A.27}$$

CONTINUOUS-TIME VERSION

If f^o, the prior pdf, is of the form

$$f^o(\gamma, q) = \left[\frac{\Gamma(a+b)}{\Gamma(a)\Gamma(b)}\gamma^{a-1}(1-\gamma)^{b-1}\right]\left[\frac{\Gamma(c+d)}{\Gamma(c)\Gamma(d)}q^{c-1}(1-q)^{d-1}\right]$$

that is, the product of two beta functions, then calculation of f, the posterior pdf, is simplified. The probability density function becomes

$$f(\gamma, q|N, v, K, T) = C\sum_{i=0}^{N-K}\binom{N-K}{i}\gamma^{K+i+a-1}(1-\gamma)^{N-K-i+b-1}$$

$$\times q^{T-K+iv+c-1}(1-q)^{K+d-1}$$

Estimates of the means and variances of γ and q can be obtained by integrating the appropriate function over the range of γ and q. The general equation is

$$E[\gamma^r q^s] = C\sum_{i=0}^{N-K}\binom{N-K}{i}\int_0^1\int_0^1 \gamma^{K+i+a+r-1}(1-\gamma)^{N-K-i+b-1}$$

$$\times q^{T-K+iv+c+s-1}(1-q)^{K+d-1}d\gamma dq \qquad (A.28)$$

This can be shown to be equal to

$$E[\gamma^r q^s] = C\sum_{i=0}^{N-K}\binom{N-K}{i}\frac{\Gamma(K+i+a+r)\Gamma(N-K-i+b)}{\Gamma(N+a+b+r)}$$

$$\times \frac{\Gamma(T-K+iv+c+s)\Gamma(K+d)}{\Gamma(T+iv+c+d+s)} \qquad (A.29)$$

Setting $r = 0$ and $s = 0$ results in the calculation of $1/C$; with $r = 1$, $s = 0$, the mean or expected value of γ is calculated; setting $r = 2$, $s = 0$ results in the expected value of γ^2, from which expected the variance of γ can be calculated; etc. Since the arguments all are (or can be) integers,[8] the terms in Equation A.29 are all factorials, which can easily be calculated.

CONTINUOUS-TIME VERSION

Likelihood Function

For the continuous-time version of Model M_I the probability of an individual failing at time t is given by

$$P_F(t) = \gamma(1 - e^{-\phi t}) \qquad (A.3')$$

[8] N, v, K and T are integers; r and s will be 0, 1, or 2 to calculate means and variances; and a, b, c and d, the parameters of the prior distribution, can be restricted to be integers as well. If a noninformative prior distribution (i.e., assuming no prior knowledge of γ and q) is used, then a, b, c and d are equal to 1, then $\bar{\gamma}$, the mean value of γ, is calculated using $r = 1$, $s = 0$; and $\bar{q}$, the mean value of q, is calculated using $r = 0$, $s = 1$.

and the probability of not failing through time t is given by

$$P_S(t) = 1 - \gamma + \gamma e^{-\phi t} \tag{A.4'}$$

The resulting likelihood function $L_C(\gamma, \phi)$, for the continuous-time version of Model M_I is, then,

$$L_C(\gamma, \phi) = \gamma^K \phi^K e^{-\phi T} \prod_{i=K+1}^{N} (1 - \gamma + \gamma e^{-\phi t_i}) \tag{A.5'}$$

where K is the number of failures; $T = \Sigma\, t_i$ is the sum of the failures' times to failure; and N is the total number in the cohort. [The last two terms in the likelihood function (Equation A.5') assume that the first K times are failure times and the last $N - K$ terms (from $K + 1$ to N) are censored observation times for the as-yet successes.]

L_C is defined in the semi-infinite strip $0 \leq \gamma \leq 1$, $\phi > 0$. From Equation A.5' it is seen that L_C is zero if γ or ϕ is zero.

Maximum Likelihood Estimation

To obtain $\hat{\gamma}$ and $\hat{\phi}$, the maximum likelihood estimates of γ and ϕ, we set the first partial derivatives of the log likelihood function to zero. The partial derivatives are

$$l_\gamma = \frac{K}{\gamma} - \sum_{i=K+1}^{N} \frac{1 - e^{-\phi t_i}}{1 - \gamma + \gamma e^{-\phi t_i}} \tag{A.10'}$$

and

$$l_\phi = \frac{K}{\phi} - T - \sum_{i=K+1}^{N} \frac{\gamma t_i e^{-\phi t_i}}{1 - \gamma + \gamma e^{-\phi t_i}} \tag{A.11'}$$

To drive them to zero the Newton–Raphson procedure is again used. The second partial derivatives in this case are

$$l_{\gamma\gamma} = -\frac{K}{\gamma^2} - \Sigma \left(\frac{1 - e^{-\phi t_i}}{1 - \gamma + \gamma e^{-\phi t_i}} \right)^2$$

$$l_{\gamma\phi} = -\Sigma \frac{t_i e^{-\phi t_i}}{(1 - \gamma + \gamma e^{-\phi t_i})^2}$$

$$l_{\phi\phi} = -\frac{K}{\phi^2} + \Sigma \frac{\gamma(1 - \gamma) t_i e^{-\phi t_i}}{(1 - \gamma + \gamma e^{-\phi t_i})^2}$$

CONTINUOUS-TIME VERSION

These equations and this procedure are used in the computer program listed in Appendix D. As before, the second partial derivatives can be used to estimate the variance–covariance matrix.[9]

If the maximum is not in the interior of the allowable region, it is on the border, along the line $\gamma = 1$. Substituting this value of γ into Equation A.5' results in

$$L_C = \phi^K e^{-\phi S} \qquad (A.9')$$

where $S = \sum_{i=1}^{N} t_i$, the sum of all times, both failure and exposure. This is a gamma distribution (Johnson & Kotz, 1970a: 166), for which the maximum likelihood estimate is $\phi = K/S$.

Maximum Likelihood Estimation for Singly Censored Data

If the data are singly censored at τ, the $N - K$ nonfailures all have the same exposure time τ, and Equation A.5' becomes

$$L_C = \gamma^K \phi^K e^{-\phi T}(1 - \gamma + \gamma e^{-\phi \tau})^{N-K} \qquad (A.6')$$

Four statistics completely determine this likelihood function, too: N, the total number in the population under study; τ, the censoring time, K, the total number of failures; and T, the total failure time of these K individuals.

The first partial derivatives of the log likelihood function are

$$l_\gamma = \frac{K}{\gamma} - (N - K)\frac{1 - e^{-\phi \tau}}{1 - \gamma + \gamma e^{-\phi \tau}} \qquad (A.17')$$

$$l_\phi = \frac{K}{\phi} - T - (N - K)\frac{\phi \tau e^{-\phi \tau}}{1 - \gamma + \gamma e^{-\phi \tau}} \qquad (A.18')$$

which can be algebraically reduced to

$$\frac{1}{x} - \frac{1}{e^x - 1} = \frac{T}{K\tau} = \frac{\bar{t}}{\tau} \triangleq \alpha \qquad (A.19')$$

where $x = \hat{\phi}\tau$, and

$$\hat{\gamma} = \frac{K}{N(1 - e^{-\hat{\phi}\tau})} \qquad (A.20')$$

As before, α is the ratio of mean failure time to censoring time; in this case it completely determines the maximum likelihood estimate $\hat{\phi}$. Equation A.19' is plotted in Figure A-5; for $\alpha < 0.1$ x can be approximated by $x = 1/\alpha$.

[9]With caution; see Note 7.

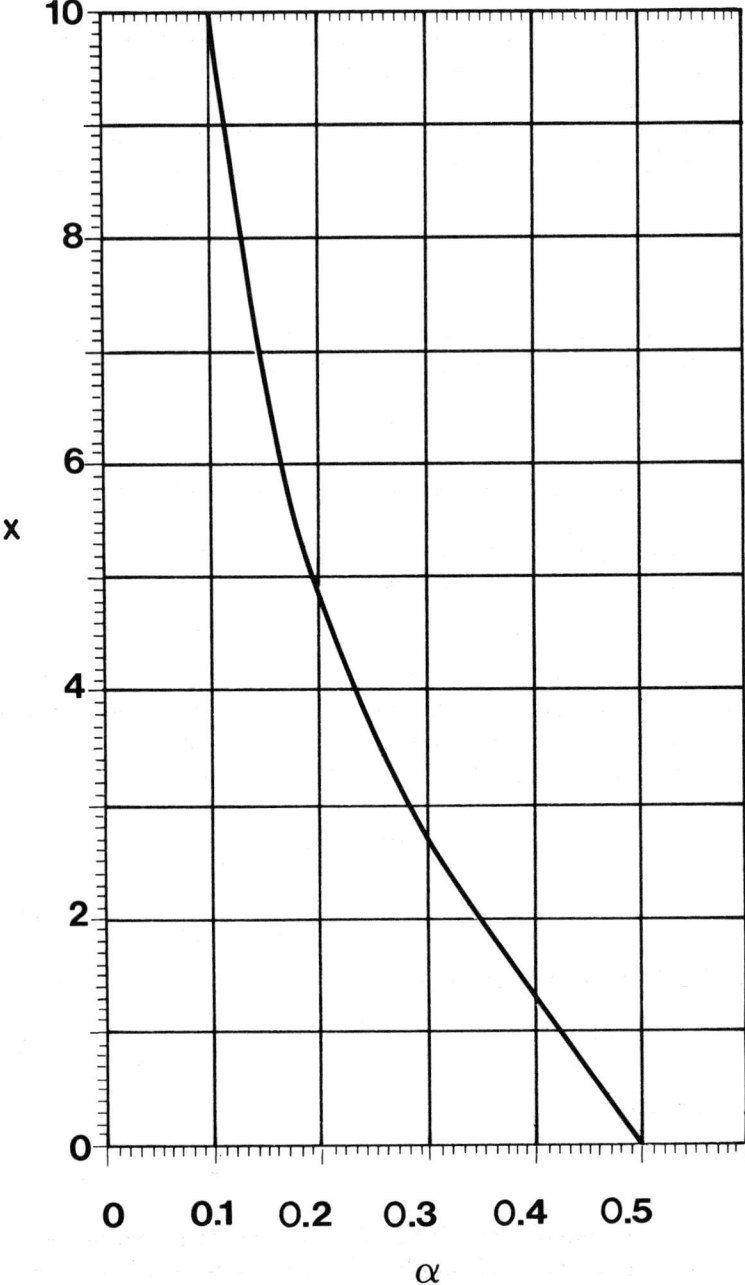

FIGURE A-5 Graph of $1/x - 1/(e^x - 1) = \alpha$.

THE "CRITICAL TIME" MODEL

$\hat{\gamma}$ is determined from Equation A.20'. As in the discrete-time case, the maximum likelihood estimate solution passes through the first and last data points.

Bayesian Estimation

Using the same approach as for the discrete-time version of Model M_I, the likelihood function for singly censored data (Equation A.6') can be represented by

$$L_C(\gamma, \phi | N, \tau, K, T) = \sum_{i=0}^{N-K} \binom{N-K}{i} \gamma^{K+i}(1-\gamma)^{N-K-i} \phi^K e^{-\phi(T+i\tau)}$$

(A.25')

This equation consists of terms which are all products of a beta function and a gamma function, which are, as before, easily calculated. If, as before, a, b, c and d are the parameters of the prior distribution,

$$f^0(\gamma, \phi) = \left[\frac{\Gamma(a+b)}{\Gamma(a)\Gamma(b)} \gamma^{a-1}(1-\gamma)^{b-1}\right]\left[\frac{d^c}{\Gamma(c)} \phi^{c-1} e^{-\phi d}\right]$$

the general equation becomes

$$E[\gamma^r \phi^s e^{-\phi u}] = C \sum_{i=0}^{N-K} \binom{N-K}{i} \frac{\Gamma(K+i+a+r)\Gamma(N-K-i+b)}{\Gamma(N+a+b+r)}$$

$$\times \frac{\Gamma(K+c+s)}{(T+i\tau+d+u)^{K+c+s}} \quad \text{(A.29')}$$

from which the appropriate moments can be calculated.

THE "CRITICAL TIME" MODEL OF RELEASEE BEHAVIOR

An alternative model of releasee behavior can be shown to produce cohort statistics that are operationally indistinguishable from Model M_I or Model M_M. Called a "critical time" model, it assumes that each individual in a cohort is subject to random failure at a constant failure rate until some critical time. After this time the individual's failure rate drops to a lower rate (also constant).[10]

In other words, if an individual can survive to the critical time without failing he or she is in some sense rehabilitated, and is thereafter subject to failure at the lower failure rate.

[10] If this lower failure rate is zero, then the critical time model is equivalent to Model M_I instead of Model M_M.

The derivation of this model for the discrete-time version is described first; the continuous-time model derivation follows.

The Discrete-Time Model

Assume that before time interval η the probability of not failing in the next time interval is w, and that in and after interval η the probability of not failing in the next interval becomes r, with $r > w$ (and $r = 1$ for Model M_1). Then the probability of failing in or before interval i is

$$P(i|\eta) = \begin{cases} 1 - w^i, & 0 < i \leq \eta \\ 1 - w^\eta r^{i-\eta}, & i > \eta \end{cases} \quad (A.30)$$

However, η is not known for any individual. Rather, we can consider η to be a random variable with some probability distribution $G(\eta)$. The unconditional probability distribution of time to failure then becomes

$$P(i) = \Sigma\, P(i/\eta)\, g(\eta)$$

where

$$g(\eta) = G(\eta) - G(\eta - 1)$$

If we assume that η is geometrically distributed, with parameter s, i.e., $G(\eta) = 1 - s^\eta$, then the probability density function becomes

$$g(\eta) = s^{\eta-1} - s^\eta = s^{\eta-1}(1 - s)$$

and the unconditional probability distribution for time to failure becomes

$$P(i) = \sum_{\eta=1}^{i} (1 - w^\eta r^{i-\eta}) s^{\eta-1}(1-s) + \sum_{\eta=i+1}^{\infty} (1 - w^i) s^{\eta-1}(1-s)$$

Since $\sum_{\eta=1}^{K} p^\eta = p(1 - p^K)/(1 - p)$, we obtain

$$P(i) = \gamma[1 - (ws)^i] + (1 - \gamma)(1 - r^i) \quad (A.31)$$

where $\gamma = (r - w)/(r - ws)$.

This equation is the geometric version of Model M_M, the mixed exponential distribution:

$$P(i) = \gamma(1 = q_1^i) + (1 - \gamma)(1 - q_2^i)$$

The relationship between the two sets of parameters is given by:

$$\gamma = \frac{r-w}{r-ws} \qquad w = \gamma q_1 + (1-\gamma)q_2$$

$$q_1 = ws \qquad r = q_2 \qquad (A.32)$$

$$q_2 = r \qquad s = \frac{q_1}{\gamma q_1 + (1-\gamma)q_2}$$

Continuous-Time Model

In this case let the critical time be denoted as θ. Then the conditional probability distribution of time to failure is

$$P(t|\theta) = \begin{cases} 1 - \exp(-\lambda_2 t), & 0 < t \le \theta \\ 1 - \exp[-(\lambda_1 - \lambda_2)\theta - \lambda_2 t], & t > \theta \end{cases} \qquad (A.30')$$

where λ_1 is an individual's (constant) failure rate until time θ, after which it is reduced to the lower failure rate λ_2—which is zero for Model M_1.

If θ is distributed exponentially, i.e., $g(\theta) = \mu \exp(-\mu\theta)$, we obtain

$$P(t) = \gamma(1 - \exp[-(\mu + \lambda_1)t]) + (1-\gamma)(1 - \exp(-\lambda_2 t)) \qquad (A.31')$$

This is identical to Equation 7.8, the mixed exponential model. The relationship between the two sets of parameters is given by

$$\phi_1 = \mu + \lambda_1, \qquad \lambda_1 = \gamma\phi_1 + (1-\gamma)\phi_2$$

$$\phi_2 = \lambda_2, \qquad \lambda_2 = \phi_2 \qquad (A.32')$$

$$\gamma = \frac{\lambda_1 - \lambda_2}{\mu + \lambda_1 - \lambda_2}, \qquad \mu = (1-\gamma)(\phi_1 - \phi_2)$$

APPENDIX B

Confidence Statements for Model M_I

This appendix explores the development of confidence regions for Model M_I. The first section discusses the concept of confidence intervals and regions in the context of this model. In the next section, the likelihood function is shown to be equivalent to the joint probability density function, for data sets with singly censored data; this permits the use of the likelihood function for making confidence statements. Extension of this ability for progressively censored data sets is discussed in the third section. The last section describes the use of a likelihood ratio test to determine whether a normal approximation to the joint density function can be used.

CONFIDENCE INTERVALS AND REGIONS

Empirical data can be used to estimate a model's parameters (Appendix A). It is also desirable to determine the reliability of the estimates, i.e., how much confidence can be placed in them. Most useful would be an interval within which a model's parameter is almost certain to be. For example, we then could state that, based on the data, (1) the best estimate of the parameter γ is .48 and (2) we are 95% confident that the true value of the parameter is in the interval .43 to .53.

However, this is not the way confidence statements are made. The data represent a single sample of the model's output, and this sample may be a highly unlikely one—that is, one found in one of the tails of the distribution. If, however, a large number of samples were drawn and intervals constructed for each of them, we could make a statement of confidence about the intervals, for example, that 95% of the intervals contained the parameter.

In other words, a confidence interval is *method*-based, not *data*-based. We can state, for example, that 95% of the intervals (constructed using an appropriate method) contain the true value of the parameter; we *cannot* state that we are 95% confident that the parameter is in a *particular* interval, based on one set of data (Mann *et al.*, 1974: 86).

A confidence *region* is an expansion of this concept to two dimensions. A 95% confidence region is one constructed from the data in such a way that, if the true parameters were known and if different data sets based on these parameters were generated, and a region constructed for each data set, 95% of these regions would contain the parameters. This explanation is graphically illustrated in the next section.

THE LIKELIHOOD FUNCTION AND THE JOINT DENSITY FUNCTION

Standard statistical practice for producing confidence intervals and regions is to assume that the model's parameters (obtained by maximum likelihood estimation) are asymtotically normally distributed,[1] and to use the information matrix to estimate the variance–covariance matrix of these parameters. However, the parameters γ and q of Model M_I are defined only in the unit square.[2] This restriction produces extreme non-normality for many cases of interest (see Figures A-1 to A-3 in Appendix A), which precludes us from using this technique.

Although we cannot use its asymptotic properties to estimate the joint probability density function of γ and q, the likelihood function itself can be used for estimation purposes. This can be demonstrated empirically.

Figures B-1 and B-2 show likelihood function contours for $\gamma = .75$, $q = .95$ and $\gamma = 1.0$, $q = .95$, respectively, for different values of observation time ($v = 12$ and 24) and sample size ($N = 100$ and 1000). Superimposed on the contours are the results of 100 simulations that use these values. That is, for Figure B-1(a) 100 cohorts were simulated, each having 100 persons, all of whom have $\gamma = .75$ and $q = .95$, all of whom are observed until failure or until $v = 12$. The four statistics (N, v, T, and K) for each of the 100 cohorts are calculated, and the maximum likelihood estimates of γ and q are made and depicted as a point on the figure. As can be seen from the figures, the likelihood function is the joint probability density function for all intents and purposes,[3] even when the likelihood function is far from normal.

The complicated shape of the likelihood function for Model M_I means that its confidence region cannot be described by a few parameters as can confidence regions for the normal distribution. Two approaches can be used to describe confidence regions for M_I. The first is actually to calculate (and plot) the con-

---

[1] If a joint probability density function is normal, its logarithm is a quadratic function centered on its maximum. By using the "asymptotic properties" of the likelihood function we are in essence expanding the logarithm of the likelihood function in a Taylor series about its maximum, and ignoring terms above second order. This gives us a quadratic equation that is used in an estimate of a normal probability density function. However, if the likelihood function does not resemble a normal distribution (i.e., if the higher order terms cannot be ignored), this approach cannot be used. This is the case with Model M_I.

[2] The discussion that follows refers to the discrete-time version of Model M_I. The same arguments apply for the continuous-time version.

[3] Except for a multiplicative constant. Normalizing the likelihood function to integrate to 1.0, however, produces the joint probability density function.

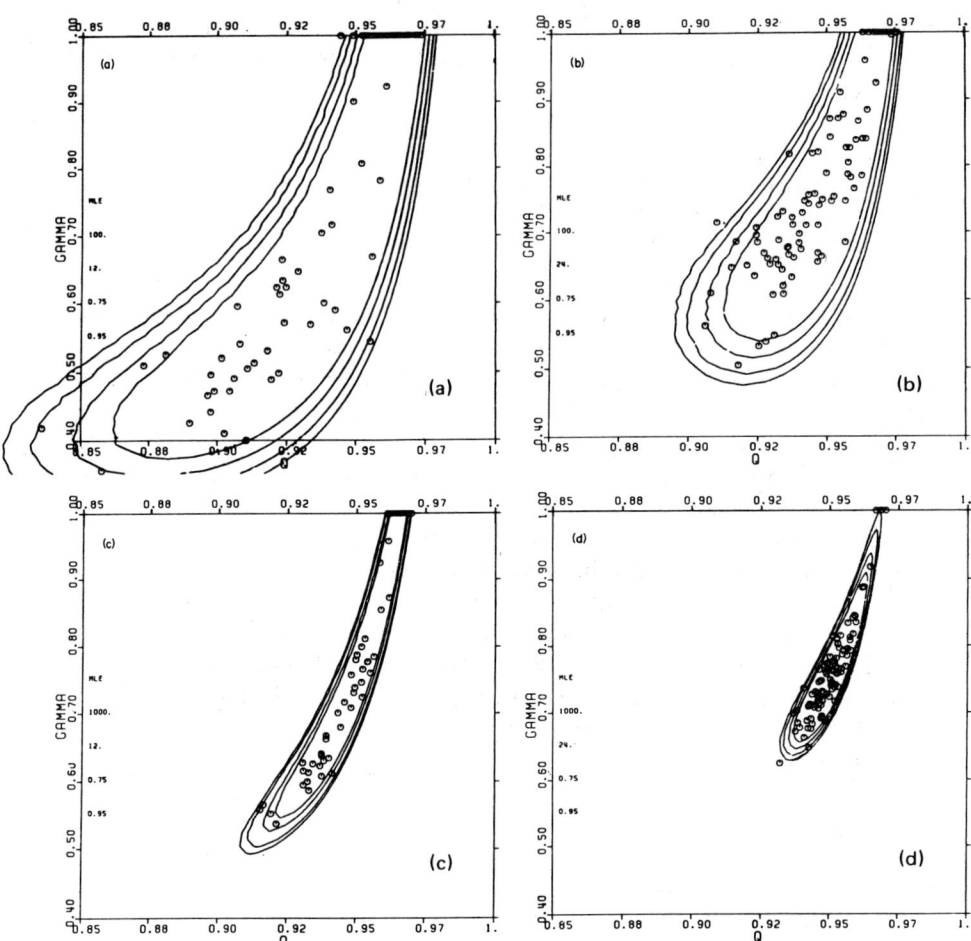

FIGURE B-1 Joint probability density function for singly censored data, $\gamma = 0.75$, $q = 0.95$, superimposed on maximum likelihood estimates of γ and q for 100 simulated cohorts: 90, 95, 98, and 99% contours shown. (a) $N = 100$ subjects, $\nu = 12$ months; (b) $N = 100$ subjects, $\nu = 24$ months; (c) $N = 1000$ subjects, $\nu = 12$ months; (d) $N = 1000$ subjects, $\nu = 24$ months.

tours of its likelihood function, as is done in Figures B-1 and B-2. This procedure is appropriate when analyzing a particular data set; in fact, the computer program that analyzes the data (Appendix D) contains an option to do just this. However, this procedure is not very helpful when trying to decide what the sample size or observation time should be—unless one had a book of the contours of all possible likelihood functions to leaf through. What would be more helpful for study design, that is, for selecting N and ν, would be tables that show the effect of these parameters on the confidence region.

The tables contained in Appendix C are an attempt to extract the most useful

THE LIKELIHOOD FUNCTION AND THE JOINT DENSITY FUNCTION 163

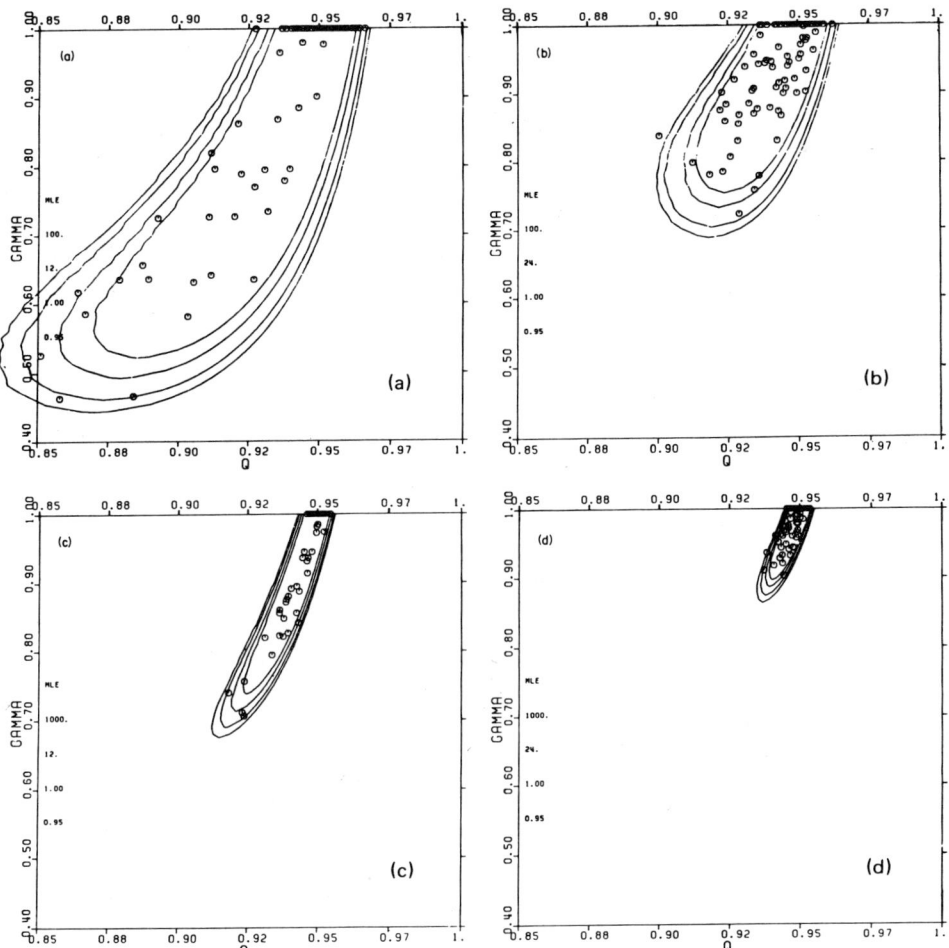

FIGURE B-2 Joint probability density function for singly censored data, $\gamma = 1.0$, $q = 0.95$, superimposed on maximum likelihood estimates of γ and q for 100 simulated cohorts: 90, 95, 98, and 99% contours shown. (a) $N = 100$ subjects, $\nu = 12$ months; (b) $N = 100$ subjects, $\nu = 24$ months; (c) $N = 1000$ subjects, $\nu = 12$ months; (d) $N = 1000$ subjects, $\nu = 24$ months.

information (for decision-making purposes) from the contours. Since the entire contour cannot be presented easily, only two points are tabulated for each contour: the maximum and minimum values of γ on a given contour. For Figure B-1(d), then, these values would be (approximately): 90%—.90 and .66; 95%—.93 and .65; 98%—.97 and .64; and 99%—1.0 and .63. Although knowledge of the confidence bounds that can be placed on q is also of importance (and should be included in any analysis of a study's data), for design purposes it is much more important to determine the confidence limits on the probability of recidivat-

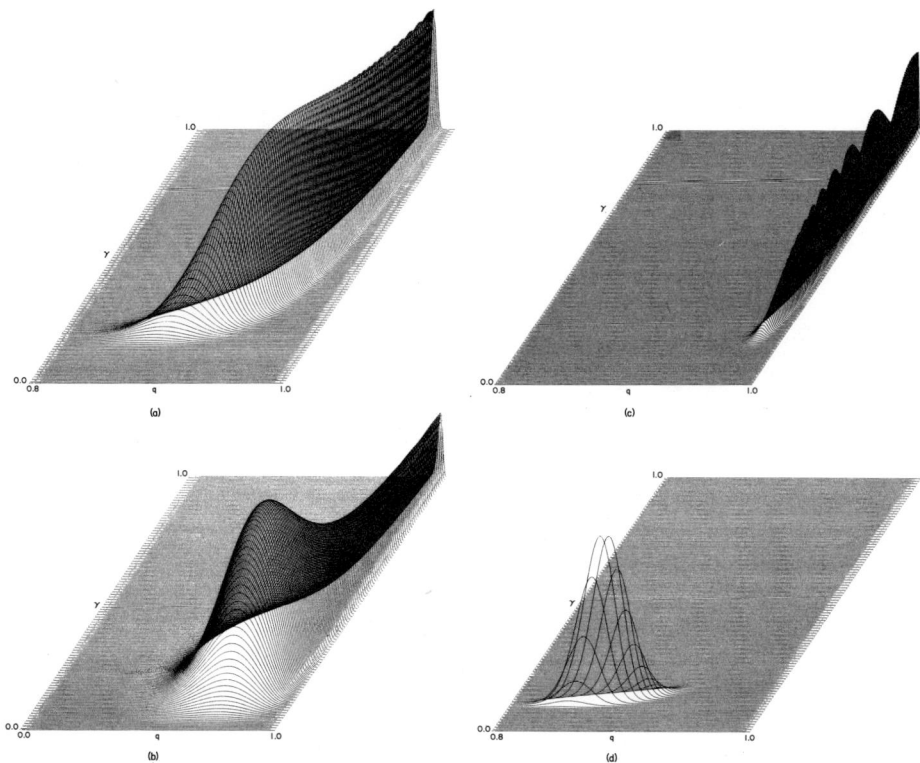

FIGURE B-3 Likelihood functions for the uniform parole report data listed in Table B-1: (a) Alabama, (b) Alaska, (c) District of Columbia, (d) Florida, (e) Georgia, (f) Idaho, (g) Illinois, (h) Iowa.

ing γ. Tables are provided in Appendix C for different values of γ that show the effect of sample size and number of observation intervals on the bounds of confidence in γ.

THE LIKELIHOOD FUNCTION AND PROGRESSIVELY CENSORED DATA

The fact that the (normalized) likelihood function is the joint probability density function means that confidence statements can be based on the likelihood function, despite its unusual shape in some cases. That the shape is not normal,

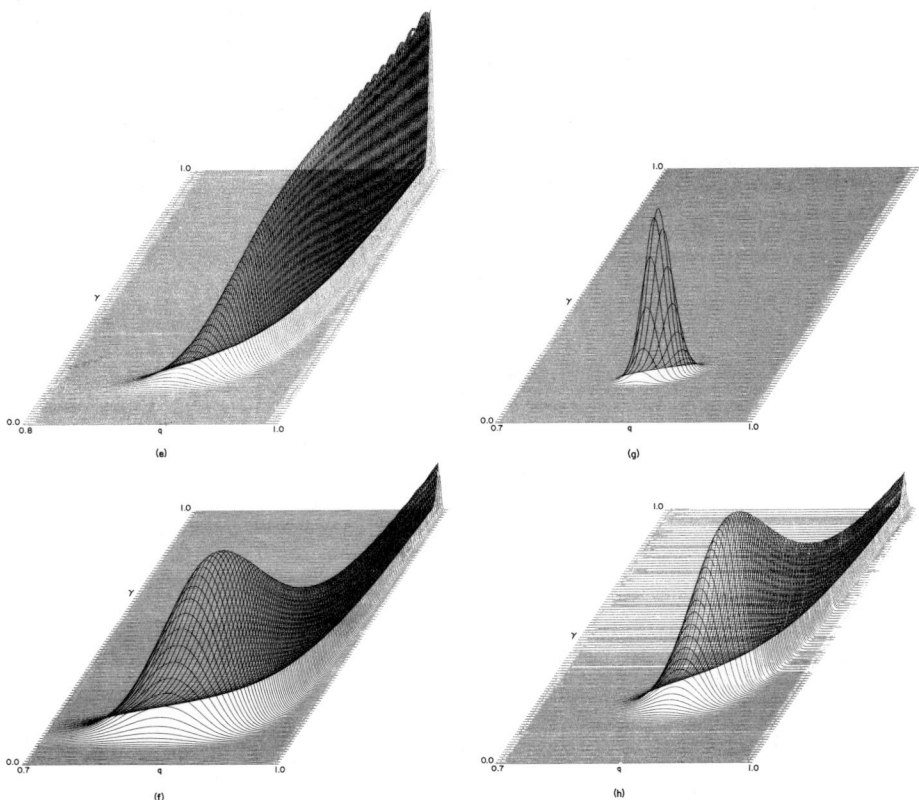

FIGURE B-3 (*Continued*)

or that it does not resemble any other tabulated distribution, means that standard confidence statements cannot be made, which is a disadvantage. But the fact that, when the data are simply censored, only four statistics (two based on the study design—N and ν—and two based on the output data—K and T) completely determine the probability density function, is a major advantage.

However, this advantage holds only if the data are singly censored. If the data are progressively censored this advantage is lost: all of the censoring (or observation) times—the m_i in Equation A.5 of Appendix A—must be used to describe the likelihood function. Of benefit would be a likelihood function for a singly censored problem that is sufficiently similar to the progressively censored likelihood function that it can be substituted for the actual likelihood function.

Fortunately, this can be done. For example, Table B-1 lists data obtained from

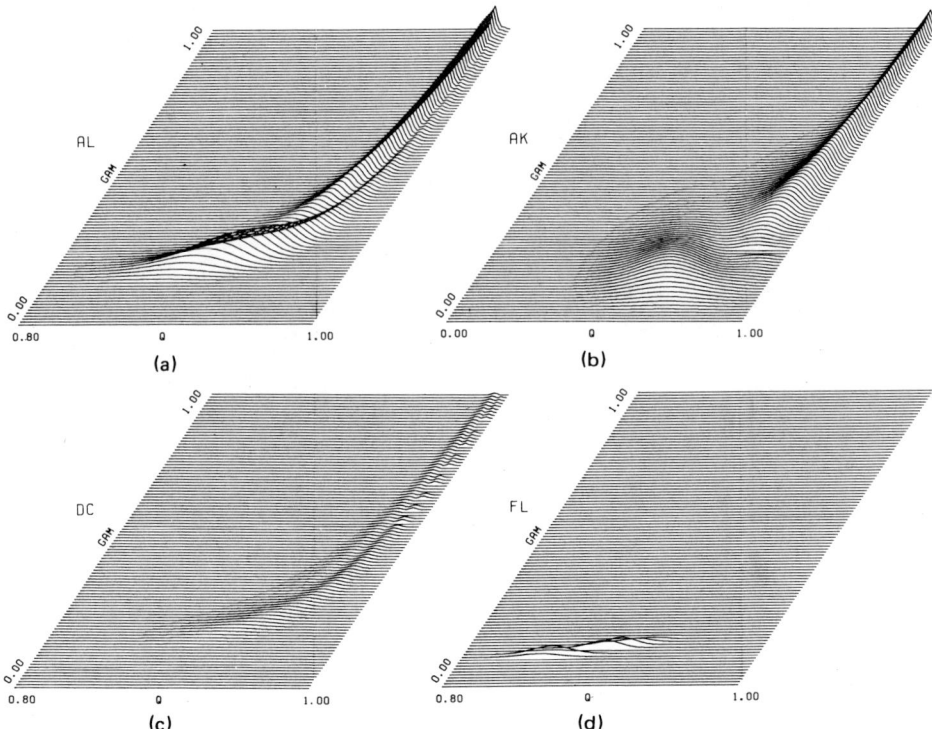

FIGURE B-4 The discrepancies between the likelihood functions of Figure B-3 and their singly censored "equivalents": (a) Alabama, (b) Alaska, (c) District of Columbia, (d) Florida, (e) Georgia, (f) Idaho, (g) Illinois, (h) Iowa.

12-month follow-ups of parolees in a number of states, obtained from the Uniform Parole Reporting Program. Figure B-3 depicts the likelihood functions for these data sets; this figure also gives an indication of the variety found in shapes of likelihood functions.[4] Figure B-4 depicts the difference between these likelihood functions and their singly censored "equivalents"; as can be seen, not much accuracy is lost if the singly censored likelihood function is used in place of the actual likelihood function.

The procedure to find the singly censored equivalent of a progressively censored likelihood function is as follows. Four statistics completely determine the likelihood function for singly censored data; therefore, four quantities from the progressively censored problem must be set equal to four quantities from the singly censored problem to obtain the singly censored equivalent. Two of these

[4]The "scalloping" in the likelihood function for Georgia is due to the step size used to plot this figure and is not a feature of its likelihood function, which is actually smooth.

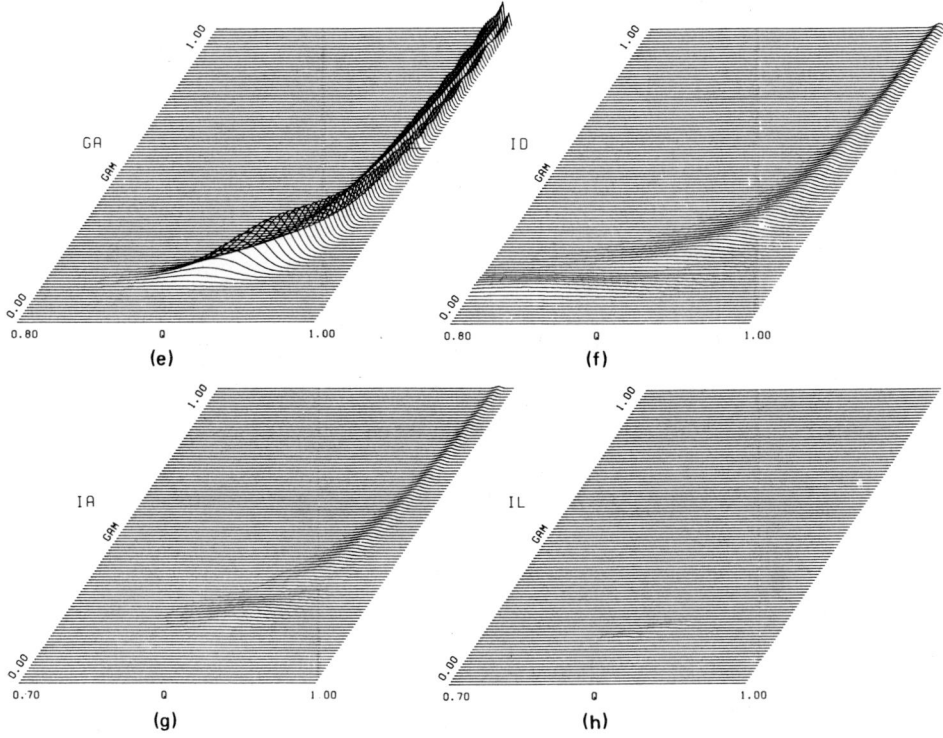

FIGURE B-4 (*Continued*)

are self-evident; we set γ and q for the progressively censored likelihood function equal to γ and q for the singly censored problem so that the peaks are at the same point. A third self-evident quantity is N: the singly censored equivalent should have the same sample size at the progressively censored problem.

The best choice for the fourth quantity is $l_{\gamma\gamma}$, the second partial derivative of the log likelihood function with respect to γ, evaluated at $\hat{\gamma}, \hat{q}$. This quantity is a measure of the curvature of the likelihood function in γ, and therefore is a good indicator of how the likelihood function varies in this direction.

The four quantities, then, are N, $\hat{\gamma}$, $\hat{q}$ and $l_{\gamma\gamma}$. It can easily be shown (by taking the partial derivative of Equation A.17 or A.17′ with respect to γ and evaluating it at $l_\gamma = 0$) that

$$l_{\gamma\gamma} = -\frac{NK}{(N-K)\hat{\gamma}^2} \tag{B.1}$$

Then the four equations to define the singly censored equivalent of the actual likelihood function are:

$$N = .N \tag{B.2}$$

$$K = \frac{N\hat{\gamma}^2 l_{\gamma\gamma}}{N + \hat{\gamma}^2 l_{\gamma\gamma}} \quad \text{(from B.1)} \tag{B.3}$$

$$v = \frac{\ln\left(1 - \dfrac{K}{N\gamma}\right)}{\ln \hat{q}} \quad \text{(from A.18)} \tag{B.4}$$

$$T = Kv\left[\frac{1}{v(1-\hat{q})} - \frac{1}{(\hat{q}^{-v}-1)}\right] \quad \text{(from A.20)} \tag{B.5}$$

For the continuous-time version of Model M_I the last two equations become

$$\tau = \frac{-\ln\left(1 - \dfrac{K}{N\hat{\gamma}}\right)}{\hat{\phi}} \tag{B.4'}$$

$$T = K\tau\left[\frac{1}{\hat{\phi}\tau} - \frac{1}{e^{\hat{\phi}\tau}-1}\right] \tag{B.5'}$$

TABLE B-1

12-Month Follow-up Data Reported by Selected States to the Uniform Parole Reporting Program[a]

State		1	2	3	4	5	6	7	8	9	10	11	12
Alabama	F	5	4	7	5	7	7	3	5	8	0	1	1
	X	1	4	5	10	11	16	14	20	12	14	12	175
Alaska	F	1	0	1	1	1	1	1	0	0	0	0	0
	X	0	0	1	2	1	0	0	2	0	0	0	14
D.C.	F	2	5	2	6	6	4	10	6	4	4	1	1
	X	1	6	4	1	0	4	5	2	4	2	3	254
Florida	F	36	26	37	38	35	24	20	29	16	4	3	2
	X	5	4	16	19	54	59	56	59	68	62	57	2160
Georgia	F	3	7	4	8	7	6	8	3	2	1	3	1
	X	2	13	24	47	46	29	23	16	20	17	14	208
Idaho	F	2	5	0	2	3	2	3	5	0	1	0	0
	X	1	0	1	1	0	1	2	4	2	2	4	144
Illinois	F	61	40	42	35	40	24	20	19	10	16	17	7
	X	2	3	0	3	1	2	2	1	2	6	2	1838
Iowa	F	5	7	6	8	5	6	5	2	5	3	2	2
	X	0	1	0	0	1	2	1	0	2	2	5	193

[a] F = number of people who failed in each month. X = number of people who were exposed for that many months without failing. (For further details see Maltz, 1981b: 183–190.)

LIKELIHOOD RATIO TEST FOR THE NORMAL APPROXIMATION

Using these relationships, one can convert a progressively censored problem into a singly censored problem. This will permit use of the tables in Appendix C and the likelihood ratio test described in the following section.

LIKELIHOOD RATIO TEST FOR THE NORMAL APPROXIMATION

When the likelihood function is approximately normal, standard confidence statements and hypothesis tests can be used to analyze the data. At which point "approximately normal" holds it somewhat arbitrary, as Figures A-1 and A-2 of Appendix A graphically illustrate. For the purposes of this discussion the point is determined by a likelihood ratio test. The value (height) of the likelihood function is calculated both at its maximum and at the highest point along the line $\gamma =$

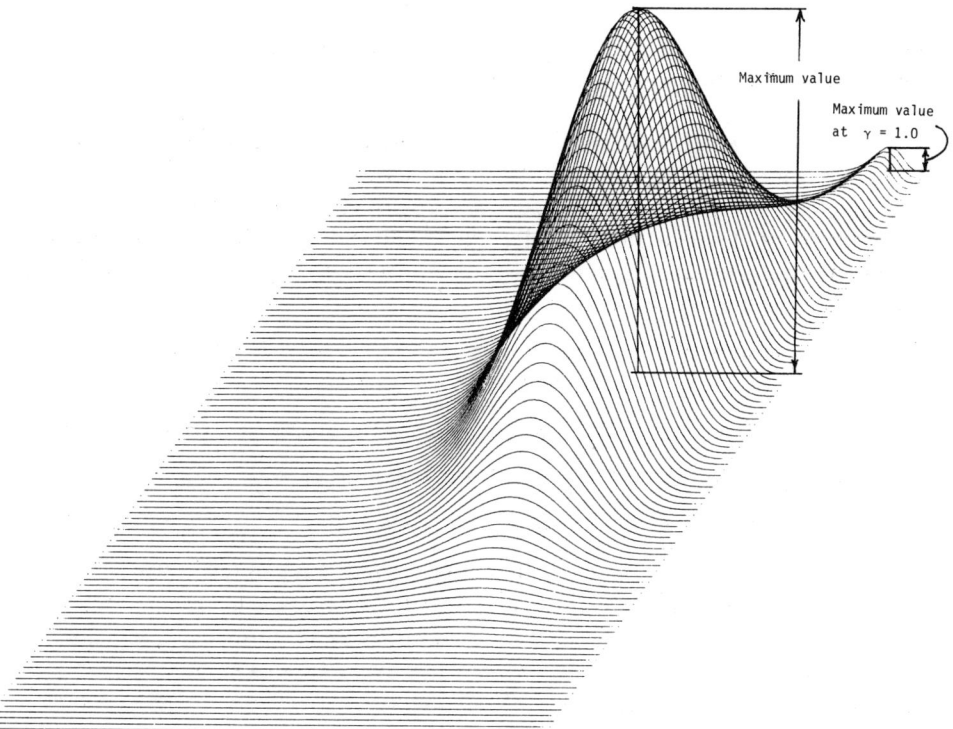

FIGURE B-5 Values of the likelihood function for model M_1 used for the likelihood ratio test.

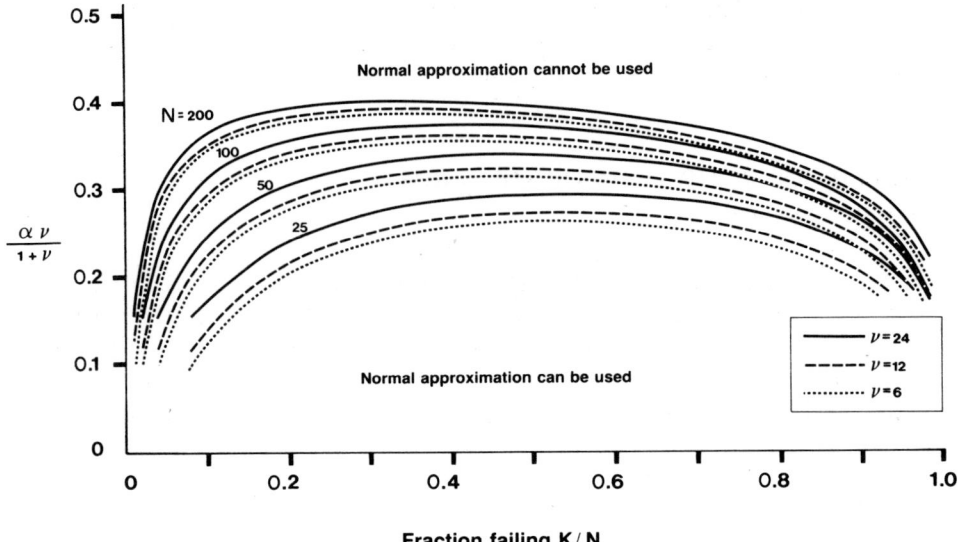

FIGURE B-6 Region in which a normal distribution is a good approximation to the joint density function of γ and q: discrete version of Model M_I.

1.0; see Figure B-5. If the ratio of the two heights is greater than 20,[5] the likelihood function is considered sufficiently normal.

Equations A.6 and A.9 of Appendix A (or A.6' and A.9' for the continuous-time version of M_I) are used to calculate the likelihood ratio. Their logarithms are taken and evaluated at $\hat{\gamma}$, $\hat{q}$ and 1, $S/(S + K)$, respectively (or at $\hat{\gamma}$, $\hat{\phi}$, and 1, K/S). The resulting equation is

$$K \ln(K/N) + (N - K) \ln(1 - K/N) + (T - K) \ln(\hat{q})$$
$$+ K \ln [(1 - \hat{q})/(1 - \hat{q}^v)]$$
$$- K \ln(K/S) - (S - K) \ln(1 - K/S) = \ln(20) = 2.996 \quad (B.6)$$

$$K \ln(K/N) + (N - K) \ln(1 - K/N) + K \ln[\hat{\phi}/(1 - e^{-\hat{\phi}\tau})] - \hat{\phi}T$$
$$- K \ln(K/S) - K = \ln(20) = 2.996 \quad (B.6')$$

Solutions to these equations are plotted in Figures B-6 and B-7, respectively, for different values of N. Note in Figure B-6 that the greater the number of observation intervals v, the larger the region in which the normal approximation can be used. For the continuous version, however, the maximum observation time τ has little effect; in fact, Figure B-7 represents the solution to Equation B.6' for $\tau = 10$ and $\tau = 500$, which are indistinguishable.

[5]The likelihood ratio for the likelihood function depicted in Figure B-5 is 15.

SUMMARY

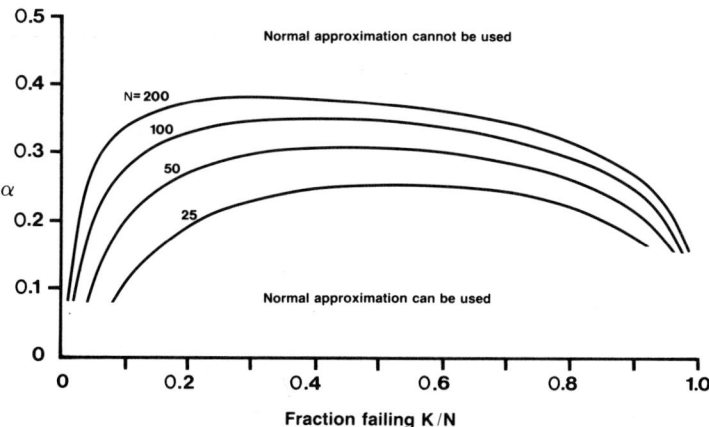

FIGURE B-7 Region in which a normal distribution is a good approximation to the joint density function of γ and ϕ: continuous version of Model M_I.

SUMMARY

This appendix describes the manner in which confidence regions for Model M_I are described. Progressively censored data sets can be handled by converting them into singly censored equivalents. This permits the analyst to use the tables in Appendix D—or to determine whether the normal approximation can be used, by using Figure B-6 or B-7.

APPENDIX C

Tables for Estimating Sample Size and Length of Observation Period

USING THE TABLES

The tables in this appendix show the relationship between confidence interval and study parameters. For example, from the first table we see that for a 24-month study of 324 subjects, in which the probability of recidivism γ is .2, we are 90% confident that the actual probability of recidivism is between .142 and .360, for a confidence interval of $(.360 - .142) = .218$. Were we to increase the observation period ν to 30 months, the 90% confidence interval would shrink to .135.

Another way to reduce the confidence interval is to increase the size of the population under study. Increasing it to 400 subjects, while keeping the observation period at 24 months, reduces the confidence interval from .218 to $(.322 - .147) = .175$. Thus we see that there are two ways to reduce the confidence interval: increasing the size of the population under study, or increasing the length of time for which it is studied.

Note that the confidence intervals for γ are asymmetric about the nominal value of .2; for $N = 324$ and $\nu = 24$ it stretches from .058 below .2 to .160 above .2. This asymmetry is even more pronounced around the upper left corner of the table, since the confidence interval is truncated at 1.00—γ cannot be greater than 1. It is for this reason that the tables give the upper and lower bounds of the confidence intervals, so that this asymmetry is not ignored.

These tables are predicted on the assumption that about 90% of all eventual recidivists will have recidivated within about 30 months.[1] This assumption is largely supported by the available data (see Figures 8-3 to 8-9), but is not always the case; for example, in Figure 8-1 it appears to be about 9 years, and in Figure 8-2, 6 years appears to be more appropriate. For cases in which it is felt that the 90% point will be reached earlier or later, one can adjust the interval size. For

---

[1]This assumption results in a value of q of .93, since $.93^{30} = .11$.

example, suppose that 90% of the eventual recidivists are expected to recidivate within 72 months. These tables can still be used, but instead of each interval representing one month, each interval will represent 72/30 = 2.4 months.

Note that intervals between the tables' rows are evenly spaced (6, 12, 18, etc.) but the intervals between the columns (16, 36, 64, etc) are not. In fact, the spacing between columns is even *for the square root of the number of subjects* (4, 6, 8, etc.). The reason for this is that the confidence interval varies approximately with $N^{-1/2}$. Using the square root of N permits the tables to include a greater range of population size without much loss of accuracy; they can readily be used to interpolate graphically, as is shown in the example below.

TRADING OFF BETWEEN POPULATION SIZE AND OBSERVATION TIME: AN EXAMPLE

You wish to run a correctional experiment that estimates the probability of eventually recidivating (γ) to within 20% (remember: because of asymmetry this does not mean ±10%), with 90% confidence. You are not certain about the expected value of γ, but expect that it will fall between .3 and .5 for the population you are studying. What size of population and length of observation time should be used?

Start with the table for $\gamma = .3$, confidence level = .90. Note that for $\nu = 18$ intervals (i.e., months) a sample size of 484 subjects will provide a confidence interval of (.225, .529), or .304. Therefore, the observation time must be greater than 18 months.[2]

At 24 months we see that the confidence interval for $N = 400$ is .236, .419), or .183 and for $N = 324$ it is .218, so we know what the number of subjects is between 324 and 400. Figure C-1(a) is a hand-drawn sketch of these points as well as those for $N = 256$ and $N = 484$ (the solid line). Curves are plotted for $\nu = 30$ and $\nu = 36$ with $\gamma = .3$, as well as for $\gamma = .4$ and $\gamma = .5$ for these three values of ν. The points at which these curves cross .2 are represented by the vertical lines, indicating the values of $N^{1/2}$ for which the confidence interval is .2.[3]

Figure C-1(b) summarizes the results of the graphical interpolation of Figure C-1(a). The three curves in this figure show the trade-off between the size of the population under study and the length of observation time for the three different values of γ. If the best guess for γ is .4, then the researcher can obtain a 20%

---

[2]Or the size of the population under study must be greater than 484 subjects, which is quite large for a correctional study.

[3]The curves would be more linear if the confidence intervals were plotted against $N^{-1/2}$ instead of $N^{1/2}$. However, since we are only producing estimates, the added accuracy is not that important.

confidence interval by observing 388 (= 19.7^2) people for 24 months, or 228 people for 30 months, or 161 people for 36 months. The trade-off between population size and observation time is thus made abundantly clear.

If for this study it is expected that 90% of the failures will fail by the fifth year, then the observation times should be adjusted to reflect this. Each of the observa-

GAMMA = .2
CONFIDENCE LEVEL = .90

NO. OF INTERVALS	NO. OF SUBJECTS									
	16	36	64	100	144	196	256	324	400	484
6	.009	.023	.035	.045	.053	.060	.066	.071	.075	.079
	1.000	1.000	1.000	1.000	1.000	1.000	1.000	1.000	1.000	1.000
12	.025	.051	.070	.084	.094	.102	.109	.114	.119	.123
	1.000	1.000	1.000	1.000	1.000	1.000	1.000	1.000	1.000	1.000
18	.037	.068	.089	.103	.114	.122	.127	.132	.136	.140
	1.000	1.000	1.000	1.000	1.000	1.000	1.000	.869	.611	.491
24	.045	.078	.099	.112	.121	.128	.136	.142	.147	.151
	1.000	1.000	1.000	1.000	1.000	.593	.429	.360	.322	.300
30	.049	.082	.102	.115	.125	.135	.142	.148	.153	.157
	1.000	1.000	1.000	.757	.434	.344	.304	.283	.270	.261
36	.051	.084	.103	.117	.129	.139	.146	.151	.156	.159
	1.000	1.000	.844	.408	.322	.289	.272	.262	.254	.249

GAMMA = .2
CONFIDENCE LEVEL = .95

NO. OF INTERVALS	NO. OF SUBJECTS									
	16	36	64	100	144	196	256	324	400	484
6	.005	.017	.029	.038	.047	.053	.059	.064	.069	.073
	1.000	1.000	1.000	1.000	1.000	1.000	1.000	1.000	1.000	1.000
12	.017	.040	.059	.075	.086	.095	.102	.107	.112	.116
	1.000	1.000	1.000	1.000	1.000	1.000	1.000	1.000	1.000	1.000
18	.026	.057	.078	.094	.105	.114	.121	.126	.130	.134
	1.000	1.000	1.000	1.000	1.000	1.000	1.000	1.000	1.000	.689
24	.033	.066	.088	.103	.114	.122	.129	.135	.141	.146
	1.000	1.000	1.000	1.000	1.000	1.000	.589	.436	.369	.331
30	.037	.070	.093	.107	.118	.127	.135	.142	.147	.152
	1.000	1.000	1.000	1.000	.617	.414	.340	.306	.286	.273
36	.039	.072	.094	.108	.121	.131	.139	.145	.150	.154
	1.000	1.000	1.000	.574	.371	.313	.287	.273	.264	.257

CONFIDENCE INTERVAL TABLES   175

tion periods mentioned in the last paragraph should be multiplied by 60/30 (see the preceding section, so that for $N = 388$ the observation period is 48 months, for N 228 it is 60 months, and for $N = 161$ it is 72 months. *(Figure C-1 is on page 190.)*

GAMMA = .2
CONFIDENCE LEVEL = .98

NO. OF INTERVALS	NO. OF SUBJECTS									
	16	36	64	100	144	196	256	324	400	484
6	.002	.011	.022	.031	.039	.047	.052	.058	.062	.066
	1.000	1.000	1.000	1.000	1.000	1.000	1.000	1.000	1.000	1.000
12	.010	.031	.050	.064	.076	.086	.093	.100	.105	.110
	1.000	1.000	1.000	1.000	1.000	1.000	1.000	1.000	1.000	1.000
18	.017	.045	.067	.084	.096	.106	.113	.119	.124	.129
	1.000	1.000	1.000	1.000	1.000	1.000	1.000	1.000	1.000	1.000
24	.023	.054	.077	.093	.106	.115	.122	.128	.134	.139
	1.000	1.000	1.000	1.000	1.000	1.000	1.000	.612	.456	.388
30	.026	.058	.081	.098	.110	.119	.127	.135	.140	.146
	1.000	1.000	1.000	1.000	1.000	.577	.409	.343	.312	.292
36	.028	.060	.084	.099	.112	.123	.131	.138	.144	.149
	1.000	1.000	1.000	1.000	.487	.357	.313	.290	.276	.267

GAMMA = .2
CONFIDENCE LEVEL = .99

NO. OF INTERVALS	NO. OF SUBJECTS									
	16	36	64	100	144	196	256	324	400	484
6	.001	.009	.018	.027	.035	.042	.048	.054	.058	.062
	1.000	1.000	1.000	1.000	1.000	1.000	1.000	1.000	1.000	1.000
12	.007	.026	.044	.059	.070	.080	.088	.095	.100	.105
	1.000	1.000	1.000	1.000	1.000	1.000	1.000	1.000	1.000	1.000
18	.013	.038	.060	.077	.090	.100	.108	.115	.120	.125
	1.000	1.000	1.000	1.000	1.000	1.000	1.000	1.000	1.000	1.000
24	.017	.046	.070	.087	.100	.110	.118	.123	.129	.135
	1.000	1.000	1.000	1.000	1.000	1.000	1.000	.861	.567	.441
30	.020	.050	.075	.091	.105	.114	.122	.130	.136	.141
	1.000	1.000	1.000	1.000	1.000	.820	.488	.383	.334	.309
36	.021	.053	.077	.094	.106	.117	.127	.134	.140	.145
	1.000	1.000	1.000	1.000	.647	.404	.333	.304	.286	.274

APPENDIX C

GAMMA = .3
CONFIDENCE LEVEL = .90

NO. OF INTERVALS	\multicolumn{10}{c}{NO. OF SUBJECTS}
	16	36	64	100	144	196	256	324	400	484
6	.023	.047	.067	.081	.093	.103	.111	.119	.125	.131
	1.000	1.000	1.000	1.000	1.000	1.000	1.000	1.000	1.000	1.000
12	.057	.098	.125	.144	.159	.170	.179	.187	.193	.198
	1.000	1.000	1.000	1.000	1.000	1.000	1.000	1.000	1.000	1.000
18	.082	.128	.157	.177	.189	.199	.206	.213	.219	.225
	1.000	1.000	1.000	1.000	1.000	1.000	.885	.698	.600	.529
24	.095	.144	.172	.189	.201	.212	.221	.229	.236	.241
	1.000	1.000	1.000	1.000	.732	.567	.490	.447	.419	.402
30	.104	.151	.177	.195	.210	.221	.231	.238	.244	.249
	1.000	1.000	1.000	.608	.485	.434	.405	.387	.375	.367
36	.108	.153	.179	.200	.216	.227	.235	.242	.248	.253
	1.000	1.000	.611	.467	.417	.393	.379	.369	.360	.354

GAMMA = .3
CONFIDENCE LEVEL = .95

NO. OF INTERVALS	\multicolumn{10}{c}{NO. OF SUBJECTS}
	16	36	64	100	144	196	256	324	400	484
6	.015	.038	.056	.071	.083	.093	.102	.110	.116	.122
	1.000	1.000	1.000	1.000	1.000	1.000	1.000	1.000	1.000	1.000
12	.043	.083	.111	.132	.147	.159	.169	.177	.184	.190
	1.000	1.000	1.000	1.000	1.000	1.000	1.000	1.000	1.000	1.000
18	.064	.111	.142	.163	.178	.190	.198	.205	.211	.217
	1.000	1.000	1.000	1.000	1.000	1.000	1.000	.931	.740	.625
24	.077	.127	.158	.178	.192	.202	.212	.221	.228	.234
	1.000	1.000	1.000	1.000	1.000	.703	.564	.494	.452	.426
30	.084	.135	.165	.184	.199	.212	.222	.230	.237	.242
	1.000	1.000	1.000	.808	.563	.472	.431	.408	.391	.380
36	.088	.138	.167	.188	.205	.218	.227	.234	.240	.246
	1.000	1.000	.838	.533	.447	.413	.393	.381	.371	.363

GAMMA = .3
CONFIDENCE LEVEL = .98

NO. OF INTERVALS	16	36	64	100	NO. OF SUBJECTS 144	196	256	324	400	484
6	.009	.028	.046	.061	.073	.083	.092	.100	.106	.112
	1.000	1.000	1.000	1.000	1.000	1.000	1.000	1.000	1.000	1.000
12	.030	.067	.096	.118	.134	.147	.158	.166	.174	.180
	1.000	1.000	1.000	1.000	1.000	1.000	1.000	1.000	1.000	1.000
18	.047	.094	.126	.149	.166	.178	.189	.197	.203	.209
	1.000	1.000	1.000	1.000	1.000	1.000	1.000	1.000	1.000	.803
24	.059	.109	.142	.165	.181	.193	.202	.211	.219	.226
	1.000	1.000	1.000	1.000	1.000	1.000	.706	.575	.506	.464
30	.066	.117	.150	.172	.187	.201	.212	.221	.228	.234
	1.000	1.000	1.000	1.000	.720	.545	.473	.435	.412	.396
36	.070	.121	.153	.175	.193	.207	.218	.226	.233	.239
	1.000	1.000	1.000	.669	.499	.442	.411	.395	.383	.374

GAMMA = .3
CONFIDENCE LEVEL = .99

NO. OF INTERVALS	16	36	64	100	NO. OF SUBJECTS 144	196	256	324	400	484
6	.006	.023	.040	.055	.067	.077	.086	.094	.100	.106
	1.000	1.000	1.000	1.000	1.000	1.000	1.000	1.000	1.000	1.000
12	.023	.058	.087	.109	.126	.140	.151	.160	.167	.174
	1.000	1.000	1.000	1.000	1.000	1.000	1.000	1.000	1.000	1.000
18	.038	.083	.116	.140	.158	.171	.182	.191	.198	.204
	1.000	1.000	1.000	1.000	1.000	1.000	1.000	1.000	1.000	.982
24	.048	.098	.132	.156	.173	.187	.196	.205	.214	.220
	1.000	1.000	1.000	1.000	1.000	1.000	.858	.654	.551	.498
30	.055	.106	.140	.164	.180	.194	.206	.215	.223	.229
	1.000	1.000	1.000	1.000	.915	.616	.508	.458	.429	.409
36	.058	.110	.144	.167	.185	.200	.211	.221	.228	.234
	1.000	1.000	1.000	.840	.552	.467	.428	.407	.392	.381

GAMMA = .4
CONFIDENCE LEVEL = .90

NO. OF INTERVALS	16	36	64	100	NO. OF SUBJECTS 144	196	256	324	400	484
6	.042	.076	.102	.121	.137	.149	.161	.171	.179	.187
	1.000	1.000	1.000	1.000	1.000	1.000	1.000	1.000	1.000	1.000
12	.097	.151	.186	.210	.229	.242	.254	.263	.270	.277
	1.000	1.000	1.000	1.000	1.000	1.000	1.000	1.000	1.000	1.000
18	.134	.194	.231	.254	.270	.281	.290	.299	.306	.313
	1.000	1.000	1.000	1.000	1.000	1.000	.868	.741	.669	.620
24	.157	.217	.251	.272	.287	.300	.311	.320	.327	.333
	1.000	1.000	1.000	.978	.746	.642	.582	.547	.524	.507
30	.169	.227	.259	.281	.299	.313	.323	.331	.337	.343
	1.000	1.000	.887	.662	.576	.533	.509	.492	.480	.472
36	.174	.231	.264	.288	.306	.319	.329	.336	.342	.348
	1.000	1.000	.659	.561	.521	.499	.484	.473	.465	.458

GAMMA = .4
CONFIDENCE LEVEL = .95

NO. OF INTERVALS	16	36	64	100	NO. OF SUBJECTS 144	196	256	324	400	484
6	.030	.063	.089	.108	.124	.137	.148	.158	.167	.175
	1.000	1.000	1.000	1.000	1.000	1.000	1.000	1.000	1.000	1.000
12	.077	.130	.168	.194	.213	.228	.241	.251	.259	.266
	1.000	1.000	1.000	1.000	1.000	1.000	1.000	1.000	1.000	1.000
18	.111	.173	.212	.238	.257	.270	.280	.289	.297	.304
	1.000	1.000	1.000	1.000	1.000	1.000	1.000	.884	.766	.691
24	.132	.196	.234	.259	.275	.288	.300	.310	.318	.325
	1.000	1.000	1.000	1.000	.913	.735	.639	.586	.553	.530
30	.143	.208	.244	.267	.287	.301	.313	.321	.329	.336
	1.000	1.000	1.000	.776	.631	.568	.533	.512	.496	.484
36	.149	.213	.248	.275	.294	.309	.319	.328	.335	.340
	1.000	1.000	.776	.606	.546	.516	.498	.485	.475	.468

GAMMA = .4
CONFIDENCE LEVEL = .98

NO. OF INTERVALS	\multicolumn{10}{c}{NO. OF SUBJECTS}
	16	36	64	100	144	196	256	324	400	484
6	.020	.050	.075	.095	.111	.124	.135	.145	.154	.162
	1.000	1.000	1.000	1.000	1.000	1.000	1.000	1.000	1.000	1.000
12	.058	.111	.149	.176	.197	.213	.226	.238	.247	.255
	1.000	1.000	1.000	1.000	1.000	1.000	1.000	1.000	1.000	1.000
18	.087	.151	.192	.221	.241	.257	.269	.279	.286	.293
	1.000	1.000	1.000	1.000	1.000	1.000	1.000	1.000	.927	.808
24	.106	.174	.215	.243	.263	.277	.289	.299	.308	.316
	1.000	1.000	1.000	1.000	1.000	.888	.731	.647	.596	.563
30	.117	.186	.227	.253	.273	.289	.302	.312	.320	.327
	1.000	1.000	1.000	1.000	.726	.621	.567	.536	.516	.500
36	.124	.192	.231	.259	.280	.297	.309	.318	.326	.332
	1.000	1.000	1.000	.688	.586	.541	.516	.500	.488	.479

GAMMA = .4
CONFIDENCE LEVEL = .99

NO. OF INTERVALS	\multicolumn{10}{c}{NO. OF SUBJECTS}
	16	36	64	100	144	196	256	324	400	484
6	.015	.042	.067	.086	.103	.116	.128	.137	.147	.155
	1.000	1.000	1.000	1.000	1.000	1.000	1.000	1.000	1.000	1.000
12	.047	.099	.137	.165	.187	.204	.218	.229	.239	.247
	1.000	1.000	1.000	1.000	1.000	1.000	1.000	1.000	1.000	1.000
18	.073	.137	.180	.210	.231	.248	.261	.272	.280	.287
	1.000	1.000	1.000	1.000	1.000	1.000	1.000	1.000	1.000	.908
24	.090	.159	.203	.232	.254	.269	.281	.292	.301	.309
	1.000	1.000	1.000	1.000	1.000	1.000	.818	.699	.633	.592
30	.102	.171	.215	.244	.263	.281	.294	.305	.314	.321
	1.000	1.000	1.000	1.000	.825	.665	.595	.556	.531	.513
36	.107	.177	.221	.248	.271	.288	.301	.311	.320	.327
	1.000	1.000	1.000	.772	.621	.562	.530	.511	.497	.486

GAMMA = .5
CONFIDENCE LEVEL = .90

NO. OF INTERVALS	NO. OF SUBJECTS									
	16	36	64	100	144	196	256	324	400	484
6	.065	.109	.140	.164	.182	.198	.212	.224	.234	.244
	1.000	1.000	1.000	1.000	1.000	1.000	1.000	1.000	1.000	1.000
12	.141	.208	.249	.280	.300	.318	.331	.342	.350	.358
	1.000	1.000	1.000	1.000	1.000	1.000	1.000	1.000	1.000	1.000
18	.194	.266	.308	.335	.354	.367	.378	.387	.396	.403
	1.000	1.000	1.000	1.000	1.000	1.000	.907	.819	.762	.720
24	.225	.296	.336	.359	.376	.391	.403	.413	.420	.427
	1.000	1.000	1.000	.981	.820	.732	.682	.650	.628	.611
30	.242	.312	.347	.372	.391	.406	.417	.426	.433	.439
	1.000	1.000	.906	.746	.675	.636	.612	.596	.584	.575
36	.250	.317	.354	.382	.400	.414	.424	.433	.439	.445
	1.000	.980	.740	.658	.622	.600	.586	.575	.567	.560

GAMMA = .5
CONFIDENCE LEVEL = .95

NO. OF INTERVALS	NO. OF SUBJECTS									
	16	36	64	100	144	196	256	324	400	484
6	.049	.091	.123	.147	.167	.183	.197	.209	.219	.229
	1.000	1.000	1.000	1.000	1.000	1.000	1.000	1.000	1.000	1.000
12	.117	.184	.228	.259	.283	.301	.315	.327	.337	.345
	1.000	1.000	1.000	1.000	1.000	1.000	1.000	1.000	1.000	1.000
18	.165	.242	.288	.317	.338	.354	.366	.376	.385	.392
	1.000	1.000	1.000	1.000	1.000	1.000	1.000	.925	.841	.783
24	.194	.273	.317	.344	.363	.379	.392	.402	.411	.418
	1.000	1.000	1.000	1.000	.938	.805	.732	.686	.656	.634
30	.212	.288	.330	.357	.378	.394	.407	.416	.424	.431
	1.000	1.000	1.000	.832	.722	.667	.635	.614	.599	.588
36	.220	.296	.336	.366	.388	.403	.414	.423	.430	.437
	1.000	1.000	.824	.698	.646	.619	.600	.588	.578	.570

GAMMA = .5
CONFIDENCE LEVEL = .98

NO. OF INTERVALS	NO. OF SUBJECTS									
	16	36	64	100	144	196	256	324	400	484
6	.035	.075	.106	.131	.151	.167	.181	.193	.204	.213
	1.000	1.000	1.000	1.000	1.000	1.000	1.000	1.000	1.000	1.000
12	.092	.160	.206	.239	.263	.283	.299	.311	.323	.332
	1.000	1.000	1.000	1.000	1.000	1.000	1.000	1.000	1.000	1.000
18	.134	.215	.264	.298	.322	.339	.353	.364	.373	.381
	1.000	1.000	1.000	1.000	1.000	1.000	1.000	1.000	.966	.874
24	.162	.246	.296	.327	.349	.365	.378	.390	.400	.408
	1.000	1.000	1.000	1.000	1.000	.921	.809	.739	.696	.666
30	.179	.263	.310	.340	.363	.380	.394	.405	.414	.421
	1.000	1.000	1.000	.974	.795	.713	.667	.637	.618	.604
36	.188	.271	.317	.348	.372	.390	.403	.413	.421	.428
	1.000	1.000	.980	.760	.682	.642	.618	.603	.591	.581

GAMMA = .5
CONFIDENCE LEVEL = .99

NO. OF INTERVALS	NO. OF SUBJECTS									
	16	36	64	100	144	196	256	324	400	484
6	.027	.065	.096	.121	.141	.158	.171	.184	.195	.205
	1.000	1.000	1.000	1.000	1.000	1.000	1.000	1.000	1.000	1.000
12	.077	.145	.192	.226	.252	.272	.288	.301	.313	.323
	1.000	1.000	1.000	1.000	1.000	1.000	1.000	1.000	1.000	1.000
18	.117	.197	.249	.285	.310	.329	.344	.356	.366	.374
	1.000	1.000	1.000	1.000	1.000	1.000	1.000	1.000	1.000	.953
24	.144	.228	.281	.315	.339	.356	.370	.382	.392	.401
	1.000	1.000	1.000	1.000	1.000	1.000	.873	.784	.728	.690
30	.158	.245	.297	.330	.352	.371	.386	.398	.407	.415
	1.000	1.000	1.000	1.000	.863	.750	.692	.656	.633	.616
36	.167	.254	.304	.336	.362	.380	.395	.406	.415	.422
	1.000	1.000	1.000	.820	.711	.661	.632	.613	.599	.589

APPENDIX C

GAMMA = .6
CONFIDENCE LEVEL = .90

NO. OF INTERVALS	16	36	64	100	NO. OF SUBJECTS 144	196	256	324	400	484
6	.090	.143	.180	.208	.230	.250	.265	.279	.292	.305
	1.000	1.000	1.000	1.000	1.000	1.000	1.000	1.000	1.000	1.000
12	.192	.268	.317	.350	.375	.395	.409	.422	.433	.442
	1.000	1.000	1.000	1.000	1.000	1.000	1.000	1.000	1.000	1.000
18	.259	.342	.389	.420	.441	.457	.468	.478	.487	.494
	1.000	1.000	1.000	1.000	1.000	1.000	.978	.910	.861	.823
24	.300	.383	.426	.452	.469	.485	.498	.507	.516	.522
	1.000	1.000	1.000	1.000	.904	.829	.782	.754	.731	.716
30	.322	.401	.441	.467	.488	.502	.514	.523	.530	.536
	1.000	1.000	.965	.837	.773	.738	.714	.698	.687	.677
36	.335	.409	.448	.478	.498	.512	.523	.531	.537	.543
	1.000	1.000	.830	.757	.722	.701	.687	.676	.668	.661

GAMMA = .6
CONFIDENCE LEVEL = .95

NO. OF INTERVALS	16	36	64	100	NO. OF SUBJECTS 144	196	256	324	400	484
6	.070	.122	.160	.189	.212	.231	.247	.261	.274	.286
	1.000	1.000	1.000	1.000	1.000	1.000	1.000	1.000	1.000	1.000
12	.161	.242	.292	.329	.355	.376	.392	.406	.418	.428
	1.000	1.000	1.000	1.000	1.000	1.000	1.000	1.000	1.000	1.000
18	.224	.313	.366	.400	.424	.442	.455	.466	.475	.483
	1.000	1.000	1.000	1.000	1.000	1.000	1.000	.997	.931	.879
24	.264	.353	.404	.435	.456	.471	.485	.496	.505	.513
	1.000	1.000	1.000	1.000	.996	.894	.830	.788	.759	.738
30	.288	.376	.422	.451	.473	.489	.503	.513	.521	.528
	1.000	1.000	1.000	.908	.818	.768	.737	.717	.701	.690
36	.299	.386	.430	.462	.484	.500	.512	.521	.529	.535
	1.000	1.000	.898	.792	.745	.719	.701	.688	.678	.670

GAMMA = .6
CONFIDENCE LEVEL = .98

NO. OF INTERVALS	16	36	64	100	144	196	256	324	400	484
6	.052	.102	.141	.170	.193	.212	.229	.243	.256	.267
	1.000	1.000	1.000	1.000	1.000	1.000	1.000	1.000	1.000	1.000
12	.131	.213	.267	.305	.333	.356	.373	.388	.401	.411
	1.000	1.000	1.000	1.000	1.000	1.000	1.000	1.000	1.000	1.000
18	.189	.283	.340	.378	.404	.425	.440	.453	.463	.471
	1.000	1.000	1.000	1.000	1.000	1.000	1.000	1.000	1.000	.958
24	.227	.324	.379	.416	.440	.457	.471	.483	.493	.502
	1.000	1.000	1.000	1.000	1.000	.986	.896	.837	.797	.769
30	.249	.346	.400	.433	.456	.475	.490	.501	.510	.519
	1.000	1.000	1.000	1.000	.880	.810	.768	.740	.721	.706
36	.261	.358	.410	.443	.468	.486	.500	.510	.519	.527
	1.000	1.000	1.000	.847	.778	.741	.719	.703	.691	.681

GAMMA = .6
CONFIDENCE LEVEL = .99

NO. OF INTERVALS	16	36	64	100	144	196	256	324	400	484
6	.042	.090	.129	.158	.182	.201	.218	.232	.245	.257
	1.000	1.000	1.000	1.000	1.000	1.000	1.000	1.000	1.000	1.000
12	.113	.195	.251	.290	.319	.342	.362	.377	.390	.401
	1.000	1.000	1.000	1.000	1.000	1.000	1.000	1.000	1.000	1.000
18	.167	.264	.324	.363	.392	.413	.430	.444	.455	.464
	1.000	1.000	1.000	1.000	1.000	1.000	1.000	1.000	1.000	1.000
24	.202	.304	.364	.402	.428	.448	.462	.475	.486	.495
	1.000	1.000	1.000	1.000	1.000	1.000	.948	.876	.825	.792
30	.224	.327	.384	.421	.445	.466	.481	.493	.504	.512
	1.000	1.000	1.000	1.000	.935	.842	.792	.758	.734	.719
36	.237	.338	.395	.430	.457	.477	.492	.504	.513	.520
	1.000	1.000	1.000	.894	.805	.759	.732	.713	.700	.690

GAMMA = .7
CONFIDENCE LEVEL = .90

NO. OF INTERVALS	16	36	64	100	NO. OF SUBJECTS 144	196	256	324	400	484
6	.117	.179	.222	.253	.279	.300	.319	.336	.352	.367
	1.000	1.000	1.000	1.000	1.000	1.000	1.000	1.000	1.000	1.000
12	.245	.331	.386	.423	.451	.472	.490	.505	.518	.529
	1.000	1.000	1.000	1.000	1.000	1.000	1.000	1.000	1.000	1.000
18	.328	.420	.474	.508	.532	.548	.562	.572	.580	.588
	1.000	1.000	1.000	1.000	1.000	1.000	1.000	.998	.957	.923
24	.379	.471	.517	.548	.567	.581	.593	.604	.612	.619
	1.000	1.000	1.000	1.000	.985	.928	.886	.856	.834	.819
30	.409	.496	.540	.566	.586	.601	.613	.622	.629	.636
	1.000	1.000	1.000	.929	.872	.838	.816	.800	.787	.777
36	.426	.508	.550	.578	.598	.612	.623	.632	.638	.644
	1.000	1.000	.917	.854	.820	.800	.785	.774	.766	.760

GAMMA = .7
CONFIDENCE LEVEL = .95

NO. OF INTERVALS	16	36	64	100	NO. OF SUBJECTS 144	196	256	324	400	484
6	.095	.155	.199	.232	.258	.280	.298	.315	.330	.344
	1.000	1.000	1.000	1.000	1.000	1.000	1.000	1.000	1.000	1.000
12	.209	.301	.358	.399	.429	.452	.470	.486	.500	.511
	1.000	1.000	1.000	1.000	1.000	1.000	1.000	1.000	1.000	1.000
18	.290	.389	.447	.486	.512	.532	.547	.559	.568	.577
	1.000	1.000	1.000	1.000	1.000	1.000	1.000	1.000	1.000	.973
24	.341	.441	.495	.529	.552	.568	.580	.592	.601	.610
	1.000	1.000	1.000	1.000	1.000	.981	.931	.891	.862	.841
30	.371	.468	.519	.550	.571	.588	.601	.612	.620	.627
	1.000	1.000	1.000	.987	.913	.867	.838	.817	.802	.791
36	.387	.483	.530	.561	.584	.600	.613	.622	.629	.636
	1.000	1.000	.976	.888	.843	.817	.799	.786	.777	.769

GAMMA = .7
CONFIDENCE LEVEL = .98

NO. OF INTERVALS	16	36	64	100	NO. OF SUBJECTS 144	196	256	324	400	484
6	.072	.132	.177	.210	.237	.259	.278	.294	.310	.324
	1.000	1.000	1.000	1.000	1.000	1.000	1.000	1.000	1.000	1.000
12	.174	.269	.330	.373	.405	.429	.449	.466	.481	.493
	1.000	1.000	1.000	1.000	1.000	1.000	1.000	1.000	1.000	1.000
18	.249	.357	.420	.460	.491	.513	.530	.544	.555	.564
	1.000	1.000	1.000	1.000	1.000	1.000	1.000	1.000	1.000	1.000
24	.298	.408	.470	.508	.534	.553	.567	.579	.590	.598
	1.000	1.000	1.000	1.000	1.000	1.000	.986	.936	.898	.871
30	.327	.437	.496	.531	.555	.573	.588	.600	.609	.618
	1.000	1.000	1.000	1.000	.968	.907	.866	.841	.822	.807
36	.344	.453	.509	.542	.568	.587	.600	.611	.620	.627
	1.000	1.000	1.000	.937	.874	.839	.817	.801	.790	.780

GAMMA = .7
CONFIDENCE LEVEL = .99

NO. OF INTERVALS	16	36	64	100	NO. OF SUBJECTS 144	196	256	324	400	484
6	.060	.118	.163	.197	.223	.246	.266	.282	.297	.310
	1.000	1.000	1.000	1.000	1.000	1.000	1.000	1.000	1.000	1.000
12	.153	.249	.312	.356	.390	.416	.436	.454	.469	.482
	1.000	1.000	1.000	1.000	1.000	1.000	1.000	1.000	1.000	1.000
18	.224	.334	.402	.445	.477	.500	.519	.533	.545	.556
	1.000	1.000	1.000	1.000	1.000	1.000	1.000	1.000	1.000	1.000
24	.270	.386	.451	.494	.522	.543	.558	.570	.581	.591
	1.000	1.000	1.000	1.000	1.000	1.000	1.000	.970	.927	.895
30	.300	.416	.479	.518	.544	.563	.579	.591	.602	.610
	1.000	1.000	1.000	1.000	1.000	.938	.889	.859	.836	.820
36	.317	.431	.494	.530	.557	.577	.592	.604	.613	.621
	1.000	1.000	1.000	.975	.900	.856	.830	.811	.798	.788

APPENDIX C

GAMMA = .8
CONFIDENCE LEVEL = .90

NO. OF INTERVALS	NO. OF SUBJECTS									
	16	36	64	100	144	196	256	324	400	484
6	.146	.216	.264	.300	.328	.353	.375	.395	.412	.428
	1.000	1.000	1.000	1.000	1.000	1.000	1.000	1.000	1.000	1.000
12	.300	.396	.455	.497	.527	.551	.571	.589	.603	.615
	1.000	1.000	1.000	1.000	1.000	1.000	1.000	1.000	1.000	1.000
18	.401	.503	.559	.597	.622	.641	.656	.668	.678	.685
	1.000	1.000	1.000	1.000	1.000	1.000	1.000	1.000	1.000	1.000
24	.464	.562	.615	.646	.667	.682	.693	.702	.710	.718
	1.000	1.000	1.000	1.000	1.000	1.000	.982	.957	.937	.920
30	.504	.596	.644	.671	.689	.703	.714	.723	.730	.737
	1.000	1.000	1.000	1.000	.967	.937	.914	.899	.888	.877
36	.525	.615	.658	.683	.702	.716	.727	.735	.741	.747
	1.000	1.000	1.000	.948	.917	.896	.882	.871	.864	.857

GAMMA = .8
CONFIDENCE LEVEL = .95

NO. OF INTERVALS	NO. OF SUBJECTS									
	16	36	64	100	144	196	256	324	400	484
6	.120	.190	.239	.276	.306	.329	.351	.370	.388	.404
	1.000	1.000	1.000	1.000	1.000	1.000	1.000	1.000	1.000	1.000
12	.260	.363	.427	.470	.503	.528	.549	.567	.583	.596
	1.000	1.000	1.000	1.000	1.000	1.000	1.000	1.000	1.000	1.000
18	.359	.469	.532	.573	.601	.622	.639	.653	.664	.673
	1.000	1.000	1.000	1.000	1.000	1.000	1.000	1.000	1.000	1.000
24	.422	.532	.590	.627	.651	.668	.681	.691	.700	.708
	1.000	1.000	1.000	1.000	1.000	1.000	1.000	.987	.962	.942
30	.460	.568	.621	.655	.675	.690	.703	.713	.721	.728
	1.000	1.000	1.000	1.000	1.000	.964	.936	.917	.902	.890
36	.483	.587	.639	.668	.689	.704	.716	.726	.733	.739
	1.000	1.000	1.000	.979	.938	.913	.896	.883	.874	.866

CONFIDENCE INTERVAL TABLES 187

GAMMA = .8
CONFIDENCE LEVEL = .98

NO. OF INTERVALS	\multicolumn{10}{c}{NO. OF SUBJECTS}
	16	36	64	100	144	196	256	324	400	484
6	.094	.164	.214	.252	.282	.307	.328	.347	.364	.380
	1.000	1.000	1.000	1.000	1.000	1.000	1.000	1.000	1.000	1.000
12	.221	.329	.396	.443	.477	.504	.526	.546	.562	.576
	1.000	1.000	1.000	1.000	1.000	1.000	1.000	1.000	1.000	1.000
18	.314	.433	.502	.547	.579	.603	.620	.636	.649	.659
	1.000	1.000	1.000	1.000	1.000	1.000	1.000	1.000	1.000	1.000
24	.374	.496	.563	.604	.632	.652	.667	.679	.689	.697
	1.000	1.000	1.000	1.000	1.000	1.000	1.000	1.000	.995	.972
30	.413	.534	.597	.634	.659	.676	.690	.701	.710	.718
	1.000	1.000	1.000	1.000	1.000	.999	.965	.940	.921	.907
36	.437	.555	.615	.650	.673	.691	.704	.715	.724	.730
	1.000	1.000	1.000	1.000	.967	.935	.913	.898	.886	.878

GAMMA = .8
CONFIDENCE LEVEL = .99

NO. OF INTERVALS	\multicolumn{10}{c}{NO. OF SUBJECTS}
	16	36	64	100	144	196	256	324	400	484
6	.079	.148	.199	.237	.267	.293	.314	.333	.350	.365
	1.000	1.000	1.000	1.000	1.000	1.000	1.000	1.000	1.000	1.000
12	.197	.306	.376	.425	.461	.489	.512	.532	.549	.563
	1.000	1.000	1.000	1.000	1.000	1.000	1.000	1.000	1.000	1.000
18	.284	.410	.483	.531	.564	.589	.609	.625	.638	.649
	1.000	1.000	1.000	1.000	1.000	1.000	1.000	1.000	1.000	1.000
24	.345	.473	.545	.588	.619	.640	.657	.670	.681	.689
	1.000	1.000	1.000	1.000	1.000	1.000	1.000	1.000	1.000	.993
30	.383	.511	.579	.620	.647	.667	.681	.693	.704	.711
	1.000	1.000	1.000	1.000	1.000	1.000	.986	.957	.935	.920
36	.405	.533	.599	.638	.663	.681	.696	.708	.717	.724
	1.000	1.000	1.000	1.000	.990	.951	.925	.908	.894	.885

APPENDIX C

GAMMA = .9
CONFIDENCE LEVEL = .90

NO. OF INTERVALS	\	\	\	\	NO. OF SUBJECTS	\	\	\	\	\
	16	36	64	100	144	196	256	324	400	484
6	.178	.254	.308	.348	.378	.406	.431	.453	.472	.489
	1.000	1.000	1.000	1.000	1.000	1.000	1.000	1.000	1.000	1.000
12	.357	.462	.526	.569	.602	.630	.653	.671	.687	.700
	1.000	1.000	1.000	1.000	1.000	1.000	1.000	1.000	1.000	1.000
18	.476	.585	.645	.684	.712	.733	.750	.764	.775	.784
	1.000	1.000	1.000	1.000	1.000	1.000	1.000	1.000	1.000	1.000
24	.553	.658	.713	.745	.767	.785	.797	.807	.815	.821
	1.000	1.000	1.000	1.000	1.000	1.000	1.000	1.000	1.000	1.000
30	.601	.701	.751	.779	.797	.811	.821	.828	.834	.839
	1.000	1.000	1.000	1.000	1.000	1.000	1.000	.994	.984	.976
36	.632	.727	.772	.797	.813	.824	.833	.840	.846	.851
	1.000	1.000	1.000	1.000	1.000	.989	.976	.968	.960	.953

GAMMA = .9
CONFIDENCE LEVEL = .95

NO. OF INTERVALS	\	\	\	\	NO. OF SUBJECTS	\	\	\	\	\
	16	36	64	100	144	196	256	324	400	484
6	.148	.226	.281	.322	.354	.380	.405	.426	.446	.463
	1.000	1.000	1.000	1.000	1.000	1.000	1.000	1.000	1.000	1.000
12	.315	.427	.495	.542	.577	.605	.629	.649	.665	.679
	1.000	1.000	1.000	1.000	1.000	1.000	1.000	1.000	1.000	1.000
18	.432	.551	.617	.660	.690	.714	.732	.747	.759	.769
	1.000	1.000	1.000	1.000	1.000	1.000	1.000	1.000	1.000	1.000
24	.508	.626	.688	.726	.750	.769	.784	.795	.803	.811
	1.000	1.000	1.000	1.000	1.000	1.000	1.000	1.000	1.000	1.000
30	.556	.671	.729	.762	.783	.798	.810	.819	.826	.831
	1.000	1.000	1.000	1.000	1.000	1.000	1.000	1.000	.999	.989
36	.587	.698	.752	.782	.801	.815	.824	.832	.839	.844
	1.000	1.000	1.000	1.000	1.000	1.000	.989	.979	.969	.962

CONFIDENCE INTERVAL TABLES

GAMMA = .9
CONFIDENCE LEVEL = .98

NO. OF INTERVALS	16	36	64	100	NO. OF SUBJECTS 144	196	256	324	400	484
6	.119 1.000	.197 1.000	.253 1.000	.295 1.000	.328 1.000	.355 1.000	.379 1.000	.400 1.000	.420 1.000	.437 1.000
12	.272 1.000	.390 1.000	.463 1.000	.513 1.000	.550 1.000	.580 1.000	.605 1.000	.625 1.000	.642 1.000	.658 1.000
18	.383 1.000	.513 1.000	.587 1.000	.634 1.000	.667 1.000	.693 1.000	.713 1.000	.729 1.000	.742 1.000	.754 1.000
24	.459 1.000	.590 1.000	.660 1.000	.702 1.000	.731 1.000	.752 1.000	.769 1.000	.781 1.000	.791 1.000	.799 1.000
30	.508 1.000	.638 1.000	.703 1.000	.742 1.000	.767 1.000	.784 1.000	.798 1.000	.808 1.000	.817 1.000	.823 1.000
36	.538 1.000	.666 1.000	.727 1.000	.764 1.000	.786 1.000	.802 1.000	.814 1.000	.823 .991	.830 .982	.837 .972

GAMMA = .9
CONFIDENCE LEVEL = .99

NO. OF INTERVALS	16	36	64	100	NO. OF SUBJECTS 144	196	256	324	400	484
6	.101 1.000	.179 1.000	.236 1.000	.278 1.000	.312 1.000	.340 1.000	.364 1.000	.385 1.000	.403 1.000	.420 1.000
12	.244 1.000	.366 1.000	.441 1.000	.494 1.000	.533 1.000	.564 1.000	.589 1.000	.610 1.000	.628 1.000	.644 1.000
18	.352 1.000	.488 1.000	.567 1.000	.617 1.000	.652 1.000	.679 1.000	.700 1.000	.717 1.000	.731 1.000	.743 1.000
24	.424 1.000	.565 1.000	.641 1.000	.687 1.000	.718 1.000	.740 1.000	.758 1.000	.771 1.000	.783 1.000	.792 1.000
30	.473 1.000	.614 1.000	.686 1.000	.728 1.000	.755 1.000	.775 1.000	.789 1.000	.800 1.000	.810 1.000	.817 1.000
36	.505 1.000	.645 1.000	.712 1.000	.751 1.000	.776 1.000	.794 1.000	.807 1.000	.816 1.000	.824 .989	.831 .980

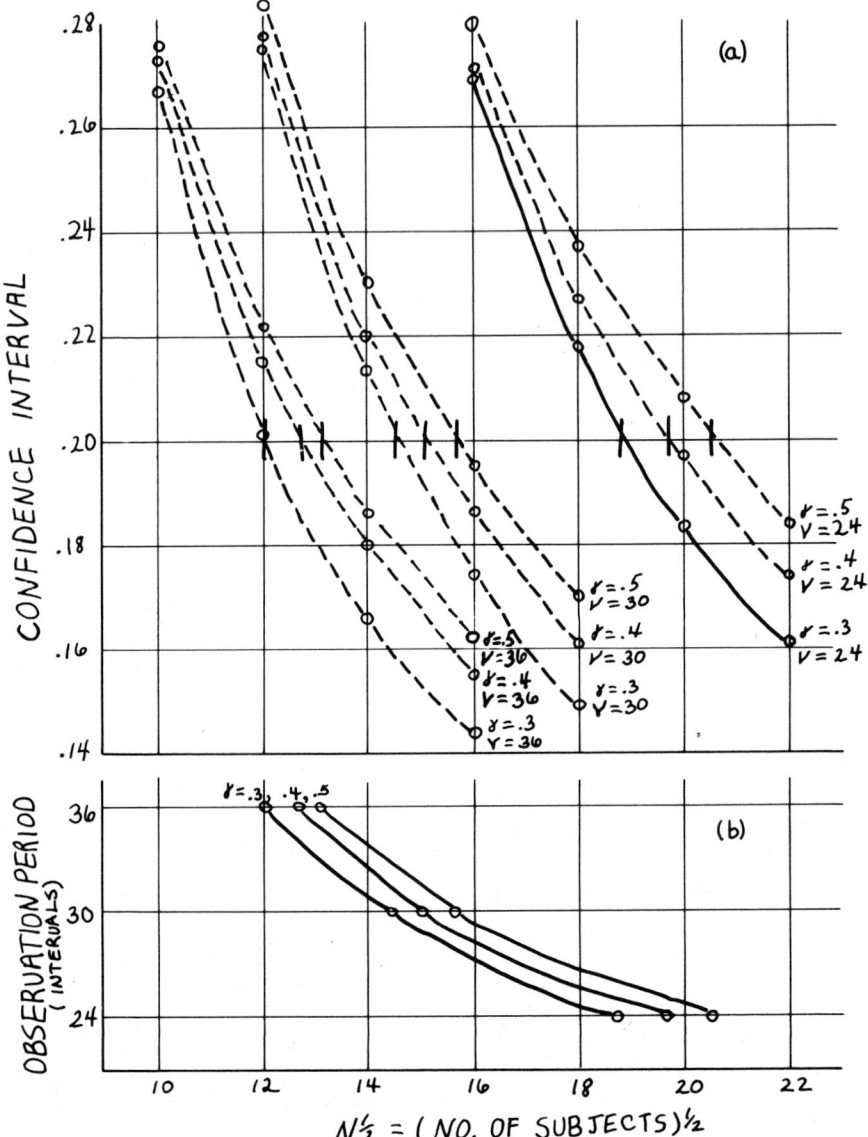

FIGURE C-1 Interpolating to determine the trade-off between population size and observation time with a 90% confidence level, for a confidence interval of .2: (a) graphical interpolation, (b) the trade-off between population size and observation time.

APPENDIX D

Programs for Analyzing Recidivism Data and Examples of Their Use

This appendix contains two programs (Listings 1 and 2, at the end of this appendix) that can be used to develop maximum likelihood estimates of recidivism parameters, and it provides examples of their use. The first program, MLEDATA.FORT, is a FORTRAN program that is used interactively to accept, format and store a set of recidivism data in a computer file. Those who wish to generate the data set automatically (from another data file, for example) need only note the data types, format, and order of storage in the program (see lines 29–30 and 101–106 in MLEDATA. FORT) and then create a data file with the same characteristics. The second program, MLECALC.FORT, reads the data from this, develops maximum likelihood estimates of the recidivism parameters (based on Model M_1), and calculates contours corresponding to confidence regions for these parameter estimates.

The programs are written in FORTRAN G and run on an IBM 3081D computer operating under JES and MVS with TSO.[1] The plotter routines are from the VERSAPLOT package, for use with the VERSATEC plotter. Those without access to a plotter but who wish to use the programs can do so by eliminating (or putting a "C" at the beginning of) lines 708–742 and 744–797 in the subroutine CONTUR of Listing 2. Since the program can print out the coordinates of the contours, they can still be plotted by hand. (Printing the coordinates of the contours can be accomplished by eliminating the "C" at the beginning of lines 705–707 of Listing 2.)

DESCRIPTION OF VARIABLES STORED BY PROGRAM MLEDATA.FORT

The following variables or arrays are stored in the data file (their format types are in parentheses):

---

[1]Versions for the Apple II+ computer and the IBM Personal Computer are under development.

1. NAME (10A4): This is the data set title; it is a string of 40 alphanumeric characters. If the confidence regions are plotted by Program MLECALC.FORT, this title is printed above the figure.

2. NN (I5): This is the total number in the group under study.

3. KK (I5): This is the number in the group who have recidivated thus far.

4. MM (I5): This is the number in the group who have not (yet) recidivated. It is the difference between the two previous variables.

5. KTYP (I5): This is the data type. If KTYP = 1 the failure time (or exposure time, for as-yet nonfailures) for each individual in the group under study is represented by a separate datum. If KTYP = 2 the data are grouped so that the ith failure datum represents the number of individuals in the group who failed in the ith time interval, and the ith exposure datum represents the number of individuals for whom contact was lost in the ith time interval.

6. KCNS (I5): This is the type of exposure time censoring. If all nonfailures have the same exposure time and this exposure time is not smaller than the largest failure time, then the data are singly censored and KCNS = 1. If some individuals have different exposure times, or if some failure times exceed the largest exposure time, then the exposure data are considered progressively censored and KCNS = 2.

7. NF (I5): If KTYP = 1, this is the number of failures; if KTYP = 2 this is the number of time intervals. In either case, this variable represents the number of data elements in the array FT (described in paragraph 10 following).

8. NX (I5): This variable plays a similar role for the exposure data, if these data are progressively censored. However, if KTYP = 2 and KCNS = 1, NX represents the number of exposure intervals experienced by all MM nonfailures. (If KTYP = 1 and KCNS = 1, its value is irrelevant.)

9. TAU (F8.2): This variable represents the length of exposure time experienced by all MM nonfailures; it has relevance only if KTYP = 1 and KCNS = 1.

10. FT (500F8.2): This is the array of individual failure times (if KTYP = 1) or the array of the number of individuals failing in each time interval (if KTYP = 2). The number of data elements in this array cannot exceed 500.

11. XT (500F8.2): This is the array of individual exposure times (if KTYP = 1) or the array of the number of individuals whose exposure times end in each time interval (if KTYP = 2). This array is empty if KCNS = 1, that is, if all nonfailures have the same exposure time TAU (if KCNS = 1) or are lost to observation in the same observation interval NX (if KCNS = 2).

EXAMPLE 1: INDIVIDUAL (KTYP = 1) SINGLY CENSORED (KCNS = 1) DATA

Table D-1 is a data set describing outcomes of a particular correctional program. The 96 subjects were tracked for a maximum of 365 days, during which 32

EXAMPLE 1

TABLE D-1

Example 1: **Hypothetical Correctional Program Data**

Data Characteristics: Individual failure times (KTYP = 1)
                      All nonfailures with same exposure time (KCNS = 1)

Failure Times in Days   (32 subjects)
  6, 7, 9, 12, 15, 15, 21, 25, 33, 39, 45, 48, 57, 71, 74, 87, 94, 95, 112, 124, 136, 140, 156, 178, 191, 198, 248, 252, 277, 298, 319, 328

Exposure Time in Days (64 subjects)
  365, for all 64 nonfailures

failed. All of the 64 subjects who did not fail were tracked for the full year; that is, none were lost to follow-up earlier.

Figure D-1 shows how the program MLEDATA.FORT was used to enter format, and store these data in a data file named EXAMPLE 1.DATA entitled, "EXAMPLE 1: HYPOTHETICAL CORRECTIONAL DAT" (the last A in "DATA" was truncated because the title was too long). The underlined words and numbers are entries made by the analyst. A representative selection of mistakes is included, along with explanations in the margin, to show how the data can be edited.

Figure D-2 shows the printed output of the program MLECALC.FORT. The input data are printed out, as are the likelihood ratio, the MLE values of γ and ϕ,

```
load mledata fort

DON'T FORGET TO ALLOCATE A FILE FOR DATA STORAGE

TYPE IN DATASET NAME,UP TO 40 CHARACTERS
example 1: hypothetical correctional data
IEC1301 FT08F001 DD STATEMENT MISSING
IHO219I IOCS - MISSING DD CARD OR DC:!
READY
alloc file(ft08f001)da(example1.data)new
READY
load mledata fort

DON'T FORGET TO ALLOCATE A FILE FOR DATA STORAGE

TYPE IN DATASET NAME,UP TO 40 CHARACTERS
example 1: hypothetical correctional data

DATA TYPES: INDIVIDUAL (1) OR GROUPED (2)

AT MOST 500 INDIVIDUAL FAILURE (AND 500 EXPOSURE) TIMES CAN BE RECORDED
IF THERE ARE MORE THAN 100-150 DIFFERENT FAILURE OR EXPOSURE TIMES
IT MAY BE BEST TO GROUP THEM INTO TIME INTERVALS (E.G., MONTHS OR WEEKS)
AND ENTER THEM AS GROUPED DATA
```

Error message:
I neglected to allocate a file for data storage

I allocated a new file named EXAMPLE1.DATA to Unit 8

FIGURE D-1 Data entry for Example 1: Individual (KTYP = 1) singly censored data (KCNS = 1).

```
TYPE 1 IF  INDIVIDUAL DATA
     2 IF GROUPED
?
1
TYPE 1 IF DATA SINGLY CENSORED
     2 IF NOT
?
1
ENTER THE NUMBER OF INDIVIDUALS WHO FAILED
?
32
ENTER  32 FAILURE  DATA, SEPARATED BY COMMAS OR RETURN
?
6,7,9,12,15,21,25,33,39,45,48,57,71,74,87,94,95,112,121,124,136,140
?
156,178,191,198,248,252,277,298,319,328
```

FAILURE DATA:

6.00	7.00	9.00	12.00	15.00	21.00	25.00	33.00	39.00	45.00
48.00	57.00	71.00	74.00	87.00	94.00	95.00	112.00	121.00	124.00
136.00	140.00	156.00	178.00	191.00	198.00	248.00	252.00	277.00	298.00
319.00	328.00

A datum is missing here

This datum is extra and should be deleted

```
IF OK TYPE 1; ELSE 2
?
2
TYPE 1 TO CHANGE DATA ELEMENT(S)
     2 TO DELETE DATA ELEMENT
     3 TO ADD DATA ELEMENT
?
2
TYPE IN ELEMENT NO. TO BE DELETED
?
19
```

FAILURE DATA:

6.00	7.00	9.00	12.00	15.00	21.00	25.00	33.00	39.00	45.00
48.00	57.00	71.00	74.00	87.00	94.00	95.00	112.00	124.00	136.00
140.00	156.00	178.00	191.00	198.00	248.00	252.00	277.00	298.00	319.00
328.00

```
IF OK TYPE 1; ELSE 2
?
2
TYPE 1 TO CHANGE DATA ELEMENT(S)
     2 TO DELETE DATA ELEMENT
     3 TO ADD DATA ELEMENT
?
3
TYPE IN DATA ELEMENT, NEW DATA
?
5,15
```

FAILURE DATA:

6.00	7.00	9.00	12.00	15.00	15.00	21.00	25.00	33.00	39.00
45.00	48.00	57.00	71.00	74.00	87.00	94.00	95.00	112.00	124.00
136.00	140.00	156.00	178.00	191.00	198.00	248.00	252.00	277.00	298.00
319.00	328.00

FIGURE D-1 (*Continued*)

EXAMPLE 2

```
IF OK TYPE 1; ELSE 2
?
1
ENTER THE NUMBER OF NONFAILURES
?
64
ENTER THE EXPOSURE TIME OF THE  64 NONFAILURES
?
365
DATA ENTERED FOR   96 INDIVIDUALS, OF WHOM   32 ARE FAILURES
     AND    64 ARE NONFAILURES

TYPE 1 IF DATA OK
     2 TO CHANGE FAILURE TIME DATA
     3 TO CHANGE NONFAILURE EXPOSURE TIME DATA
?
1
READY
```

FIGURE D-1 (*Continued*)

estimates of these two parameters' standard deviations and of their correlation coefficient. Note that the standard deviations and the correlation coefficient are only of utility if the normal approximation is valid, as in this case they are. Otherwise they are not printed out and the computed contours must be used to depict the confidence regions.

Figure D-3 is the graphical output of the program. The MLE solution is indicated by the circle, which is surrounded by the 99, 98, 95, and 90% confidence regions. Note that the confidence contours are somewhat skewed as γ approaches 1. Although the likelihood ratio is quite large (86), which suggests that the likelihood function can be approximated by a normal distribution, because of the skewness it is still better to use the contours themselves for the confidence regions.

```
NN    KK    MM KTYP KCNS    NF    NX      TAU
96    32    64   1    1     32    64    365.00

                              FAILURE   DATA

  6.00    7.00    9.00   12.00   15.00   15.00   21.00   25.00   33.00   39.00
 45.00   48.00   57.00   71.00   74.00   87.00   94.00   95.00  112.00  124.00
136.00  140.00  156.00  178.00  191.00  198.00  248.00  252.00  277.00  298.00
319.00  328.00
                                                   Title truncated
   EXAMPLE 1: HYPOTHETICAL CORRECTIONAL DAT       to 40 characters
LIKELIHOOD RATIO = 0.86E+02,  NORMAL APPROXIMATION MAY BE USED

          GAMMA = 0.3670,   S.D. =0.05897
            PHI =0.00654,   S.D. =0.00191
            RHO =-0.4393
```

FIGURE D-2 Printed output for Example 1: Individual (KTYP = 1) singly censored data (KCNS = 1).

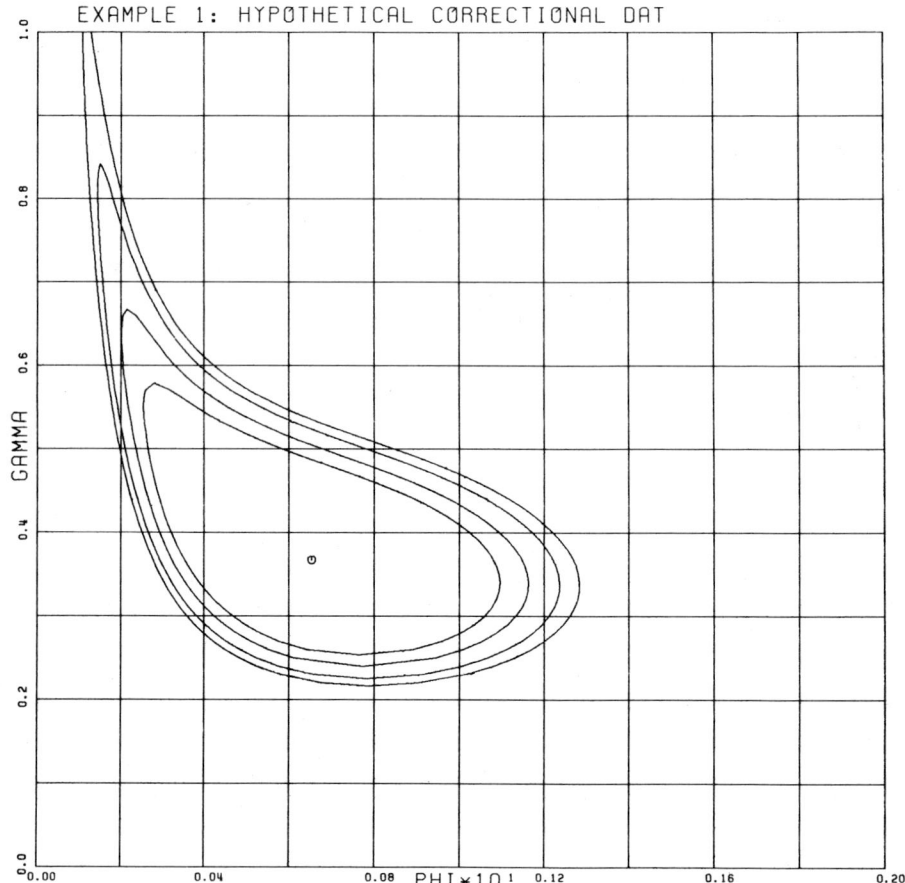

FIGURE D-3 Plotted output for Example 1: Individual (KTYP = 1) singly censored data (KCNS = 1).

EXAMPLE 2: GROUPED (KTYP = 2) SINGLY CENSORED (KCNS = 1) DATA

Table D-2 is based on the same data as the last example. The individual times of Table D-1 were grouped by month (taken to be 30.5 days). Figure D-4 shows how MLEDATA.FORT is used to enter this type of data. Figure D-5 is the printed output of MLECALC.FORT for this data set, and Figure D-6 is the graphical output. As can be seen, the value of γ obtained using grouped data (γ = .3678) is about the same as that obtained when the data are entered individually in Example 1 (γ = .3670); and the value of q obtained in Example 2

EXAMPLE 2

TABLE D-2

Example 2: Hypothetical Correctional Program Data

Data characteristics: Grouped failure times (KTYP = 2)
All nonfailures in same exposure interval (KCNS = 1)

No. of Failures in Each (Monthly) Interval   (32 subjects)
8, 5, 3, 3, 3, 2, 2, 0, 3, 1, 2, 0

No. of Nonfailures Lost to Follow-up in Each (Monthly) Interval   (64 subjects)
All 64 lost to follow-up in the 12th month

```
alloc fi(ft08f001)da(example2.data)new
READY
load mledata fort

DON'T FORGET TO ALLOCATE A FILE FOR DATA STORAGE

TYPE IN DATASET NAME, UP TO 40 CHARACTERS
example 2: grouped version of ex. 1

DATA TYPES: INDIVIDUAL (1) OR GROUPED (2)

AT MOST 500 INDIVIDUAL FAILURE (AND 500 EXPOSURE) TIMES CAN BE RECORDED
IF THERE ARE MORE THAN 100-150 DIFFERENT FAILURE OR EXPOSURE TIMES
IT MAY BE BEST TO GROUP THEM INTO TIME INTERVALS (E.G., MONTHS OR WEEKS)
AND ENTER THEM AS GROUPED DATA

TYPE 1 IF INDIVIDUAL DATA
     2 IF GROUPED
?
2
TYPE 1 IF DATA SINGLY CENSORED
     2 IF NOT
?
1
ENTER THE MAXIMUM NO. OF OBSERVATION INTERVALS
?
12
ENTER 12 FAILURE DATA, SEPARATED BY COMMAS OR RETURN
?
8,3,5,3,3,2,2,0,3,1,2,0
              FAILURE  DATA:
    8.00   3.00   5.00   3.00   3.00   2.00   2.00   0.0   3.00   1.00
    2.00   0.0

IF OK TYPE 1; ELSE 2
?
2
```

The second and third data are reversed

FIGURE D-4 Data entry for Example 2: Grouped (KTYP = 2) singly censored data (KCNS = 1).

```
TYPE 1 TO CHANGE DATA ELEMENT(S)
     2 TO DELETE DATA ELEMENT
     3 TO ADD DATA ELEMENT
?
1
TYPE IN DATA ELEMENT, NEW DATA
WHEN DONE TYPE 0,0
?
3,3
?
2,5
?
0,0
                    FAILURE DATA:
  8.00    5.00    3.00    3.00    3.00    2.00    2.00    0.0    3.00    1.00
  2.00    0.0

IF OK TYPE 1; ELSE 2
?
1
ENTER THE NUMBER OF NONFAILURES AT THE END OF  12 OBSERVATION INTERVALS
?
64
DATA ENTERED FOR  96 INDIVIDUALS, OF WHOM   32 ARE FAILURES
      AND    64 ARE NONFAILURES

TYPE 1 IF DATA OK
     2 TO CHANGE FAILURE TIME DATA
     3 TO CHANGE NONFAILURE EXPOSURE TIME DATA
?
1
READY
```

FIGURE D-4 (*Continued*)

```
 NN    KK    MM  KTYP KCNS    NF    NX     TAU
 96    32    64    2    1     12    12     0.0
                                 FAILURE  DATA
 8.00   5.00   3.00   3.00   3.00   2.00   2.00   0.0   3.00   1.00
 2.00   0.0

   EXAMPLE 2: GROUPED VERSION OF EX. 1
LIKELIHOOD RATIO = 0.77E+02, NORMAL APPROXIMATION MAY BE USED

         GAMMA = 0.3678,  S.D. =0.05474
             Q = 0.8209,  S.D. =0.02403
           RHO = 0.2440
```

FIGURE D-5 Printed output for Example 2: Grouped (KTYP = 2) singly censored data (KCNS = 1).

EXAMPLE 3

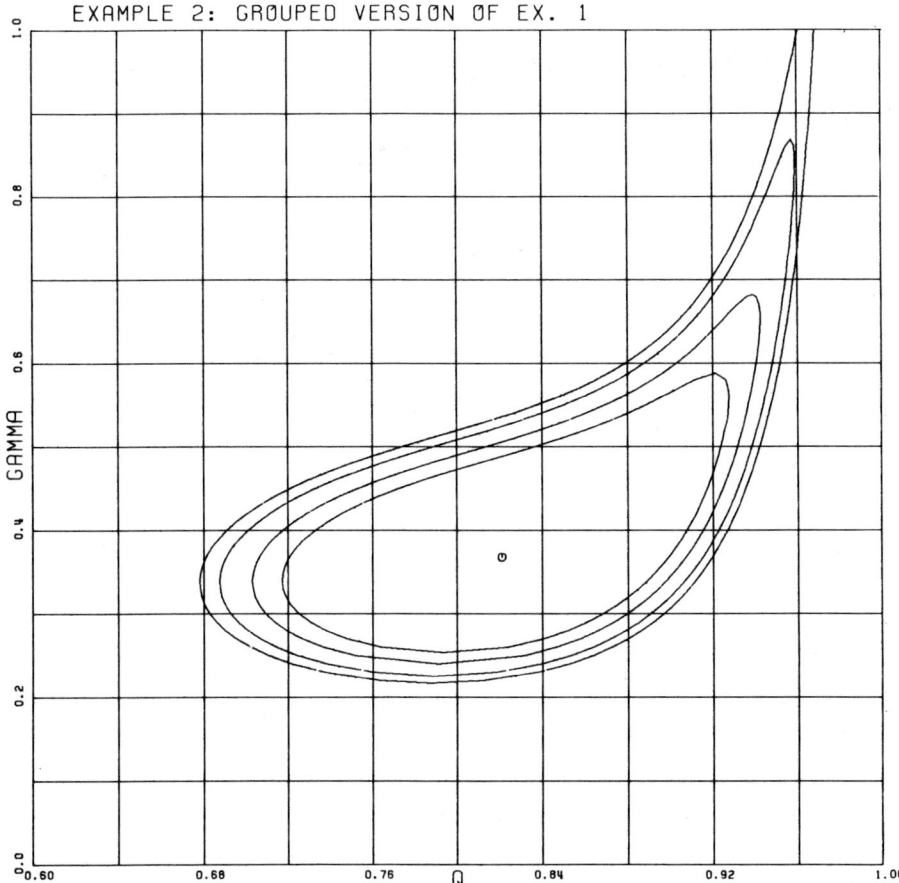

FIGURE D-6 Plotted output for Example 2: Grouped (KTYP = 2) singly censored data (KCNS = 1).

(q = .8209) is equivalent to the value of ϕ in Example 1, since if we estimate a month to be 30.5 days we estimate q from Example 1 to be exp($-$.00654 $\times$ 30.5) = .8192, well within one standard deviation of q. Furthermore, data entry is easier with 12 entries instead of 32.

EXAMPLE 3: INDIVIDUAL (KTYP = 1) PROGRESSIVELY CENSORED (KCNS = 2) DATA

This example shows how progressive censoring can affect the parameter estimates. Of the 64 nonfailures in Table D-1, suppose that 41 of them actually had exposure times less than 365 days, as shown in Table D-3. Data entry for this

TABLE D-3

Example 3: Hypothetical Correctional Program Data

Data Characteristics:	Individual failure times (KTYP = 1)
	Individual exposure times (KCNS = 2)

Failure Time in Days   (32 subjects)
  6, 7, 9, 12, 15, 15, 21, 25, 33, 39, 45, 48, 57, 71, 74, 87, 94, 95, 112, 124, 136, 140, 156, 178, 191, 198, 248, 252, 277, 298, 319, 328

Exposure Time in Days   (64 subjects)
  14, 21, 48, 52, 52, 71, 80, 86, 94, 97, 102, 108, 111, 114, 130, 138, 142, 146, 160, 177, 192, 196, 200, 204, 227, 242, 245, 248, 252, 260, 278, 281, 288, 289, 296, 304, 304, 304, 321, 325, 338, 365, 365, 365, 365, 365, 365, 365, 365, 365, 365, 365, 365, 365, 365, 365, 365, 365, 365, 365, 365, 365, 365,

case is shown in Figure D-7 and the printed and pictorial output are shown in Figures D-8 and D-9, respectively. The estimate of the probability of eventual failure, γ, is significantly higher, and as can be seen the likelihood function cannot be approximated accurately by a bivariate normal distribution.

```
alloc fi(ft08f001)da(example3.data)new
READY
load mledata fort

DON'T FORGET TO ALLOCATE A FILE FOR DATA STORAGE

TYPE IN DATASET NAME,UP TO 40 CHARACTERS
example 3: ex.1, with progressive cnsrng

DATA TYPES: INDIVIDUAL (1) OR GROUPED (2)

AT MOST 500 INDIVIDUAL FAILURE (AND 500 EXPOSURE) TIMES CAN BE RECORDED
IF THERE ARE MORE THAN 100-150 DIFFERENT FAILURE OR EXPOSURE TIMES
IT MAY BE BEST TO GROUP THEM INTO TIME INTERVALS (E.G., MONTHS OR WEEKS)
AND ENTER THEM AS GROUPED DATA

TYPE 1 IF INDIVIDUAL DATA
     2 IF GROUPED
?
1
TYPE 1 IF DATA SINGLY CENSORED
     2 IF NOT
?
2
ENTER THE NUMBER OF INDIVIDUALS WHO FAILED
?
32
```

FIGURE D-7 Data entry for Example 3: Individual (KTYP = 1) progressively censored data (KCNS = 2).

EXAMPLE 3

```
ENTER  32 FAILURE  DATA, SEPARATED BY COMMAS OR RETURN
?
6,7,9,12,15,15,21,25,33,39,45,48,57,71,74,87,94,95,112,124
?
136,140,156,178,191,198,248,252,277,298,319,328
```

               FAILURE DATA:

```
   6.00    7.00    9.00   12.00   15.00   15.00   21.00   25.00   33.00   39.00
  45.00   48.00   57.00   71.00   74.00   87.00   94.00   95.00  112.00  124.00
 136.00  140.00  156.00  178.00  191.00  198.00  248.00  252.00  277.00  298.00
 319.00  328.00
```

IF OK TYPE 1; ELSE 2
?
1
ENTER THE NUMBER OF NONFAILURES
?
64
ENTER 64 EXPOSURE DATA, SEPARATED BY COMMAS OR RETURN
?
14,21,48,52,52,71,80,86,94,97,102,108,111,114,130,138,142,146,160,177
?
192,196,200,204,227,242,245,248,252,260,278,281,288,289,296,304,304,304,321,325
?
338,365,365,365,365,365,365,365,365,365,365,365,365,365,365,365,365,365,365
?
365,365,365,365

               EXPOSURE DATA:

```
  14.00   21.00   48.00   52.00   52.00   71.00   80.00   86.00   94.00   97.00
 102.00  108.00  111.00  114.00  130.00  138.00  142.00  146.00  160.00  177.00
 192.00  196.00  200.00  204.00  227.00  242.00  245.00  248.00  252.00  260.00
 278.00  281.00  288.00  289.00  296.00  304.00  304.00  304.00  321.00  325.00
 338.00  365.00  365.00  365.00  365.00  365.00  365.00  365.00  365.00  365.00
 365.00  365.00  365.00  365.00  365.00  365.00  365.00  365.00  365.00  365.00
 365.00  365.00  365.00  365.00
```

IF OK TYPE 1; ELSE 2
?
1
DATA ENTERED FOR   96 INDIVIDUALS, OF WHOM   32 ARE FAILURES
     AND   64 ARE NONFAILURES

TYPE 1 IF DATA OK
     2 TO CHANGE FAILURE TIME DATA
     3 TO CHANGE NONFAILURE EXPOSURE TIME DATA
?
1
READY

FIGURE D-7 (*Continued*)

NN	KK	MM	KTYP	KCNS	NF	NX	TAU
96	32	64	1	2	32	64	0.0

FAILURE DATA

6.00	7.00	9.00	12.00	15.00	15.00	21.00	25.00	33.00	39.00
45.00	48.00	57.00	71.00	74.00	87.00	94.00	55.00	112.00	124.00
136.00	140.00	156.00	178.00	191.00	198.00	248.00	252.00	277.00	298.00
319.00	328.00								

EXPOSURE DATA

14.00	21.00	48.00	52.00	52.00	71.00	80.00	86.00	94.00	97.00
102.00	108.00	111.00	114.00	130.00	138.00	142.00	146.00	160.00	177.00
192.00	196.00	200.00	204.00	227.00	242.00	245.00	248.00	252.00	260.00
278.00	281.00	288.00	289.00	296.00	304.00	304.00	304.00	321.00	325.00
338.00	365.00	365.00	365.00	365.00	365.00	365.00	365.00	365.00	365.00
365.00	365.00	365.00	365.00	365.00	365.00	365.00	365.00	365.00	365.00
365.00	365.00	365.00	365.00						

EXAMPLE 3: EX.1, WITH PROGRESSIVE CNSRNG

LIKELIHOOD RATIO = 2.792,. NORMAL APPROXIMATION SHOULD NOT BE USED

GAMMA = 0.5235

PHI = 0.00427

FIGURE D-8 Printed output for Example 3: Individual (KTYP = 1) progressively censored data (KCNS = 2).

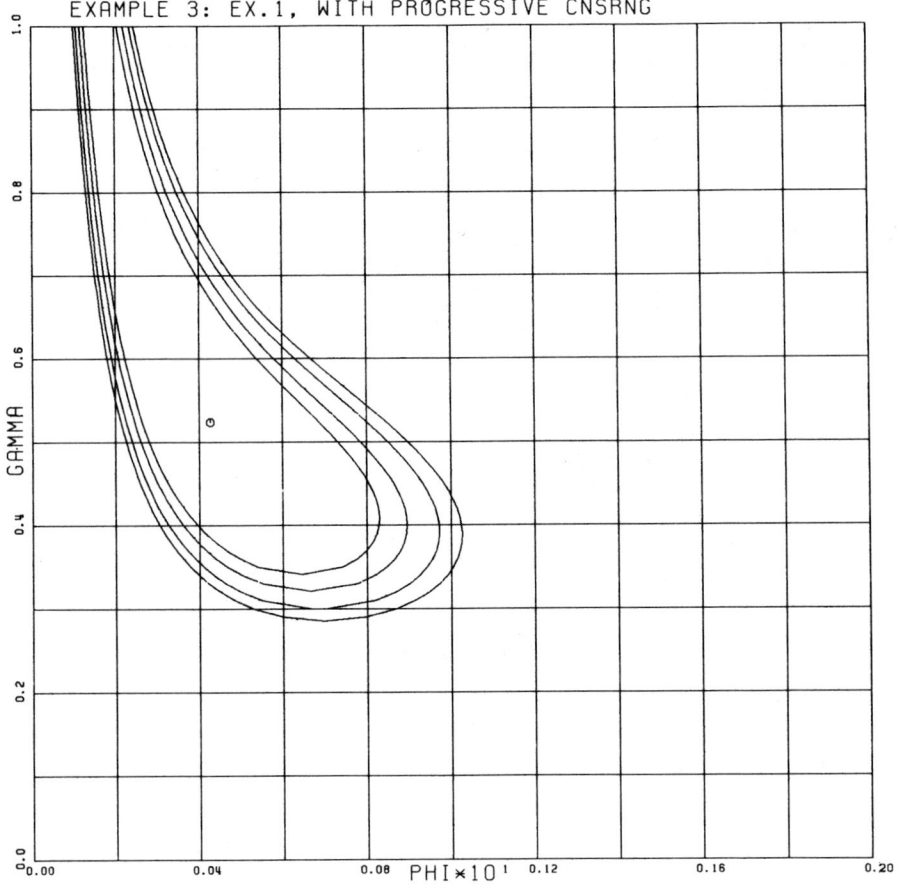

FIGURE D-9 Plotted output for Example 3: Individual (KTYP = 1) progressively censored data (KCNS = 2).

EXAMPLE 4

TABLE D-4

Example 4: Hypothetical Correctional Program Data

Data Characteristics: Grouped failure times (KTYP = 2)
Grouped exposure times (KTYP = 2)

No. of Failures in Each (Monthly) Interval   (32 subjects)
8, 5, 3, 3, 3, 2, 2, 0, 3, 1, 2, 0

No. of Nonfailures Lost to Follow-up in Each (Monthly) Interval   (64 subjects)
2, 3, 3, 6, 4, 2, 4, 1, 5, 5, 5, 24

EXAMPLE 4: GROUPED (KTYP = 2) PROGRESSIVELY CENSORED (KCNS = 2) DATA

The data of Table D-3 are grouped by month in Table D-4, as before. Figures D-10, D-11, and D-12 show the data entry and printed and pictorial output, respectively. There is a greater difference between the solutions using individual data (Example 3) and grouped data (Example 4) for these cases of progressive censoring than their was for Examples 1 and 2, where the data were singly censored. The estimates of γ are .5235 and .5038, and those of q are $[\exp(-.00427 \times 30.5) =]$ .8779 and .8752 for Examples 3 and 4, repestively. Data entry for Example 4 is considerably easier than for Example 3; instead of entering 96 data, only 24 need be entered.

```
alloc fi(ft08f001)da(example4.data)new
READY
load mledata fort

DON'T FORGET TO ALLOCATE A FILE FOR DATA STORAGE

TYPE IN DATASET NAME,UP TO 40 CHARACTERS
example 4: example 3, with grouped data

DATA TYPES: INDIVIDUAL (1) OR GROUPED (2)

AT MOST 500 INDIVIDUAL FAILURE (AND 500 EXPOSURE) TIMES CAN BE RECORDED
IF THERE ARE MORE THAN 100-150 DIFFERENT FAILURE OR EXPOSURE TIMES
IT MAY BE BEST TO GROUP THEM INTO TIME INTERVALS (E.G., MONTHS OR WEEKS)
AND ENTER THEM AS GROUPED DATA

TYPE 1 IF INDIVIDUAL DATA
     2 IF GROUPED
?
2
```

FIGURE D-10 Data entry for Example 4: Grouped (KTYP = 2) progressively censored data (KCNS = 2).

```
TYPE 1 IF DATA SINGLY CENSORED
     2 IF NOT
?
2
ENTER THE MAXIMUM NO. OF OBSERVATION INTERVALS
?
12
ENTER  12 FAILURE  DATA, SEPARATED BY COMMAS OR RETURN
?
8,5,3,3,3,2,2,0,3,1,2,0

                    FAILURE   DATA:

   8.00      5.00     3.00    3.00    3.00   2.00    2.00    0.0    3.00   1.00
   2.00      0.0

IF OK TYPE 1; ELSE 2
?
1
ENTER  12 EXPOSURE DATA, SEPARATED BY COMMAS OR RETURN
?
2,3,3,6,4,2,4,1,5,5,5,24

                    EXPOSURE DATA:

   2.00      3.00     3.00    6.00    4.00   2.00    4.00    1.00   5.00   5.00
   5.00     24.00

IF OK TYPE 1; ELSE 2
?
1
DATA ENTERED FOR   96 INDIVIDUALS, OF WHOM   32 ARE FAILURES
     AND    64 ARE NONFAILURES

TYPE 1 IF DATA OK
     2 TO CHANGE FAILURE TIME DATA
     3 TO CHANGE NONFAILURE EXPOSURE TIME DATA
?
1
READY
```

FIGURE D-10 (*Continued*)

```
NN    KK     MM  KTYP KCNS    NF     NX     TAU
96    32     64    2    2     12     12     0.0

                             FAILURE   DATA

 8.00    5.00    3.00     3.00     3.00    2.00    2.00    0.0    3.00    1.0
 2.00    0.0

                             EXPOSURE DATA

 2.00    3.00    3.00     6.00     4.00    2.00    4.00    1.00   5.00    5.0
 5.00   24.00

     EXAMPLE 4: EXAMPLE 3, WITH GROUPED DATA
LIKELIHOOD RATIO = 3.204, NORMAL APPROXIMATION SHOULD NOT BE USED

          GAMMA = 0.5038
              Q = 0.8752
```

FIGURE D-11 Printed output for Example 4: Grouped (KTYP = 2) progressively censored data (KCNS = 2).

EXAMPLE 4

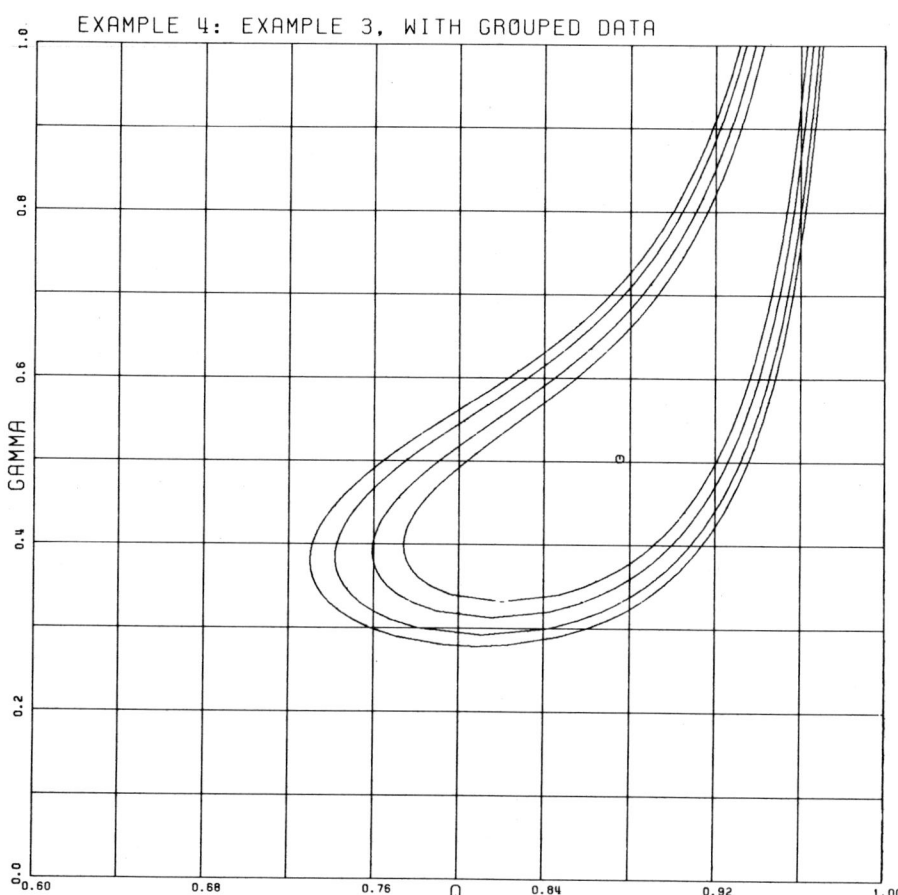

FIGURE D-12 Plotted output for Example 4: Grouped (KTYP = 2) progressively censored data (KCNS = 2).

LISTING 1:

Data Entry Program, MLEDATA.FORT

```
1.      C ******************************************************************
2.      C *                                                                *
3.      C *                      PROGRAM MLEDATA.FORT                      *
4.      C *                                                                *
5.      C ******************************************************************
6.      C *                                                                *
7.      C * MLEDATA IS AN INTERACTIVE PROGRAM DESIGNED TO ACCEPT FAILURE AND *
8.      C * EXPOSURE DATA AND STORE THEM IN A FORM SUITABLE FOR ANALYSIS. THE *
9.      C * FAILURE (AND EXPOSURE) TIME DATA CAN BE IN ONE OF TWO FORMS. EACH *
10.     C * INDIVIDUAL'S TIME CAN BE ENTERED AS AN INDIVIDUAL DATUM (KTYP = *
11.     C * 1), OR DATUM NO. I CAN REPRESENT THE NUMBER OF INDIVIDUALS WITH *
12.     C * FAILURE (OR EXPOSURE) TIME WITHIN INTERVAL I -- THAT IS, GROUPED *
13.     C * DATA (KTYP = 2).                                                *
14.     C * SOME STUDIES ARE DESIGNED SO THAT ALL INDIVIDUALS ARE STARTED  *
15.     C * (RELEASED) SIMULTANEOUSLY, SO THAT INDIVIDUALS WHO HAVE NOT FAILED *
16.     C * BY THE END OF THE DATA COLLECTION PERIOD ALL HAVE THE SAME     *
17.     C * EXPOSURE TIME.  IN THIS CASE THE DATA ARE SINGLY CENSORED (KCNS = *
18.     C * 1). ALTERNATIVELY, SOME MAY HAVE DIFFRENT EXPOSURE TIMES (KCNS = *
19.     C * 2), I.E., PROGRESSIVELY OF MULTIPLY CENSORED DATA.             *
20.     C *                                                                *
21.     C ******************************************************************
22.             DIMENSION FT(500),XT(500),NAME(10),MF(2),MX(2)
23.             DATA MF,MX/'FAIL','URE ','EXPO','SURE'/
24.             WRITE(6,100)
25.     100     FORMAT(/' DON''T FORGET TO ALLOCATE A FILE FOR DATA STORAGE'/)
26.             WRITE(6,110)
27.     110     FORMAT(' TYPE IN DATASET NAME,UP TO 40 CHARACTERS')
28.             READ(5,120)NAME
29.     120     FORMAT(10A4)
30.             WRITE(8,120)NAME
31.             WRITE(6,130)
32.     130     FORMAT(/' DATA TYPES:  INDIVIDUAL (1) OR GROUPED (2)'//
33.            1       ' AT MOST 500 INDIVIDUAL FAILURE (AND 500 EXPOSURE) TIMES',
34.            2       ' CAN BE RECORDED'/' IF THERE ARE MORE THAN 100-150',
35.            3       ' DIFFERENT FAILURE OR EXPOSURE TIMES'/' IT MAY BE BEST',
36.            4       ' TO GROUP THEM INTO TIME INTERVALS (E.G., MONTHS OR',
37.            5       ' WEEKS)'/' AND ENTER THEM AS GROUPED DATA'//' TYPE 1 IF ',
38.            6       ' INDIVIDUAL DATA'/6X,'2 IF GROUPED')
39.             READ(5,*)KTYP
40.             WRITE(6,140)
41.     140     FORMAT(' TYPE 1 IF DATA SINGLY CENSORED'/6X,'2 IF NOT')
42.             READ(5,*)KCNS
43.             IF(KTYP.EQ.2)GO TO 300
44.             WRITE(6,200)
45.     200     FORMAT(' ENTER THE NUMBER OF INDIVIDUALS WHO FAILED')
46.             READ(5,*)KK
47.             NF=KK
48.             WRITE(6,210)NF,MF
49.     210     FORMAT(' ENTER',I4,1X,2A4,' DATA, SEPARATED BY COMMAS OR RETURN')
50.             READ(5,*)(FT(I),I=1,NF)
51.     220     CALL EDIT(KTYP,KK,NF,MF,FT)
52.     225     WRITE(6,230)
53.     230     FORMAT(' ENTER THE NUMBER OF NONFAILURES')
54.             READ(5,*)MM
55.             NX=MM
56.             IF(KCNS.EQ.2)GO TO 350
57.     240     WRITE(6,250)MM
58.     250     FORMAT(' ENTER THE EXPOSURE TIME OF THE',I4,' NONFAILURES')
```

LISTING 1

```
59.            READ(5,*)TAU
60.            DO 260 I=1,NF
61.            IF(FT(I).GT.TAU)GO TO 270
62.     260    CONTINUE
63.            GO TO 500
64.     270    WRITE(6,280)I,FT(I),TAU
65.     280    FORMAT(' FAILURE NO.',I3,' (',F6.2,') OCCURS AFTER THE MAXIMUM'/
66.           1    'OBSERVATION TIME OF',F6.2//' TYPE 1 TO CHANGE FAILURE DATA',
67.           2    /6X,'2 TO CHANGE ONLY MAXIMUM OBSERVATION TIME')
68.            READ(5,*)I
69.            IF(I.EQ.1)GO TO 220
70.            GO TO 240
71.     300    WRITE(6,310)
72.     310    FORMAT(' ENTER THE MAXIMUM NO. OF OBSERVATION INTERVALS')
73.            READ(5,*)NF
74.            NX=NF
75.            WRITE(6,210)NF,MF
76.            READ(5,*)(FT(I),I=1,NF)
77.            CALL EDIT(KTYP,KK,NF,MF,FT)
78.            IF(KCNS.EQ.2)GO TO 350
79.            WRITE(6,320)NX
80.     320    FORMAT(' ENTER THE NUMBER OF NONFAILURES AT THE END OF',I4,
81.           1    ' OBSERVATION INTERVALS')
82.            READ(5,*)MM
83.            GO TO 500
84.     350    WRITE(6,210)NX,MX
85.            READ(5,*)(XT(I),I=1,NX)
86.     360    CALL EDIT(KTYP,MM,NX,MX,XT)
87.     500    NN=KK+MM
88.            WRITE(6,510)NN,KK,MM
89.     510    FORMAT(' DATA ENTERED FOR',I5,' INDIVIDUALS, OF WHOM',I5,
90.           1    ' ARE FAILURES'/'       AND',I5,' ARE NONFAILURES')
91.            WRITE(6,520)
92.     520    FORMAT(/' TYPE 1 IF DATA OK'/6X,'2 TO CHANGE FAILURE TIME DATA'
93.           1    /6X,'3 TO CHANGE NONFAILURE EXPOSURE TIME DATA')
94.            READ(5,*)I
95.            GO TO (600,550,560),I
96.     550    CALL EDIT(KTYP,KK,NF,MF,FT)
97.            GO TO 500
98.     560    IF(KCNS.EQ.2)GO TO 360
99.            IF(KTYP.EQ.2)GO TO 300
100.           GO TO 225
101.    600    WRITE(8,610)NN,KK,MM,KTYP,KCNS,NF,NX,TAU
102.    610    FORMAT(7I5,F8.2)
103.           WRITE(8,620)(FT(I),I=1,NF)
104.    620    FORMAT(/(10F8.2))
105.           IF(KCNS.EQ.1)STOP
106.           WRITE(8,620)(XT(I),I=1,NX)
107.           STOP
108.           END
109.           SUBROUTINE EDIT(KTYP,LL,NT,MT,TT)
110.           DIMENSION TT(500),MT(2)
111.     10    WRITE(6,20)MT
112.     20    FORMAT(/20X,2A4,' DATA:'/)
113.           WRITE(6,30)(TT(I),I=1,NT)
114.     30    FORMAT((10F8.2))
115.           WRITE(6,40)
116.     40    FORMAT(/' IF OK TYPE 1; ELSE 2')
117.           READ(5,*)I
118.           IF(I.EQ.1)GO TO 400
119.           WRITE(6,50)
120.     50    FORMAT(' TYPE 1 TO CHANGE DATA ELEMENT(S)'/6X,
```

```
121.              1  '2 TO DELETE DATA ELEMENT'/6X,'3 TO ADD DATA ELEMENT')
122.              READ(5,*)II
123.              GO TO (100,200,300),II
124.      100     WRITE(6,110)
125.      110     FORMAT(' TYPE IN DATA ELEMENT, NEW DATA'/' WHEN DONE TYPE 0,0')
126.      120     CONTINUE
127.              READ(5,*)IZ,ZZ
128.              IF(IZ.LE.0)GO TO 10
129.              IF(IZ.GT.NT)GO TO 100
130.              TT(IZ)=ZZ
131.              GO TO 120
132.      200     WRITE(6,210)
133.      210     FORMAT(' TYPE IN ELEMENT NO. TO BE DELETED')
134.              READ(5,*)IZ
135.              IF(IZ.LE.0)GO TO 10
136.              IF(IZ.GT.NT)GO TO 200
137.              IZ1=IZ+1
138.              IF(IZ1.GT.NT)GO TO 230
139.              DO 220 I=IZ1,NT
140.              IL=I-1
141.      220     TT(IL)=TT(I)
142.      230     NT=NT-1
143.              GO TO 10
144.      300     WRITE(6,310)
145.      310     FORMAT(' TYPE IN DATA ELEMENT, NEW DATA')
146.              READ(5,*)IZ,ZZ
147.              IF(IZ.LE.0)GO TO 10
148.              IF(IZ.GT.NT+1)GO TO 300
149.              NT=NT+1
150.              IZ1=IZ+1
151.              IF(IZ.EQ.NT)GO TO 330
152.              DO 320 I=IZ1,NT
153.              IR=NT+IZ1-I
154.              IL=IR-1
155.      320     TT(IR)=TT(IL)
156.      330     TT(IZ)=ZZ
157.              GO TO 10
158.      400     LL=NT
159.              IF(KTYP.EQ.1)RETURN
160.              LL=0
161.              DO 410 I=1,NT
162.      410     LL=LL+TT(I)
163.              RETURN
164.              END
```

LISTING 2:

Data Analysis Program, MLECALC.FORT

```
1.      C ************************************************************
2.      C *                                                          *
3.      C *                    PROGRAM MLECALC.FORT                  *
4.      C *                                                          *
5.      C ************************************************************
6.      C *                                                          *
7.      C * THIS PROGRAM IS DESIGNED TO ACCEPT RECIDIVISM DATA AS STORED (AND *
8.      C * FORMATTED) BY PROGRAM MLEDATA.FORT, AND TO CALCULATE THE MAXIMUM *
9.      C * LIKELIHOOD ESTIMATE (MLE) OF THE PARAMETERS OF MODEL MI, THE *
10.     C * INCOMPLETE EXPONENTIAL DISTRIBUTION. THIS MODEL HAS TWO  *
11.     C * PARAMETERS.  THE FIRST, GAMMA, IS THE PROBABILITY OF AN  *
12.     C * INDIVIDUAL EVENTUALLY RECIDIVATING. WHEN APPLIED TO A GROUP *
13.     C * UNDER STUDY, IT IS AN ESTIMATE OF THE FRACTION OF THE GROUP *
14.     C * EXPECTED TO EVENTUALLY RECIDIVATE.                       *
15.     C *                                                          *
16.     C * THE SECOND PARAMETER REFLECTS THE RAPIDITY WITH WHICH THE *
17.     C * INDIVIDUALS WHO DO EVENTUALLY RECIDIVATE ARE EXPECTED TO DO SO. *
18.     C * IF THE DATA REPRESENT INDIVIDUAL TIMES OF FAILURE (OR EXPOSURE, *
19.     C * FOR THOSE WHO HAVE NOT FAILED), I.E., IF KTYP=1, THEN THE SECOND *
20.     C * PARAMETER IS PHI, THE FAILURE RATE.  ITS UNITS ARE 1/(T.U.), *
21.     C * WHERE T.U. IS THE TIME UNIT OF THE DATA, E.G., DAYS.     *
22.     C *                                                          *
23.     C * IF THE DATA ARE GROUPED (KTYP=2), THE ITH FAILURE DATUM  *
24.     C * REPRESENTS THE NUMBER OF INDIVIDUALS WHO FAILED WITHIN THE ITH *
25.     C * TIME INTERVAL (E.G., MONTH) AND THE ITH EXPOSURE DATUM   *
26.     C * REPRESENTS THE NUMBER OF INDIVIDUALS LOST TO FOLLOW-UP WITHIN THE *
27.     C * ITH TIME INTERVAL.  IN THIS CASE THE SECOND PARAMETER IS Q, THE *
28.     C * PROBABILITY THAT AN EVENTUAL FAILURE DOES NOT FAIL IN THE NEXT *
29.     C * TIME INTERVAL.                                           *
30.     C *                                                          *
31.     C ************************************************************
32.             COMMON FT(500),XT(500),TPQ(100),STD(100),HLF(100),NAME(10)
33.             COMMON NN,KK,MM,TT,KTYP,KCNS,NF,NX,TAU,XK,XTT,XNU,XTAU
34.             DIMENSION CL(4),CH(4),KF(2),KX(2)
35.             DATA CL/.99,.98,.95,.90/,KF/'FAIL','URE '/,KX/'EXPO','SURE'/
36.     C
37.     C    DATA READ IN
38.     C
39.             READ(8,10)NAME
40.      10     FORMAT(10A4)
41.             READ(8,15)NN,KK,MM,KTYP,KCNS,NF,NX,TAU
42.      15     FORMAT(7I5,F8.2)
43.             WRITE(6,20)NN,KK,MM,KTYP,KCNS,NF,NX,TAU
44.      20     FORMAT('    NN    KK    MM KTYP KCNS    NF    NX    TAU'/7I5,F8.2)
45.             READ(8,25)(FT(I),I=1,NF)
46.      25     FORMAT(/(10F8.2))
47.             WRITE(6,30)KF,(FT(I),I=1,NF)
48.      30     FORMAT(//35X,2A4,' DATA'//(10F8.2))
49.             IF(KCNS.EQ.2)READ(8,25)(XT(I),I=1,NX)
50.             IF(KCNS.EQ.2)WRITE(6,30)KX,(XT(I),I=1,NX)
51.             IF(KTYP.EQ.2)GO TO 300
52.     C
53.     C    INDIVIDUAL TIME DATA
54.     C
55.             TT=0
56.             DO 100 I=1,NF
57.     100     TT=TT+FT(I)
58.             ICT=0
```

```
59.            IF(KCNS.EQ.2)GO TO 200
60.      C
61.      C  SINGLY CENSORED DATA, NEWTON-RAPHSON SEARCH FOR MLE SOLUTION
62.      C  FOR GAMMA AND PHI
63.      C
64.            ALFA=TT/(KK*TAU)
65.            X=1/ALFA
66.      120   ICT=ICT+1
67.            IF(ICT.GT.20)GO TO 130
68.            T1=1/X
69.            T2=T1*T1
70.            T3=EXP(X)
71.            T4=1/(T3-1)
72.            TOP=T1-T4-ALFA
73.            BOT=T2-T3*T4*T4
74.            DX=TOP/BOT
75.            X=X+DX
76.            IF(ABS(DX/X).GT.1E-4)GO TO 120
77.            PHI=X/TAU
78.            GAM=KK/(NN*(1-EXP(-X)))
79.            T1=KK/PHI-TT
80.            HGG=-NN*KK/(MM*GAM*GAM)
81.            HGP=-NN*T1/(MM*GAM)
82.            HPP=-KK/(PHI*PHI)+T1*TAU*(1-GAM)*NN/MM
83.            DET=HGG*HPP-HGP*HGP
84.            GO TO 240
85.      C
86.      C  LOCAL MAXIMUM OF LF NOT FOUND; FIND GLOBAL MAXIMUM AT GAMMA = 1
87.      C
88.      130   T=TT+MM*TAU
89.      140   PHI=KK/T
90.            GAM=1
91.            SG=0
92.            SP=SQRT(FLOAT(KK))/T
93.            RHO=0
94.            PQ=PHI
95.            GO TO 500
96.      C
97.      C  PROGRESSIVELY CENSORED DATA, NEWTON-RAPHSON SEARCH FOR MLE SOLUTION
98.      C  FOR GAMMA AND PHI
99.      C
100.     200   T=TT
101.           DO 210 I=1,NX
102.     210   T=T+XT(I)
103.           PHI=KK/T
104.           GAM=FLOAT(KK)/NN
105.     220   ICT=ICT+1
106.           IF(ICT.GT.30)GO TO 140
107.           HG=KK/GAM
108.           HP=KK/PHI-TT
109.           HGG=-HG/GAM
110.           HPP=-KK/(PHI*PHI)
111.           HGP=0
112.           DO 230 I=1,NX
113.           TI=XT(I)
114.           EI=EXP(-PHI*TI)
115.           DEN=1-GAM*(1-EI)
116.           T1=(1-EI)/DEN
117.           T2=GAM*TI*EI/DEN
118.           HG=HG-T1
119.           HP=HP-T2
120.           HGG=HGG-T1*T1
```

LISTING 2

```
121.            HPP=HPP+(1-GAM)*TI*T2/DEN
122.      230   HGP=HGP-T2/(GAM*DEN)
123.            DET=HGG*HPP-HGP*HGP
124.            DG=-(HPP*HG-HGP*HP)/DET
125.            DP=(-HGP*HG+HGG*HP)/DET
126.            GAM=GAM+DG
127.            PHI=PHI+DP
128.            IF((DG/GAM)**2+(DP/PHI)**2.GT.1E-8)GO TO 220
129.      240   SG=SQRT(-HPP/DET)
130.            SP=SQRT(-HGG/DET)
131.            RHO=HGP/SQRT(HGG*HPP)
132.            PQ=PHI
133.            GO TO 500
134.      C
135.      C     GROUPED TIME DATA
136.      C
137.      300   TT=0
138.            DO 310 I=1,NF
139.      310   TT=TT+I*FT(I)
140.            ICT=0
141.            IF(KCNS.EQ.2)GO TO 400
142.      C
143.      C     SINGLY CENSORED DATA, NEWTON-RAPHSON SEARCH FOR MLE SOLUTION
144.      C     FOR GAMMA AND Q
145.      C
146.            ALFA=TT/(KK*NX)
147.            QQ=1-KK/TT
148.      320   ICT=ICT+1
149.            IF(ICT.GT.30)GO TO 340
150.            QC=1-QQ
151.            QN=QQ**NX
152.            QNC=1-QN
153.            TOP=1/(NX*QC)-QN/QNC-ALFA
154.            BOT=-1/(NX*QC*QC)+(NX/(QQ*QNC))*(QN/QNC)
155.            DQ=TOP/BOT
156.            QQ=QQ+DQ
157.            IF(ABS(DQ/QQ).GT.1E-5)GO TO 320
158.            GAM=KK/(NN*(1-QQ**NX))
159.            HGG=-NN*KK/(MM*GAM*GAM)
160.            HGQ=NN*NN*NX*QN/(MM*QQ)
161.            QC=1-QQ
162.            TK=TT-KK
163.            S1=TK/QQ-KK/QC
164.            HQQ=-TK/(QQ*QQ)-KK/(QC*QC)-S1*(S1/MM-(NX-1)/QQ)
165.            DET=HGG*HQQ-HGQ*HGQ
166.            GO TO 440
167.      C
168.      C     LOCAL MAXIMUM OF LF NOT FOUND; FIND GLOBAL MAXIMUM AT GAMMA = 1
169.      C
170.      340   T=TT+MM*NX
171.      350   QQ=1-KK/T
172.            SQ=SQRT(KK*(T-KK)/T)/T
173.            GAM=1.0
174.            SG=0
175.            RHO=0
176.            PQ=QQ
177.            GO TO 500
178.      C
179.      C     PROGRESSIVELY CENSORED DATA, NEWTON-RAPHSON SEARCH FOR MLE SOLUTION
180.      C     FOR GAMMA AND Q
181.      C
182.      400   T=TT
```

```
183.            DO 410 I=1,NX
184.      410   T=T+I*XT(I)
185.            QQ=1-KK/T
186.            GAM=FLOAT(KK)/NN
187.      420   ICT=ICT+1
188.            IF(ICT.GT.30)GO TO 350
189.            HG=KK/GAM
190.            TK=TT-KK
191.            QC=1-QQ
192.            HQ=TK/QQ-KK/QC
193.            HGG=-HG/GAM
194.            HGQ=0
195.            HQQ=-TK/(QQ*QQ)-KK/(QC*QC)
196.            QI=1
197.            DO 430 I=1,NX
198.            XM=XT(I)
199.            QL=QI
200.            QI=QI*QQ
201.            IF(XM.EQ.0)GO TO 430
202.            QIC=1-QI
203.            DEN=1-GAM*QIC
204.            T1=QIC/DEN
205.            HG=HG-XM*T1
206.            T2=GAM*I*QL/DEN
207.            HQ=HQ+XM*T2
208.            HGG=HGG-XM*T1*T1
209.            HGQ=HGQ+XM*T2/(GAM*DEN)
210.            HQQ=HQQ-XM*T2*(T2-(I-1)/QQ)
211.      430   CONTINUE
212.            DET=HGG*HQQ-HGQ*HGQ
213.            DG=-(HQQ*HG-HGQ*HQ)/DET
214.            DQ=-(-HGQ*HG+HGG*HQ)/DET
215.            GAM=GAM+DG
216.            QQ=QQ+DQ
217.            IF((DG/GAM)**2+(DQ/QQ)**2.GT.1E-8)GO TO 420
218.      440   SG=SQRT(-HQQ/DET)
219.            SQ=SQRT(-HGG/DET)
220.            RHO=HGQ/SQRT(HGG*HQQ)
221.            PQ=QQ
222.      500   IF(KCNS.EQ.2)GO TO 505
223.      C
224.      C     CALCULATE LIKELIHOOD RATIO FOR SINGLY CENSORED DATA
225.      C
226.            XK=KK
227.            XTAU=TAU
228.            XTT=TT
229.            XNU=NX
230.            GO TO 520
231.      C
232.      C     CALCULATE LIKELIHOOD RATIO FOR PROGRESSIVELY CENSORED DATA
233.      C
234.      505   T1=-GAM*GAM*HGG
235.            XK=NN*T1/(NN+T1)
236.            IF(KTYP.EQ.2)GO TO 510
237.            XTAU=-ALOG(1-XK/(NN*GAM))/PHI
238.            X=PHI*XTAU
239.            XTT=XK*XTAU*(1/X-1/(EXP(X)-1))
240.            GO TO 520
241.      510   XNU=ALOG(1-XK/(NN*GAM))/ALOG(QQ)
242.            QC=1-QQ
243.            QN=QQ**XNU
244.            QNC=1-QN
```

LISTING 2

```
245.           XTT=XK*XNU*(1/(XNU*QC)-QN/QNC)
246.    520    XM=NN-XK
247.           HMX=VALLF(GAM,PQ,1)
248.           CALL LINMAX(1.0,PQ1,DQ)
249.           RATIO=1/VALLF(1.0,PQ1,2)
250.    C
251.    C   PRINT OUT RESULTS
252.    C
253.           IF(RATIO.LT.20)GO TO 600
254.           WRITE(6,530)NAME,RATIO
255.    530    FORMAT(//5X,10A4//' LIKELIHOOD RATIO = ',E8.2,
256.           1    ', NORMAL APPROXIMATION MAY BE USED')
257.           WRITE(6,570)GAM,SG
258.    570    FORMAT(//10X,' GAMMA =',F7.4,', S.D. =', F7.5)
259.           IF(KTYP.EQ.1)WRITE(6,580)PHI,SP
260.    580    FORMAT(/13X,'PHI =',F7.5,', S.D. =',F7.5)
261.           IF(KTYP.EQ.2)WRITE(6,590)QQ,SQ
262.    590    FORMAT(/15X,'Q =',F7.4,', S.D. =',F7.5)
263.           WRITE(6,595)RHO
264.    595    FORMAT(/18X,'RHO =',F7.4)
265.           GO TO 700
266.    600    WRITE(6,610)NAME,RATIO
267.    610    FORMAT(//5X,10A4//' LIKELIHOOD RATIO =',F6.3,
268.           1    ', NORMAL APPROXIMATION SHOULD NOT BE USED')
269.           WRITE(6,620)GAM
270.    620    FORMAT(//10X,' GAMMA =',F7.4)
271.           IF(KTYP.EQ.1)WRITE(6,630)PHI
272.    630    FORMAT(/13X,'PHI =',F7.5)
273.           IF(KTYP.EQ.2)WRITE(6,640)QQ
274.    640    FORMAT(/15X,'Q =',F7.4)
275.    700    CALL NTGRTN(GAM,PQ,CL,CH)
276.           CALL CONTUR(CL,CH,GAM,PQ)
277.           STOP
278.           END
279.           FUNCTION VALLF(G,PQ,IX)
280.    C ***************************************************************
281.    C *                                                             *
282.    C *                    FUNCTION VALLF                           *
283.    C *                                                             *
284.    C ***************************************************************
285.    C *                                                             *
286.    C * THIS FUNCTION CALCULATES THE VALUE OF THE LIKELIHOOD FUNCTION AT *
287.    C * ANY POINT G (= GAMMA), PQ(= PHI OR Q, DEPENDING ON KTYP). IF *
288.    C * IX=1, THE VALUES OF G AND PQ ARE THE MLE VALUES AND THE LOGARITHM *
289.    C * OF THE LIKELIHOOD FUNCTION THERE (AT ITS MAXIMUM) IS CALCULATED; *
290.    C * IF IX=2 THE VALUE OF THE LIKELIHOOD FUNCTION RELATIVE TO THE *
291.    C * MAXIMUM VALUE IS CALCULATED.                                *
292.    C *                                                             *
293.    C ***************************************************************
294.           COMMON FT(500),XT(500),TPQ(100),STD(100),HLF(100),NAME(10)
295.           COMMON NN,KK,MM,TT,KTYP,KCNS,NF,NX,TAU,XK,XTT,XNU,XTAU
296.           IF(KTYP.EQ.2)GO TO 30
297.           X=KK*ALOG(G*PQ)-PQ*TT
298.           IF(KCNS.EQ.2)GO TO 10
299.           Y=MM*ALOG(1-G*(1-EXP(-PQ*TAU)))
300.           GO TO 60
301.    10     Y=0
302.           DO 20 I=1,NX
303.    20     Y=Y+ALOG(1-G*(1-EXP(-PQ*XT(I))))
304.           GO TO 60
305.    30     X=KK*ALOG(G*(1-PQ))+(TT-KK)*ALOG(PQ)
306.           IF(KCNS.EQ.2)GO TO 40
```

```
307.              Y=MM*ALOG(1-G*(1-PQ**NX))
308.              GO TO 60
309.        40    Y=0
310.              PQI=1
311.              DO 50 I=1,NX
312.              PQI=PQI*PQ
313.              IF(XT(I).EQ.0)GO TO 50
314.              Y=Y+XT(I)*ALOG(1-G*(1-PQI))
315.        50    CONTINUE
316.        60    X=X+Y
317.              IF(IX.GT.1)GO TO 70
318.        C
319.        C  VALUE OF LOG LF AT MAXIMUM IS RETURNED
320.        C
321.              HMX=X
322.              VALLF=X
323.              RETURN
324.        C
325.        C VALUE OF LF RELATIVE TO MAXIMUM IS RETURNED, IF GREATER THAN EXP(-10)
326.        C
327.        70    VALLF=0
328.              E=X-HMX
329.              IF(E.LT.-10.)RETURN
330.              VALLF=EXP(E)
331.              RETURN
332.              END
333.              SUBROUTINE LINMAX(G,PQ,SD)
334.        C ****************************************************************
335.        C *                                                              *
336.        C *                    SUBROUTINE LINMAX                         *
337.        C *                                                              *
338.        C ****************************************************************
339.        C *                                                              *
340.        C * THIS SUBROUTINE CALCULATES THE VALUE OF PHI (KTYP=1) OR Q (KTYP=2) *
341.        C * THAT MAXIMIZES THE LIKELIHOOD FUNCTION ALONG THE LINE G (GAMMA)    *
342.        C * = CONSTANT.  IT ALSO RETURNS THE STANDARD DEVIATION OF PHI OR Q.   *
343.        C *                                                              *
344.        C ****************************************************************
345.              COMMON FT(500),XT(500),TPQ(100),STD(100),HLF(100),NAME(10)
346.              COMMON NN,KK,MM,TT,KTYP,KCNS,NF,NX,TAU,XK,XTT,XNU,XTAU
347.              IF(G.LT.0.999)GO TO 100
348.              IF(KTYP.EQ.2)GO TO 30
349.              Y=MM*TAU
350.              IF(KCNS.EQ.1)GO TO 20
351.              Y=0
352.              DO 10 I=1,NX
353.        10    Y=Y+XT(I)
354.        20    T=TT+Y
355.              P=KK/T
356.              PQ=P
357.              V=KK/(T*T)
358.              GO TO 240
359.        30    Y=MM*NX
360.              IF(KCNS.EQ.1)GO TO 50
361.              Y=0
362.              DO 40 I=1,NX
363.        40    Y=Y+I*XT(I)
364.        50    T=TT+Y-KK
365.              Q=T/(T+KK)
366.              PQ=Q
367.              V=T*KK/(T+KK)**3
```

LISTING 2

```
368.            GO TO 240
369.     100    ICT=0
370.            IF(KTYP.EQ.2)GO TO 200
371.     110    ICT=ICT+1
372.            IF(ICT.GT.30)STOP 110
373.            HP=KK/P-TT
374.            HPP=-KK/(P*P)
375.            IF(KCNS.EQ.2)GO TO 120
376.            EI=EXP(-P*TAU)
377.            DEN=1-G*(1-EI)
378.            TX=G*TAU*EI/DEN
379.            HP=HP-MM*TX
380.            HPP=HPP+MM*(1-G)*TAU*TX/DEN
381.            GO TO 140
382.     120    DO 130 I=1,NX
383.            TI=XT(I)
384.            EI=EXP(-P*TI)
385.            DEN=1-G*(1-EI)
386.            TX=G*TI*EI/DEN
387.            HP=HP-TX
388.     130    HPP=HPP+(1-G)*TI*TX/DEN
389.     140    DP=-HP/HPP
390.            P=P+DP
391.            IF(ABS(DP/P).GT.1E-4)GO TO 110
392.            PQ=P
393.            V=-1/HPP
394.            GO TO 240
395.     200    ICT=ICT+1
396.            IF(ICT.GT.30)STOP 200
397.            QC=1-Q
398.            TK=TT-KK
399.            HQ=TK/Q-KK/QC
400.            HQQ=-TK/(Q*Q)-KK/(QC*QC)
401.            IF(KCNS.EQ.2)GO TO 210
402.            QN=Q**NX
403.            T1=G*NX*QN/Q
404.            DEN=1-G*(1-QN)
405.            T2=T1/DEN
406.            HQ=HQ+MM*T1/DEN
407.            HQQ=HQQ+MM*T2*((NX-1)/Q-T2)
408.            GO TO 230
409.     210    QI=1
410.            DO 220 I=1,NX
411.            QL=QI
412.            QI=QI*Q
413.            XM=XT(I)
414.            IF(XM.EQ.0)GO TO 220
415.            T1=G*I*QL
416.            T2=T1/(1-G*(1-QI))
417.            HQ=HQ+XM*T2
418.            HQQ=HQQ+XM*T2*((I-1)/Q-T2)
419.     220    CONTINUE
420.     230    DQ=-HQ/HQQ
421.            Q=Q+DQ
422.            IF(ABS(DQ/Q).GT.1E-4)GO TO 200
423.            PQ=Q
424.            V=-1/HQQ
425.     240    SD=SQRT(V)
426.            RETURN
427.            END
428.            SUBROUTINE NTGRTN(GMX,PQX,CL,CH)
```

```
C ***********************************************************************
C *                                                                     *
C *                        SUBROUTINE NTGRTN                            *
C *                                                                     *
C ***********************************************************************
C *                                                                     *
C *   THIS SUBROUTINE CALCULATES THE VOLUME OF THE LIKELIHOOD FUNCTION   *
C *   WITHIN A SET OF HEIGHTS.  WHEN HT=0 THE VOLUME CALCULATED IS THE   *
C *   ENTIRE VOLUME.  THE FRACTION OF VOLUME WITHIN EACH CONTOUR CAN     *
C *   THEN BE CALCULATED FOR THE NINE REMAINING HEIGHTS.  THESE HEIGHTS  *
C *   ARE THEN INTERPOLATED TO APPROXIMATE THE HEIGHT OF THE CONTOUR     *
C *   (CH) THAT WILL PRODUCE THE APPROPRIATE CONFIDENCE LEVELS (CL).     *
C *   FOUR CONFIDENCE LEVELS ARE CALCULATED -- .99, .98, .95, AND .90.   *
C *                                                                     *
C ***********************************************************************
      COMMON FT(500),XT(500),TPQ(100),STD(100),HLF(100),NAME(10)
      COMMON NN,KK,MM,TT,KTYP,KCNS,NF,NX,TAU,XK,XTT,XNU,XTAU
      DIMENSION HT(10),SLICE(10),VOL(10),CL(4),CH(4)
      DATA HT/0.,.005,.01,.015,.02,.03,.05,.1,.15,.2/
      DO 10 I=1,10
   10 VOL(I)=0
      GAM=1.01
      IG=101
C
C   THE L.F. IS DIVIDED INTO 100 "SLICES" FOR NUMERICAL INTEGRATION
C
   20 GAM=GAM-0.01
      IG=IG-1
      IF(GAM.LE.0.001)GO TO 100
C
C   FIND PTOP OR QTOP THAT MAXIMIZES THE L.F. FOR THAT GAMMA
C
      CALL LINMAX(GAM,PQTOP,SDX)
      TPQ(IG)=PQTOP
      STD(IG)=SDX
C
C   CALCULATE RELATIVE HEIGHT OF L.F. AT THAT POINT
C
      HREL=VALLF(GAM,PQTOP,2)
      HLF(IG)=HREL
      IF(HREL.GT.0)GO TO 30
      IF(GAM.LT.GMX)GO TO 100
      GO TO 20
   30 DO 40 I=1,10
      SLICE(I)=0
      IF(HREL.GT.HT(I))SLICE(I)=HREL
   40 CONTINUE
C
C   FIRST INTEGRATE SLICE TO RIGHT OF SLICE MAXIMUM, FOR EACH HEIGHT
C
      DPQ=.02*SDX
      PQ=PQTOP
      ISW=1
   50 PQ=PQ+DPQ
      IF(PQ.LE.0)GO TO (70,80),ISW
      IF((KTYP.EQ.2).AND.(PQ.GE.1))GO TO (70,80),ISW
      HREL=VALLF(GAM,PQ,2)
      IF(HREL.LE.0)GO TO (70,80),ISW
      DO 60 I=1,10
      IF(HREL.LT.HT(I))GO TO 50
   60 SLICE(I)=SLICE(I)+HREL
```

LISTING 2

```
490.              GO TO 50
491.       C
492.       C   NEXT INTEGRATE SLICE TO LEFT OF SLICE MAXIMUM
493.       C
494.       70    DPQ=-DPQ
495.             PQ=PQTOP
496.             ISW=2
497.             GO TO 50
498.       80    DO 90 I=1,10
499.       90    VOL(I)=VOL(I)+SLICE(I)*ABS(DPQ)
500.             GO TO 20
501.       100   DO 110 I=2,10
502.       110   VOL(I)=VOL(I)/VOL(1)
503.             VOL(1)=1
504.             DO 140 IC=1,4
505.             DO 120 I=1,10
506.             IF(VOL(I).LE.CL(IC))GO TO 130
507.       120   CONTINUE
508.             STOP 120
509.       C
510.       C   THIS NEXT SECTION INTERPOLATES TO OBTAIN THE APPROPRIATE
511.       C   CONTOUR HEIGHTS (CH) FOR THE SPECIFIED CONFIDENCE LEVELS (CL)
512.       C
513.       130   J=I-1
514.             SLOPE=(HT(I)-HT(J))/(VOL(I)-VOL(J))
515.       140   CH(IC)=HT(J)+SLOPE*(CL(IC)-VOL(J))
516.             RETURN
517.             END
518.             SUBROUTINE CONTUR(CL,CH,GMX,PQX)
519.       C ********************************************************************
520.       C *                                                                  *
521.       C *                    SUBROUTINE CONTUR                             *
522.       C *                                                                  *
523.       C ********************************************************************
524.       C *                                                                  *
525.       C * THIS SUBROUTINE CALCULATES THE CONFIDENCE REGIONS SURROUNDING THE*
526.       C * MAXIMUM LIKELIHOOD ESTIMATES OF GAMMA AND PHI (OR Q).  THEY ARE  *
527.       C * REPRESENTED BY CONTOURS OF THE LIKELIHOOD FUNCTION CORRESPONDING *
528.       C * TO THE CONFIDENCE LEVELS -- CL.  THE LEVELS AT WHICH THEY ARE    *
529.       C * PLOTTED -- CH -- HAVE PREVIOUSLY BEEN CALCULATED, IN THE         *
530.       C * SUBROUTINE 'NTGRTN'.                                             *
531.       C *                                                                  *
532.       C ********************************************************************
533.             COMMON FT(500),XT(500),TPQ(100),STD(100),HLF(100),NAME(10)
534.             COMMON NN,KK,MM,TT,KTYP,KCNS,NF,NX,TAU,XK,XTT,XNU,XTAU
535.             DIMENSION CL(4),CH(4),LL(4),PQC(203,4),GC(203,4),PX(203),PY(203)
536.             DATA NG/100/
537.                PQMIN=10000
538.                PQMAX=0
539.             DG=1./NG
540.             PQL=0
541.             PQR=0
542.             DO 200 IH=1,4
543.             IF(CH(IH).EQ.0)GO TO 200
544.             IC=2
545.             JC=204
546.             I1=0
547.             GF=0
548.       C
549.       C   'TEST' IS THE HEIGHT OF THE CONTOUR FOR THIS PARTICULAR CONF. LEVEL
550.       C
```

```
551.              TEST=CH(IH)
552.              DO 100 IG=1,NG
553.              IF(HLF(IG).LT.TEST)GO TO 100
554.              GI=IG*DG
555.       C
556.       C ISIDE = 1 TO CALCULATE RIGHT SIDE OF CONTOUR
557.       C       = 2 TO CALCULATE LEFT  SIDE OF CONTOUR
558.       C
559.              ISIDE=1
560.              PQI=PQR
561.       10     IF(PQI.NE.0)GO TO 20
562.       C
563.       C IF NO BETTER STARTING POINT EXISTS, START 2 S.D.S FROM MAX
564.       C
565.              PQI=TPQ(IG)+2.0*ISIDE*STD(IG)
566.       20     ISTEP=0
567.       C
568.       C FIRST STEP SIZE IS 0.1 S.D.
569.       C
570.              DPQ=0.1*ISIDE*STD(IG)
571.              HNEW=0
572.       30     STEP=DPQ
573.       40     PQI=PQI+STEP
574.              HLAST=HNEW
575.              HNEW=VALLF(GI,PQI,2)
576.              IF(HLAST.EQ.0)GO TO 40
577.       C
578.       C HAVE THE LAST 2 STEPS BRACKETED THE STEP HEIGHT?
579.       C
580.              IF((HNEW-TEST)*(HLAST-TEST).LE.0)GO TO 50
581.              IF(HNEW.GT.TEST)GO TO 30
582.              STEP=-DPQ
583.              GO TO 40
584.       C
585.       C INTERPOLATE TO ESTIMATE VALUE WHERE L.F. CROSSES TEST HEIGHT
586.       C
587.       50     PQI=PQI+DPQ*(HNEW-TEST)/(HNEW-HLAST)
588.              IF(ISTEP.GT.0)GO TO 60
589.              HNEW=VALLF(GI,PQI,2)
590.              ISTEP=1
591.       C
592.       C REDUCE STEP SIZE TO 0.01 S.D. AND AGAIN BRACKET AND INTERPOLATE
593.       C
594.              DPQ=0.1*DPQ
595.              GO TO 30
596.       C
597.       C STORE INTERPOLATED VALUE OF POINT ON CONTOUR IN ARRAY
598.       C
599.       60     IF(ISIDE.NE.1)GO TO 80
600.       C
601.       C POINT IS ON RIGHT SIDE OF CONTOUR
602.       C
603.              PQC(IC,IH)=PQI
604.              GC(IC,IH)=GI
605.       C
606.       C START THE RIGHT SIDE SEARCH AT PQR NEXT TIME
607.       C
608.              PQR=PQI
609.       C
610.       C FIND THE LARGEST (RIGHTMOST) VALUE OF PQI
611.       C
612.              IF(PQI.GT.PQMAX)PQMAX=PQI
```

LISTING 2

```
613.      C
614.      C   FIND THE SMALLEST VALUE OF GAMMA ON THIS CONTOUR
615.      C
616.              IF(GF.NE.0)GO TO 70
617.              GF=GI
618.              I1=IG
619.              PQ1=TPQ(IG)
620.              R1=HLF(IG)
621.      C
622.      C   FIND THE LARGEST VALUE OF GAMMA ON THIS CONTOUR
623.      C
624.       70     IZ=IG
625.              GL=GI
626.      C
627.      C   INCREMENT THE CONTOUR POINT COUNTER
628.      C
629.              IC=IC+1
630.              PQI=PQL
631.      C
632.      C   SWITCH TO SEARCH ON LEFT SIDE
633.      C
634.              ISIDE=-1
635.              GO TO 10
636.      C
637.      C   DECREMENT THE OTHER CONTOUR POINT COUNTER AND STORE THE
638.      C   INTERPOLATED VALUES IN THE CONTOUR ARRAY FOR THE LEFT SIDE
639.      C
640.       80     JC=JC-1
641.              PQC(JC,IH)=PQI
642.              GC(JC,IH)=GI
643.      C
644.      C   START THE LEFT SIDE SEARCH AT PQL NEXT TIME
645.      C
646.              PQL=PQI
647.      C
648.      C   FIND THE SMALLEST (LEFTMOST) VALUE OF PQI
649.      C
650.              IF(PQI.LT.PQMIN)PQMIN=PQI
651.      100    CONTINUE
652.      C
653.      C   STARTING POINTS FOR NEXT CONTOUR
654.      C
655.              PQR=PQC(1,IH)
656.              PQL=PQC(203,IH)
657.              LVL=100*CL(IH)+0.1
658.      C
659.      C   THIS SECTION CALCULATES THE FIRST POINT OF THE CONTOUR
660.      C
661.              PQC(1,IH)=PQC(2,IH)
662.              GC(1,IH)=GC(2,IH)
663.              I2=I1-1
664.              IF(I2.LE.0)GO TO 140
665.              PQ2=TPQ(I2)
666.              R2=HLF(I2)
667.              FACTR=(R1-CH(IH))/(R1-R2)
668.              PQC(1,IH)=PQ1+(PQ2-PQ1)*FACTR
669.              GC(1,IH)=GF-DG*FACTR
670.      C
671.      C   THIS SECTION CALCULATES THE CONTOUR'S MIDPOINT
672.      C
673.      140    KC=IC-1
674.              PQC(IC,IH)=PQC(KC,IH)
```

```
675.            GC(IC,IH)=GC(KC,IH)
676.            IF(IZ.GE.NG)GO TO 150
677.            PQ1=TPQ(IZ)
678.            R1=HLF(IZ)
679.            I2=IZ+1
680.            PQ2=TPQ(I2)
681.            R2=HLF(I2)
682.            FACTR=(R1-CH(IH))/(R1-R2)
683.            PQC(IC,IH)=PQ1+(PQ2-PQ1)*FACTR
684.            GC(IC,IH)=GL+DG*FACTR
685.      C
686.      C     THIS SECTION PACKS THE TWO HALVES OF THE CONTOUR TOGETHER
687.      C
688.       150  IL=2*IC-2
689.            IC=IC+1
690.            JEX=207-2*IC
691.            DO 160 I=IC,IL
692.            JJ=I+JEX
693.            PQC(I,IH)=PQC(JJ,IH)
694.       160  GC(I,IH)=GC(JJ,IH)
695.            IL=IL+1
696.      C
697.      C     THE LAST POINT REJOINS THE FIRST POINT OF THE CONTOUR
698.      C
699.            PQC(IL,IH)=PQC(1,IH)
700.            GC(IL,IH)=GC(1,IH)
701.            LL(IH)=IL
702.      C
703.      C     CONTOUR POINTS ARE PRINTED OUT AND STORED ON DATA FILE
704.      C
705.      C          WRITE(8,170)LVL,(I,GC(I,IH),PQC(I,IH),I=1,IL)
706.      C          WRITE(6,170)LVL,(I,GC(I,IH),PQC(I,IH),I=1,IL)
707.      C170      FORMAT(//I5,' PERCENT CONTOUR'/(5(I6,F6.3,F8.5)))
708.      C
709.      C     SCALE FACTORS FOR THE CONTOUR ARE PLOTTED
710.      C
711.            IF(IH.NE.1)GO TO 190
712.            IF(KTYP.EQ.2)GO TO 180
713.            SF=1E-5
714.            ISF=5
715.       171  SF=10*SF
716.            ISF=ISF-1
717.            IF(PQMAX.GT.SF)GO TO 171
718.            STEP=.1*SF
719.            BMAX=0
720.       172  BMAX=BMAX+STEP
721.            IF(PQMAX.GT.BMAX)GO TO 172
722.            BMIN=BMAX
723.            I=0
724.       173  BMIN=BMIN-STEP
725.            I=I+1
726.            IF(PQMIN.LT.BMIN)GO TO 173
727.            IF(I.NE.2*(I/2))BMIN=BMIN-STEP
728.            RANGE=BMAX-BMIN
729.            FIRST=BMIN
730.            GO TO 190
731.       180  FIRST=1
732.            SF=1
733.       185  FIRST=FIRST-0.2
734.            IF(PQMIN.LE.FIRST)GO TO 185
735.            FIRST=AMAX1(FIRST,0.0)
736.            RANGE=1.0-FIRST
737.       190  I1=IL+1
```

LISTING 2

```
738.              PQC(I1,IH)=FIRST
739.              GC(I1,IH)=0
740.              I2=I1+1
741.              PQC(I2,IH)=.125*RANGE
742.              GC(I2,IH)=.125
743.       200    CONTINUE
744.              CALL BGNPLT(7,'CONTOUR')
745.       C
746.       C  THE REST OF THE PROGRAM PLOTS THE DATA
747.       C
748.              CALL PLOT(6.5,1.0,-3)
749.       C
750.       C  THE MLE VALUES ARE PLOTTED AS A CIRCLED POINT
751.       C
752.              CALL SYMBOL((PQX-PQC(I1,4))/PQC(I2,4),8*GMX,.07,1,0,-1)
753.       C
754.       C  THE CONTOURS ARE PLOTTED NEXT
755.       C
756.              DO 210 IH=1,4
757.              L=LL(IH)+2
758.              DO 205 I=1,L
759.              PX(I)=PQC(I,IH)
760.       205    PY(I)=GC(I,IH)
761.       210    CALL LINE(PX,PY,LL(IH),1,0,1)
762.              CALL PLOT(8.,8.,3)
763.       C
764.       C  THE GRID IS PLOTTED NEXT
765.       C
766.              DO 220 I=1,5
767.              Y=(6-I)*1.6
768.              CALL PLOT(0.,Y,2)
769.              CALL PLOT(0.,Y-.8,3)
770.              CALL PLOT(8.,Y-.8,2)
771.       220    CALL PLOT(8.,Y-1.6,3)
772.              CALL PLOT(0.,0.,2)
773.              DO 230 I=1,5
774.              X=1.6*I
775.              CALL PLOT(X-1.6,8.,2)
776.              CALL PLOT(X-.8,8.,3)
777.              CALL PLOT(X-.8,0.,2)
778.       230    CALL PLOT(X,0.,3)
779.              CALL PLOT(X,8.,2)
780.       C
781.       C  THIS SECTION PLOTS THE SCALES ALONG THE AXES
782.       C
783.              DO 240 I=1,6
784.              TIC=0.2*(I-1)
785.              PQ=(FIRST+0.2*(I-1)*RANGE)/SF
786.       240    CALL NUMBER(8.*TIC-.07,-.13,.07,PQ,0.,2)
787.              DO 250 I=1,6
788.              TIC=0.2*(I-1)
789.       250    CALL NUMBER(-.1,8.*TIC-.07,.07,TIC,90.,1)
790.              CALL SYMBOL(-.1,3.7,.14,'GAMMA',90.,5)
791.              CALL SYMBOL(.4,8.1,.14,NAME,0.,40)
792.              IF(KTYP.EQ.2)GO TO 260
793.              CALL SYMBOL(3.6,-.2,.14,'PHI*10',0.,6)
794.              CALL NUMBER(4.4,-.13,.07,FLOAT(ISF),0.,-1)
795.              GO TO 270
796.       260    CALL SYMBOL(3.96,-.2,.14,'Q',0.,1)
797.       270    CALL ENDPLT
798.              RETURN
799.              END
```

References

(Entries marked with an asterisk were used in the development of Table 6-1)

Adams, R., and H. J. Vetter (1971). "Probation Caseload Size and Recidivism Rate." *British Journal of Criminology,* 11, 390–393.
*Adams, Stuart (1959). "Effectiveness of the Youth Authority Special Treatment Program: First Interim Report." Research Report No. 5, California Youth Authority. (Cited in Lipton *et al.,* 1975.)
*Adams, Stuart (1961). "Effectiveness of Interview Therapy with Older Youth Authority Wards: An Interim Evaluation of the PICO Project." Research Report No. 20, California Youth Authority. (Cited in Lipton *et al.,* 1975.)
*Adams, Stuart (1964). "An Experimental Assessment of Group Counseling with Juvenile Probationers." Paper presented at the 18th Convention of the California State Psychological Association. (Cited in Lipton *et al.,* 1975.)
*Adamson, LaMay, and Warren H. Dunham (1956). "Clinical Treatment of Male Delinquents: A Case Study in Effort and Result." *American Sociological Review,* 21, 312–320. (Cited in Lipton *et al.,* 1975.)
Akaike, H. (1974). "A New Look at Statistical Model Identification." *IEEE Transactions on Automatic Control* AC-19, 716–723.
Alschuler, Albert (1978). "Sentencing Reform and Prosecutorial Power: A Critique of Recent Proposals for 'Fixed' and 'Presumptive' Sentencing." *University of Pennsylvania Law Review,* 126, 550–577.
Amemiya, T., and M. Boskin (1974). "Analysis When the Dependent Variable is Truncated Lognormal, with Application to the Duration of Welfare Dependency." *International Economic Review,* 15, 485–496.
American Correctional Association (1981). *Standards for Adult Correctional Institutions* (second edition). American Correctional Association (in cooperation with the Commission on Accreditation for Corrections), College Park, Maryland.
American Friends Service Committee (1971). *Struggle for Justice.* Hill and Wang, New York.
Anscombe, F. J. (1961). "Estimating a Mixed-Exponential Response Law," *Journal of the American Statistical Association,* 56, 493–502.
Avi-Itzhak, B., and R. Shinnar (1973). "Quantitative Models in Crime Control." *Journal of Criminal Justice,* 1, 185–217.
Babst, Dean, and John W. Mannering (1965). "Probation Versus Imprisonment for Similar Types of Offenders: A Comparison by Subsequent Violations." *Journal of Research in Crime and Delinquency,* 2, 60–71.
Baer, D. J., P. J. Jacobs, and F. E. Carr (1975). "Instructors' Ratings of Delinquents after Outward Bound Survival Training and Their Subsequent Recidivism." *Psychology Reports,* 36, 547–553.
Bagozzi, Richard (1980). *Causal Models in Marketing.* Wiley, New York.
Baldus, D., and J. W. Cole (1975). "A Comparison of the Work of Thorsten Sellin and Isaac Ehrlich on the Deterrent Effect of Capital Punishment." *Yale Law Journal,* 85, 170–186.
*Banks, Charlotte (1964). "Reconviction of Young Offenders." *Current Legal Problems 1964,* 61–79. (Cited in Lipton *et al.,* 1975.)

Barlow, Richard, and Frank Proschan (1975). *Statistical Theory of Reliability and Life Testing: Probability Models*. Holt, Rinehart and Winston, New York.
Barnett, Arnold (1981a). "Further Standards of Accountability for Deterrence Research." In J. A. Fox, Ed., *Methods in Quantitative Criminology* Academic Press, New York.
Barnett, Arnold (1981b). "The Deterrent Effect of Capital Punishment: A Test of Some Recent Studies." *Operations Research*, 29, 346–370.
Barnett, Arnold (1982). "An Underestimated Threat to Multiple Regression Analysis Used in Job Discrimination Cases." *Industrial Relations Law Journal* 5(1), 156–173.
Barnett, Arnold (1983). "The Linear Model and Some of Its Friends." *Interfaces*, 13(1), 61–65.
Barry, Donald M., and Alexander Greer (1981). "Sentencing Versus Prosecutorial Discretion: The Application of a New Disparity Measure." *Journal of Research in Crime and Delinquency*, 18, 254–271.
Barton, Russell R. (1978). "Exoffender Postrelease Performance Evaluation with Related Theoretical Topics in Variable Selection and Followup Intervals for Regression Models Using Grouped Censored Survival Data." Ph.D. dissertation, School of Operations Research and Industrial Engineering, Cornell University, Ithaca, New York. (University Microfilms, Ann Arbor, Michigan.)
Barton, Russell R., and Bruce W. Turnbull (1979). "Evaluation of Recidivism Data: Use of Failure Rate Regression Models." *Evaluation Quarterly*, 3, 629–641.
Barton, Russell R., and Bruce W. Turnbull (1981). "A Failure Rate Regression Model for the Study of Recidivism." In J. A. Fox, Ed., *Models in Quantitative Criminology*, Academic Press, New York, 81–101.
Beck, James, and Peter Hoffman (1976). "Time Served and Release Performance: A Research Note." *Journal of Research in Crime and Delinquency*, 13, 127–132.
Belkin, Jacob, Alfred Blumstein, and William Glass (1973). "Recidivism as a Feedback Process: An Analytical Model and Empirical Validation." *Journal of Criminal Justice*, 1, 7–26.
Bennett, Lawrence, and Max Ziegler (1975). "Early Discharge: A Suggested Approach to Increased Efficiency in Parole." *Federal Probation*, 39, 27–30.
*Benson, Sir George (1959). "Prediction Methods and Young Prisoners." *British Journal of Delinquency*, 9, 192–199. (Cited in Lipton *et al.*, 1975.)
Berk, Richard A., Sheldon L. Messinger, David Rauma, and E. John Berecochea (1982). "Prisons as Self-Regulating Systems: A Comparison of Historical Patterns in California for Male and Female Offenders." Paper presented at the Joint Meeting of the Operations Research Society of America and the Institute of Management Science, San Diego, October.
Berkson, Joseph, and Robert P. Gage (1952). "Survival Curve for Cancer Patients Following Treatment." *Journal of the American Statistical Association*, 47, 501–515.
*Bernsten, Karen, and Karl O. Christiansen. "A Resocialization Experiment with Short-Term Offenders." *Scandinavian Studies in Criminology*, 1, 35–54. (Cited in Lipton *et al.*, 1975.)
Blalock, Hubert M. Jr. (1972). *Social Statistics*. McGraw-Hill, New York.
Bloom, Howard S. (1979). "Evaluating Human Service and Criminal Justice Programs by Modeling the Probability and Timing of Recidivism." *Sociological Methods and Research*, 8, 179–208.
Bloom, Howard S., and Neil M. Singer (1979). "Determining the Cost-Effectiveness of Correctional Programs: The Case of Patuxent Institution." *Evaluation Quarterly*, 3(4) 609–627.
Blumstein, Alfred (1975). "A Model to Aid in Planning for the Total Criminal Justice System." In L. Oberlander, Ed., *Quantitative Tools for Criminal Justice Planning*. Law Enforcement Assistance Administration, Washington, D.C.
Blumstein, Alfred, and Jacqueline Cohen (1973). "A Theory of the Stability of Punishment." *Journal of Criminal Law and Criminology*, 64, 198–207.
Blumstein, Alfred, and Jacqueline Cohen (1979a). "Control of Selection Effects in the Evaluation of Social Programs." *Evaluation Quarterly* 3(4), 583–608.

Blumstein, Alfred, and Jacqueline Cohen (1979b). "Estimation of Individual Crime Rates from Arrest Records." *Journal of Criminal Law and Criminology,* 70, 561–585.

Blumstein, Alfred, Jacqueline Cohen, and Daniel Nagin (1977). "The Dynamics of a Homeostatic Punishment Process." *Journal of Criminal Law and Criminology,* 67, 317–354.

Blumstein, Alfred, and Elizabeth Graddy (1982). "Prevalence and Recidivism in Index Arrests: A Feedback Model." *Law and Society Review* 16(1), 265–290.

Blumstein, Alfred, and Richard C. Larson (1971). "Problems in Modeling and Measuring Recidivism." *Journal of Research in Crime and Delinquency,* 8, 124–132.

Blumstein, Alfred, and Soumyo Moitra (1980). "An Analysis of the Time Series of the Imprisonment Rate of the States of the United States: A Further Test of the Stability of Punishment Hypothesis." *Journal of Criminal Law and Criminology,* 70, 376–390.

Boag, John W. (1949). "Maximum Likelihood Estimates of the Proportion of Patients Cured by Cancer Therapy." *Journal of the Royal Statistical Society,* 11, 15–53.

Boland, Barbara, and James Q. Wilson (1978). "Age, Crime, and Punishment." *The Public Interest,* 51, 22–34.

*Boston University, Law-Medicine Institute, Training Center in Youth Development (1966). "Educational Counselors: Training for a New Definition of After-Care of Juvenile Parolees." (Cited in Lipton *et al.,* 1975.)

Bowers, William J., and Glenn L. Pierce (1975). "The Illusion of Deterrence in Isaac Ehrlich's Research on Capital Punishment." *Yale Law Journal,* 85, 187–208.

Box, George E. P., and George C. Tiao (1973). *Bayesian Inference in Statistical Analysis.* Addison-Wesley, Reading, Massachusetts.

Brown, Lawrence D. (1978). "The Development of a Parole Classification System Using Discriminant Analysis." *Journal of Research in Crime and Delinquency,* 15, 92–108.

*Burkhart, Walter R., and Arthur Sathmary (1964). "An Evaluation of a Treatment Control Project for Narcotics Offenders: Phases 1 and 2." *Journal of Research in Crime and Delinquency,* 1, 47–52. (Cited in Lipton *et al.,* 1975.)

Bury, Karl (1975). *Statistical Models in Applied Science.* Wiley, New York.

*California Adult Authority, Division of Adult Paroles (1956). "Special Intensive Parole Unit, Phase I: Fifteen Man Caseload Study." (Cited in Lipton *et al.,* 1975.)

*California Department of Corrections (1958). "Intensive Treatment Program: Second Annual Report." (Cited in Lipton *et al.,* 1975.)

*California Department of Corrections (1958). "Special Intensive Parole Unit, Phase II: Thirty Man Caseload Study." (Cited in Lipton *et al.,* 1975.)

*Cambridge University, Department of Criminal Science (1952). *Detention in Remand Homes.* Macmillan, London. (Cited in Lipton *et al.,* 1975.)

Campbell, Donald T., and Albert Erlebacher (1970). "How Regression Artifacts in Quasi-Experimental Evaluations Can Mistakenly Make Compensatory Education Look Harmful." In J. Hellmuth, Ed., *Compensatory Education: A National Debate.* Volume 3, *Disadvantaged Child.* Brunner/Mazel, New York, 185–210.

Campbell, Donald T., and H. Laurence Ross (1968). "The Connecticut Crackdown on Speeding: Time-Series Data in Quasi-Experimental Analysis." *Law and Society Review,* 3, 33–53.

Carr-Hill, G. A., and R. A. Carr-Hill (1972). "Reconviction as a Process." *British Journal of Criminology,* 12, 35–43.

Chaiken, Jan M. (1978). "Estimates of Offender Characteristics Derived from the Rand Prison Inmate Survey." A working paper prepared for the U.S. Department of Justice, the Rand Corporation, Santa Monica, January, 1978.

Chaiken, Jan M. (1980). *Two Patrol Car Deployment Models: History of Use 1975–1979.* Report P-6458, The Rand Corporation, Santa Monica, California.

Chaiken, Jan M., and Marcia R. Chaiken (1982a). *Varieties of Criminal Behavior.* Report R-2814-NIJ, The Rand Corporation, Santa Monica, California.

Chaiken, Jan M., and Marcia R. Chaiken, with Joyce E. Peterson (1982b). *Varieties of Criminal Behavior: Summary and Policy Implications.* Report R-2814/1-NIJ, The Rand Corporation, Santa Monica, California.

Chaiken, Jan M., and John E. Rolph (1980). "Selective Incapacitation Strategies Based on Estimated Crime Rates." *Operations Research,* 28, 1259–1274.

Chaiken, Marcia R. (1982). *The Chicago Area Project and the Enigma of Delinquency Prevention: Some Exploratory Findings.* Draft report, The Rand Corporation, Santa Monica, California.

Chambers, Marcia (1981). "How the Police Target Young Offenders." *The New York Times Magazine,* September 20, 116–124.

Christie, Nils (1976). "Is It Time to Stop Counting?" In *Evaluation Research in Criminal Justice.* United Nations Social Defence Research Institute, Rome, 63–76.

Chung, Min Keun (1983). *Alternative Methodologies for Occupational Injury Analysis.* Department of Industrial and Operations Engineering, University of Michigan, Ann Arbor.

Cirel, Paul, Patricia Evans, Daniel McGillis, and Debra Whitcomb (1977). *An Exemplary Project: Community Crime Prevention in Seattle, Washington.* National Institute of Law Enforcement and Criminal Justice, Washington, D.C.

Clarke, Stevens H. (1974). "Getting 'Em Out of Circulation: Does Incarceration of Juvenile Offenders Reduce Crime?" *Journal of Criminal Law and Criminology,* 65(4), 528–535.

Coates, Robert B., Alden D. Miller, and Lloyd E. Ohlin (1978). *Diversity in a Youth Correctional System: Handling Delinquents in Massachusetts.* Ballinger, Cambridge, Massachusetts.

Cockerill, R. W. (1975). "Probation Effectiveness in Alberta." *Canadian Journal of Criminology and Corrections,* 17, 284–291.

Cohen, Jacqueline (1978). "The Incapacitative Effect of Imprisonment: A Critical View of the Literature." In Alfred Blumstein, Jacquline Cohen, and David Nagin, Eds. *Deterrence and Incapacitation: Estimating the Effects of Criminal Sanctions on Crime Rates,* National Academy of Sciences Press, Washington, D.C., 187–243.

Cohen, Jacqueline (1982). "Avoiding the Pitfalls of Prediction: The Incapacitative Potential of Targeting on Charged Offense." Paper presented at the American Society of Criminology, Toronto, November 1982.

Conrad, John P. (1981). *Justice and Consequences.* Lexington Books, Lexington, Massachusetts.

Cook, Philip J. (1980). "Research in Criminal Deterrence: Laying the Groundwork for the Second Decade." In N. Morris and M. Tonry, Eds., *Crime and Justice: An Annual Review of Research* (Volume 2). University of Chicago Press, Chicago, 211–268.

Cook, Thomas D., and Donald T. Campbell (1979). *Quasi-Experimentation: Design and Analysis Issues for Field Settings.* Rand McNally, Chicago.

*Coombs, Keith A. (1965). "An Analysis of the Academic Educational Program in Washington State Adult Correctional Institutions." Research Review No. 20, State of Washington, Department of Institutions. (Cited in Lipton *et al.,* 1975.)

Cox, D. R., and H. D. Miller (1965). *The Theory of Stochastic Processes.* Wiley, New York.

Cox, George H. (1977). *The Relative Impact of Georgia's Institutional Training Programs on the Post-Release Behavior of Adult Male Offenders.* Georgia Department of Offender Rehabilitation, Atlanta.

Cutler, Sidney J., and Lillian M. Axtell (1963). "Partitioning of a Patient Population with Respect to Different Mortality Risks." *Journal of the American Statistical Association,* 58, 701–712.

Daniel, C., and F. S. Wood (1971). *Fitting Equations to Data.* Wiley, New York.

Davis, J. C., and A. J. Cropley (1976). "Psychological Factors in Juvenile Delinquency." *Canadian Journal in Behavioral Science,* 8, 68–77.

Deutsch, Stuart J. (1979). "Lies, Damn Lies, and Statistics: A Rejoinder to the Comment by Hay and McCleary." *Evaluation Quarterly,* 3(2), 315–328.

Deutsch, Stuart J., and Francis B. Alt (1977). "The Effect of the Massachusetts Gun Control Law on Gun-Related Crimes in the City of Boston." *Evaluation Quarterly,* 1(4), 543–568.

*Ditman, Keith S., and George Crawford (1965). "The Use of Court Probation in the Management of the Alcohol Addict." Alcoholism Research Clinic, UCLA Health Services Center, Los Angeles. (Cited in Lipton *et al.*, 1975.)

*Dombross, E. E., and J. R. Silver (1966). "Excerpt from Final Report of the San Francisco Rehabilitation Project for Offenders." Northern California Service League, San Francisco. (Cited in Lipton *et al.*, 1975.)

Eck, John E. (1979). "Regulating Punishment: An Aggregate Population Dynamics Model of a Prison System." Paper presented at the Joint Meeting of the Operations Research Society of America and the Institute of Management Science, Milwaukee, October 1979.

Ehrlich, Isaac (1973). "Participation in Illegitimate Activities: A Theoretical and Empirical Investigation." *Journal of Political Economy*, 81, 521–565.

Ehrlich, Isaac (1975). "Deterrence: Evidence and Inference." *Yale Law Journal*, 85, 209–227.

Empey, Lamar T., and Maynard L. Erickson (1972). *The Provo Experiment*. Lexington Books, Lexington, Massachusetts.

Empey, Lamar T., and Steven G. Lubeck (1971). *The Silverlake Experiment*. Aldine, Chicago.

*Ericson, Richard C., *et al.* (1966). "The Application of Comprehensive Psycho-Social Vocational Services in Rehabilitation of Parolees—January 1, 1965 through December 31, 1965." Minneapolis Rehabilitation Center. (Cited in Lipton *et al.*, 1975.)

Erikson, Kai T. (1966). *Wayward Puritans: A Study in the Sociology of Deviance*. Wiley, New York.

Eysenck, S. B. G., and H. J. Eysenck (1974). Personality and Recidivism in Borstal Boys." *British Journal of Criminology*, 14, 385–387.

*Feistman, Eugene G. (1966). "Comparative Analysis of the Wilowbrook-Harbor Intensive Services Program, March 1, 1965 through February 28, 1966." Los Angeles County Probation Department. (Cited in Lipton *et al.*, 1975.)

Feller, William (1957). *An Introduction to Probability Theory and Its Applications* (Volume I, Second Edition). Wiley, New York.

Feller, William (1966). *An Introduction to Probability Theory and Its Applications* (Volume II). Wiley, New York.

Fienberg, Stephen, and Patricia Grambsch (1979). "Appendix: An Assessment of the Accuracy of *The Effectiveness of Correctional Treatment*." In Lee Sechrest, Susan D. White, and Elizabeth D. Brown, Eds., 1979, *The Rehabilitation of Criminal Offenders: Problems and Prospects*. National Academy of Sciences, Washington, D.C., 119–147.

Fishman, Robert (1977). *Criminal Recidivism in New York City: An Evaluation of the Impact of Rehabilitation and Diversion Services*. Praeger, New York.

Fogel, David (1979). *We Are the Living Proof* (Second Edition). Anderson, Cincinnati.

Forst, Brian (1976). "Participation in Illegitimate Activities: Further Empirical Findings." *Policy Analysis*, 2, 477–492.

*Fox, Vernon (1950). "Michigan's Experiment in Minimum Security Penology." *Journal of Criminal Law, Criminology and Police Science*, 41, 150–166. (Cited in Lipton *et al.*, 1975.)

Frazier, Laura A. (1981). "The Confidentiality of Juvenile Records: An Opposing View." Unpublished masters paper, Department of Criminal Justice, University of Illinois at Chicago.

*Freeman, Howard E., and H. Ashley Weeks (1956). "Analysis of a Program of Treatment of Delinquent Boys." *American Journal of Sociology*, 62, 56–61. (Cited in Lipton *et al.*, 1975.)

*Garrity, Donald Lee (1956). "The Effects of Length of Incarceration upon Parole Adjustment and Estimation of Optimum Sentence: Washington State Corrections Institutions." Unpublished Ph.D. dissertation, University of Washington. (Cited in Lipton *et al.*, 1975.)

Gass, Saul I. (1983). "Decision-Aiding Models: Validation, Assessment, and Related Issues for Policy Analysis." *Operations Research* 31 (4), 603–631.

Gass, Saul I., and B. W. Thompson (1980). "Guidelines for Model Evaluation: An Abridged Version of the U.S. General Accounting Office Exposure Draft." *Operations Research* 28(3), 431–439

REFERENCES

*Gearhart, J. Walter, Harold L. Keith, and Gloria Clemmons (1967). "An Analysis of the Vocational Training Program in the Washington State Adult Correctional Institutions." Research Review No. 23, State of Washington, Department of Institutions. (Cited in Lipton et al., 1975.)

Glaser, Daniel (1965). *The Effectiveness of a Prison and Parole System*. Bobbs-Merrill, Indianapolis.

Glaser, Daniel. (1965). "Correctional Research: An Elusive Paradise." *Journal of Research in Crime and Delinquency*, 2, 1–11.

Goldstein, Paul J. (1982). "Habitual Criminal Activity and Patterns of Drug Use." Paper presented at the 34th Annual Meeting of the American Society of Criminology, Toronto.

Golomb, Henry D., and Howard M. Bunch (1978). *Stochastic Analysis of Future Vehicle Populations*. Report to the Highway Safety Research Institute, University of Michigan, Ann Arbor.

Goodman, Leo A. (1961). "Statistical Methods for the Mover–Stayer Model." *Journal of the American Statistical Association*, 56, 841–868.

Gordon, Andrew C., David McDowall, Michael D. Maltz, and Richard McCleary (1978). "Evaluating a Delinquency Intervention Program: A Comment." *Criminal Justice Newsletter*, 9, 1–4.

Gottfredson, D. M., and K. B. Ballard (1966). "Differences in Parole Decisions Associated with Decision-Makers." *Journal of Research in Crime and Delinquency*, 3(2), 112–119.

*Great Britain, Home Office (1964). *The Sentence of the Court: A Handbook for Courts on the Treatment of Offenders*. Her Majesty's Stationery Office, London. (Cited in Lipton et al., 1975.)

Green, Linda, and Peter Kolesar (1983). "Validating a Queuing Model of Police Patrol." Paper presented at the Joint Meeting of the Operations Research Society of America and the Institute of Management Science, Chicago.

Greenberg, David F. (1975). "The Incapacitative Effect of Imprisonment: Some Estimates." *Law and Society Review*, 9, 541–580.

Greenberg, David F. (1977). "The Correctional Effects of Corrections: A Survey of Evaluations." In D. F. Greenberg, Ed., *Corrections and Punishment*. Sage, Beverly Hills, California.

Greenberg, David F. (1978). "Recidivism as Radioactive Decay." *Journal of Research in Crime and Delinquency*, 24, 124–125.

Greenberger, M., M. A. Crenson, and B. L. Crissey (1976). *Models in the Policy Process*. Russell Sage Foundation, New York.

Greenwood, Peter W. (1979). *Rand Research on Criminal Careers: Progress to Date*. Report No. N-1286-DOJ, The Rand Corporation, Santa Monica, California.

Greenwood, Peter W., with Allan Abrahamse (1982). *Selective Incapacitation*. Report R-2815-NIJ, The Rand Corporation, Santa Monica, California.

Greenwood, Peter W., Jan M. Chaiken, and Joan Petersilia (1977). *The Criminal Investigation Process*. Lexington Books, Lexington, Massachusetts.

Greenwood, Peter W., Joan Petersilia, and Franklin E. Zimring (1980). *Age, Crime and Sanctions: The Transition from Juvenile to Adult Court*. Report No. R-2642-NIJ, The Rand Corporation, Santa Monica, California.

Griswold, David B. (1978). "A Comparison of Recidivism Measures." *Journal of Criminal Justice*, 6, 247–252.

Grizzle, Gloria A. (1979). "A Typology of Performance Measures for Correctional Programs," Working Paper 79-1. "Criteria for Rating Corrections Performance Measures." Working Paper 79-2. "A Conceptual Framework for Correctional Performance Measurement," Working Paper 79-3. Reports to the National Institute of Law Enforcement and Criminal Justice, the Osprey Company, Raleigh, North Carolina.

Gross, Alan J., and Virginia A. Clark (1975). *Survival Distributions: Reliability Applications in the Biomedical Sciences*. Wiley, New York.

Gross, Donald, and Carl M. Harris (1974). *Fundamentals of Queuing Theory*. Wiley, New York.

Gross, Hyman, and Andrew von Hirsch, Eds. (1981). *Sentencing*. Oxford University Press, New York.

Gulland, J. A. (1955). "On the Estimation of Population Parameters from Marked Members." *Biometrika*, 43, 269–270.

*Guttman, Evelyn S. (1961). "MMPI Measured Changes in Treated and Untreated Youth Authority Wards Judged in Need of Psychiatric Treatment." Research Report No. 25, California Youth Authority. (Cited in Lipton *et al.*, 1975.)

*Guttman, Evelyn S. (1963). "Effects of Short-Term Psychiatric Treatment on Boys in Two California Youth Authority Institutions." Research Report No. 36, California Youth Authority. (Cited in Lipton *et al.*, 1975.)

Haight, Frank A. (1967). *Handbook of the Poisson Distribution*. Wiley, New York.

*Hansen, Hans A., and Karl Teilmann (1954). "A Treatment of Criminal Alcoholics in Denmark." *Quarterly Journal of Studies on Alcohol* 25(2):246–287. (Cited in Lipton *et al.*, 1975.)

Harris, Carl M., Ali R. Kaylan, and Michael D. Maltz (1981). "Advances in the Statistics of Recidivism Measurement." In J. A. Fox, Ed., *Models in Quantitative Criminology*. Academic Press, New York, 61–79.

Harris, Carl M., and Jay Mandelbaum (1979). "Asymptotic Behavior of Maximum-Likelihood Estimators of Mixed Weibull Parameters." Project Memo CMH1-UICC-DOJ, Center for Research in Criminal Justice, University of Illinois at Chicago Circle, Chicago.

Harris, Carl M., and Soumyo Moitra (1978a). "Improved Statistical Techniques for the Measurement of Recidivism." *Journal of Research in Crime and Delinquency*, 15, 194–213.

Harris, Carl M., and Soumyo Moitra (1978b). "On the Transfer of Some OR/MS Technology." *Interfaces*, 9, 78–86.

*Havel, Joan (1963). "A Synopsis of Research Report No. 10 SIPU Phase 4—The High Base Expectancy Study." Administrative Abstract No. 10, California Department of Corrections. (Cited in Lipton *et al.*, 1975.)

*Havel, Joan (1965). "Special Intensive Parole Unit—Phase Four: 'The Parole Outcome Study.' " Research Report No. 13, California Department of Corrections. (Cited in Lipton *et al.*, 1975.)

Hay, Richard A., Jr., and Richard McCleary (1979). "Box-Tiao Time Series Models for Impact Assessment." *Evaluation Quarterly*, 2(3), 277–314.

Haybittle, J. L. (1965). "A Two-Parameter Model for the Survival Curve of Treated Cancer Patients." *Journal of the American Statistical Association*, 60, 16–26.

Heims, Steve J. (1980). *John von Neumann and Norbert Wiener: From Mathematics to the Technologies of Life and Death*. MIT Press, Cambridge, Massachusetts.

Herman, Robert, and Ilya Prigogine (1979). "A Two-Fluid Approach to Town Traffic." *Science*, 204, 148–151.

Hirsley, Michael (1983). "He Hired a Killer to Avenge His Parents, and He'd Do It Again." *Chicago Tribune*, June 23, 1, 4.

Hoffman, Peter B., and James L. Beck (1974). "Parole Decision-Making: A Salient Factor Score." *Journal of Criminal Justice*, 2, 195–206.

Hoffman, Peter B., and Barbara Stone-Meierhoefer (1979). "Post-Release Arrest Experiences of Federal Prisoners: A Six-Year Followup." *Journal of Criminal Justice*, 7, 193–216.

Hoffman, Peter B., and Barbara Stone-Meierhoefer (1980). "Reporting Recidivism Rates: The Criterion/Followup Issue." United States Parole Commission Research Unit, Washington, D.C.

Hoge, Warren (1979). "Brazil's Crime Rate Produces Lynchings." *The New York Times*, December 2, 1, 11.

*Hood, Roger (1966). *Homeless Borstal Boys: A Study of Their After-Care and After-Conduct*. G. Bell and Sons, London. (Cited in Lipton *et al.*, 1975.)

Hopkins, Andrew (1976). "Imprisonment and Recidivism: A Quasi-Experimental Study." *Journal of Research in Crime and Delinquency*, 13, 13–32.

REFERENCES

Howard, Ronald (1970). "Educational Issues." *Management Science*, October, 17, 2, B1–B53.
Inciardi, James (1971). "Use of Parole Prediction with Institutionalized Narcotics Addicts." *Journal of Research in Crime and Delinquency*, 8, 65–73.
Iowa Statistical Analysis Center (1979). *Recidivism*. Volume VIII of *Crime and Criminal Justice in Iowa*. State of Iowa Statistical Analysis Center.
Jacobs, James B. (1978). *Stateville: The Penitentiary in Mass Society*. University of Chicago Press, Chicago.
*Jacobson, Frank, and Eugene McGee (1965). "Englewood Project: Re-Education: A Radical Correction of Incarcerated Delinquents." Federal Correctional Institution, Englewood, Colorado (mimeo). (Cited in Lipton *et al.*, 1975.)
*Johnson, Bertram (1962). "Parole Performance of the First Year's Releases, Parole Research Project: Evaluation of Reduced Caseloads." Research Report No. 27, California Youth Authority. (Cited in Lipton *et al.*, 1975.)
*Johnson, Bertram (1962). "An Analysis of Predictions of Parole Performance and of Judgments of Supervision in the Parole Research Project." Research Report No. 32, California Youth Authority. (Cited in Lipton *et al.*, 1975.)
Johnson, Norman L., and Samuel Kotz (1970a). *Distributions in Statistics: Continuous Univeriate Distributions*—2. Wiley, New York.
Johnson, Norman L., and Samuel Kotz (1970b). *Distributions in Statistics: Continuous Univariate Distributions*—1. Wiley, New York.
Joplin, G. H. (1973). "Self-Concept and the Highfields Project: Recidivists vs. Non-Recidivists." *Criminology*, 9, 491–495.
Kahneman, Daniel, and Amos Tversky (1974). "Judgment Under Uncertainty: Heuristics and Biases." *Science* 185, 1124–1131. (Reprinted in D. Kahneman, P. Slovic, and A. Tversky, Eds., *Judgment Under Uncertainty: Heuristics and Biases*. Cambridge University Press, New York, 1982.)
Kalbfleisch, John D., and Ross L. Prentice (1980). *The Statistical Analysis of Failure Time Data*. Wiley, New York.
Kantrowitz, Nathan (1977). "How to Shorten the Follow-up Period in Parole Studies." *Journal of Research in Crime and Delinquency*, 14, 222–236.
Kaplan, Abraham (1964). *The Conduct of Inquiry*. Chandler, San Francisco.
Kaplan, Edward H. (1979). "Models for the Evaluation of Treatment Release Corrections Programs." Technical Report No. 162, Operations Research Center, Massachusetts Institute of Technology, Cambridge.
Kaplan, E. L., and P. Meier. (1958). "Nonparametric Estimation from Incomplete Observations." *Journal of the American Statistical Association*, 53, 457–481.
*Kawaguchi, Ray M., and Leon M. Siff (1967). "An Analysis of Intensive Probation Services—Phase II." Research Report No. 29, Los Angeles County Probation Department. (Cited in Lipton *et al.*, 1975.)
Kelling, George L., Tony Pate, Duane Dieckmann, and Charles E. Brown (1974). *The Kansas City Preventive Patrol Experiment: Summary Report*. Police Foundation, Washington, D.C.
Kelly, F. J., and D. J. Baer (1971). "Physical Challenge as a Treatment for Delinquency." *Crime and Delinquency*, 17, 437–445.
Kiernan, L. (1979). "Study Says Youth Crime Falls After Incarceration." *Washington Star*, November 19, A4.
Kitchener, Howard, Annesley K. Schmidt, and Daniel Glaser (1977). "How Persistent Is Post-Prison Success?" *Federal Probation*, 41, 9–15.
Kitsuse, J., and A. Cicourel (1963). "A Note on the Use of Official Data." *Social Problems*, 11, 131–139.
Klein, Lawrence R., Brian Forst, and Victor Filatov (1978). "The Deterrent Effect of Capital Punishment: An Assessment of the Estimates." In Alfred Blumstein, Jacqueline Cohen, and

Daniel Nagin, Eds., *Deterrence and Incapacitation: Estimating the Effects of Criminal Sanctions on Crime Rates*, National Academy of Sciences, Washington, D.C. 336–360.

Klein, Malcolm W. (1974). "Labeling, Deterrence, and Recidivism: A Study of Police Dispositions of Juvenile Offenders." *Social Problems*, 22(2), 292–303.

Klockars, Carl B. (1975). "The True Limits of the Effectiveness of Correctional Treatment." *Prison Journal*, 55, 53–64.

*Kovacs, Frank W. (1967). "Evaluation and Final Report of the New Start Demonstration Project." Colorado Department of Employment. (Cited in Lipton *et al.*, 1975.)

Kozol, H. L., R. J. Boucher, and R. F. Garofalo (1972). "The Diagnosis and Treatment of Dangerousness." *Crime and Delinquency*, 18, 371–392.

*Kusuda, Paul H., and Dean V. Babst (1964). "Wisconsin Base Expectancies for Adult Male Parolees: Preliminary Findings on the Relationship of Training, Work and Institutional Adjustment at Wisconsin State Prison to Later Parole Violation Experience, 1958 and 1959 Releases." Wisconsin Department of Public Welfare. (Cited in Lipton *et al.*, 1975.)

Larson, Richard C. (1975). "What Happened to Patrol Operations in Kansas City? A Review of the Kansas City Preventive Patrol Experiment." *Journal of Criminal Justice*, 3, 267–297.

Larson, Richard C., and Amadeo R. Odoni (1981). *Urban Operations Research*. Prentice-Hall, Englewood Cliffs, New Jersey.

Law Inforcement Assistance Administration, National Criminal Justice Information and Statistics Service (1977). *Criminal Victimization in the United States 1974*. U.S. Government Printing Office, Washington D.C.

LeClair, Daniel P. (1977). *An Analysis of Recidivism Rates Among Residents Released from Massachusetts Correctional Institutions During the Year 1974*. Massachusetts Department of Corrections, Boston.

Lerman, Paul (1968). "Evaluative Studies of Institutions for Delinquents." *Social Work*, 13(3), 55–64.

Lindgren, Bernard W. (1976). *Statistical Theory*. Macmillan, New York.

Lipton, Douglas, Robert Martinson, and Judith Wilks (1975). *The Effectiveness of Correctional Treatments: A Survey of Treatment Evaluation Studies*. Praeger, New York.

Lloyd, Michael R., and George Joe. (1979). "Recidivism Comparisons Across Groups: Methods of Estimation and Tests of Significance for Recidivism Rate and Asymptotes." *Evaluation Quarterly*, 3(1), 105–117.

*Lohman, Joseph D., *et al.* (1967). "The Intensive Supervision Caseloads: A Preliminary Evaluation." School of Criminology, University of California, Berkeley. (Cited in Lipton *et al.*, 1975.)

Maltz, Michael D. (1972). *Evaluation of Crime Control Programs*. U.S. Government Printing Office, Washington, D.C.

Maltz, Michael D. (1975). "Measures of Effectiveness for Crime Reduction Programs." *Operations Research* 23(3), 452–474.

Maltz, Michael D. (1977). "Crime Statistics: A Historical Perspective." *Crime and Delinquency* 23(1), 32–40.

Maltz, Michael D. (1980). "Beyond Suppression: More Sturm und Drang on the Correctional Front." *Crime and Delinquency* 26(3), 389–397.

Maltz, Michael D. (1981a). "Transportation Smuggling in Analyzing an Economic Crime." In James A. Fox, Ed., *Methods in Quantitative Criminology*. Academic Press, New York, 77–97.

Maltz, Michael D. (1981b). *On Recidivism: Exploring Its Properties as a Measure of Correctional Effectiveness*. Center for Research in Criminal Justice, University of Illinois at Chicago.

Maltz, Michael D., Andrew C. Gordon, David McDowall, and Ricard McCleary (1980). "An Artifact in Pretest-Posttest Designs: How It Can Mistakenly Make Delinquency Programs Look Effective." *Evaluation Review*, 4, 225–240.

REFERENCES

Maltz, Michael D., and Richard McCleary (1977). "The Mathematics of Behavioral Change: Recidivism and Construct Validity." *Evaluation Quarterly*, 1, 421–438.
Maltz, Michael D., and Richard McCleary (1978). "Comments on 'Stability of Parameter Estimates in the Split Population Exponential Distribution'." *Evaluation Quarterly*, 2, 650–654.
Maltz, Michael D., Richard McCleary, and Stephen M. Pollock (1979). "Recidivism and Likelihood Functions: A Reply to Stollmack." *Evaluation Quarterly*, 3, 124–131.
Maltz, Michael D., and Stephen M. Pollock (1980). "Artificial Inflation of a Delinquency Rate by a Selection Artifact." *Operations Research*, 28(3), 547–559.
Mann, Nancy, Ray E. Schafer, and Nozer Singpurwalla (1974). *Methods for Statistical Analysis of Life Data*. Wiley, New York.
Marcus, Richard, and Saul Blumenthal (1974). "A Sequential Screening Procedure." *Technometrics*, 16, 229–234.
Marsh, J. and M. Singer (1972). "Soft Statistics and Hard Questions." Paper No. HI-1712-DP, Hudson Institute, Croton-on-Hudson, New York.
Martin, Susan E., Lee B. Sechrest, and Robin Redner, Eds. (1981). *New Directions in the Rehabilitation of Criminal Offenders*. National Academy Press, Washington, D.C.
Martinson, Robert (1974). "What Works? Questions and Answers about Prison Reform." *The Public Interest*, Spring, 22–54.
Martinson, Robert (1975). Letter to the Editor, *Prison Journal*, 55, 65.
Martinson, Robert (1979). "New Findings, New Views: A Note of Caution Regarding Sentencing Reform." *Hofstra Law Review*, Winter, 7(2), 243–258. (Reprinted in P. C. Kratcoski, Ed., *Correctional Counseling and Treatment*. Duxbury Press, Monterey, California, 1981.)
Martinson, Robert, Ted Palmer, and Stuart Adams (1976). *Rehabilitation, Recidivism, and Research*. National Council on Crime and Delinquency, Hackensack, New Jersey.
Martinson, Robert, and Judith Wilks (1977). "Save Parole Supervision." *Federal Probation* 41, 23–27.
Marx, Gary, and Dane Archer (1971). "Citizen Involvement in the Law Enforcement Process: The Case of Community Police Patrols." *American Behavioral Scientists*, 15, 52–72.
Marx, Gary, and Dane Archer (1973). "The Urban Vigilante." *Psychology Today*, January, 45–50.
*Massimo, Joseph L., and Milton F. Shore (1963). "The Effectiveness of a Comprehensive Vocationally Oriented Psychotherapeutic Program for Adolescent Delinquent Boys." *American Journal of Orthopsychiatry*, 33, 634–642. (Cited in Lipton *et al.*, 1975.)
McCleary, Richard (1978). *Dangerous Men*. Sage, Beverly Hills, California.
McCleary, Richard, Andrew C. Gordon, David McDowall, and Michael D. Maltz (1979). "How a Regression Artifact Can Make Any Delinquency Program Look Effective." In L. Sechrest *et al.*, Eds., *Evaluation Studies Review Annual* (Volume IV). Sage, Beverly Hills, California.
McCord, William, and Joan McCord, with Irving Kenneth Zola (1959). *Origins of Crime*. Columbia University Press, New York.
*McCorkle, Lloyd W., Albert Elias, and F. Lovell Bixby (1958). *The Highfields Story: An Experimental Treatment for Youthful Offenders*. Henry Holt, New York. (Cited in Lipton *et al.*, 1975.)
*McEachern, Alexander W., and Edward M. Taylor (1967). "The Effects of Probation." Youth Studies Center, University of Southern California, Los Angeles. (Cited in Lipton *et al.*, 1975.)
Meade, A. (1973). "Seriousness of Delinquency: The Adjudicative Decision and Recidivism—A Longitudinal Configuration Analysis." *Journal of Criminal Law, Criminology and Police Science*, 64, 478–485.
Merritt, Frank S. (1980). "Parole Revocation: A Primer." *University of Toledo Law Review*, 11, 893–938.
Miley, Alan D. (1978). "Stability of Parameter Estimates in the Split Population Exponential Distribution." *Evaluation Quarterly*, 2, 646–649.

Miller, Stuart J., and Simon Dinitz (1973). "Measuring Institutional Impact." *Criminology*, 11, 417–426.

Miller, Stuart J., and Simon Dinitz (1982). *Careers of the Violent: The Dangerous Offender and Criminal Justice*. Lexington Books, Lexington, Massachusetts.

Minnesota Governor's Commission on Crime Prevention and Control, Evaluation Unit (1976). *Residential Community Corrections Programs in Minnesota*. Minnesota Governor's Commission, St. Paul.

Moberg, David, O., and Richard C. Ericson (1972). "A New Recidivism Outcome Index." *Federal Probation*, 36, 50–57.

Morris, Norval (1974). *The Future of Imprisonment*. University of Chicago Press, Chicago.

Morris, W. T. (1967). "On the Art of Modeling." *Management Science*, August, 13(12), B707–B717.

Moseley, William, and Margaret Gerould (1975). "Sex and Parole: A Comparison of Male and Female Parolees." *Journal of Criminal Justice*, 3, 47–58.

Murray, Charles A. (1978a). Statement before the U.S. Senate Subcommittee on Juvenile Delinquency, April 12, 1978.

Murray, Charles A. (1978b). Letter to the Editor, *Criminal Justice Newsletter*, 9(16), 4–5.

Murray, Charles A. (1979). Interview by Garrick Utley, NBC "Today" program, November 16, 1979.

Murray, Charles A., and Louis A. Cox, Jr. (1979a). *Juvenile Corrections and the Chronic Delinquent*. American Institutes for Research, Washington, D.C.

Murray, Charles A., and Louis A. Cox, Jr. (1979b). *Beyond Probation: Juvenile Corrections and the Chronic Delinquent*. Sage, Beverly Hills, California.

Murray, Charles A., Doug Thomson, and Cindy B. Israel (1978). *UDIS: Deinstitutionalizing the Chronic Juvenile Offender*. American Institutes for Research, Washington, D.C.

Muthén, Bengt, and Karl D. Jöreskog (1983). "Selectivity Problems in Quasi-Experimental Studies." *Evaluation Review*, 7(2), 139–174.

*Narloch, R. P., S. Adams, and K. J. Jenkins (1959). "Characteristics and Parole Performance of California Youth Authority Early Releases." Research Report No. 7, California Youth Authority. (Cited in Lipton *et al.*, 1975.)

National Advisory Commission on Criminal Justice Standards and Goals (1973). *Corrections*. U.S. Government Printing Office, Washington, D.C.

National Institute of Justice (1977). "Highlights of Interim Findings and Implications." PROMIS Research Publication No. 1, National Institute of Justice, Washington, D.C.

Neithercutt, Mark G., William H. Moseley, and Ernst A. Wenk (1975). "Uniform Parole Reports: A National Correctional Data System." National Council on Crime and Delinquency Research Center, San Francisco.

Nelson, Wayne (1982). *Applied Life Data Analysis*. Wiley, New York.

New York Times (1978). Editorial, June 19, 1978; Letter to the Editor, June 30, 1978.

*New York State, Division of Parole, Department of Corrections (1964). "Parole Adjustment and Prior Educational Achievement of Male Adolescent Offenders, June 1957–June 1961." (Cited in Lipton *et al.*, 1975.)

Office of Technology Assessment (1978). *A Preliminary Assessment of the National Crime Information Center and the Computerized Criminal History System*. U.S. Government Printing Office, Washington, D.C.

Palmer, Ted (1975). "Martinson Revisited." *Journal of Research in Crime and Delinquency*, 12, 133–152.

Palmer, Ted (1978). *Correctional Intervention and Research: Current Issues and Future Prospects*. Lexington Books, Lexington, Massachusetts.

Partanen, Juha (1969). "On Waiting Time Distributions." *Acta Sociologica*, 12, 132–143.

Passell, Peter (1975). "The Deterrent Effect of the Death Penalty: A Statistical Test." *Stanford Law Review*, 28(1), 61–80.
*Persons, Roy W. (1967). "Relationship between Psychotherapy with Institutionalized Boys and Subsequent Community Adjustment." *Journal of Consulting Psychology*, 31, 137–141. (Cited in Lipton *et al.*, 1975.)
Petersilia, Joan (1980). "Criminal Careers Research: A Review of Recent Evidence." In N. Morris and M. Tonry, Eds., *Crime and Justice: An Annual Review of Research* (Volume 2). University of Chicago Press, Chicago, 321–379.
Pew, M. L., D. C. Speer, and J. Williams (1973). "Group Counseling for Offenders." *Social Work*, 18, 74–79.
Pierce, Glenn L., and William J. Bowers (1979). *The Impact of the Bartley-Fox Law on Gun and Non-Gun Related Crime in Massachusetts*. Center for Applied Social Research, Northeastern University, Boston. (See also Bowers and Pierce (1981). "The Bartley-Fox Gun Law's Short-Term Impact on Crime in Boston." *Annals*, 455, 120–137.)
*Pilnick, Saul, *et al.* (1967). "Collegefields: From Delinquency to Freedom." Laboratory for Applied Behavioral Science, Newark State College. (Cited in Lipton *et al.*, 1975.)
Philpotts, G. J. O., and L. B. Lancucki (1979). *Previous Convictions, Sentence and Reconviction*. Home Office Research Study No. 53. Her Majesty's Stationery Office, London.
Pollock, Stephen M. (1976). "Mathematical Modeling: Applying the Principles of the Art Studio." *Engineering Education*, 67(2), 167–171.
Pollock, Stephen M., and Robert Farrell (1984). "Past Intensity of a Terminated Poisson Process." *Operations Research Letters*, 2(6), in press.
Press, S. James (1971). *Some Effects of an Increase in Police Manpower in the 20th Precinct*. Report No. R-704-NYC, The Rand Corporation, Santa Monica.
Pritchard, David A. (1979). "Stable Predictors of Recidivism." *Criminology* 17(1), 15–21.
Proschan, Frank (1963). "Theoretical Explanation of Observed Decreasing Failure Rate." *Technometrics*, 5(3), 375–383.
Quetelet, L. A. J. (1842). *A Treatise on Man and the Development of His Faculties*. W. and R. Chambers, Edinburgh, Scotland. (Reprinted in *Comparative Statistics in the 19th Century*. Gregg International Publishers Limited, 1973.)
Rawls, John (1972). *A Theory of Justice*. Harvard University Press, Cambridge, Massachusetts.
Reed, David E. (1978). *Whistlestop: A Community Alternative in Crime Control*. Unpublished Ph.D. dissertation, Department of Sociology, Northwestern University, Evanston, Illinois.
Regal, Ronald R., and Kinley Larntz (1978). "Likelihood Methods for Testing Grouped Problem Solving Models with Censored Data." *Technometrika*, 43(3), 353–366.
Reiss, Albert J., Jr. (1982). "How Serious Is Serious Crime." *Vanderbilt Law Review* 35(3), 541–585.
Rezmovic, Eva L. (1979). "Methodological Considerations in Evaluating Correctional Effectiveness: Issues and Chronic Problems." In L. Sechrest *et al.*, Eds., *The Rehabilitation of Criminal Offenders: Problems and Prospects*. National Academy of Sciences, Washington, D.C.
Robins, Lee N., and Eric Wisk (1977). "Childhood Deviance as a Developmental Process: A Study of 223 Urban Black Men from Birth to 18." *Social Forces* 56(2), 448–471.
Rohatgi, V. (1975). *An Introduction to Probability Theory and Mathematical Statistics*. Wiley, New York.
Rubenstein, M. L., and T. J. White (1979). "Plea Bargaining: Can Alaska Live Without It?" *Judicature*, 62, 266–279.
*Rudoff, Alvin (1960). "The Effect of Treatment on Incarcerated Young Adult Delinquents as Measured by Disciplinary History." Unpublished Master's thesis, University of Southern California. (Cited in Lipton *et al.*, 1975.)
Saint-Exupery, Antoine de (1939). *Wind, Sand and Stars*. Reynal and Hitchcock, New York.

Schmidt, Peter, and Ann D. Witte (1978). "Determinants of Criminal Recidivism: Further Investigations." Report to the North Carolina Department of Corrections. Department of Economics, University of North Carolina, Chapel Hill.

Schmidt, Peter, and Ann D. Witte (1980). "Evaluating Correctional Programs: Models of Criminal Recidivism and an Illustration of Their Use." *Evaluation Quarterly,* 4(5), 585–600.

*Schwitzgebel, R., and D. A. Kolb (1964). "Inducing Behavior Change in Adolescent Delinquents." *Behavior Research Therapy,* 1, 297–304. (Cited in Lipton *et al.,* 1975.)

Sechrest, Lee, Susan O. White, and Elizabeth D. Brown, Eds. (1979). *The Rehabilitation of Criminal Offenders: Problems and Prospects.* National Academy of Sciences Press, Washington, D.C.

Sellin, Thorsten (1931). "The Basis of a Crime Index." *Journal of Criminal Law and Criminology,* September, 346.

Sellin, Thorsten, and Marvin E. Wolfgang (1964). *The Measurement of Delinquency.* Wiley, New York.

*Shelley, Ernest L. V., and Walter F. Johnson, Jr. (1961). "Evaluating an Organized Counseling Service for Youthful Offenders." *Journal of Counseling Psychology,* 8, 351–354. (Cited in Lipton *et al.,* 1975.)

Shinnar, R., and S. Shinnar (1975). "The Effects of the Criminal Justice System on the Control of Crime: A Quantitative Approach." *Law and Society Review,* 9, 581–611.

*Shoham, Shlomo, and Moshe Sandberg (1964). "Suspended Sentences in Israel: An Evaluation of the Preventive Efficacy of Prospective Imprisonment." *Crime and Delinquency,* 10, 74–83. (Cited in Lipton *et al.,* 1975.)

Simon, Frances H. (1972). "Statistical Methods of Making Prediction Instruments." *Journal of Research in Crime and Delinquency,* 9, 46–53.

Sokal, Robert R. (1974). "Classification: Purposes, Principles, Progress, Prospects." *Science,* 185, 1115–1123.

Stamp, Sir Josiah (1929). *Some Economic Factors in Modern Life.* P. S. King and Son, Ltd., London.

*Stanton, John M. (1956). "An Empirical Study of the Results of the Special Narcotics Project." New York State Division of Parole. (Cited in Lipton *et al.,* 1975.)

Stein, William E., and Michael R. Lloyd (1981). "The Maltz–McCleary Model of Recidivism: A Reexamination." *Evaluation Review* 5(1), 132–144.

Stollmack, Stephen (1979). "Comments on 'The Mathematics of Behavioral Change'." *Evaluation Quarterly,* 3, 120–124.

Stollmack, Stephen, and Carl M. Harris (1974). "Failure-Rate Analysis Applied to Recidivism Data." *Operations Research,* 22, 1192–1205.

Sullivan, Clyde E., and Wallace Mandell (1967). "Restoration of Youth through Training: A Final Report." Wakoff Research Center, Staten Island, New York. (Cited in Lipton *et al.,* 1975.)

Sutherland, Edwin, and Donald T. Cressey (1970). *Criminology.* Lippincott, Philadelphia.

Taylor, C. U. (1971). "The Early Violators: Who Are They?" Illinois Department of Corrections (mimeo), Springfield, Illinois.

Terry, R. M. (1967). "The Screening of Juvenile Offenders." *Journal of Criminal Law, Criminology and Police Science,* 58, 173–181.

Tierney, Luke (1983). "A Selection Artifact in Delinquency Data Revisited." *Operations Research* 31(5), 852–865.

Turnbull, Bruce W. (1977). "A Note on the Nonparametric Analysis of the Stollmack-Harris Recidivism Data." *Operations Research,* 25, 706–708.

U.S. Department of Justice, Law Enforcement Assistance Administration, National Criminal Justice Information and Statistics Service (1977). *Criminal Victimization in the United States 1974.* U.S. Government Printing Office, Washington, D.C.

Van Alstyne, David J., and Michael R. Gottfredson (1978). "A Multi-Dimensional Contingency Table Analysis of Parole Outcome: New Methods and Old Problems in Criminological Prediction." *Journal of Research in Crime and Delinquency*, 15, 171–193.

*Van Couvering, Nancy, et al. (1966). "One-to-One Project: Final Report." (Cited in Lipton et al., 1975.)

von Hirsch, Andrew (1976). *Doing Justice: The Choice of Punishments*. Hill and Wang, New York.

Wainer, Howard. (1981). "A Parameterization of Recidivism." *Evaluation Review*, 5(6), 810–821.

*Waldo, Gordon P., and Theodore G. Chiricos (1977). "Work Release and Recidivism: An Empirical Evaluation of a Social Policy." *Evaluation Quarterly*, 1, 87–108.

Wattley, Philip (1982). "Mob Beats Suspected Rapist." *Chicago Tribune*, December 23, 2, 1.

Weber, Max (1949). *The Methodology of Social Science* (E. A. Shils and H. A Finch, Translators and Editors). The Free Press, New York.

Werner, Eric, and Ted Palmer (1976). "Psychological Characteristics of Successful and Unsuccessful Parolees: Implications of Heteroscedastic and Non-linear Relationships." *Journal of Research in Crime and Delinquency*, 13, 165–178.

Westin, Alan F., and Michael A. Baker (1972). *Databanks in a Free Society*. Quadrangle Books, New York.

*Wilkins, Leslie T. (1958). "A Small Comparative Study of the Results of Probation." *British Journal of Criminology*, 8, 201–209. (Cited in Lipton et al., 1975.)

Wilkins, Leslie T. (1969). *Evaluation of Penal Measures*. Random House, New York.

Wilson, James Q. (1968). *Varieties of Police Behavior*. Harvard University Press, Cambridge, Massachusetts.

Witte, Ann D., and Peter Schmidt (1977). "An Analysis of Recidivism, Using the Truncated Lognormal Distribution." *Applied Statistics*, 26, 302–311.

Wolfgang, Marvin E., Robert M. Figlio, and Thorsten Sellin (1972). *Delinquency in a Birth Cohort*. University of Chicago Press, Chicago.

Wright, James D., Peter H. Rossi, and Kathleen Daly (1983). *Under the Gun: Weapons, Crime, and Violence*. Aldine, New York.

*Zivan, Morton (1966). "Youth in Trouble: A Vocational Approach." Children's Village, Dobbs Ferry, New York. (Cited in Lipton et al., 1975.)

Zimring, Franklin E., and Gordon J. Hawkins (1973). *Deterrence: The Legal Threat in Crime Control*. University of Chicago Press, Chicago.

*Zumbrun, Alvin J. T., and John Berry (1958). "A Follow-Up Study of Men Released in 1954 from the State Reformatory for Males by Reason of Parole and Expiration of Sentence." Criminal Justice Commission, Baltimore, Maryland. (Cited in Lipton et al., 1975.)

Index

A

Absconsion, 52, 61, 63, 65
Arrest rates, 32, 36, 62
  traffic, 35
Artifact, *see* Selection artifact

B

Bayesian estimation, 105, 150, 157

C

Capital punishment, models of, 14
Casablanca, 57
Censored data, 95n, 118, 121, 143, 150, 155, 164
  biasing effects of, 74
Chi-square test, *see* Goodness of fit
Chronic juvenile offenders, 30, 36
Conditional release, 43, 47
Confidence intervals, *see* Confidence regions

Confidence regions, 121, 160, 171, 172
Constant failure rate (CFR), defined, 76
Corrections
  goals of, 7
    correctional administration, 17
    desert, 16
    deterrence
      general, 13
      special, 11, 17n
    employment, 24
    forestalling vengeance, 14
    incapacitation, 11
    moral and social education, 15
    proportionality, 16
    reducing recidivism, 10, 13, 20, 27, 32
    rehabilitation, 8
    retribution, 16, 30
    sentence equity, 16
  medical model of, 8, 19
Covariate models, 77n, 127
Crime seriousness, 16, 23
Criminal behavior, *see* Offender behavior

237

Criminal history records, 11
Critical time model, 156

D

Data
    analysis, 116, 127, 139
    censored, see Censored data
    collection, 114
    criminal justice, 11, 59
    grouped (discrete time), 117, 120, 143
    individual (continuous time), 117, 153
    quality of, 22, 56, 58, 60, 114, 128, 141
    requirements, 24, 115
    state-specific, 59, 65
    stochastic properties of, 69, 77
Death Wish, 14
Decreasing failure rate (DFR), defined, 76
Desert, 16
Distributions, see Statistical distributions

E

Employment, as a measure of correctional effectiveness, 24
Evaluation
    criteria, 20
    design, 10, 21, 30, 128, 138, 190
    experimental, 21, 31
    impact, 10
    measures, 26
    of correctional studies, 27
    pretest–posttest, 20n, 27
    process, 9
    quasi-experimental, 21, 30
    values in, 18, 56
    voluntarism as a confounding factor, 21
Eyeballing, see Model, selection of

F

Failure, as a measure of correctional effectiveness, 20, 23
Failure rate, 71, 75
First offender, 56
Follow-up period, 22n, 52, 71, 72, 116
Forecasting, 99

G

Gagnon v. *Scarpelli*, 47
γ (gamma), defined, 80, 112
Goodness of fit, 91, 92
Graphical parameter estimation, 118, 151, 157, 173, 190
Gun control, 14, 15

I

Incapacitation
    as a goal of corrections, 11
    models of, 12
    selective, 12
Increasing failure rate (IFR), defined, 76
Intervention, 30, 37, 41

J

Juvenile offenders, 56; see also Chronic juvenile offenders

L

Law of Parsimony, 70
Likelihood function for Model M_1
    for grouped (discrete) time data, 143, 158
    for individual (continuous) time data, 153, 159
Logical construct of offender rehabilitation, 9

M

Markov model, 33
Maximum likelihood estimation, 117, 147, 154
Model, 68; see also Offender behavior
    characteristics, 68
    covariate, 127
    development, 69
    interpretability, 112, 133
    selection, 70, 88
        chi-square goodness-of-fit test, 92
        eyeballing, 91
        split-sample, 97
    stochastic properties of, 77
    versatility, 107
Money, definitions of, 64
Moral and social education, 15
Morrissey v. *Brewer*, 47

N

National Academy of Sciences, Panel on Research on Rehabilitative Techniques, 10, 29, 30, 40, 41
National Advisory Commission on Criminal Justice Standards and Goals, 22n, 54, 72
National Crime Information Center (NCIC), 60, 61
Newton-Raphson procedure, 117, 148
Nonparametric methods, 135

O

Occam's razor, see Law of Parsimony
Offender Based State Correctional Information System (OBSCIS), 59
Offender Based Transaction System (OBTS), 55
Offender behavior
   empirical data, 12, 26, 66, 73, 89, 90, 93, 96, 119
   mathematical models of, 12, 19, 33, 34, 69, 71, 75, 77, 89, 127, 157

P

Parameter estimation
   Bayesian, see Bayesian estimation
   graphical, see Graphical parameter estimation
   maximum likelihood, see Maximum likelihood estimation
Parole, 42
   discretion, 47, 52
   supervision, 44, 47, 49
   violation of, as measure of recidivism, 22, 65
ϕ (phi), defined, 80, 112
Point process, 39, 90n
Poisson process, 39, 90n
Police contacts, 32n
Probability distributions, see Statistical distributions
Probation, 62, 63n
Proportionality, 16
Prosecutor's Management Information System (PROMIS), 59, 66n

Q

q, defined, 143

R

"Rap sheets," see Criminal history records
Rate, 71, 75
Recidivism
   as measure of correctional effectiveness, 7, 20, 27, 50
   as measure of special deterrence, 11, 17n
   definitions of, 1, 22, 32, 51, 54, 138
   effect of parole supervision on, 49
   effect of sentencing on, 48
   effect of timing of release on, 49
   event, 64, 115
   individual versus group, 56, 70, 77, 128
   time of, 52, 64, 65, 115
Recidivism rate, 71, 75n
   as a measure of correctional effectiveness, 26
   measuring, imbalance in precision, 3, 25, 71n, 75, 77
   "normal," 23
   one-year, 2n, 71
Reconviction, 62
Regression to the mean, 14, 32, 34, 35
Rehabilitation, 8
   assumptions of, 19
Release event, 64
Reliability theory, 89
Retribution, 16
Return to prison, 65

S

Salient Factor Score, 12, 99
Selection artifact, 32, 34, 40
Selective incapacitation, see Incapacitation
Sentencing, 43, 46, 48, 57n
   equity in, 16
Special Intensive Parole Unit, 49
Speeding, analogy to juvenile offenses, 35
Split sample model validation, 97
Statistical distributions
   beta, 147, 153, 157
   exponential (Model M_E), 78, 159
   gamma, 157
   hyperexponential (Model M_H), 81, 106

Statistical distributions (cont'd)
  incomplete exponential (Model M_I), 79, 89, 99, 105, 114, 129, 142, 159
  incomplete geometric (discrete time) (Model M_I), 81, 120, 143, 158
  lognormal (Model M_L), 82, 134
  mixed exponential (Model M_M), 84, 105
  normal, 124, 144, 169
  properties, 87
  Weibull (Model M_W), 81
Statistical methods
  Bayesian, see Bayesian estimation
  covariate, see Covariate methods
  maximum likelihood, see Maximum likelihood estimation
  nonparametric, see Nonparametric methods
Success, as a measure of correctional effectiveness, 20, 23, 71n
  measuring, 23

Sufficient statistics, 144
Suppression effect, 30, 32

T

Type I and II errors, 12, 57

U

Unified Delinquency Intervention Services (UDIS), 30, 40n
Uniform Parole Reporting System, 45, 166
United States Parole Commission, 99

V

Validation, see Model validation
Validity, threat to, see Regression to the mean
Vengeance, 14
Violation of probation or parole, 62, 65

QUANTITATIVE STUDIES IN SOCIAL RELATIONS
(Continued from page ii)

J. Ronald Milavsky, Ronald C. Kessler, Horst H. Stipp, and William S. Rubens, **TELEVISION AND AGGRESSION:** *A Panel Study*

Ronald S. Burt, **TOWARD A STRUCTURAL THEORY OF ACTION:** *Network Models of Social Structure, Perception, and Action*

Peter H. Rossi, James D. Wright, and Eleanor Weber-Burdin, **NATURAL HAZARDS AND PUBLIC CHOICE:** *The Indifferent State and Local Politics of Hazard Mitigation*

Neil Fligstein, **GOING NORTH:** *Migration of Blacks and Whites from the South, 1900–1950*

Howard Schuman and Stanley Presser, **QUESTIONS AND ANSWERS IN ATTITUDE SURVEYS:** *Experiments on Question Form, Wording, and Context*

Michael E. Sobel, **LIFESTYLE AND SOCIAL STRUCTURE:** *Concepts, Definitions, Analyses*

William Spangar Peirce, **BUREAUCRATIC FAILURE AND PUBLIC EXPENDITURE**

Bruce Jacobs, **THE POLITICAL ECONOMY OF ORGANIZATIONAL CHANGE:** *Urban Institutional Response to the War on Poverty*

Ronald C. Kessler and David F. Greenberg, **LINEAR PANEL ANALYSIS:** *Models of Quantitative Change*

Ivar Berg (Ed.), **SOCIOLOGICAL PERSPECTIVES ON LABOR MARKETS**

James Alan Fox (Ed.), **METHODS IN QUANTITATIVE CRIMINOLOGY**

James Alan Fox (Ed.), **MODELS IN QUANTITATIVE CRIMINOLOGY**

Philip K. Robins, Robert G. Spiegelman, Samuel Weiner, and Joseph G. Bell (Eds.), **A GUARANTEED ANNUAL INCOME:** *Evidence from a Social Experiment*

Zev Klein and Yohanan Eshel, **INTEGRATING JERUSALEM SCHOOLS**

Juan E. Mezzich and Herbert Solomon, **TAXONOMY AND BEHAVIORAL SCIENCE**

Walter Williams, **GOVERNMENT BY AGENCY:** *Lessons from the Social Program Grants-in-Aid Experience*

Peter H. Rossi, Richard A. Berk, and Kenneth J. Lenihan, **MONEY, WORK, AND CRIME:** *Experimental Evidence*

Robert M. Groves and Robert L. Kahn, **SURVEYS BY TELEPHONE:** *A National Comparison with Personal Interviews*

N. Krishnan Namboodiri (Ed.), **SURVEY SAMPLING AND MEASUREMENT**

QUANTITATIVE STUDIES IN SOCIAL RELATIONS

Beverly Duncan and Otis Dudley Duncan, SEX TYPING AND SOCIAL ROLES: *A Research Report*

Donald J. Treiman, OCCUPATIONAL PRESTIGE IN COMPARATIVE PERSPECTIVE

Samuel Leinhardt (Ed.), SOCIAL NETWORKS: *A Developing Paradigm*

Richard A. Berk, Harold Brackman, and Selma Lesser, A MEASURE OF JUSTICE: *An Empirical Study of Changes in the California Penal Code, 1955–1971*

Richard F. Curtis and Elton F. Jackson, INEQUALITY IN AMERICAN COMMUNITIES

Eric Hanushek and John Jackson, STATISTICAL METHODS FOR SOCIAL SCIENTISTS

Edward O. Laumann and Franz U. Pappi, NETWORKS OF COLLECTIVE ACTION: *A Perspective on Community Influence Systems*

Walter Williams and Richard F. Elmore, SOCIAL PROGRAM IMPLEMENTATION

Roland J. Liebert, DISINTEGRATION AND POLITICAL ACTION: *The Changing Functions of City Governments in America*

James D. Wright, THE DISSENT OF THE GOVERNED: *Alienation and Democracy in America*

Seymour Sudman, APPLIED SAMPLING

Michael D. Ornstein, ENTRY INTO THE AMERICAN LABOR FORCE

Carl A. Bennett and Arthur A. Lumsdaine (Eds.), EVALUATION AND EXPERIMENT: *Some Critical Issues in Assessing Social Programs*

H. M. Blalock, A. Aganbegian, F. M. Borodkin, Raymond Boudon, and Vittorio Capecchi (Eds.), QUANTITATIVE SOCIOLOGY: *International Perspectives on Mathematical and Statistical Modeling*

N. J. Demerath, III, Otto Larsen, and Karl F. Schuessler (Eds.), SOCIAL POLICY AND SOCIOLOGY

Henry W. Riecken and Robert F. Boruch (Eds.), SOCIAL EXPERIMENTATION: *A Method for Planning and Evaluating Social Intervention*

Arthur S. Goldberger and Otis Dudley Duncan (Eds.), STRUCTURAL EQUATION MODELS IN THE SOCIAL SCIENCES

Robert B. Tapp, RELIGION AMONG THE UNITARIAN UNIVERSALISTS: *Converts in the Stepfathers' House*

QUANTITATIVE STUDIES IN SOCIAL RELATIONS

Kent S. Miller and Ralph Mason Dreger (Eds.), **COMPARATIVE STUDIES OF BLACKS AND WHITES IN THE UNITED STATES**
Douglas T. Hall and Benjamin Schneider, **ORGANIZATIONAL CLIMATES AND CAREERS:** *The Work Lives of Priests*
Robert L. Crain and Carol S. Weisman, **DISCRIMINATION, PERSONALITY, AND ACHIEVEMENT:** *A Survey of Northern Blacks*
Roger N. Shepard, A. Kimball Romney, and Sara Beth Nerlove (Eds.), **MULTIDIMENSIONAL SCALING:** *Theory and Applications in the Behavioral Sciences,* Volume I — Theory; Volume II — Applications
Peter H. Rossi and Walter Williams (Eds.), **EVALUATING SOCIAL PROGRAMS:** *Theory, Practice, and Politics*